REPRESENTING REALITY

REPRESENTING REALITY

Discourse, Rhetoric and
Social Construction

Jonathan Potter

SAGE Publications
London • Thousand Oaks • New Delhi

ISBN 0-8039-8410-3 (hbk)
ISBN 0-8039-8411-1 (pbk)
© Jonathan Potter 1996
First published 1996
Reprinted 1997, 2000, 2003, 2004, 2005

1004783441

SAGE Publications Ltd
1 Oliver's Yard,
55 City Road
London EC1Y 1SP

SAGE Publications Inc
2455 Teller Road
Thousand Oaks,
California 91320

SAGE Publications India Pvt Ltd
B–42 Panchsheel Enclave
PO Box 4109
New Delhi 110 017

British Library Cataloguing in Publication data
A catalogue record for this book is available from the British Library

Typeset by M Rules, Southwark, London
Printed and bound in Great Britain by
Athenaeum Press Ltd., Gateshead, Tyne & Wear.

For Michael Mulkay and Peter Stringer

Contents

Acknowledgements

This is the first description in a book about the business done with descriptions. The book is asking how people construct their world in their talk and texts, and what is done with those constructions. Acknowledgements do business of all sorts and are often the occasion for some pretty ambitious psychology and sociology. They are fenced around by conventions – even the ironies on the conventions are conventional! How is it possible to acknowledge influence and debt? What is visible and what is transparent? What discourses should be drawn upon to constitute the world of acknowledgement?

Let me start more psychoanalytically with my parents – Mary and Percy. Of course, if this was a serious psychoanalytic account I would refer to their toilet training but, given that this might be family reading, I will stress, instead, their wonderful combination of (almost) thoroughgoing scepticism and sense of social responsibility.

For a somewhat more recent socialization account, I want to thank my PhD supervisors. Indeed, I have dedicated the book to them. In Peter Stringer and Michael Mulkay I was blessed with two supervisors (at different times) who each combined enormous originality of their own with wonderful support for me, personally and intellectually. I cite them occasionally in the book that follows – but that does not do justice to the enduring impact that they have had on my thinking and approach to social science.

To bring out some issues in sociology and ideology, I would like to thank my wife for staying at home and giving me such wonderful support. I can't thank her, however, as I am not married. Margaret Wetherell who was originally going to write this with me got bored with waiting and wrote a book about men and masculinity instead (surely a coincidence!). So I blame the shortcomings in my book on her lack of input, but have to accept that many of its qualities are a result of the specific comments that she made on draft chapters as well as her general intellectual example.

By rights, Sue Jones and Ziyad Marar from Sage ought to be part of an economic and practical account. But, by chance or otherwise, I have dealt with two Sage editors who were genuine academics who made valuable contributions to the content of this work.

My immediate social network has been great. I have written so much with Derek Edwards recently that it seems odd to be writing something without him. Luckily he was there with detailed suggestions and long discussions about the ideas developed here. The book would have been very different without his intellect, support and wit. Mick Billig and Malcolm Ashmore provided further intellect and humour in spades.

Over the years Loughborough's Discourse and Rhetoric Group has provided a nurturing, although always argumentative, environment for exploring these ideas. I am particularly conscious of the input from Anne Smith, Ava Horowitz, Belinda Cripps, Dave Middleton, Jon Fong, Katie Macmillan, Mick Roffe, Mike Gane, Sumiko Mushakoji. Outside of Loughborough, I received helpful comments on various drafts from Anna Madill, Alexa Hepburn, Kathy Doherty, David Bamberg, Hedwig te Moulder, Nancy Budwig and Nigel Edley.

In direct institutional terms, the United Kingdom Economic and Social Research Council provided support (grant R000231439) for the work on making a current affairs television film that is drawn on occasionally through the book. More importantly, the Social Sciences Department at Loughborough University has housed, paid and supported me throughout.

Last, but by no means least, I am particularly grateful to the various people who allowed their talk to be recorded and used for the research on which this book depends. Without them nothing would have been possible.

Introduction

In virtually any situation appeal to the facts, to what really happened and what is only invention, can be a powerful device. Factual accounting is the stuff of arcane scientific disputes over whether neutrinos have been detected, of mundane domestic conflict over who last washed the dishes, and of ideological concern as particular versions of the economy are assembled and undermined. Descriptions are so bound up with our lives that virtually any conversation includes reports of events and actions. We read newspapers and watch television programmes which overflow with real life stories and varied factual claims. Factual reports are a commonplace currency of occupations as varied as doctors, teachers, engineers and police officers. And fiction, too, ironically but interestingly, is full of realist description striving to make characters believable and plots coherent.

This book is concerned with two closely related sets of questions. First, how are descriptions produced so they will be treated as factual? That is, how are they made to appear solid, neutral, independent of the speaker, and to be merely mirroring some aspect of the world? How can a factual description be undermined? And what makes a description difficult to undermine? Second, how are these factual descriptions put together in ways that allow them to perform particular actions? What kinds of activities are commonly done using descriptions? And why might descriptions be suitable for doing those activities?

There are three main objectives for the book. First, it provides an overview of the main traditions of work on fact construction: the sociology of scientific knowledge, the closely related perspectives of ethnomethodology and conversation analysis, and the 'structural tradition' of semiology, post-structuralism and postmodernism. The coverage is necessarily selective. I am trying to capture the main thrust of the arguments, and pull out the issues which are particularly relevant to the study of fact construction, while avoiding getting bogged down in unnecessary technicalities. The coverage is comparative and points of convergence and conflict are emphasized where possible. Anyone hoping for a full integration will be disappointed; however, I do draw on elements of all three traditions in the more specific discussion in the later chapters.

The second objective of the book is to give an account of some of the basic procedures through which the factuality of descriptions is built up, and how those descriptions are involved in actions. This combines a detailed discussion of a range of relevant research on fact construction – some derived from the traditions reviewed earlier, some with more disparate roots – with novel analyses of my own. In particular, a set of themes in the construction of facts are identified and illustrated with sample analyses. My hope is that these will both provide an organizing framework for making sense of the different studies and highlight some issues which any research using descriptions would wish to discuss. Further, they should provide some considerations which anyone analysing descriptions and accounts of any kind are likely to find helpful.

The third objective is more diffuse, but perhaps more important. I hope the book will show both how significant the role of descriptions and factual accounts is in our lives and what a rich and fascinating topic it is to study. I have deliberately chosen to draw on materials from a wide range of factual descriptions to illustrate the generality of the questions I am raising. At the same time, many of the examples should be familiar to most readers (for example, newspaper reports and relationship disputes) which I hope will make the points more accessible as well highlighting their generality. I have come to see that factual discourse, even in casual, mundane settings, such as in an argument between a husband and wife, is organized in enormously fine detail and with great subtlety. If I can convey some of that subtlety and intricate organization here I will be very happy.

Before starting with Chapter 1, there are three tasks. First, I will provide a small number of brief examples to illustrate more explicitly what is involved in studying fact construction, and to raise some of the themes that will come up later. Second, I will comment on some background issues relevant to the book and discuss one or two precursors to the work described here. Finally, I will give a brief overview of the book as a whole.

Welcome to the Fact Factory

A Fictional Undercover Cop

In Quentin Tarantino's film, *Reservoir Dogs*, a central character is a young undercover cop, Freddy. His mentor, Holdaway, has helped get him access to a gang of jewel thieves and is teaching him a story that he can use to make his criminal identity convincing.

Freddy:	I gotta memorize all this? There's over four fuckin' pages of shit here.
Holdaway:	It's like a fuckin' joke, man. You remember what's important and the rest you make your own. You can tell a joke, can't ya?
Freddy:	I can tell a joke.
Holdaway:	Well just think about it like that. Now the things you hafta remember are the details. It's the details that sell your story. Now your story takes place in a men's room. So you gotta know the details about that men's room. You gotta know if they got paper towels or a blower to dry your hands. You gotta know if the stalls got doors or not. You gotta know if [*Holdaway continues . . .*] Now what you

gotta do is take all them details and make 'em your own. This story's gotta be about you, and how you perceived the events that took place. (Tarantino, 1994: 71)

What lessons are there here? The first is very basic, and easily missed. It takes work to produce a description that is convincing; it can be done well and it can be done badly. There are more or less standard procedures that can be drawn on when establishing the veracity of an account. Note the emphasis that Holdaway places on detail. It is not the general pattern of events so much as the details that makes the story credible. These are the sorts of things that someone who was there to witness events would know but which are not intrinsic to the general narrative. This is a theme that will be explored in Chapter 6.

A further consideration is that Freddy is working up an invented story. It is tempting to consider this to be totally different from someone recounting an actual story. That is, we might consider the actual story as the standard, natural form and the fake one as a derived form or parasite. However, both the conversation analyst Harvey Sacks and the philosopher Derrida offer reasons for not accepting this hierarchy too readily. It may be that an authentic story draws on the same resources as a subversive alternative that pretends to authenticity. And maybe the way authentic stories are organized is partly a consequence of the possibility of inauthentic alternatives.

Two final issues are highlighted with this example: the contrast between fact and fiction and reflexivity. This is not a real dialogue between an undercover cop and his boss – it is invented, and it is part of a fiction where a whole set of considerations about the dialogue will be at work over and above whether it is the sort of thing that might actually be said in a real-life example of this kind (does it work dramatically? does it develop the characters? and so on). Indeed, there are all sorts of reasons to think that a real life conversation between cops like this would be very different. Most basically, a comparison between transcripts of actual conversations and playscript dialogue is likely to show the actual conversation to appear messier than the fictional one – it will be full of corrections, hesitations, pauses, ungrammatical constructions. However, that does not mean that actual conversation will not be organized in subtle and artful ways; nor, for that matter, that the fictional example is uninteresting. Both are fascinating, and both throw light on each other.

One of the interesting and paradoxical features of fiction is that it is a major domain for fact construction. Novelists and playwrights produce texts which need to be credible and believable on some level. For example, the vivid detail and witnessed perspective that Holdaway emphasizes is also a central feature in the literary skill of making a story convincing. Tarantino's text is both *about* the cop's process of learning fact construction and, simultaneously, *doing* fact construction as it vividly paints this interaction for us with its swearing, colloquialisms and displayed anxieties. And this reflexive relationship is repeated here in the introduction to the current book, where it is both standing as an example of fact construction and contributing to the credibility of this text. Freddy is convincing the jewel thieves; Tarantino is convincing cinema goers; I am trying to convince readers.

Economies of Truth

In the course of the famous 'Spycatcher' court case in Australia, in which the British government attempted to prevent publication of a book claiming the security organization MI5 was run by a traitor, Sir Robert Armstrong famously responded that he had been 'economical with the truth' when examined by defence attorney Malcolm Turnbull. The following is reconstructed from partial reports in different newspapers:

> *Mr Turnbull*:　Did the letter contain an untruth?
>
> *Sir Robert*:　It does not say we already had a copy of the book.
>
> *Mr Turnbull*:　It contains an untruth.
>
> *Sir Robert*:　It does not contain that truth.
>
> *Mr Turnbull*:　It gives a misleading impression.
>
> *Sir Robert*:　It was a misleading impression in that respect, but a lie is a straightforward untruth.
>
> *Mr Turnbull*:　And what is the difference between an untruth and a misleading impression?
>
> *Sir Robert*:　The question is rather one of being *economical with the truth*.

This example illustrates a number of relevant themes. Note first that the phrase was produced as a response to cross examination. That is, it is part of the interaction, it is occasioned by its context where it is a response to an accusation. It addresses inconsistencies in testimony while resisting the implication that the speaker had been lying. The simple point here is that people do not produce descriptions out of the blue; they produce them for what they can do in some stream of activity. Sir Robert's claim should not be understood as an abstract claim about truth that he will stand behind in whatever future context he might find himself; it is produced *on* this occasion *for* this occasion.

A second point is related to the idea of being economical with the truth itself. It captures in a very neat way how the business done by a description can relate to both what is described and what is left out. The point of the being 'economical with the truth' in this version is that you can provide an answer to a question which does not contain actual falsehoods, but works by leaving out something that would give a very different impression. For example, in this case Sir Robert denied that the government had a copy of a book without telling the questioner that it had the proofs of the book; that is, although it did not have an actual bound copy it did know what it would contain. This is a feature of factual accounting that we will return to in detail in Chapter 7.

This example also shows up the sorts of skills that people have for undermining and resisting factual versions. Although this phrase was used as part of a distinction between lying and giving a misleading impression by withholding information (Sir Robert later claimed to have been drawing on Edmund Burke's distinction between 'falsehood and delusion' and 'economy of truth'), it was widely taken as a softened admission of lying. Indeed, since then 'economical with the truth' has become a popular pejorative phrase for certain kinds of official lying and deception. Here are just three examples from around 50 thrown up by a brief search through just three months of two newspapers on CD-ROM.

> For ministers to point out that four out of five prescriptions are not paid for by individuals is surely being *economical with the truth*. Forty percent of the population pays for prescriptions. (*Guardian*, 19 February 1994)

> Mr Paul Marland . . . also disputed claims that Lloyd's never made Names bankrupt. He said the market was being '*economical with the truth*'. (*Daily Telegraph*, 17 January 1994)

> Grave doubts have been cast on the financing methods used to purchase Venables' stake at Spurs by indicating that he has been somewhat *economical with the truth* when he claimed he had put all his money into Spurs. (*Daily Telegraph*, 19 January 1994)

The phrase is not always directly quoted in this way; it can be modified to do different tasks. For example, an editorial about a minister's disputed hotel bill (the issue being whether his visit was an undeclared gift) describes him as being '*miserly with the truth*', and a cartoon about a government law officer's criticism of an official inquiry features one commuter saying to another, 'he feels they have been *extravagant with the truth*'. By modifying the phrase, reporters, cartoonists and others can draw delicately on the original and familiar meaning to ironize some claims and arguments.

More generally, the notion of an economy of truth serves as an appropriate metaphor for the topic of this book. Like money on the international markets, truth can be treated as a commodity which is worked up, can fluctuate, and can be strengthened or weakened by various procedures of representation.

The Anecdotalizer

This extract is from a light-hearted article where the author confesses to be a compulsive anecdotalizer.

> Anecdotalising. It's an addiction. Every minuscule detail of my life is transformed into another party piece. Pubs, bus stops, the office, are all turned into impromptu theatre spaces. . . .
> Often there is no incident. Having a point, an event or bizarre coincidence is reserved for beginners. Anyone can string out a tale about the time they were locked out of the house naked while a Salvation Army brass band marched down their street.
> Only a true raconteur will hold forth on a failed attempt to adjust a wall thermostat. (*Guardian Weekend*, 6 January 1993)

One point that this extract neatly illustrates is that descriptions are not just

involved in situations of conflict, or where there is a strong concern with factual accuracy. People in their everyday talk tell stories to one another; they
construct narratives – anecdotes – to make points, for entertainment and
laughter.

In the continuation of the article the writer tells a story about recklessly
starting an anecdote and only halfway through realizing that there is no point
or punch line. This again stresses the theme of reflexivity. The article about
the compulsive anecdotalizer is *itself* constructed as an anecdote, where a relatively trivial matter – not having a good ending to a story – is turned into a
major disaster: 'like the captain of a sinking ocean liner, I refuse to acknowledge defeat, tell the band to play on'. And again, note, this narrative is being
set to work in the current text that I am writing.

Another issue highlighted here is the flexibility of descriptions.
Descriptions are not determined by events but are worked up, and this working up can itself be skilful. Thus the achievement of making the failed
thermostat adjustment is turned into an interesting and involving story.
However, while the surface implication of the article is that the compulsive
anecdotalizer is a rather special figure, I will argue that issues involving the
construction of versions are endemic in conversation. People package their
lives into narratives which they tell for a whole range of different purposes.
For example, one of the materials which will be used in several chapters
below is taken from a relationship counselling session in which a couple each
gives versions of an evening where the woman may have been flirting and the
man may have attempted suicide (as we will see, these are already highly contentious descriptions). The anecdotalizing in this case is geared to actions
such as assigning blame and showing who needs to change their behaviour.

These three examples are intended to provide an initial orientation to the
themes that will be explored in detail later in the book. Before then there are
some final introductory issues that need airing.

Preparations

Philosophy

It is important to emphasize that this is not a work of philosophy. In particular I am not trying to resolve classic philosophical disputes between, say,
advocates of realism and anti-realism. And I am certainly not trying to
answer ontological questions about what sorts of things exist. The focus is on
the way people construct descriptions as factual, and how others undermine
those constructions. This does not require an answer to the philosophical
question of what factuality is. Nevertheless, this approach cannot fail to have
implications for broader debates about the status of realism and relativism,
and about the appropriate ontology for social sciences. Work of this kind contributes to the respecification of the nature of philosophical discourse as
rhetoric (following Richard Rorty, 1991). Conversely, one move in linguistic
philosophy has been to rework unmanageable and enduring metaphysical

questions as issues which can be addressed through a consideration of people's discourse. For example, rather than trying to solve the philosophical question of free will, John Austin (1961) suggested it might be more constructive to consider the way people account for freedom and constraint.

Rather than arguing directly with realism, the sorts of rhetorical devices that are used to shore up a realist position have been analysed (Gergen, 1994; Potter, 1992). There are certain common tropes that realists use to attack the coherence of the sort of constructionist position developed in this book, most notably the *furniture argument* ('see this [bangs on table]; you're not telling me that's a social construction') and the *death argument* ('what about the victims of the Holocaust, the fleeing Iraqis on the Basra Road, victims of amnesia – surely you don't want to deny their reality'). Again, the response that Derek Edwards, Malcolm Ashmore and I (1995) developed to these arguments was not to argue directly against them, but to take apart the rhetoric on which they are based; decoupling the implied equivalence between relativism and lack of political commitment, and emphasizing that constructionist arguments are not aimed at denying the existence of tables (a very realist idea!) but at exploring the various ways in which their reality is constructed and undermined. Interesting though they are, these debates move away from the main issues of this book, and they will not be further explored here.

Definitions and Etymology

The simplest way of characterizing the main theme of this book is in terms of the way descriptions are made factual, and what those descriptions are used to do. However, the words *fact* and *description* (and related terms such as *report* and *account*) have a complex history, and their current sense is only the start-point for research. *Fact* in the sense of 'a thing done or performed' (*Oxford English Dictionary*, 2nd edition on CD-ROM; henceforth *OED*) goes back to the sixteenth century; while the seventeenth century starts to see the more familiar modern sense, 'something that has really occurred or is actually the case', and contrasts made between facts and inferences or fictions: 'a particular truth known by actual observation or authentic testimony, as opposed to what is merely inferred, or to a conjecture or fiction' (*OED*). The interest in facts in this book is attributional rather than actual. That is, the topic is what participants *count as* factual rather than what is *actually* factual.

The term *description* can refer to both action and object: on the one hand, it is 'the action of setting forth in words by mentioning recognizable features or characteristic marks' and, on the other, it is 'a statement which describes, sets forth, or portrays; a graphic or detailed account of a person, thing, scene, etc.' (*OED*). Both of these senses date back to the fourteenth century. The terms *account* and *report* are described in a similar fashion. To *report* something is 'to relate, narrate, tell, give an account of (a fact, event, etc.); while an *account* is 'a particular statement or narrative of an event or thing; a relation, report, or description' (*OED*). Note the way the definition of *description* uses the term *describes* as well as the term *account*, the definition of *report* uses *account*, and the definition of *account* uses *report* and *description*. There is a lot of circularity. However, the contrast that I want to pick out is the way *fact* implies truth and real occurrence while *description* does not. This book covers the interactional space between these two notions, the business of building up a description as a fact.

Specificity versus Universalism

One of the tensions in this book is that between specificity and generality. I will argue that to understand the way factual accounts are constructed, and the way they are bound up with activities, it is important to understand their specific features, and the way those features relate to the setting in which they are used. Harvey Sacks (1992) has effectively shown the way much of the business of interaction is carried by what might at first sight seem to be the details. In talk, for example, this may be the selection of one specific word from a group of words with similar meanings, or the appearance of delays and overlaps, hesitations and corrections. Much of the book will be concerned with specific features of talk such as this, or with the particular constructions that appear in newspaper reports or texts of other kinds.

As a counterpoint to this focus on specificity, I have deliberately chosen to cover a very wide variety of forms of factual discourse. In the chapters that follow, I discuss scientific discourse, newspaper articles of various kinds, a couple's relationship counselling sessions, novels and films, everyday talk and talk amongst documentary film makers. My use of this wide selection of materials is driven by the conviction that there are general features of fact construction. That is, there are considerations that are likely to be attended to whatever the type of discourse. By casting the net widely in this way these general patterns are more likely to be revealed along with limitations on their generality. It is notable that the main traditions discussed in Chapters 1 to 3 combine major theoretical differences with differences in the kinds of material they are focused on: sociology of scientific knowledge obviously deals with scientific practices; ethnomethodology and conversation analysis have come to focus on talk in everyday and institutional settings; and work in post-structuralism and postmodernism has concentrated on literary and philosophical texts. I have opted for a comparative approach at both the level of theory and material.

Transcription

A number of the chapters below discuss examples of transcribed talk. Most use the increasingly standard system of transcription developed by the conversation analyst Gail Jefferson (1985; for an overview see Psathas, 1995). In some cases the origin is published articles; in other cases the examples are reproduced from original transcript. Either way there is a dilemma over its presentation. Many people find the sorts of detail, and the transcription symbols that go along with it, interfere with its readability. That would be a reason for simplifying the transcript: stripping off the extraneous symbols and elements. However, given the sorts of arguments about specificity I have just noted, this kind of detail needs to be recognized as an intrinsic part of a good transcript. The transcribed detail is not just an empiricist flourish to demonstrate completeness or conscientiousness or rigour (although it might do those things – see Bogen, 1992); it is an intrinsic and essential part of the interaction. In addition, anyone wishing to evaluate the claims and interpretations I make about sections of transcript might want to do so without being handicapped by information lost through judgements about what is extraneous.

I have been mindful of both of these concerns, and I have retained transcription symbols and information unless it is a major handicap to the intelligibility of the example. I hope that those readers unfamiliar with the Jeffersonian system (briefly described in an Appendix) will soon come to see it as clear and, indeed, invaluable for giving a sense of the talk as situated, voiced and, most importantly, a co-constructed part of an interaction (Schegloff, 1995).

Reflexivity

This is a book about constructing facts. One of its themes is the way descriptions are organized to make some version seem credible and objective. This also is a book full of descriptions (of theory, of disciplines, of literatures, of findings, of bodies of belief, and so on). It is a book, then, that refers to itself. This immediately raises the issue of reflexivity. Let me put this in its sharpest form. If the book is revealing that facts are constructed by devices, what of the devices that it uses to construct the fact that facts are constructed by devices? Put another way, do the conclusions of the book have any implications for the book itself? Is it, for example, entirely self-destructive?

Without getting too far ahead of arguments that will be aired more thoroughly later, I do think that there are reflexive implications from work on fact construction for this book and for social sciences more generally. Indeed, I even think there is an element of self-destruction. At the end of the book the ideal reader should be able to turn their gaze back on the book itself and decompose the techniques and tropes that it draws on so freely. For I have opted to use a conventional mode of presentation. It is not a new literary form; no alternative voices will pop up to argue with the main authorial voice (Mulkay, 1985); and it is not (I hope!) a parody of a social science book (Ashmore, 1989). I hope that erratic, but persistent, references to reflexive issues in the course of the text will underline their pertinence.

That is not to say that a novel literary form would have been inappropriate; more than anything it is the sheer difficulty of achieving one without making the text reader-unfriendly that put me off. So, as it stands the book has a single authorial voice (although thinkers such as Mikhail Bakhtin, 1981, might dispute whether any book actually has a single voice) and draws on many of the familiar tropes of social science writing and fact construction more generally. It is (almost) unashamed of *drawing* on the kinds of visual metaphors that imbue recent western writing about knowledge: it is concerned with *throwing*

light on *murky* topics, tracing out a new *point of view*, and *seeing* how far a
constructionist argument can be pushed (Derrida, 1982; Rorty, 1980).

Omissions

As I will discuss in detail later on, academic writing tends to draw on textual
forms – tropes – which construct a god-like, all-seeing, all-knowing, all-com-
prehending stance, which is at the same time disinterested and fair. Real
authors are, of course, located in history, in particular communities, constrained by their grasp (or lack of grasp) of bodies of ideas, by the quality of
their libraries and so on. Writing is full of serendipity and is inseparable from
academic biography. Even noting this can have the same quality: 'look, here
is a stance *so* disinterested and so god-like that it can even understand and
admit its own limitations!' Nevertheless, this is an opportunity to highlight
(confess?) some limitations. (I am not going to confess prejudices – I am sure
they will be all too apparent.)

The first limitation is in my coverage and use of the work of Mikhail
Bakhtin. He makes a couple of brief appearances, but I have a strong sense
that his work could be made much more relevant to a number of the arguments used here (cf. Shotter, 1992). The second limitation is in the failure to
address seriously the Actor Network Theory developed by Bruno Latour,
Michel Callon and John Law (for example, Callon, 1995; Latour, 1993; Law,
1994). This is an exciting approach to facts and knowledge which has important implications for any study of fact construction. Yet I have been unable to
decide whether it provides an organizing frame within which some of the
ideas that I discuss could be situated, or whether those ideas raise problems
for that frame. My rather weak solution in this text is to attempt neither situation nor critique.

A third limitation is of a rather different order. I long envisaged this book
to have a chapter on images or visual rhetoric. The fact that it does not is not
because I do not think this is an important topic – I do; it is because the book
has grown and was already in danger of becoming unwieldy. This chapter was
the one that could be abandoned with least disturbance to the overall argument. If had been included, it would undoubtedly have covered the recent
sociology of science work on practices of 'making visual' in research settings
such as staining cells, graphing animal habitats and charting features of the
sea bed (Aman and Knorr Cetina, 1988; Atkinson, 1995; Lynch, 1985, 1988;
Myers, 1990; Goodwin, 1995 – see also references in Ashmore et al., 1995). A
common theme here is the collaborative work that goes into producing
observable images that provide for stable interpretations. The chapter would
also have covered some of the classic work on semiology, such as Roland
Barthes's essays on photography (Barthes, 1977, 1981) and more recent semi-
ologically inspired developments (Hodge and Kress, 1988; Shapiro, 1988;
Williamson, 1978). This body of work in particular provides a major attack
on the idea of photography as an innocent medium of factual representation.
Some other time . . .

Precursors

It is useful to situate what comes next in terms of two of its most important precursors: John Austin's speech act philosophy in *How to Do Things with Words* and Peter Berger and Thomas Luckmann's phenomenological development of the sociology of knowledge in *The Social Construction of Reality*. These two books are part of what made the current project possible.

Austin and Speech Acts

One of the main elements in Austin's philosophical project was an attack on views of language that made referential issues of truth and falsity paramount. In place of the overwhelming philosophical concern with the 'truth value' of statements taken in the abstract, Austin emphasised the *practical* nature of language. Language is used to do things; it is a medium of action.

Initially, he built a plausible distinction between two classes of utterances. On the one hand, there are utterances that state things: 'Loughborough is in the middle of England'; on the other, there are utterances that do things: 'I bet you five pounds that Labour win the election.' But in the course of a brilliantly argued set of lectures he showed that the distinction could not be sustained. He proposed a general theory of speech acts which treats all utterances to be both performing actions and having features that depended on issues of truth and falsity. Thus 'I bet you five pounds that Labour wins the election' is part of the act of betting – but depends on there being a sensible referent for the words '*Labour*' and '*election*'; at the same time 'Loughborough is in the middle of England' is a statement that may be evaluated for its truth or falsity – but when uttered performs the act of stating.

This is the crucial and radical point. Austin's work starts to move the discussion away from the idea of statements – descriptions, reports – hanging in some conceptual space where they can be compared to some feature of the world and focuses attention on statements as actions performed in settings with particular outcomes. As he put it 'the total speech act in the total speech situation is the only actual phenomenon which, in the last resort, we are engaged in elucidating' (1962: 148).

It would be most unfair to criticize Austin for not doing something that he was not trying to do; after all, his targets were particular traditions in philosophy. Nevertheless, it is worth noting some limitations in his work, and the burgeoning literature it spawned, for the enterprise I am concerned with.

First, despite the expressed commitment to elucidating the total speech act in the total speech situation, Austin worked with made-up examples, which tend to be typifications (the standard bet) or institutionally determined (*I do* in the marriage ceremony) and which are considered outside of their production in actual settings. Again, this is not a problem for Austin in so far as he is seen as developing a philosophical argument, but it starts to become an important problem when Austin's work is drawn on as the basis for an analytic programme for studying language practices in general and factual language in particular (for example, see, Duranti, 1992). It cuts across the sorts of sense making that go on in everyday interaction by having the meaning of the target utterance determined by fiat. This approach will be discussed more in Chapter 2. Austin's emphasis on idealized cases as the best start point for understanding language has been effectively criticized by Jacques Derrida in a series of arguments discussed in Chapter 3.

Another problem lies with Austin's treatment of statements as actions. This is a radical first step in the study of fact construction, but the procedure of basing arguments on decontextualized invented examples leads him to miss one of the fundamental features of statements. Statements are used to do things. This can be seen as a subclass of one of the classic problems with speech act theory, that of indirection. Speech act theorists have struggled to account successfully for one of the most pervasive phenomena in language use which is, to put it crudely, the separation of form and function. Thus when we say 'can you pass the salt' we are not asking a question about abilities, we are making a request for the salt to be passed; while if we are making an offer we often couch it as a request: 'have a drink'. As we will see, statements are a more or less indirect way of performing a huge range of different actions: complimenting, complaining, inviting, blaming and so on. Showing that statements are actions is just the preliminary; what comes next is an examination of the many different actions that statements can do; where Austin finishes this book starts.

Berger and Luckmann and Social Construction

Berger and Luckmann's classic, *The Social Construction of Reality*, made a hugely influential contribution to the sociology of knowledge. It provided a systematic argument to the effect that the worlds in which we all live are not just there, not just natural objective phenomena, but are constructed by a whole range of different social arrangements and practices. For our present purposes it had the important role of establishing processes of social construction as a central topic of study.

A second important feature of the book is its emphasis on taking a 'symmetrical' stance to knowledge that is treated as true and false. As they put it: 'It is our contention, then, that the sociology of knowledge must concern itself with whatever passes for "knowledge" in a society, regardless of the ultimate validity or invalidity (by whatever criteria) of such "knowledge"' (1966: 15).

As we will see in Chapter 1 when discussing the sociology of scientific knowledge, this stance is an extremely important one when dealing with fact construction because it frees the researcher from taking sides with particular groups whose beliefs are better established than others and, more fundamentally, from deciding what should be counted as true or not. The social researcher is thus excused the difficult task of being a better physicist than the physicists that are being studied, a better surgeon, or whatever.

Like Austin, however, Berger and Luckmann were better at opening up the potential for analysing fact construction as a topic than following through that analysis. There are a number of potentially problematic features of their argument. First, the book is not an analytic book. It does not contain much in the way of analysis of how reality is constructed. Instead it provides general arguments for such construction and explores their implications for social life. Again, it would be unfair to criticize Berger and Luckmann for something they were not attempting, but this is an important difference from the approach to fact construction that I have adopted.

Second, Berger and Luckmann's study is focused on the phenomenology of individuals' experience. That is, rather than see processes of construction at work in talk and texts, it emphasizes people's perception and understanding:

> The reality of everyday life is organized around the 'here' of my body and the 'now' of my present. This 'here and now' is the focus of my attention to the reality of everyday life. What is 'here and now' presented to me in everyday life is the *realissimum* of my consciousness. (1966: 36)

The sorts of problems that this kind of 'cognitivism' generates are discussed in various places below, but particularly in Chapters 4 and 8. For the moment, I will just note that it tends to obscure the interactional and rhetorical nature of fact construction, while reifying a mental world which itself a major element in factual discourse. In other words, people produce versions of their mental life – their motives, their beliefs and so on – in the course of establishing the factuality of particular claims (see Edwards, 1996).

A final problem with Berger and Luckmann is that their constructionism is a rather limited affair. Although they spend a lot of time considering the various assumptions that a garage mechanic, for example, makes about 'his' world and its nature, they themselves can see round the edges of this construction without any problems. They do not, that is, consider the implications of treating social construction as a general feature of knowledge, including that of sociologists. I have already stressed the value of reflexivity; Berger and Luckmann ignore any epistemological troubles it faces them with. Despite these limitations, both Austin and Berger and Luckmann played a crucial role in opening up for study the issues that are the topic of this book.

Overview of the Book

The first three chapters in the book cover the main traditions of work involved in fact construction. Chapter 1 covers the sociology of scientific knowledge which exploded, especially in Britain, in the late 1970s and throughout the 1980s, stimulated by earlier developments in philosophy of science. This offered a radical reappraisal of traditional views of scientific facts and is still a site for heated debate between sociologists, philosophers and scientists. The chapter describes traditional sociology of science, and a range of challenges to it from philosophers. These challenges reconceptualized the nature of observation, stressed the interconnected nature of scientific claims, and emphasized the importance of scientific community and practice. The work of Harry Collins and the 'Empirical Relativist Programme' is discussed in detail, particularly his studies of the social construction and destruction of replication, along with 'constructionist' and 'interest' theories of scientific knowledge. This chapter highlights the value of taking a relativist perspective which starts without preconceptions about what facts are true, and illustrates some of the ways in which rhetoric is both emphasized and underplayed in sociology of science.

Chapter 2 takes ethnomethodology and conversation analysis as its topic. Stimulated by the pioneering work of Garfinkel and Sacks during the 1960s, these perspectives offered a novel account of both social interaction and the procedures that people use to understand the nature of their world and to display their conduct as coherent. It laid a particular emphasis on the way the stable, orderly nature of human life is achieved by people's practices. The chapter describes the central ethnomethodological concepts of indexicality, reflexivity and the documentary method of interpretation, and reviews some studies of the organized practices through which facts are made, concentrating on the example of suicide statistics. Another important topic is Melvin Pollner's work on 'mundane reason'; that is, the pattern of methods and assumptions that people use to sustain the sense of a stable and agreed underlying reality. Conversation analysis is introduced with a focus on the way it has conceptualized accounts as a structural element in particular kinds of interaction. This provides a developed research example where one class of descriptions (accounts) can be understood as performing a particular action, and having features that facilitate the performance of that action.

The loose tradition of semiology, post-structuralism and postmodernism continues to exert a major influence across the human sciences and wider cultural debates. Here the nature of human understanding has been redefined more than once. Chapter 3 introduces the basic ideas of semiology with a discussion of Ferdinand de Saussure's foundational work and some of Roland Barthes's later refinements to the approach. A range of post-structuralist thinkers are discussed including Roland Barthes (again), Michel Foucault and Jacques Derrida. I try and provide a feel for what is common and what is unique with respect to their work as it relates to fact construction, using the example of intertexuality and war to explore some of their insights. The section on postmodernism concentrates on Jean-François Lyotard's diagnosis of the postmodern condition and Donna Haraway's political and feminist exploration of the nature of factuality and stories given that condition. Some of the issues raised are addressed through a discussion of David Byrne's movie *True Stories*.

Chapter 4 provides a transition from the reviewing and systematizing in the first three chapters to the focus on specific procedures that makes up the chapters that follow. It outlines a set of considerations that need to be taken into account, and distinctions that need to be made, in research on fact construction. Some of these derive from the earlier traditions and some are new. One of its roles is to describe different ways in which the metaphor of construction has been used in linguistics, ethnomethodology and post-structuralism. It suggests that a complete constructionist account of fact construction will need to consider both the procedures through which versions are stabilized and made credible and the resources that those procedures draw on. The chapter develops an argument for taking an analytic approach to fact construction which focuses on texts and talk in action (discourse) rather than mental models, representations and ideas (cognition), and for treating that discourse as having two rhetorical orientations: an offensive orientation concerned with undermining alternative descriptions and a defensive orientation concerned with resisting discounting. Chapter 4 ends by introducing a distinction between the action orientation of descriptions (what the description is doing) and the epistemological orientation of descriptions (how the description attends to its own factuality). It is also intended to serve as a compact introduction to the themes that will be explored in the next three chapters.

Chapters 5 and 6 concentrate on the various procedures that are involved in constructing (and undermining) factual accounts. In Chapter 5 the topics of interest management and category entitlement are discussed. The referencing of a speaker's interest in their description is one major procedure for discounting it. The discussion focuses on a range of different ways in which writers and speakers resist such discounting. Categories of persons are often closely connected to their epistemological rights (doctors know about medicine, people with good memories can be trusted to give accurate accounts, and so on), and building a category entitlement for the producer of a description can be an important way of building up its factuality. This chapter also discusses the notion of footing – for example, is the speaker claiming or merely reporting? This has an important role in fact construction. The discussion here concentrates on the way neutrality with respect to a claim may be built up or undermined by various techniques of quoting.

In Chapter 6 the general concern is with the procedures that people use to separate descriptions from their own interests and produce them as neutral and external; that is, to give them a quality of out-there-ness. There are a range of these procedures, or externalizing devices. I focus on the use of empiricist discourse (impersonal constructions characteristic of science and some news reporting), constructions of consensus and corroboration (independent observers agree in their descriptions), and the use of narrative involving either rich detail or general formulations (rich detail can be used to sustain the category entitlement 'witness', general formulations can be used to resist easy rebuttal). In each case the emphasis will be on the way they can be worked up or undermined; these devices are not 'plug and play' modules that work irrespective of context.

While Chapters 5 and 6 concentrate on the epistemological orientation of descriptions, Chapter 7 is focused on their action orientation. As this is such a huge topic I restrict coverage to three themes. The chapter discusses the connected issues of categorization and ontological gerrymandering. A lot of the business of a description is done through its categorization; different categories imply different stories of motive and responsibility and have different implications for what should come next. At the same time categorizations can work to exclude potentially relevant considerations; they can gerrymander what is taken into account in a way that contributes to business at hand. A second theme is extrematization and minimization. This involves building some description to present bigness or smallness, violence or passivity, goodness or badness and so on. The third and final theme is normalization. How can some event or conduct be made out as normal and commonplace, or how can it be undermined as strange or deviant?

The final chapter returns to the nature of constructionism and asks how it should be conceptualized in the light of the arguments in the book. It also considers the significance of these arguments for the conduct and presentation of social science, taking work on public opinion and on social representations as two contrasting examples where a concern with the business done by descriptions can have important consequences. Finally, the chapter explores the broader implications of these arguments for politics and practice, highlighting tensions between different kinds of criticism and the reflexive exploration of social science texts.

The book is organized in two groups of chapters (1–3, 5–7) and two individual chapters. Chapters 1, 2 and 3 focus on the main theoretical and analytic traditions, and each could be read separately as a review which emphasizes the way descriptions are established as factual. Chapter 4 is a linking chapter which provides brief illustrations of the themes that are developed in detail in the following three chapters. This could be read as an introduction to what comes later and stands as a relatively compact summary of the perspective on fact construction developed in the book. Chapters 5 and 6 concentrate on procedures for fact construction, while Chapter 7 focuses on the way descriptions are fitted to activities.

These three chapters contain much of what is novel in the book, and they can be read as a relatively self-contained whole without losing too much. Although they draw on a range of different arenas where factual descriptions are used, for simplicity they will return repeatedly to a small number of examples: the relationship counselling sessions of a couple called Connie and Jimmy, the talk of various people involved in making a film about the failure of cancer research, and a range of different kinds of television and newspaper reporting. These will be combined with repeated discussion of two pathbreaking studies – Dorothy Smith's (1990) study of the workings of an account describing someone's mental illness, and Robin Wooffitt's (1992) study of the construction of accounts of paranormal experiences. Chapter 8 ends the book by raising the broader questions of constructionism, social science representation and criticism.

1

Social Studies of Science

If we are asked to think of something that epitomizes the world of facts, before very long we are likely to consider science. Colossal investments of time, money and people seem to have led to facts which are sharply specified and precisely defined, sustaining the weight of prodigious technological advances. Looked at in this way science becomes a 'hard case' against which to test an argument about the constructed nature of facts. If you can succeed in showing that scientific fact generation deviates from idealized models, then you expect that fact generation in other realms is likely to be even further from those models (Collins, 1985). If even white-coated scientists, with all their training and technical back-up, produce facts which are in some way problematic, then what hope for barristers, newspaper reporters or 'ordinary people'?

This argument makes many assumptions and can easily be viewed as a piece of rather transparent rhetoric used by some social researchers into science to build up the importance of their work. However, with the proviso that we should not take the 'hard case' argument too seriously, the social study of science is an excellent place to start examining fact construction. Not only has it been a melting pot for different theories of knowledge generation but it has also led to numerous detailed case studies of the work of scientists. Many of the themes and problems that arise in science recur in other fields of fact making.

Social studies of science have broadly based origins. Although much of it is characterized as the sociology of science, or the sociology of scientific knowledge, in the last two decades one of the notable features of the field is the wide interdisciplinary collaboration among sociologists, philosophers and historians of science, psychologists, linguists and literary analysts. Indeed, the traditional sociology of science, which held sway until the 1970s, now seems striking in its conservatism and its resistance to a thoroughgoing exploration of the social basis and context of facts. It is worth briefly considering the nature of this earlier work to provide a contrast to what came later.

Traditional Sociology of Science

Typically, traditional sociology of science was concerned with two questions. How is science organized as a social institution in such a way that scientists regularly and successfully produce objective facts? And, conversely, what distorting social factors might result in the production of scientific errors? The figure in the sociology of science who was most involved in formulating and attempting to answer these questions was Robert Merton (1970, 1973). I will take his solutions in turn.

Norms and the Scientific Ethos

Merton wanted to understand the way particular social conditions paved the way for the emergence of modern science. He suggested that the rise of Puritanism in the seventeenth century generated an ethos characterized by values such as utility, rationality, empiricism and individualism which was ideally suited for science. Merton argued that, when they conformed to these values, people were starting to view their world more in the manner of modern scientists, and thus starting to act in a way that facilitated the production of objective facts.

In an extension of this argument, Merton suggested that modern science is sustained by a more developed set of puritan values, which he called the *norms of science*. The argument is that modern science is constrained by four particular institutional imperatives: universalism, communism, disinterestedness and organized scepticism. While historically developed from the Protestant ethos, the role of these imperatives is to generate the conditions which allow facts to be produced in a reliable way. Communism requires that knowledge is freely and openly shared; organized scepticism, that all knowledge claims are assessed for their theoretical coherence and empirical adequacy; disinterestedness and universalism, that everyone's knowledge claims are assessed by essentially the same impersonal criteria and thus that scientific status is gained through merit rather than patronage or social position.

This account of science has continued to generate a large critical literature (for recent discussion, see, for example, Fuller, 1995; Lynch, 1993). And stories have been told about the origins of science which are strikingly different from Merton's (Shapin and Schaffer, 1985; Latour, 1993). The major point of interest for us is the way in which the problem of fact production was initially constructed in Merton's work. Essentially, it started from a received view of the nature of scientific facts – that they are impersonal, empirically warranted, rigorously tested – and then asked what kind of social organization could produce such things. In what has often been called a storybook (Mitroff, 1974) view of science, scientific activity is taken as given, and the problem for the sociologist is to outline a social system that will explain it.

The problem with starting with the storybook view of scientific facts, as many subsequent analysts have pointed out, is that it is just that: a storybook account which does not describe the actual practices of scientists. For example, it is possible to view norms such as universalism very differently, by not treating them as clear-cut constraints, but as symbolic and open-ended resources that have to be interpreted differently according to the context in which they are used (Mulkay, 1976, 1980). Moreover, it is possible to consider scientific accounts which invoke such norms as vocabularies of justification

(Mulkay and Gilbert, 1981; Potter, 1984). That is, norms can be seen as one element in the persuasive armoury that scientists draw on when they are arguing with other scientists or attempting to legitimate the practice of science as a whole.

This brings us to the question right at the heart of this current book. How are descriptions made to seem literal and factual? In this case, how can scientists describe their individual activities in a way that presents them as following from the impersonal rule of 'proper' science? Before focusing directly on that, however, I will turn to the other major feature of Mertonian sociology of science, which is its concentration on error.

Sociology of Error

Although Merton stressed the importance of the set of norms for guiding the scientific activity of fact finding, he also stressed that scientists do not always conform to these norms. At times there is fraud; scientists may keep results to themselves or pass them only to selected associates; there may also be prejudice against particular individuals or groups. However, these deviations were treated as exceptions – indeed, for Merton they *must* be exceptions, for without their general effectiveness scientific facts would not have the special status they do.

Merton suggested that these deviations from the norms provide a sociological or psychological way of explaining scientific error. Prejudice against a group of researchers may result in the maintenance of a mistaken theory in the face of a correct alternative, or individual ambition may lead a scientist to falsify findings to fit into a desired model. What is interesting here is the asymmetrical way in which researchers in the Mertonian tradition approached what they construed as true and false belief. False belief could be directly explained through a 'social fact' (personality, prejudice and so on) disrupting the proper operation of scientific norms. True belief was dealt with quite differently. For scientists governed by the norm system, true belief arises directly from a careful investigation of how the world is. Put simply, in this view of science, the facts themselves determine truth, while error is explained by processes of a psychological or sociological nature. The consequence of this is that with true belief there was nothing to explain save for how the conditions for proper scientific inquiry came about and how those conditions are undermined. Social researchers only come into their own when they apply their skills in understanding group processes and psychodynamics to understand how false belief came about. This set of assumptions has been most effectively identified and criticized by the sociologist David Bloor (1991).

In effect, then, the tradition represented by Merton and others bracketed off the study of facts themselves and contented itself with examining their sociological context. A full sociological analysis of the *content* of science – of scientific ideas, theories, methods and so on – was reserved only for falsehoods. With the benefit of hindsight, we can see that these sociologists embraced scientists' own stories about the distinctive and privileged nature of their knowledge and were led to focus their attention on facts that scientists had already discarded as mistaken for one reason or another. Given this self-imposed limit on analysis it is perhaps not surprising that the crucial developments that paved the way to a full social study of scientific facts came from philosophy and history of science rather than sociology.

Philosophy and Scientific Facts

It is important not to give the impression that philosophers and historians of science have been more sceptical about scientific activities than sociologists. For, with some notable exceptions, they have found scientists' stories as congenial and as self-evident as Merton. Philosophers have been primarily concerned with the justification of scientific knowledge; while historians have been traditionally interested in the thoughts and procedures that led 'great' scientists to 'great' discoveries. Philosophers in particular have traditionally taken it as given that scientific knowledge is special; and have seen their role as being to show how this special nature can be rigorously demonstrated. However, in their attempts to provide such a demonstration through the detailed exploration of classic scientific episodes, philosophers and historians started to build a radically different view of science. I will focus here on three facets of this novel view: the breakdown of the distinction between observation and theory; the notion that scientific beliefs are bound together in complex networks; and an emphasis on scientific communities and practices.

Observations and Theories

One of the most powerful and bewitching ways of understanding facts has been to think of them as observations of how the world is. Do I see a table there or not? Was that a blip on the photon scintillator or not? Observation has been thought to provide two basic rewards. First, it appeared to offer direct and unmediated access to the world and its features. It is the evidence of one's own eyes. Second, it seemed to allow for a basic process of corroboration: any observer who takes a particular viewing position ought to be able to see the same thing. Taken together, these appear to allow observation to work as a foundation for knowledge building; whatever else might be going on, we can see some particular properties of the world, and also others can check our observations by substituting themselves for us (Mulkay, 1979).

The idea that facts are a product of observation (the doctrine of empiricism) is so taken for granted, and so fundamental to scientists' understanding of their current practice, that it is difficult indeed to resist viewing it as self-evident. Indeed, both our scientific and everyday language of knowledge and understanding are permeated with visual metaphors: *looking* for the truth, *seeing* the point, *viewing* it as self-evident, and so on. Yet this idea of knowledge based on observation has a complex historical pedigree. Its self-evidence to us now is not something natural; it has been built up over a long period of time.

For example, Steven Shapin and Simon Schaffer (1985) documented the way that, in the middle of the seventeenth century, Robert Boyle drew on ideas from the judicial process to provide a new way of justifying his scientific claims about air pressure and the existence of a vacuum. They quote from Boyle:

> For, though the testimony of a single witness shall not suffice to prove the accused party guilty of murder; yet the testimony of two witnesses, though but of equal credit . . . shall ordinarily suffice to prove a man guilty; because it is thought reasonable to suppose, that, though each testimony single be but probable, yet a concurrence of such probabilities, (which ought in reason to be attributed to the truth of what they jointly tend to prove) may well amount to a moral certainty, *i.e.*, such a certainty, as may warrant the judge to proceed to the sentence of death against the indicted party. (1985: 56)

The truth of the scientific claims is established for Boyle, then, through using a number of witnesses who can concur in their support. It should be noted, however, that not just any witness would do; for Boyle, reliable witnesses were members of the appropriate communities, while 'Papists and atheists' were apt to find their stories questioned. Note also that, for Boyle, this way of understanding scientific observation was not self-evident. He had to argue for it and he imported the practice from the more familiar legal setting.

In this century the utility of observation as a foundation for scientific knowledge has started to come under threat from philosophical, historical and sociological analysis (for example, Barnes, 1977; Hacking, 1983; Kuhn, 1970; Rorty, 1980). In questioning the idea that visual experience is somehow a direct and unproblematic facsimile of aspects of the world, philosophers drew on psychological research on visual perception, and in particular work showing the sorts of reversals in how one sees an image that take place with visual illusions along with the role of cultural expectations in categorizing what is seen. We are all familiar with line drawings that can be seen as either a duck or a rabbit, or as either the top or bottom of a set of steps. Here the visual experience changes, although the drawing stays the same, and this is taken to raise the possibility of fundamental disagreements over the meaning of the same scene (Hanson, 1969; Kuhn, 1970). Cultural expectations are shown to operate in contexts where, for example, people quickly have to identify playing cards from a pack in which the colour of the ace of spades has been changed to red. The tendency is to report the ace of spades as black in line with expectations. The lesson, and the problem for empiricism, is that we may see what we *expect* rather than just what is there.

These are rather artificial examples and their relation to actual scientific practice is open to question. Practices of observation in the sorts of settings that scientists actually work in are much more complex than these simple, isolated visual exposures imply (for example, Goodwin, 1995; Lynch and Woolgar, 1990; Knorr Cetina and Aman, 1990). For example, Michael Lynch (1994) notes the way in astronomy the term *observation* serves as a rather loose device for collecting together a range of actions such as setting up the position of a telescope, connecting a particular sensor to it, building up patterns of dots on an oscilloscope, converting a series of these into a chart and then gaining the support of colleagues over a particular interpretation. Unlike the snap judgement made of a single projected image, observation is 'temporally extended, socially and equipmentally distributed, and contingently fated' (1994: 138). Nevertheless, the sorts of psychological examples used by Kuhn and others worked as powerful rhetorical counters to the idea that what is seen is determined by the object, or even its image on the retina.

The problem with the idea that perception provides a firm and unproblematic foundation for knowledge becomes more apparent when we consider that, whatever the images on scientists' retinas, when observations enter the currency of science they do so in terms of utterances or some form of written discourse. Even at its simplest this involves some form of categorization; it is not just seeing what is before the eyes but seeing it *as something*; not just a particular colour sensation but a descriptive choice: red, brown with golden speckles, or whatever. And in science, as with 'common sense', our categories are not some neutral and abstract set of descriptive pigeon-holes; they are derived from theories and broad cosmologies. Philosophers such as Mary Hesse (1974) have argued that scientists work with descriptive terms – mass, mitochondria, muscle fibre – that presuppose a whole set of theoretical assumptions; and if we try to unpack these assumptions, and ground them in terms of other observations, these too are theory dependent (see Chalmers, 1992; Mulkay, 1979, for useful summaries of these arguments).

In addition to this range of problems with observation there is another issue which is increasingly apparent with modern science. Much of the time scientific 'observations' (and, as I have noted, this term starts to become increasingly misleading) are dependent on intricate recording apparatus such as electron microscopes, oscilloscopes and bubble chambers whose workings are themselves dependent on a range of elaborate theories which are presupposed in every observation (Feyerabend, 1975). Take Karin Knorr Cetina's (1996) ethnographic study of the use of a particle detector in high energy collider experiments at CERN. The detector is immensely complex, and the physicists spend much more of their time trying to make sense of *its* behaviour than they do looking for the hypothesized and almost unimaginably small particles that are their research topic. They run the huge equipment over and over again to find out about its blemishes and idiosyncrasies. The term *observation* here stands only in the loosest relation to research practices in this community.

The Web of Belief

Another facet of this critique of empiricism considers the way scientific statements or beliefs are connected together in a network. In the early part of the twentieth century the philosopher of science Pierre Duhem argued that scientific claims were never evaluated purely in relation to the findings of particular experiments. Instead, claims are evaluated by considering a whole range of issues, including experimental findings, theories, ideas about method, statistics and so on (Duhem, 1962). For example, if a finding is consistent with a well-established body of theory, it is more likely to be accepted without discussion than if it is thought to contradict an established theory. An 'observation' of 'dark matter' in space is more likely to be rigorously repeated if it is seen as contradicting basic postulates of modern astrophysics; astronomers will search for alternative interpretations that sustain the coherence of their general account of the universe. In contrast, an observation that meshes with a large body of theory may be accepted with relatively little discussion.

In the 1950s, the American philosopher Willard van Orman Quine developed Duhem's ideas about the interconnection of beliefs and the role of experience into a famous metaphor, often elaborated as the Quine–Duhem thesis (1961; see also Hesse, 1974; Quine and Ullian, 1970). Quine suggested that scientific beliefs should be regarded as stretched in a fabric, rather like the skin of a drum. The fabric is pulled toward the edge of the drum by experience; however, this experience does not determine the organization of the fabric, for it adjusts all the time to ease tension. Sometimes adjustments arise because of new observations pulling from the edge; at other times theoretical developments lead to reorganization of the fabric.

The crucial, and radical, point of the metaphor is that no *single* scientific observation will have a determinate effect on the web of belief. The impact of observations will depend on the state of the fabric as a whole. This way of understanding science suggests that there could never be a crucial experiment, a study which *on its own* definitively forced the choice between two competing theories; indeed historical work has suggested that experiments commonly thought of as crucial are often viewed in this way only some time *after* the abandonment of the earlier theory (Collins and Pinch, 1993). The general consequence is to undermine the idea that observation provides a conclusive foundation for knowledge. At the same time it provides a novel pragmatic emphasis on issues like the coherence of one belief with others and the overall simplicity of the system.

Community and Practice

A final and somewhat ironic consequence of these philosophical reassessments of science was an increasing recognition of the crucial role of scientific community and practice. While sociologists were led away from concerns with the content of scientific knowledge by Mertonian ideas, philosophers were finding that their concerns led them to psychology and sociology. The best-known proponent of this view was the philosopher and historian Thomas Kuhn (1970), whose ideas can be usefully seen as an extension of the Quine–Duhem thesis. The notion of a web of beliefs is a very abstract one. Kuhn's important modification was to stress that such a network does not hang in some abstract conceptual space, but is embodied in the knowledge and practices of specific groups of scientists. Scientific beliefs are expressed in debate and inscribed in scientific writing.

If the network is going to be readjusted in the way Quine suggests, this will involve groups of scientists changing their theoretical commitments, learning new methods, abandoning favoured and laboriously acquired standard models of problem solving ('paradigms') and so on. Kuhn argued, on the basis of historical case studies, that instead of putting the network into a state of minor but continual disruption, the community of scientists will carry on doing 'normal science' in the face of anomalies and problems that arise from research until at some point the whole system will be so stressed that it will be forced to undergo radical readjustments. Only after this period of 'revolutionary science' can the serenity of normal science return. Kuhn not only claimed that science actually worked in this way, but also that it was sensible for it to do so.

Kuhn's community-based model of science was not the only one developed by philosophers. For example, Imre Lakatos (1970) argued that the central social unit for doing science is the 'research programme': a developing series of studies organized around a set of more of less basic theoretical assumptions. Others, notably Karl Popper (1959), suggested that it is not the social and intellectual organization of science which is important but the *manner* in which scientists carry out their activities. For Popper, science is distinguished from non-science by the *activity* of trying critically to test hypotheses and resisting the temptation to make continual *ad hoc* modifications to keep hypotheses going in the face of counter-evidence. For example, he argued that scientists should not have postulated new but invisible planets to keep Newtonian theory going in the face of seeming deviations in planetary orbits from predictions. In fact, Popper was strongly critical of Kuhn's suggestion that periods of 'normal', stable and unquestioning science are necessary for its development; for him this was simply bad science (Popper, 1970).

This brief characterization of developments in the philosophy of science does scant justice to the complexity and richness of what has been one of the most exciting areas of modern philosophy. Controversy continues, and there are many in philosophy who would reject some or even all of the points above. I have covered it in this way because it fits into the general narrative I am constructing about facts in two ways.

First, it is intended to show the way that even philosophers, whose basic concern has been the justification of the unique status of scientific facts, have raised fundamental problems for simple storybook models of science and its development. The simplicity of empiricism – the lone contemplative scientist and the world ready for inspection – is compromised by observations blurring into theories, by theories being interconnected, and by the recognition of how this is dependent on a community of scientists and their actions. The value of this work does not arise from a demonstration of how facts are warranted – for it has left only a vague outline of how this is done – but from its revelation of the limits of the classic empiricist story of science.

Second, this work shows how an abstract epistemological concern with the relation between an observation statement and some part of reality has turned into a psychological and sociological concern with the role of expectations, machineries and communal practices. Unlike the traditional sociology of science, which effectively locked the content of factual knowledge away from the prying eyes of analysts, the new philosophy of science was an invitation to open the box and grapple with the specifics of scientific knowledge. And, particularly in Britain where Mertonian theory had anyway not been so well established, the invitation was accepted with relish.

Sociology of Scientific Knowledge

Modern sociology of scientific knowledge (or SSK, as it is widely called) is characterized by a number of overlapping theoretical concerns, analytic methods and research focuses. It is an area of lively internal debate, quite apart from sporadic controversies with more traditional sociologists and philosophers of science (Bunge, 1992; Laudan, 1990) as well as with scientists themselves (Labinger, 1995; Wolpert, 1993). I will start by discussing Harry Collins' work because it raises effectively many of the fundamental issues in SSK, as well as providing some powerful examples of this position in analytic practice.

The Empirical Relativist Programme

The clearest way to introduce this work is through a contrast to the traditional sociology of science, which focused on the social conditions or norms that enable the generation of true knowledge, and on the way particular social or psychological factors such as prejudices and personal ambitions led to scientific errors. For Harry Collins, the problem with this work is that it adopts scientists' own distinctions between what is true and what is false and sets itself the twin problems of explaining how the errors came to be made and what the social conditions are which sustain the truth. His point was that this traditional work legitimated any current *status quo* by presupposing the correctness of any current state of belief. It assumes that what scientists take as valid scientific knowledge needs no *social* explanation, for it is adequately accounted for by the nature of the *natural* phenomena that are being studied (Collins 1981; Collins and Cox, 1976).

Collins argued that, if they are to avoid becoming public relations managers for science, then social analysts need to adopt a *relativist* stance. Now relativism is a complex and fiercely contested notion in the social sciences, and one which is often treated as a straightforward term of abuse: someone has 'fallen into' a relativist position; the 'spectre of relativism' has to be avoided (Edwards et al., 1995; Smith, 1988). Collins wanted to rescue the notion from its theoretical dungeon.

Collins proposed that a form of *methodological* relativism is crucial for SSK. That is, scientists' claims about what is true and false should not be taken as the start point for analysis but should become a topic of analysis in their own right. One of the most striking consequences of approaching scientific knowledge from a stance of methodological relativism is that it immediately frees up the whole scientific field for study. The social analyst is no longer restricted to picking up the scraps rejected from the scientific table as false beliefs or having to be content with routine studies of its organizational psychology. Furthermore, the analyst no longer has to sort out the scientific issues in a more definitive manner than the scientists themselves. In fact, what might have seemed at first sight to be an unnecessary and even rather eccentric start point for social research quickly comes to seem sensible and, indeed, indispensable. The value of methodological relativism immediately becomes apparent as we concentrate on the sorts of tangles that we can easily get into as we attempt to make unproblematic judgements about scientific truth and falsity. It is worth briefly noting some of these difficulties before we proceed.

In many of the most exciting areas of contemporary science there is no consensus over what is correct or not; instead there is heated controversy. Indeed, it is often the controversy that generates the excitement. There are also large scientific fields in which there is apparent consensus over matters of truth and falsity. Yet even here the analyst often does not have to look too hard to find an appreciable number of dissenting voices. Furthermore, the content of the consensual view may be varied; that is, scientists may espouse the 'same' theory, but what they mean by that theory may be radically different (Gilbert and Mulkay, 1984; Latour, 1987). Moreover, if we take a longer historical perspective, many scientific claims which are widely accepted at one time have later been drastically revised or entirely abandoned (Feyerabend, 1975; Kuhn, 1970). Sometimes the process has happened in reverse; initially ridiculed ideas become accepted.

Collins has focused much of his research on scientific fields in which there is ongoing controversy. This has two benefits. First, in controversies the rules and competencies that underlie science are thrown into question and may thus be explicitly formulated in ways rare in more consensual areas. That is, the researcher can use the controversy to bring into the open what is elsewhere often tacit. Second, the researcher is better able to maintain the relativistic stance of indifference to the way things 'really are' because this is precisely what is in dispute.

The advantage of controversies is underlined by the use of a powerful analogy, which has implications for the analysis of fact production more generally. Collins (1985) suggested that when we deal with scientific knowledge it is often like studying the sorts of traditional ships in bottles that sailors make. After all the glue has dried and the strings have been cut they seem almost magical. There is no easy way of seeing how they came to be made. The advantage of looking at controversies, according to Collins, is that they are situations where we might be able to catch a glimpse of the glue being inserted and the strings being pulled.

Collins suggests that there are three stages to providing a sociological account of a controversy (Collins, 1983a). The first stage involves documenting the flexible ways in which experimental results can be interpreted. How can particular findings be made out as supporting a theory or not? How can a replication be constructed as confirming a finding or dismissed as incompetent? Such flexibility is just what is to be expected in the light of the Quine–Duhem thesis which stresses that the findings of an individual experiment will be judged against bodies of theory as a whole. There are all sorts of ways in which tensions in the network introduced by novel findings can be reduced.

The second stage focuses on the way this open-endedness is dealt with so that one particular outcome results. How, ultimately, is the controversy settled? Here Collins departs from the Quine–Duhem view. Recent versions of the Quine–Duhem thesis (Hesse, 1980; Knorr Cetina, 1982a; cf. Kuhn, 1977) suggest that although there may be varied responses to the findings of individual experiments, there can be an orderly and rational response to accumulations of findings from a range of studies. This response depends on the application of general criteria which encourage the network to change in ways that emphasize coherence, say, or simplicity. However, for Collins the flexibility in dealing with research results combined with the holistic nature of scientific belief systems provides an opportunity for a variety of rhetorical devices and techniques of persuasion to be used. The debate is not closed by these rational considerations but by the sorts of strategies that might be used to sell a political programme to an electorate.

The third stage of the programme is much less developed in Collins' work. It concerns the attempt to relate the closure of controversies to wider social and political structures in society. I will return to this theme later in the chapter, when examining another tradition in sociology of scientific knowledge which has tried to relate the choice of theories and development of controversies to scientists' group allegiances and, ultimately, the broader societal context. For the moment it will be useful to move away from these rather abstract and programmatic claims and illustrate what they add up to when Collins researches a specific controversy. There are a number of case studies of controversies that have been carried out within this framework (for example, Collins and Pinch, 1982; Pickering, 1981; Pinch, 1986); I will concentrate on one of Collins' own studies which is well known and well respected and concerns a dispute over the detection of gravitational radiation (Collins, 1975, 1981, 1985).

Gravitational Radiation and the Sociology of Facts

One prediction adduced from Einstein's theory of relativity is that gravity ought to be detectable as a form of radiation. The movements of large objects should create a flux or discharge of this radiation. The problem for researchers is that this flux is almost unimaginably weak, making detection an exceptionally difficult task. However, massive galactic events such as exploding stars should generate quantities of radiation that might be detectable on the Earth. In 1969 the American physicist Joseph Weber claimed to have been the first person to detect it. Put very simply, he had hung up a very large aluminium bar in a sealed chamber and measured minute vibrations using strain gauges. The bar is like a stick floating at the edge of a pond; if there is a big splash near the middle of the pond it should bob up and down.

Following Weber's claim, a number of other groups of scientists attempted to find gravitational radiation using similar apparatus. None of them found success. Collins examined the published papers and disputes between these scientists as well as interviewing a number of the key figures. Much of his argument was directed against what might be called the orthodox scientific interpretation of what went on – namely, that a number of studies had tried and failed to replicate the original, and thus the original was mistaken. Collins raised two difficulties with this orthodox view.

First, in practice what was described as 'repeating the experiment' did not involve using precisely the same apparatus and measurement techniques as Weber's original. So-called replications generally attempt to improve on the original apparatus, or address its potential shortcomings; there is often no profit for the researcher in doing a mere duplication. In fact, scientists often move between two different ways of characterizing a replication. When considering its methodological role in demonstrating the trustworthiness (or not) of some findings they often characterize the replication as a mere duplication; but elsewhere they may emphasize its novelty or sophistication when compared with the original (see also Ashmore, 1988; Mulkay, 1985).

Collins' study raised a second and more fundamental problem with the orthodox account of replication. For it turned out that there was a lack of agreement over what counted as a competently conducted experiment. Collins documented a range of 'extra-scientific considerations' which were drawn on as evidence of scientific competence or lack of it. It could be the personality and intelligence of the experimenters, a previous history of failures, the prestige of their home university, and so on. He notes that these judgements seem also to be closely related to the scientists' prior beliefs about the existence of gravity waves. Thus scientists who *believed* in measurable gravity waves tended to treat replications claiming to find them as *competent* and replications failing to find them as *incompetent*. Mirroring this, those scientists who did *not* believe gravity waves were measurable thought that the replications which did *not* find them were *competent*, while those which *did* find them were *incompetent*. In this situation the status of replications does not stand outside the controversy in a way that can neutrally close it down in one way or another; rather, the controversy extends to the status of replications.

Collins concluded that the best way to understand what was going on was not to think of it in terms of simple attempts to replicate but as a negotiation about *what counts as* a competent experiment in the field. Rather than replication being an arbiter of dispute, it becomes a focus of dispute in its own right. And as judgements of the competence of experiments were bound up with judgements about the nature of gravitational radiation, in effect the experiments were negotiations about the nature of the phenomena. Collins expressed this perspective on replication in gravity-wave research in the following manner:

the most fruitful way of interpreting the activity of scientists . . . is not as attempts to competently replicate, or competently test . . . findings, but rather as *negotiations about the meaning of a competent experiment* in the field. *Ipso-facto*, they are nego-tiating the character of gravitational radiation and building the culture of that part of science which may become known as 'gravitational wave observation' (Collins, 1975: 216).

This element of the research can be seen as part of the first stage of the empirical programme which demonstrates the potential flexibility in the interpretation of experimental findings.

In a later part of the study, Collins (1981, 1985) went on to the second stage of the programme and tried to show how particular strategies had been used to close the controversy down to the point where it was essentially dead. His crucial sociological point was that there were no purely *rational* or *scientific* reasons that compelled gravity-wave scientists to disbelieve Weber's claims. The incredibility of these claims had to be *socially produced* by the use of a range of different rhetorical strategies.

According to Collins, the critical actor in the controversy was a scientist he called Quest (the pseudonym is to protect his anonymity). Quest was instru-mental in closing down the controversy. However, this was not because of the technical merit of his work, or the novelty of his evidence, or the sophistica-tion of his experimental design; rather, it was because Quest devoted himself to a high-profile campaign, using skilful rhetorical presentations in both sci-entific and more popular outlets. Collins quotes different scientists in the field in support of this interpretation of the effect of Quest's work.

1   . . . as far as the scientific community in general is concerned, it's probably Quest's publication that generally clinched the attitude. But in fact the exper-iment they did was trivial – it was a tiny thing . . . but the thing was the way they wrote it up. . . .

2   Quest had considerably less sensitivity so I would have thought he would have made less impact than anyone, but he talked louder than anyone and he did a very nice job of analysing his data.

3   [Quest's paper] was very clever because its analysis was actually very convinc-ing to other people, and that was the first time that anyone had worked out in a simple way just what the thermal noise from the bar should be. . . . It was done in a very clear manner, and they sort of convinced everybody.

(All from Collins, 1985: 92)

Collins' general conclusion is that, although there were a variety of findings and studies that went against Weber, it was not these that were crucial; it was the *manner* in which they were marshalled by a particular scientist, Quest, alongside his own work, in such a way that they appeared to settle unam-biguously the non-existence of measurable gravity waves. With the campaign a success, the controversy was effectively over, pushed out of the market (one might say) like a weak brand in the face of a sustained bout of television advertising from a stronger competitor.

Collins, Relativism and Facts

At this juncture it is useful for us to take stock of what is valuable in Collins' approach in order to consider how far it could provide the basis for a more general account of fact making. There are two important features of this work which I will carry forward throughout this book. The first is the stance of methodological relativism. Collins does not start from the assumption that Weber's research is flawed or that his critics were misguided. The empirical programme of relativism is intended to be indifferent to both of these possibilities. When he considers the success of Quest and failure of Weber, he is not wanting to argue that this is because Quest is, in fact, *right* or, indeed, that Weber is *wrong*. The alternative to methodological relativism would be to assume a knowledge of astrophysics greater than the participants (a tempting but unlikely claim!) or simply to treat the beliefs of whoever is currently successful as right. That would mean that the social analyst would be forever providing a sociological gloss on the current scientific *status quo*; that is, they would be repeating the Mertonian sociology of error discussed above.

The second feature of Collins' approach I want to emphasize and support is his more general emphasis on deriving conclusions from a detailed analysis of specific fact-making practices. He is avoiding the theoretical or conceptual stipulations that are present in much philosophy of science along with much of the sociology of knowledge tradition (for a useful discussion of that tradition, see Dant, 1991). Such stipulations may be useful if the enterprise is the normative one of specifying what *should* count as a good fact; if, however, the concern is with what *participants* count as factual in particular social settings, and how their versions are warranted, then a strongly analytic stance will be indispensable. Throughout this book I will emphasize the virtues of understanding fact construction through considering actual cases.

Both methodological relativism and the analytic focus are very important. However, Collins' work raises some equally interesting but much more problematic issues (see also Ashmore, 1989; Mulkay et al., 1983). It is worth spending time on them as they have implications for how my argument will continue. I will take three areas of difficulty in turn: Collins' use of a realist perspective to understand the social world; the leaking away of his relativism in analytic practice; his treatment of accounts of rhetoric as non-rhetorical. To address these points we will need to become more and more entangled in some of the rich but complex detail involved in the study of fact making. In fact, we can start to see that much of the descriptive language that we have used up to now in talking about science is far from neutral in its implication about what is going on.

The Problem of Social Realism   Collins adopts a realist stance when conceptualizing the activities and beliefs of scientists. His scientific world is furnished with individual scientists; these scientists have specific beliefs and are organized into collectivities within which there are controversies with sides; they may be persuaded by rhetoric or by evidence; and a controversy can be up and running or closed down. Collins is treating science as you might a car engine: here is the distributor, over there the spark plugs, when the pistons move they turn the crankshaft, and so on. Thus Collins takes issue with the stories that scientists tell about gravity waves, the quality of experiments, and more generally how science progresses; yet, at the same time, he is accepting their general common-sense understanding of the relevant categories, objects and processes.

This is an important point, so it is worth spelling out carefully what is being suggested. Take categories of scientists, for example. It is possible to take a category such as 'gravity-wave scientists' as a neutral descriptive term that collects together all the scientists who actually work on gravity waves. That would be to treat the category realistically. However, the category can also be treated as a construction; that is, as a category that different scientists use with different boundaries, say, and as part of different activities. Some versions of the category may be widely accepted, while others may be fiercely contested.

There are numerous theoretical reasons for questioning the kind of social realism Collins uses, some of which derive from traditions of social analysis that we will cover in later chapters (such as ethnomethodology and deconstruction). But for the moment I will focus on the analytic problems that confront Collins in his attempt to produce a unitary and realist version of what is happening in the social worlds of 'gravity-wave scientists'.

To understand these problems better it is necessary briefly to consider Collins' analytic method. Although the gravity-wave study was conducted mainly through two major interview tours, along with extensive reading of the gravity-wave literature, Collins characterizes what he is doing as developing his *participant comprehension* of the field (Collins, 1983b). That is, he is not treating his interviews simply as a means of finding out what is going on in the field; instead he is using them as a setting in which to develop his participants' understanding of what is involved in gravity physics. He learns what is involved in being a member of this community, albeit somewhat vicariously, and then uses this developing understanding to guide his analysis. This means that when he presents extracts from interviews they are not meant to be the *data* on which the analysis is based but an *exemplification* of his participants' understanding. Given that they are meant to be ideal cases, is it possible to re-read them in a way that reveals a different story? That is, is it possible to trouble Collins' realist story? I want to argue that it is.

When we start to look for it, it is not hard to find considerable variability in the way events, people and developments in the gravity-wave field are constructed by the participants. For example, I quoted above some participants who present Quest as having been effective in closing down the controversy; others characterized their response to Quest very differently:

4   [Quest and his group] are so obnoxious, and so firm in their belief, that only their approach is the right one and that everyone else is wrong, that I immediately discount their veracity on the basis of self delusion. (Collins, 1981: 47)

Variability of this kind is profoundly troubling for the kind of realist story Collins is telling. It poses the question of how Collins decided on his particular version of Quest's effectiveness, or on his version of what is happening in the field more generally. To construct his realist account in the face of variability of this kind Collins is forced into selectively reifying (reading as literally true) some accounts and ironizing (treating as mistakes, lies or rhetoric) other accounts. I will discuss these two terms in more detail in Chapter 4. Collins was led to work in this way by the demands of producing a realist version from the competing and fragmentary texts at his disposal. This also leads him into difficulties sustaining his relativist stance.

The Problem of Relativism Leakage   Although the relativist position allows Collins to be disinterested in the truth or otherwise of scientists' utterances about the natural world, his need to provide a definitive version of what is going on in the social world forces him to make exactly such judgements concerning scientists' utterances about the social world. The difficulty with this is in keeping the two sorts of judgements separate. For example, Collins claimed that the technical arguments against Weber's experiments were not sufficient to end the controversy – it had to be finished off rhetorically. However, this appears to be moving beyond a mere judgement about what is happening in the field socially towards the provision of a definitive version of the adequacy of particular experiments. Indeed, it is the sort of version that Weber could use in defence of his position; he might say: 'They have not shown me to be wrong scientifically; I am a victim of a political vendetta.'

The particular concern with the way relativist analysis may favour one party in a dispute has been developed by Brian Martin, Evelleen Richards and Pam Scott (1991). They give examples of the way relativist studies of scientific controversies – for example, over the value of vitamin C in cancer treatment – can be treated as asymmetrical by the participants. As studies of this kind are showing the flexibility in the interpretation of experimental findings, and the rhetorical means through which disputes are closed down, they can be drawn on by the participants on the weaker side in the controversy to help criticize the stronger side. The demonstration of the social contingency of an argument is more troubling for an argument that has been established as solid and rationally justified than for one that has been widely treated as unreliable and inadequately justified. Martin et al. (1991) refer to the phenomena of participants in a controversy taking over SSK arguments within the controversy as *capturing*.

The point I am making is slightly different from that of Martin et al.; it is not that Collins' work has been captured by participants but that it is inevitably involved in making judgements about the content of science, because these are inseparable from judgements about what is happening socially. Accepting evaluations of the relative worth of sets of experiments (for instance, that Quest's research was trivial but rhetorically effective) amounts to the same thing as evaluating the relative worth of different versions of the natural world. To paraphrase Collins' own conclusion about replication:

negotiations about the value (rhetorical or genuine) of a particular experiment are, *ipso facto*, negotiations about the character of gravitational radiation.

The Problem of Non-rhetorical Rhetoric   The final issue is with the way Collins uses the notion of rhetoric. Rhetoric is central to his account because it provides closure to controversies; without it the indeterminate nature of experimental findings would allow the controversy to drift on and on. Yet although rhetoric is one of his major concepts for understanding social life, he does not explore its senses or develop an elaborate theoretical account of the notion. When he provides examples of rhetoric they are often in the form of rhetoric *attributions*. That is, he gives examples of people claiming that such and such an experiment or publication had its effect through rhetoric – but takes the claims themselves as *non*-rhetorical. Michael Billig (1989) has suggested that rhetoric attributions of this kind are themselves a powerful rhetoric.

I will be devoting more space in later chapters to the role of rhetoric in social analysis. For the moment let me start with a preliminary, but useful, definition of rhetoric as discourse used to bolster particular versions of the world and to protect them from criticism. Using this notion, let us look again at the extracts (1–3 above) which Collins uses to illustrate his claim that it was Quest's rhetoric that was crucial in finishing the gravity-wave controversy rather than the intrinsic quality of his research findings.

1b   . . . as far as the scientific community in general is concerned, it's probably Quest's publication that generally clinched the attitude. But in fact the experiment they did was trivial – it was a tiny thing . . . but the thing was the way they wrote it up. . . .

2b   Quest had considerably less sensitivity so I would have thought he would have made less impact than anyone, but he talked louder than anyone and he did a very nice job of analysing his data.

3b   [Quest's paper] was very clever because its analysis was actually very convincing to other people, and that was the first time that anyone had worked out in a simple way just what the thermal noise from the bar should be. . . . It was done in a very clear manner, and they sort of convinced everybody.

(All from Collins, 1985: 92)

In each of these extracts we see the speaker focusing on the effect of Quest's work on *other* scientists. These scientists do not characterize *themselves* as taken in by what they see as the work's style; indeed, they are keen to praise Quest's clarity, his very nice job of data analysis and his novel problem solution. We therefore have to take on trust that these speakers can give an accurate account, not only of the influence of Quest's work on a large number of other scientists, but also exactly what feature of the papers was responsible for the influence. The irony in Collins' analysis, then, is that he is elevating rhetoric to a position as the crucial lubricant for controversy closure – yet he is treating the accounts which supposedly show this as non-rhetorical.

This discussion has taken us some way from central features of Collins' Empirical Programme of Relativism. However, its value is in introducing issues which will appear repeatedly in different guises in the course of work on fact construction. If we think back to the use of a car engine as a metaphor for the social world of science, we can now be clear just how limited it is. Rather than there being carburettors, plugs and so on which are simply *there* to study (or so the garage tells us!), we would need to treat these things as *constructions*. The social world of science is produced in the talk and writing of the different scientists. And the production is very much a part of the business at hand. Weber can use the sort of construction that Collins has worked up as part of his defence that his research was undermined by rhetoric rather than proper scientific argument; Quest can characterize his arguments as effective because they so clearly show Weber's flaws. From this perspective it makes sense for us as analysts to treat *both* gravity waves *and* social processes equally as constructions.

Oh, and there is another construction here, of course. It would be very odd, to say the least, for me to expend this effort in showing some of the difficulties of Collins' mixture of realism and constructionism, and then to repeat them precisely in my own text. My version of Collins' work is a story put together for the purposes of this text, it is designed to make a particular argument. Collins, the Empirical Programme of Relativism, philosophy of science – all these things are simplifying and clarifying categories that allow me to build a story. That is not to say that the story is wrong or untrue or inaccurate – for those judgements presuppose that there is a definitive 'Collins', a definitive philosophy, and so on that this account could be compared with. It is a story that works here.

For the rest of this chapter I will discuss, rather more briefly, two of the main contemporary alternatives to the Empirical Programme of Relativism: constructionism and interest theory. As well as being important players in contemporary SSK, they will allow us to address further central issues that are involved in the study of fact construction.

Constructionist and Interest Theories of Scientific Fact Making

These two approaches to the sociology of scientific knowledge have their own distinctive features; yet they share with Collins' work a rejection of the principal assumptions of traditional Mertonian sociology of science. They reject the view that a set of broad social norms will ensure the production of true knowledge, as well as the idea that the task of the social analyst is to account only for scientific errors. Constructionist work will be considered first. This is best exemplified by the work of Karin Knorr Cetina (1981, 1996) and that of Bruno Latour and Steve Woolgar (1986). While Collins' research is based largely on interview studies (although, as I have indicated, he gives them an ethnographic spin), Knorr Cetina and Latour and Woolgar derived their conclusions mainly from ethnographic studies performed in laboratories involved in biochemistry and high energy physics. As Knorr Cetina put it, ethnography 'furnished the optics for viewing the process of knowledge production as "constructive" rather than descriptive; in other words, for viewing it as constitutive of the reality knowledge was said to "represent"' (1995a: 141). Such studies involved spending time with scientists watching their actions at the lab bench, sitting with them at their workstations as they analyse data, and trying to make sense of what is going on in much the same way that an anthropologist might make sense of an exotic culture. Indeed, it is hard to think of a culture more exotic than the high-energy physicists at CERN with their vast detection machines and extraordinary cosmologies.

The Construction of Knowledge

The term 'constructionism' is used with a number of distinct and sometimes contradictory shades of meaning across the social sciences and even within SSK itself. I have already briefly introduced the phenomenological variety of constructionism of Berger and Luckmann (1966), which was concerned with the life world of individuals; how a person's experience takes the form of solid and enduring entities and structures. In SSK a constructionist approach is typically contrasted to a descriptive approach. In this case what is being stressed is a contrast to parts of the standard or storybook view which treats science as producing increasingly accurate and powerful descriptions of an external reality. Knorr Cetina expressed this contrast as follows:

> Rather than view empirical observation as questions put to nature in a language she understands, we will take all references to the 'constitutive' role of science seriously, and regard scientific inquiry as a process of production. Rather than considering scientific products as somehow capturing what is, we will consider them as selectively carved out, transformed and constructed from whatever is. And rather than examine the external relations between science and the 'nature' we are told it describes, we will look at those internal affairs of scientific enterprise which we take to be *constructive*. (1981: 1, emphasis in original)

In opposition to the standard view, Knorr Cetina and others in this tradition have suggested that the products of science are fabricated through social interaction between specific individuals in accordance with *ad hoc* criteria in idiosyncratic circumstances that are dealt with in an opportunistic manner. Much of a researcher's time will be occupied with 'tinkering'; that is, using the local resources – apparatus, raw materials, available skills – to 'make things work', where the criteria of something 'working' will itself have been developed. The analytic studies in this area have concentrated on documenting the role of these different constructive activities in fact production.

This perspective has two related consequences for how epistemology is understood in practice; that is, for the status of scientific knowledge. On the one hand, the argument is that there is nothing epistemologically special about scientific work. Scientific knowledge production does not have principled differences from knowledge in legal or everyday settings. Not surprisingly, this is a claim that has not always been taken in good spirit by practising scientists (for example, Wolpert, 1993). Knorr Cetina quotes Richard Rorty's provocative formulation: '"no interesting epistemological difference" could be identified between the pursuit of knowledge and the pursuit of power' (1995a: 151). On the other hand, the argument breaks up the supposed uniformity of scientific practices. Rather than science being characterized by a small set of methods that are followed, whether in bio-chemistry, astronomy or sociology, constructionists have stressed that scientific disciplines and sub-disciplines operate with a disparate set of epistemic cultures. For example, molecular biologists and high-energy physicists work with strikingly different notions of the empirical: compare the hypothetical events in the particle collider which may be reconstructed within several concurrently available theoretical systems and the search for change in bacteria growth on a high-protein culture in a petri dish (Knorr Cetina, 1995b).

Constructionists also emphasize the importance of negotiation in the making of scientific knowledge. Again, the point here is generally to build a contrast with the storybook view that scientists' decisions are governed in a mechanical or simple manner by the outcome of experiments, observations, replications and so on. Just as Collins argued that what counts as a competent replication should be seen as a product of negotiation, so various constructionist researchers have shown that a wide range of features of scientific life do not have universal determinate meanings, but are subject to processes of negotiation and interaction. For example, Michael Lynch (1985) has studied the interactions taking place where neuroscientists decide whether observations made by microscope are genuine phenomena or really artefactual. These interactions are not merely an adjunct to the decisions, but are part of the constitution of their nature.

Exactly what is being suggested about the nature of knowledge and truth by workers in this perspective is not always clear. For example, at times Knorr Cetina (for example, 1982b) has characterized her work as complementary to that of Collins; yet at other points she has distanced herself from his work, and seems to be more interested in following up the sociological implications of accepting the Quine–Duhem thesis (Knorr Cetina, 1982a). Although she has adopted the methodological relativism which is widespread in SSK she did not follow Collins in hypothesizing that the 'natural world' makes no difference to science. As she puts it, 'facts are not made by pronouncing them to be facts but by being intricately constructed against the *resistances* of the natural (and social!) order' (1995b: 148, emphasis added). For her, the natural world is an emergent product of laboratory practices, but this does not mean that these practices are not revealing high quality, powerful or at least useful knowledge in some not quite precisely specified sense.

Whatever the detailed epistemological differences between an empirical relativist and a constructionist position, their difference in research emphasis is reasonably clear. While empirical relativists have looked mainly at controversies, constructionists have concentrated on 'unfinished knowledge'. This has involved them approaching fact making through ethnographic and observational studies of scientists at work in laboratories. This emphasis fits, of course, with the theoretical stress on the opportunistic, *ad hoc*, situated nature of knowledge manufacture. If scientific products are closely dependent on the contingencies of their location of production then that is the sensible place in which to study them. The observer needs to be on the spot because that is where knowledge is actually manufactured. This is a contrast to Collins who, in his work on controversies, sees the end of a controversy as the moment when a fact is finally stabilized; that is, when the last strings are pulled out of the bottle, the glue is set and the ship is standing magically. Knorr Cetina sees facts as fabricated through procedures taking place somewhere within the laboratory; while the controversy is merely the place in which they are later argued over, rationalized and accepted or rejected.

We have already noted that Collins is rather vague in his use of notions such as rhetoric and negotiation in the outcome of controversies. There are often similar ambiguities over the exact explanatory role of some of the features constructionists emphasize when studying the production of specific facts in laboratories. As Knorr Cetina herself notes, the notion of negotiation is used with a range of different inflections and the precise procedures at work in any situation are not always well specified. Part of the problem is that constructionists, like Collins, are often attempting to produce a unitary, realist version of how facts are manufactured out of idiosyncratic local resources; and as such they are subject to the same problems that we documented above with respect to Collins. In particular, constructionists are forced into a mixture of ironizing and reifying accounts as they produce a singular realist narrative, and this means that they have not always attended carefully to the rhetorical orientation of scientists' accounts. This is not to claim that the general perspective, or individual studies done within it, have not made important contributions to understanding fact making. Far from it. The work of Latour, Woolgar and Knorr Cetina has provided a powerful alternative to the accounts of science given by traditional philosophers and historians. Moreover, the general perspective I will be using in this book is a variant of constructionism. To end the chapter, let us now turn to the final SSK perspective concerned with social interests.

The Theory of Social Interests

The best-known researchers in this tradition are Barry Barnes (1977, 1982), David Bloor (1982, 1991) and Steven Shapin (1982; Shapin and Schaffer, 1985). These and others have tried to explain the content of scientific knowledge in terms of various kinds of interests. Put simply, perhaps rather too simply, these researchers suggested that scientists are making certain claims about reality because it is in their interest to make those claims. Some of these interests may be a product of the local disciplinary context in which a scientist works – scientists may have an interest in getting their work published, for example, as this will further their careers. And studies of scientific practice which are concerned with interests of this type (for example, Pickering, 1984) overlap to a considerable extent with those in the empirical relativist and constructionist traditions. What is distinctive and provocative in the theory of social interest is the emphasis it places on the role of scientists' background culture and broader social allegiances – their group memberships and political viewpoints. And it is this aspect of the approach which I will concentrate on here.

The Quine–Duhem thesis has again proved a useful reference point for interest theorists (Barnes, 1982), although they refer to 'Hesse nets' in recognition of the important development of these ideas by the philosopher Mary Hesse (1980). As I noted earlier in the chapter, the Quine–Duhem thesis suggests we regard scientific beliefs as lying in an extensive interconnected network or web of belief. Although observations provide a boundary condition for this network, no individual observation has a determinate effect because of the interconnected nature of the network. Any particular belief statement may thus be retained in the face of a contradictory observation statement by making a readjustment somewhere else in the network: by modifying or abandoning a theory, say, or even in the extreme case a logical law (Quine, 1961).

One important consequence of the Quine–Duhem model, which I have not stressed so far, is that there will be a strongly *conventional* aspect to scientific judgement. When a novel observation or theoretical statement is introduced into the network there are a range of different ways in which adjustments could be made. The adjustments that are actually made will be dependent on some general notions about what sort of transformations in the network are acceptable. Interest theorists have argued that such general notions themselves are neither a product of 'observation' nor 'pure reason' (Barnes, 1981). In his original article Quine talked rather vaguely of the network tending towards 'simplicity' and 'conservatism'. Interest theorists have suggested that such general notions are not sufficient to force determinate choices between theories; they have to be supplemented by the operation of social interests. They will modify their networks in ways that serve their interests and they will also use their interests as standards against which to evaluate extensions of the network (Pickering, 1992: 4).

From this perspective certain scientific laws or theories will be retained, perhaps in the face of what some scientists would see as contradictory evidence, because of their perceived use in justifying social world views. That is, the social background of a group of scientists may lead them to see a certain configuration of theory as appropriate because it fits in with their social understanding. Interest theorists argue that this will result in homologies between the structure of knowledge and the structure of society (Bloor, 1982). Scientists will be literally rediscovering or redescribing the structure of their society in their test-tubes and cloud chambers.

This is all rather abstract – let me try and flesh it out using a highly regarded study of the relation of interests to scientific knowledge. Brian Wynne (1979) tried to demonstrate the crucial role of social interests in a debate about the nature of the 'ether' in late Victorian times. Many astrophysicists in Victorian Britain believed in the existence of the ether, an invisible medium that filled space and explained a variety of physical and astronomical phenomena. Wynne claims that the theory of ether was drawn on by its proponents at Cambridge University as a part of a moral discourse to legitimate their own social ideals. Ether theory reflected their general social and religious beliefs which stressed 'the organic unity of knowledge, metaphysical realism, and the unseen world' (Wynne, 1979: 176). These social beliefs opposed the fast-growing secular ideology of scientific naturalism and individualism which, according to Wynne, was a by-product of industrialization and the increasing power of the bourgeois middle class. Thus there is a two-way causal connection: ether theory was influenced by broader social concerns, and it was also used to effect those concerns. Put simply, it was believed because of the ideology of its proponents, and these proponents used the theory to justify that ideology.

Interest theory has made an important contribution to SSK and has stimulated a number of fascinating case studies of scientific episodes. However, it raises some of the same issues that we noted above with respect to constructionism and, in more detail, with respect to the empirical programme of relativism (see also Woolgar, 1981; Yearley, 1982). It represents another attempt to develop a realist version of a particular arena of scientific work; indeed, it is even more ambitious, for not only does it depend on producing a realist account of scientific events, beliefs and groupings but it also has to co-ordinate this with a similarly definitive account of the nature of particular social groupings, classes and their ideologies. Whether such a version is *in principle* possible or not, in practice, interest analysts are also involved in processes of selective ironization and reification as they assemble an account from particular historical documents. In addition, because of their emphasis on the central role of group allegiances they are led to provide clear-cut group and sometimes social class categorizations for each scientist.

For example, Wynne uses a variety of what we might call 'homogenizing devices' to sustain his unified account of the beliefs of Cambridge physicists. The principal device is to treat everyone who taught at Cambridge or went to Cambridge at some point as sharing the same social beliefs. Furthermore, Wynne's attribution of social interests is particularly problematic. He is concerned to show that scientific beliefs are a product of interests and not purely understandable as produced by technical concerns. To warrant this he quotes scientific judgements that the ether theory cannot be warranted purely in terms of the contemporary state of theory and evidence; however, in doing this he is moving away from a relativistic stance and starting to side with critics of ether theory who at times argued exactly this. Yet rather than see these critics' accounts as themselves factual constructions designed for rhetorical purposes (showing the inadequacy of ether theory), Wynne is treating them, for the purposes of his own argument, as definitive documents of the actual situation for ether theory.

So we see again in the theory of social interests the combination of social realism, relativism leakage and selective reification and ironization that we identified in Collins' work. Nevertheless, this is an ambitious theory, and one of the most successful existing attempts to relate the content of scientific knowledge to the broader social climate in which those ideas were produced.

Realism, Relativism and Rhetoric

I have not tried to provide a thorough review of SSK in this chapter. Sociology of scientific knowledge is now a major area of social research and one that has boomed during the 1980s and continues to grow, most recently with a major concern with technology (Bijker and Pinch, 1992). Research in SSK is conducted from several different perspectives of a complexity to which it is hard to do justice in a single chapter. (For very different summaries, see Ashmore, 1989; Jasanoff et al., 1995; Woolgar, 1988b). Some work that is often treated as part of SSK is dealt with elsewhere. For example, Donna Haraway's more postmodern explorations of the intersections between science and society appear in Chapter 3, while discourse analytic work done by Nigel Gilbert and Michael Mulkay is discussed in Chapter 6.

In this chapter I have tried to show how SSK emerged out of issues in the philosophy of science which raised questions about traditional images of science and its operation. Although it focused on the breakdown of the conventional distinction between observation and theory, the stress on the way scientific claims are organized together in interconnected networks, and the emphasis on scientific practice and its communal nature, there are several other themes in recent philosophy of science that would have led in the same direction (Chalmers, 1992). The sociological work which I have reviewed picks up this attack on the storybook view of science and develops it in various directions.

The Empirical Programme of Relativism stresses the flexibility in dealing with scientific findings and the central role of rhetoric in the ending (or sustaining) of controversies. Constructionist work stresses the local and *ad hoc* nature of scientific work along with the importance of negotiating the meaning of observations, methods, replications, policy implications and virtually everything else *in situ*, in laboratories and on work benches. Interest theory reconnects scientists to their broader social allegiances by suggesting that their choice of theory is related to their understanding of society.

Three theoretical and analytic themes will be taken forward into later chapters. First, the argument for methodological relativism is crucial not just for work on science, but for work on fact construction generally. Methodological relativism means that the analyst is not starting with a set of assumptions about what is true and false in any particular social setting and then trying to work out what led some people to get it wrong. Instead, the analyst will be indifferent to whether some set of claims is widely treated by participants as 'true' or 'false'. Truth and falsity can be studied as moves in a rhetorical game, and will be treated as such rather than as prior resources governing analysis, to avoid subordinating the analyst to a current scientific orthodoxy.

Second, one of the positive points about SSK is its strongly analytic, or empirical, orientation. Even though it raises questions about traditional ways of understanding the nature of empirical research, it shows the value of conducting detailed studies of fact construction. One of the distinctive features of the field is its assumption that the best way to study fact construction is to research its operation in particular settings, and I will follow this principle throughout this book. So, although there are important and live philosophical questions to do with realism, epistemology, the nature of truth and so on, these will be bracketed off in favour of concrete investigations of factual accounts. As it turns out, many of them reappear as practical concerns for people as they construct and undermine versions of the world.

The third and final point concerns social realism. The discussion of the work of Collins focused on problems with his combined emphasis on social realism and rhetoric. Collins told a story of controversy resolution which drew on notions of sides, strategies, rhetoric and so on. His goal was the actual story of how the controversy was closed down. And his most central explanatory tool was rhetoric: the scientists were described as mobilizing political strategies. Yet Collins' realism became problematic precisely because of the importance of the rhetoric. Scientists will be constructing powerful arguments not just about gravity waves and experiments but also about the groupings that they fall into, about the rhetoric in each other's papers, and about the very closure of the controversy itself. The problem is in treating the deadness of the controversy as simply there, a social *fact*; when its deadness itself is part of what is at issue. That is, the deadness can be a rhetorical *accomplishment*, but not, as Collins claimed, through rhetorical strategies enabling one side to win, but instead attempting to constitute the controversy as dead is itself one move in the controversy.

Consider this another way. Collins has to limit carefully the effectiveness of rhetoric to make his social realism work. If the rhetoric is too weak, then it is either not strong enough to force the closure of controversies or, even worse for Collins' argument, the controversies are being closed because of the accumulation of rational considerations such as telling evidence, novel analysis of data, successful theorizing. However, if the rhetoric is too strong, the realism breaks down because the social furniture – the groups, closed debates, strategies – becomes subject to rhetorical reworking. In this book the consequences of a strong notion of rhetoric will be explored where nothing (the data, the sides in the controversy, the text I am currently writing) is excluded a priori from being considered as a rhetorical construction. The next chapter discusses the perspectives that have most to say about facts as an accomplishment: ethnomethodology and conversation analysis.

2
Ethnomethodology and Conversation Analysis

Facts have long been a central topic for ethnomethodological study and theorizing. In one of the earliest ethnomethodological writings, Harvey Sacks (1963) stressed that self-characterizations are central to social life. The social world is imbued with stories, versions and representations whose topic is the social world itself. Moreover, these are not merely free-floating images, they are both highly organized and highly consequential; these characterizations are there to do things. Sacks went on to argue that the descriptive activities underlying these characterizations should become an important area for study, and in the course of his lectures he returned again and again to this topic. Harold Garfinkel (1967) developed the same theme in somewhat different directions. One of the basic objectives of his programme for ethnomethodology was to study the methods that people use to produce descriptions of the social world which seem rational, appropriate and justifiable. Ethnomethodology is the study of people's methods for conducting social life in an accountable way; one of its principal topic areas is thus the methods people use for producing and understanding factual descriptions.

Although ethnomethodological research has roots very different from most of the social studies of science discussed in the previous chapter, there are some notable similarities in its arguments against more traditional views of facts and fact construction. Recent studies of science have attacked the storybook model which has science based around some form of simple empiricism. In parallel to this, ethnomethodology has been marshalled against a long-standing view of language which treats what is important about description as the abstract relationship between a word, or utterance, and an object. In this tradition, what descriptions do is 'stand for' something in the world; and as such what it treats as interesting about descriptions is the quality of their 'standing in': are they accurate, distorted, vague, truthful or what?

Interestingly, the consequences of this traditional view of language for social analysis have been similar to the effects of the Mertonian model in sociology of science. It leads to a social science focused on error where what is factual requires no explanation because it is merely a product of language mirroring the world in some way. Put another way, it is assumed that there is literally nothing for the social scientist to explain about factual *accounts* because they are merely the linguistic imprints left by the factual *object*. In this tradition, it is accounts that are in error which need social analysis, for if they are distorted or confabulated, not guaranteed by 'the world', some social or psychological processes have to be invoked to explain their deviation from reality: 'the cult were brainwashed into seeing Koresh as God', for example, or 'her love had blinded her to his violent past', or even 'false consciousness prevents the workers seeing their exploitation'. Just as sociology of scientific knowledge (SSK) has attempted to build a form of analysis which purges their field of this assumption, so ethnomethodologists have attempted the same type of decontamination on a wider scale. They too stress the importance of taking a *symmetrical* approach which attempts to understand utterances considered true and false in the same way.

In this chapter I intend to explore themes from both ethnomethodology and the related tradition of conversation analysis. This will focus on those themes where the procedures by which descriptions are assembled as factual are considered in detail, as well as the role of facts, reports or descriptions in carrying out certain activities. It will start with some of the basic concepts in ethnomethodology as outlined in Harold Garfinkel's classic work. It discusses Melvin Pollner's important work on the way basic assumptions about an intersubjectively available reality are maintained in interaction. The latter part of the chapter will focus on conversation analysis, the more analytically orientated discipline that developed out of ethnomethodology; and it will end with a discussion of some of the limitations of a purely ethnomethodological approach to factual discourse.

Ethnomethodology

In this exposition I am going to focus on three ethnomethodological concepts – indexicality, reflexivity and the documentary method of interpretation – which are pivotal to its radically different understanding of the nature of facts. After that I will discuss some ethnomethodological studies of fact production in organizations.

Indexicality

The central idea of indexicality is that the meaning of a word or utterance is dependent on its context of use. This is true whether the utterance is conventionally thought of as a description, a question, an order or whatever. Put another way, the study of what an utterance means will not reach a satisfactory conclusion without some understanding of the occasion on which the utterance is used. And it is important to note that when ethnomethodologists talk of 'occasion' and 'context' they are meaning more than gross institutional features of the setting of talk – for example, whether it is spoken in a classroom or courtroom. They are highlighting the specifics of the interaction in which the participants are engaged. So to say an utterance is 'occasioned' is to say that it is fitted to a sequence of talk, which is part of a broader social setting.

When philosophers consider meaning they have traditionally distinguished two elements: sense and reference. Ethnomethodologists stress that both of these elements vary in accordance with the occasion of use. For example, if we consider the utterance 'my tummy hurts' said by a child, Sam, there are issues of both sense and reference. Most basically, we should note that Sam made the utterance rather than his friend, Sophie. If she had been the speaker although the same words were used, a different tummy would have been referred to (or 'indexed' – hence 'indexicality'). Moreover, when Sam says 'my tummy hurts' the precise reference could be his stomach, chest or lower abdomen; we might well need some further conversation to sort this out. The use of the word 'tummy' does not, on its own, guarantee a particular referent. Likewise, the sense of the phrase can vary widely. In the appropriate settings we might take it to be a plea for food or, given Sam has already had a second apple *and* an ice-cream, we might take it as a plea for *no* more food. Sam might use this phrase as a way of indicating that he needs the toilet; or it might be a sign of a less conventional form of pain which could involve more expert medical ratification to provide for it a definitive sense, as, say, appendicitis.

John Heritage (1984) makes the important point that indexicality should not be seen as some sort of flaw in ordinary language. We should not think that language is not good enough – not determinate enough or elaborate enough – to refer precisely in all contexts. Rather, this is one of ordinary language's great strengths. Its indexical nature allows a relatively small number of descriptive terms to be used in different ways in a huge variety of different occasions to give just the required inflexion to an account. General and open-ended terms are given precise sense and reference by their use in context. Indeed, without this feature an enormous number of unique descriptive terms would be needed, each of which would have to be learned and understood by both speakers and potential listeners.

Put simply, the basic point is that it is the *combination* of words and context which give the utterance sense. As it stands this is rather a truism (although one which has implications regularly ignored in social science). One of the successes of ethnomethodological work has been its demonstration of the important consequences for both social theory and analysis that flows from this basic point. In terms of theory, we have arrived at a view of language use and understanding which departs radically from the kinds of traditional semantic theories which take sense to be derived from operations on the abstract meaning of words. What ethnomethodology offers instead is a model of understanding which depends on sense being recovered from utterances in context using a range of methods of sense making (Heritage, 1984). Language understanding in this view is not a product of shared semantic representations – a sort of mental dictionary that all speakers can look up – but is the consequence of shared procedures for generating meaning in context (Edwards, 1996). In terms of analysis, this view of language encourages us to examine these procedures directly – ethnomethodologists call them 'members' methods'. In terms of our particular interest in fact construction, the focus shifts to the *practical* nature of factual discourse. The ethnomethodological approach directs us to look at the methods through which factual discourse is constructed, the occasions in which it is embedded, and the uses to which it is put.

Indexical Descriptions in Court

I will illustrate the importance of the indexical nature of factual descriptions by briefly considering some material from an ethnomethodological study of the use of descriptions in a legal setting, specifically a Small Claims Court case in which a litigant is claiming compensation for his flat which has been damaged by water. Anita Pomerantz's (1987) research took as its focus descriptions of the time at which flooding took place in the flat. These initially simple seeming descriptions allowed her to demonstrate clearly the indexical nature of descriptions.

In the following pair of extracts Adj. is the Adjudicator (the equivalent of the judge) and Pla. is the Plaintiff, who has taken the case to the court.

1 *Adj.*:   at two o'clock in the morning.
   Pla.:   on the eleventh.
(Pomerantz, 1987: 227)

2 *Adj.*:   in March last year where early in the morning
(Pomerantz, 1987: 228)

These descriptions were offered in relation to the attempt to settle who should be held responsible for water damage to the flat. Pomerantz notes that there are subtle differences between the descriptions, and suggests that we should understand the reason for these differences in terms of the detailed contexts in which the descriptions were offered. In particular, she attempts to undermine the superficially attractive view that the description in Extract 1 is more accurate and precise than the one in Extract 2. Pomerantz suggests instead that, rather than understanding them as descriptions *abstractly* related to events, we should see them as doing particular kinds of work, performing particular activities, in their specific occasion of use. Furthermore, these differences are not an accident (like water coming through your ceiling) – the descriptions are designed this way *precisely* to accomplish these activities in the best way possible.

Let me illustrate this by providing more of the sequence of interaction in which the descriptions are embedded. Extract 1 occurs in the context of the adjudicator clarifying and formulating the details of the circumstances, and soliciting the plaintiff's testimony.

3 *Adj.*:   This flooding I think occurred at *two o'clock in the morning (0.4)*
   Pla.:   <u>On</u> the eleven⌈ th
   Adj.   ⌊ On: the eleventh
   Pla.:   ((*clears throat*)) This is true.
   Adj.:   And what – Did you go upstairs to find out what was happening?
(Pomerantz, 1987: 232, previously quoted section emphasized. Note: a full explanation of the transcription symbols used is in the Appendix.)

Pomerantz suggests that in identifying the time of day with a number – 'two o'clock' – the adjudicator is using the preferred type of description for testimony. The number here is used as a 'colourless' formulation of how things are; that is, of the 'facts'. The context of Extract 2 is rather different; it is part of the adjudicator's summing up of the case:

4   *Adj.*:   Now this is a case where one must have a good deal of sympathy for Mr
             M. He's been a tenant of S Council for a very long time, and here we
             have an incident *in March last year where early in the morning* water
             starts coming in through the ceiling of their flat and causes damage to
             their carpets and their decorations.

(Pomerantz, 1987: 238, previously quoted section emphasized)

Here, instead of the numerical description 'two o'clock in the morning' the characterization 'early in the morning' is used. Pomerantz suggests that this characterization is not used accidentally; it is not a *sloppy* way of formulating the time; rather, it is used because it provides an understanding of what it is for water to come gushing through your roof at two in the morning. It is not just any time, it is a time that will get you up out of bed when you are fast asleep. Getting up that early in the morning is pretty miserable at the best of times; it is downright horrible when it seems to be raining indoors!

The point, then, is that the adjudicator provides a sense of the event from the plaintiff's perspective, and in doing so displays sympathy. It is not that one description is accurate and one vague; it is that each description is precisely formulated do the relevant actions: legal recording and offering sympathy. The simple but important point to be taken from this study, then, is that to understand the sense of the alternative descriptions of the time of day the water came through the roof is inseparable from the context in which they are uttered. This is the significance of indexicality – it reminds us that utterances are occasioned and to treat them as otherwise will lead to confusions.

There is one further point that it is important to address. The form of analysis used here, and the descriptions of language use, can easily make it seem that the focus is on *strategic* language use. The phrase 'descriptions are designed in this way precisely to accomplish these activities' is suggestive of conscious planning; it can easily be taken to imply that someone is doing the designing. I will address this in more detail at the end of the discussion of conversation analysis. For the moment, just note that it is possible to consider utterances being fitted to contexts in ways that perform actions without necessarily involving the speaker in thought-out, strategic planning. For example, most of us are familiar and skilled at ending telephone conversations, which have been shown by conversation analysts to have a quite complex organization of turns (Schegloff and Sacks, 1973). Yet we would be hard put to make explicit quite how we do it, or what it involves, if we were asked in the abstract. The task would not be too dissimilar from trying to describe how we ride a bicycle. We rarely spend time plotting how to end a phone conversation, or how to stop one ending. It is a practical skill – the sort of thing that the philosopher Gilbert Ryle (1949) calls *know-how*. It makes sense to talk of skill and design, without implying planning and strategy.

Reflexivity

The second major ethnomethodological concept I will consider is reflexivity. This notion draws attention to the fact that descriptions are not just *about* something but they are also *doing* something; that is, they are not merely *representing* some facet of the world, they are also *involved* in that world in some practical way (Garfinkel, 1967; Wieder, 1974). In stressing the reflexive nature of discourse, ethnomethodologists are attempting to undermine the commonly assumed dualism between a description and what it is a description of. Consider again Pomerantz's study of the Small Claims Court. The adjudicator's characterization 'early in the morning' is certainly a description of some feature of the world; but it is not merely that. It also does some business by displaying that sympathy is appropriate and, as such, it is a contribution to the general set of events which consists of the water damage, the court case, the reparations and so on. It is a *constitutive* part of the events; that is, the sense of the events is, in part, constituted by the description. It is this combination of being both *about* and a *part of* to which reflexivity is drawing attention.

A simple way of thinking about this is to consider that people do not use descriptions just for their own sake. Descriptions are performed as parts of actions which are, in turn, embedded in broader sequences of interaction. The notions of reflexivity and indexicality are closely connected. Once you start to treat descriptive utterances as occasioned, you are ceasing to treat them as having a disembodied, abstract relation to some part of the world. Instead you are attending to how they are practically involved with ongoing activities. It might be objected at this point that in the practices of science, at least, the goal is to achieve a straightforward description. However, as the philosophical and sociological work discussed in the last chapter shows, scientific descriptions are produced in a context of varied theoretical and practical concerns, and scientific descriptions are successful in so far as they build on those concerns.

When presented in this way, the reflexive nature of discourse may seem unexceptional or even self-evident. However, like indexicality, its implications are not always well recognized by social scientists. For example, a large amount of research has been done by social psychologists under the general rubric of attribution theory (Hewstone, 1989). Such work typically involves asking people to give explanations for events and then attempting to account for the explanations they chose in terms of the kind of information they had available to them and the information processing they performed on it. One of the striking things about the overwhelming majority of this work has been its failure to consider the reflexive dimension to people's talk and writing (Edwards and Potter, 1992, 1993; Potter and Edwards, 1990). That is, it fails to consider participants' 'explanations' and 'attributions' in terms of the actions they are part of.

Take, for example, the following piece of 'explanatory' discourse from the then British Prime Minister. This is part of an 'answer' in a television interview to a 'question' concerning her involvement in the resignation of her chief finance minister (the quotes around 'explanatory', 'answer' and 'question' are because the nature of the actions being performed is precisely what is at issue here).

> 5   *Thatcher*:   I tried very hard to dissuade the Chancellor from going (0.2) .hh but he had made up his mind and in the end I had to accept his resignation and appoint someone else.
>
> (Edwards and Potter, 1992: 133)

This extract could, with a bit of effort perhaps, be read as a mere description: a neutral telling of the facts. However, in the context of a question which formulates the possibility of the Prime Minister being to blame for the resignation, the description can be heard as designed to display her lack of blame. That is, the description is offered, and put together in just this way, to attend to the current activities of blame and mitigation. Events are being constructed and reality formulated to satisfy the *current* requirement of responding to an accusation.

Reflexivity and Formulations

Ethnomethodologists, and more recently conversation analysts, have not only considered the reflexive nature of formulations of objects and events outside of the ongoing interaction (such as the resignation in Extract 5), but have studied the way what is happening in the current interaction is formulated. We are all familiar with conversational moves such as 'so what you are saying then is . . .'. They preface a formulation of what has just been said. As is to be expected from the reflexive possibilities inherent in talk, such formulations are not neutral, abstract summaries (whatever they might be) but are designed as they are, in order to have specific upshots relevant to future actions (Heritage and Watson, 1979, 1980). Indeed, it would be extremely surprising if they were anything other than this; what would be the point of producing abstract disembodied description of slices of previous interaction? – they would be merely *non sequiturs*.

Formulations, then, are actions done in talk that 'package' the previous interaction, perhaps specifying its nature and upshot, in a way that prepares for future interaction. Telephone closings provide a simple example where it is common for the end of the call to include some turns which formulate what the call has been about and/or check on an agreed plan for future action (Schegloff and Sacks, 1973). I expect most people would recognize the following style of call ending with the formulation of the important business in the call (arrowed) followed by a number of what Schegloff and Sacks call passing and pre-closing turns:

> 6   →   *Ken*:   So, expect me aroun' then
> *Gordon*:   Alright sh::
> *Ken*:   O:kay?
> *Gordon*:   I will do
> *Ken*:   I'll, see you ↓later.

```
Gordon:  I: sh'll see ↓you.
Ken:     Okay?
Gordon:  Sherrio:,
Ken:     °R't° Bye
```
(Simplified from a transcript by Elizabeth Holt: SO88: 1:9:4–5)

Similar sorts of processes appear in institutional contexts. For example, Derek Edwards and Neil Mercer (1987) have described the way that summaries of classroom lessons, which describe the activities, findings and conclusions that have been done, are used by teachers to reformulate capricious and problematical classroom events according to their originally planned outcomes. In effect, what they are often doing is articulating classroom events in terms of what 'ought' to have happened. Others have examined the role of formulations in legal, media and scientific contexts (Atkinson and Drew, 1979; Greatbatch, 1986; Watson, 1990; Yearley, 1981, 1985). In each case the formulation is both *about* some piece of interaction and also a contribution *to* that interaction; that is, it is reflexive.

I have spent some time on the central ethnomethodological concepts of indexicality and reflexivity. It is important now to explore a third concept to flesh out more fully the radical nature of the ethnomethodological reworking of notions of description and fact. This is Harold Garfinkel's notion of a 'documentary method of interpretation'.

The Documentary Method of Interpretation

Harold Garfinkel's (1967) claim that people use a 'documentary method of interpretation' to make sense of the world emphasizes that when people come to understand events and actions, they do so in terms of background expectancies, models and ideas. However, these background expectancies are, in turn, modified by the understanding which is gained. That is, there is a sort of circular process continually taking place where a particular utterance is seen as evidence of an underlying pattern and, in turn, the fact that the utterance is part of this underlying pattern is used to make sense of it. Garfinkel expresses this as follows:

> The [documentary] method consists of treating an actual appearance as 'the document of,' as 'pointing to,' as 'standing on behalf of' a presupposed underlying pattern. Not only is the underlying pattern derived from its individual documentary evidences, but the individual documentary evidences, in their turn, are interpreted on the basis of 'what is known' about the underlying pattern. Each is used to elaborate the other. (1967: 78)

This might initially strike us as simply poor reasoning: a process of confirming expectations. However, Garfinkel's point is that there is no way out of this cycle. It is what all of us make do with in our everyday lives. The only access to underlying patterns is through instances and the only way of understanding instances is in terms of the patterns to which they belong. There is an analogy here with the Quine–Duhem thesis and philosophical critiques of empiricism which stress that observation statements are always necessarily imbued with theory (see pages 20–4 above). Neither observations nor theories determine beliefs – it is the overall organization of the network. But while the Quine–Duhem thesis treats this as a rather abstract process of coming to know, ethnomethodology's emphasis on indexicality and reflexivity situates such understanding in sequences of actions.

Garfinkel illustrated the documentary method in his well-known 'experiments' which were designed to exaggerate and make graphic this process and 'to catch the work of "fact production" in flight' (1967: 79).

The Fake Therapist 'Experiment' and the Documentary Method

Garfinkel's study has superficial similarities to a large amount of the social psychological research conducted in the last four decades. Student volunteers were recruited and placed in a situation where they thought they were taking part in an exercise with a trainee counsellor. They first discussed the background to some problem on which they wanted advice and then were asked to pose, through an intercom, a series of yes/no type questions to the counsellor, who was supposed to be in the adjoining room (the cover story used by Garfinkel to make sense of this bizarre situation is never made fully explicit, and it is doubtful that this study would have been passed by the ethics committee of a modern university). After each question, there was a standardized pause (to give the impression of the therapist thinking it over) and then the answer was delivered – 'yes' or 'no'.

After each answer the participant was asked to switch the intercom off and record a comment on the answer and how effectively it dealt with their problem. The central trick in the study was, of course, that there was no counsellor and the yes/no responses were delivered in entirely random order with no consideration given to the nature of the question. This set-up displays the operation of the documentary method of interpretation. The participants typically used the pattern of yes and no responses to assemble some notion of the underlying pattern of assessment and advice that the counsellor was supposedly making, and in turn, they used their developing and changing notion of the underlying pattern to reinterpret the yes and no responses. The apparent lurches produced by the randomization of responses were intended to force the operation of the documentary method out into the open.

Garfinkel's write-up and transcripts of some of the sessions point to a number of features of the documentary method; I will concentrate on three. The first and most basic is its flexibility. None of the undergraduates had any difficulty in getting through the exchange; none of them broke off and said that there was something funny going on, that this made no sense. They all claimed to have heard the randomized yes/no answers as answers to *their* questions which provided advice on *their* problem. In daily life, of course, there are various procedures for checking out and repairing problems that crop up in understanding interaction (Schegloff, 1992a); part of the role of the experimental set-up was precisely to stop these procedures from coming into play.

The second feature of the exchanges in the study is that they had what Garfinkel termed a *retrospective-prospective* orientation. By this he means that the subjects did not view their understanding of the fake therapist's answers as definitive. When an answer was not obvious or was unclear they would reconsider their understanding of previous responses to try and make sense of it, or they would ask additional questions to try and explicate the meaning of a problematic answer. That is, the sense of what had passed was constantly open to reworking, while the sense of what was to come was dependent on the framing of current understandings. One radical implication from this is to call into question simple notions of the passing of time. Instead of the past being set solid, like a strip of cooling plastic being extruded from a nozzle, it becomes a set of provisional forms that can be reformulated and reworked in the light of later events.

Third, and most generally, the participants can be seen to be generating meaning in the replies they received; they started with the expectation that these replies would fall into an understandable pattern and this expectation was maintained, although the pattern needed frequent reworking. Furthermore, the pattern generated expectations about what it is normal and proper for counsellors to say, what kind of advice it is appropriate for them to give, and about the nature of the world in which the advice is to be implemented. That is, the undergraduates *constructed* the sense of the adviser's answers to fit in with their normative expectations. According to Garfinkel, in an important sense they are reproducing the basic assumptions of local culture in the course of their interpretations.

Of course, this specific situation is highly artificial, with more of the flavour of a party game than a piece of natural interaction; the kind of party game, for example, where a dupe has to guess a party guest's fantasy – and where the dupe will usually confidently elaborate the fantasy on the basis of answers to yes/no questions, which are in fact delivered according to whether the dupe's question ends in a vowel or consonant. The result is often extraordinarily elaborate and sometimes excruciatingly embarrassing. Garfinkel's particular 'game' is meant to exemplify processes which go on continually, and necessarily, as people come to make sense of their worlds. Social facts – that the National Health Service is under threat, that our partner is depressed, that a joke was meant insultingly – are inevitably produced using methods such as the documentary method. Garfinkel stresses that there is no 'time out' from such methods. The significance of the basic processes highlighted in the counsellor study have been explored in a rather different, and more analytically focused, way in the more naturalistic arena of everyday talk by conversation analysts, as we will see later in this chapter.

Organizational Practices of Fact Making

Although the documentary method study is based around interaction between two individuals, some important ethnomethodological studies have concentrated on fact production in more institutional settings. Here the topic

has been the institutional processes involved in the production of records, statistics and various other forms of official data, whether by agencies such as
the police and social workers, by doctors, or by social researchers themselves
(for a range of such studies, see Atkinson, 1995; Cicourel, 1974; Garfinkel,
1967; Mehan, 1986; Sudnow, 1967). I will address this theme here, first using
a simple example of 'rape statistics' and then a more developed research illustration from Max Atkinson's (1978) work on suicide attribution and the
construction of suicide statistics.

A variety of social processes contribute to the make-up of official records
of rape. To become a 'rape case', and hence a statistic, the victim has to present herself to the police and be believed. Thus the official incidence will
depend, among many other things, on the skills and prejudices of the police
and on the perceptions and fears of the victim. Thus an 'increase in the
occurrence of rape' shown by the statistics could be due to a range of different things. It *could* be due to an increase in sexual violence, yet it could also
be to do with a change in perception of the police, or a change in the sensitivity of the police, leading more victims to report the crime so that they
become cases; alternatively, it could be due to changes in the criteria used
when recording rape cases. Unfortunately, these statistics are still misleadingly
called simply rape statistics rather than (perceptions of) police (in)sensitivity
statistics, or something even more cumbersome.

Although some of these features of social statistics are increasingly widely
recognized in popular discussions of such material, their potentially critical
implications are widely ignored – no doubt because of the problems they
pose to the process of making clear inferences from such materials. At the
same time, such a discussion can undermine the rhetorical use of such statistics; for example, working up statistics by various procedures can be a device
for justifying extra resources. The central point, then, is that in the production
of an official record, such as a rape statistic, a variety of institutional
processes will take place which will have an important bearing on the nature
of the record.

Max Atkinson (1978) provides one of the best, and clearest, illustrations of
the various social processes that contribute to the recording of 'official facts',
in this case the facts of interest being suicide statistics (which have long been
considered important for throwing light on the quality of particular patterns
of social life). Atkinson starts by noting various general problems with interpreting cross-national and cross-cultural suicide statistics. For example, styles
of suicide vary markedly in the ease in which they can be classified as suicide
or some other form of death. While hanging may be relatively unambiguous,
at the other extreme, drowning can easily be an accident. Self-killing in cars,
given the carnage that happens in the perfectly normal course of things on the
road, is particularly hard to identify. Furthermore, the stigma of suicide
varies across nations and social groups. In strongly Catholic cultures, families
may be very reluctant to interpret a death in that way; and this may have an
important influence on the coroner and on the practice of suicide itself and
on the method chosen. Thus, just as rape statistics reflect views about the

police, so suicide statistics reflect cultural fashions in self-killing as well as its local significance. The point here is that the records are systematically related to a wide range of factors that become embodied in their construction; or, in more ethnomethodological terms, they reflect a variety of *members' methods* that are used in their construction.

Atkinson follows this general point with a more subtle one about the processes of suicide attribution. He notes that for coroners to classify a death as a suicide they have to draw on a range of information: they have a version of the biography of the deceased, possibly a suicide note, and information about the circumstances of the death. How they deal with these materials will depend on their own lay theories and assumptions about suicide. For example, in an ambiguous set of circumstances (a drowning in a canal which could have been suicide or an accident) information to the effect that the victim had been depressed could encourage a suicide verdict, or indeed, particulars such as the weather: they probably would not normally be walking next to the canal when it was raining; while a set of cigarette butts on the bank may be taken to indicate a final weighing up of the situation before the fatal plunge.

The important point that Atkinson takes from this study is that in the discovery and attribution of suicide the coroner and other relevant reporters (family, police, witnesses) draw on their own theories of the nature and causes of suicide. This means that suicide statistics are *already* a reflection of theorized versions of suicide. So social scientists who are attempting to use the figures to clarify what suicide is, and how it relates to phenomena such as psychiatric illness, are inevitably involved in a process of *rediscovery*. Put another way, the 'facts' about suicide are inseparable from the methods through which these facts were constructed (see also Smith, 1983). In some respects this parallels the breakdown of the fact/theory distinction noted by philosophers of science. In each case the standard view is of facts being there for the researcher to discover and to guide their theories, but as we come to a more subtle understanding we realize that the seemingly independent facts have already been constructed on the basis of a set of theoretical assumptions and decisions.

Pollner and Mundane Reason

One of the most important developments in ethnomethodology with respect to the study of facts is Melvin Pollner's (1987) work on what he calls *mundane reason*. The principal idea is a simple one. Pollner notes that when we are discussing features of our world with others – what went on, who did what and so on – we make a fundamental assumption. We assume that we all have at least potential access to the same underlying reality. Any neutral, competent observer, placed in the same position, will see the same thing. This is one of the basic assumptions of empiricism; and it is what Pollner means by mundane reason.

Now at first sight we may consider it odd to talk of this as a form of *reason* at all; for surely, we might think, that is just the way things are. After all, every time we give directions to someone to meet us for lunch we assume that the paths, doors and buildings will be pretty much the same for both of us. We do not think that the path will have moved 200 metres south, let alone that it will have turned into a river. However, Pollner puts quite a lot of work into convincing us that this is indeed a form of reasoning, a specific method for understanding; and, moreover, that it is one which is fundamental because it is at the centre of a web of beliefs about reality, self and other people.

One of the devices he uses to show up the working of mundane reason is to examine situations where there are fundamental conflicts over basic facts; he calls these *reality disjunctures*.

Reality Disjunctures

To start to reveal the operation of mundane reason, Pollner turns a basic assumption on its head: rather than asking how we could believe anything *else* given the overwhelming support for mundane reason, he asks how mundane reason can be maintained in the face of frequent counter examples. For example, how can this assumption that we all have at least potential access to the same underlying reality be maintained in the face of the sorts of basic conflicts in accounts that are commonplace in settings such as law courts? We can see here that Pollner is getting leverage on this issue by using a similar methodological relativism to that which we saw deployed effectively by social studies of science researchers in the previous chapter. In this case, he is resisting using 'what we all know' as a start point for social analysis and is instead asking how 'what we all know' is maintained. In ethnomethodological terms, the question is: what methods are used to sustain mundane realism in the face of the threat posed to it by reality disjunctures?

Pollner studied this process at work in the practices of a traffic court. In this situation mundane realism was repeatedly under threat from the reality disjunctures which abounded as defendants disagreed on basic matters with police officers and witnesses. However, the judges did not take this wealth of evidence as an opportunity for reworking their basic epistemological assumptions: the judges did not pronounce the world to be plural and open-ended; rather they made a variety of *practical* resolutions of these disjunctures in a way which sustained mundane reason.

The following example from Pollner's court materials has a defendant dealing with an accusation that he was aiding and abetting illegal drag racing; he asserts that there was no drag racing at all taking place. From within the assumptions of mundane reason it is a scene that cannot exist: two contrary things happening simultaneously. The conflict in reports generates the fundamental mundane problematic. In the extract that follows, J is the judge and D the defendant, while twenty-five or five is twenty-five dollars or five days in jail.

7 *J*:   How do you plead?
   D: Could I plead guilty with an explanation?

J: All right sir.
D: Well it's true that I was at the scene of this incident, but it's not true that I was guilty. . . . What happened is . . . I saw my mother and a friend parked. . . . They were just down there to see what was happening . . . and then the police barricaded both ends of the street off so we couldn't leave, then they charged me with aiding and abetting a drag racing contest, and there was no drag racing at all taking place.
J: Well, the officers appeared at the scene of extensive drag racing and gave an estimate of three hundred people present. Were there about three hundred people there?
D: No, ma'am, there wasn't.
J: Then, well perhaps –
D: I would say approximately a hundred and fifty and I –
J: Er, what were a hundred and fifty people doing at Riverside and Fletcher Drive?
D: Oh, well maybe there had been drag racing part of the time, but . . . while I was there, there was no drag racing at all, not even anyone driving a car on the street.
J: That'll be twenty-five or five.
(Pollner, 1987: 38–9, slightly shortened)

There are many fascinating features of this interchange. For Pollner, the interest is in how this apparent assault on the fundamentals of mundane reason is managed. After all, in the face of an initially basic conflict between versions, which poses the question of whether there is the same thing in the world to be seen, the Judge and Defendant emerge with their basic epistemology intact, although one is twenty-five dollars poorer. Of course, as *we* read this extract we have to work hard at maintaining the sceptical stance that Pollner is striving for; we are not even a *little* surprised by the conflict that occurs between versions. But this is part of Pollner's point.

Despite our minimal knowledge of the participants and the events described, and even the *kind* of putative event it is (we may have never been to a drag race, let alone an illegal one), we have a ready-made set of ways of interpreting the account which explains why these are competing versions of a single actual event rather than the symptoms of a basic fault in epistemology. For example, the setting is one in which the Defendant can be seen as having a strong *interest* in rebutting the police version. In Chapter 5 I will spend some time focusing on how the attribution of interest is bound up with the construction and destruction of factual accounts. In Pollner's terms, our use of this interpretative method of interest imputation has sustained the basic assumption of mundane reason against threat.

In his discussion of the account Pollner notes that the participants themselves use another kind of method to reconcile the threatened reality disjuncture. The Defendant produces an account which leaves his version and that of the police relating to different periods in time. The police report what happened at the height of the drag racing, while the defendant claims to have been present only after drag racing had finished and people were drifting away. This is a prototypical form of resolution of disjunctures: 'the conflict is made to "disappear", because the two accounts no longer describe an identical referent' (Pollner, 1987: 40).

Pollner suggests that there are a wide range of methods that participants use to resolve conflicts between versions which threaten to turn into fully fledged reality disjunctures. He groups these into three levels. First there is the level of the *object*. Here dissonant reports are dealt with by treating them as not concerning the same object or scene. Extract 7 is an example of this. Alternatively, it may be the same object but the conflict may be a product of the different positions of the observer. Second, there is the level of *experience*. This can involve some sort of distortion of mental processes. For example, the speaker may be reporting something that they hallucinated, or they may be presented as having been too drunk to remember something properly. Third, there is the level of *accounts*. Here the concern is with various intentional effects that speakers may be trying to achieve. They might be joking or using a metaphor; or, as in our discussion of Extract 7, they may be lying. We use all of these methods at these different levels to make sense of events and to sort out 'the facts' in different situations. Pollner's point is not that there is anything wrong with this; rather, it is that we should understand that these are indeed *methods of sense making* and, furthermore, that they are reflexively used to sustain mundane reason.

The Politics of Puzzle Resolution

One of the features of mundane reason that Pollner stresses is that although there is a wide variety of techniques for the resolution of the reality puzzles which arise through competing reports of how things are, they in no way ensure that there will be consensual resolution of the puzzles. When accused of imagining an embarrassing scene that happened at the previous evening's party because you were drunk you can respond that the accuser does not want to admit it happened because they were involved and they were sober! Because of the interconnected nature of beliefs and assumptions such a dispute can unfold into a clash between basic *moral* or *ideological* conflicts.

This is well illustrated in a study by Hugh Mehan (1990), which focused on a psychiatric interview in which a patient is being assessed for potential release by a group of mental health workers. The patient is upset because, as he put it, he is quite unreasonably being kept in the hospital against his wishes and the doctors are systematically misunderstanding his point of view. In the psychiatrists' discourse, the patient is described as a paranoid schizophrenic who plainly has delusions about the role of the doctors, and should continue to be incarcerated. Robert DeNiro plays a very similar scene in the film of Oliver Sacks' *Awakenings;* he gets crosser and crosser about his continued incarceration, and the doctors treat his anger as a good reason to continue it. In effect, both the patient and doctors have systems of understanding which are relatively impermeable because they reinterpret the perceptions and actions of the other in their own terms. In this case, there is no resolution of the conflict as such; rather, there is an asymmetrical relationship of power in defining what the situation is. The psychiatrists are the ones deciding the fate of the patients who are limited by their world view. Mehan sums up this situation by reworking the famous aphorism: 'all people define situations as real; but when powerful people define situations as real, then they are real *for everybody involved* in their consequences' (Mehan, 1990: 160).

Indeed, the traffic courts which Pollner takes as his focus exhibit precisely this feature. When the Judge in Extract 7 comes to her decision it is not a consensual one, although she has spent some time exploring the Defendant's account; the Defendant is ultimately fined for aiding and abetting a drag-racing contest, *despite his protestations to the contrary.*

In everyday, non-institutionally organized settings, however, power is not so clearly defined and backed up, so reality disjunctures are not so straightforwardly managed. In the light of Pollner's observation that methods of conflict resolution can themselves provide a new focus of conflict, John Heritage (1984) poses the question of how it is that these conflicts do not continually expand into major disputes. His answer is that there are a variety of methods that people use to minimize disagreement and to forestall potentially blaming implications. We will move on to considering some of these in this and later chapters.

Conversation Analysis

Pollner represents one very distinctive development in ethnomethodological thinking about facts which is concerned with reworking basic sociological and epistemological issues about reality and understanding. Pollner's use of his analytic work in the traffic courts reflects this. He determinedly avoids getting too involved with the many fascinating features of the passages he is studying. For example, he outlines general classes of resolution to reality disjunctures, but he puts little effort into looking at the ways any particular resolution is achieved; nor does he much concern himself with the possibility that there might be systematic properties of resolutions. For instance, he does not investigate the possibility that a particular type of claim by a police witness might regularly be countered by a particular style of formulation of events from the Defendant (cf. Drew, 1992). It is this lack of interest in the detail of how a particular action is managed, and how its management is sensitive to features of the activity sequences which, in part, is what distinguishes Pollner's work from that of conversation analysts.

One way of understanding the nature of conversation analysis is to think of it as a development of ethnomethodology which has followed through the insights about the indexical and reflexive nature of action and applied them specifically to conversational interaction. Thus the concern with indexicality is here manifested in a concern with how utterances relate to the *conversational sequences* to which they belong; and the concern with reflexivity emerges in the close attention paid to the various kinds of *interactional work* utterances and whole sequences accomplish. Furthermore, Harvey Sacks, and his associates Emanuel Schegloff and Gail Jefferson, who have been most closely involved in developing conversation analysis, also adopted the general ethnomethodological idea that interaction is *methodically based*. Thus, in studying conversation they started with the assumption that what is said is not the way it is accidentally, that forms of words are not rough and ready make-dos, but are *designed in their detail* to be sensitive to their sequential context and to their role in interaction (Sacks, 1992; Sacks et al., 1974).

It is important to note that this is radically different from the approach to language found in most research conducted in the social sciences, philosophy and even, or perhaps especially, linguistics. Language has often been seen as a carrier of meanings or ideas such that, on receipt of an utterance, the messy stuff of particular phrasing, intonation and so on in which the meaning was packaged can be stripped off to leave the elegant goods within. Survey research is often predicated on this kind of notion of communication where participants' untidy conversational 'responses' to questions are filtered and coded into a set of clear-cut categories and positions (see, for example, Cicourel, 1964, 1974; Heritage, 1974; Suchman and Jordan, 1990). Conversation analysis, guided by ethnomethodology, undermines any such distinction between the meaning and the utterance. Rather than the 'detail' of delivery, intonation and so on being a sort of fuzzy aura that can be stripped off, conversation analysts have tried to show that these specifics are there *precisely* because they serve the action that is being performed.

Conversation analysts have argued that talk-in-interaction (as they prefer to call language use) is very far from being messy. In fact it is incredibly orderly; and the principal ambition of conversation analysis is to reveal and account for this orderliness. Although the argument applies to language use generally, my interest will be in how this perspective allows us to make sense of factual or descriptive discourse: the sort of thing that in everyday terms we might gloss as reports, observations, portraits and so on. The relevance becomes apparent if we consider the example of accounts in the context of adjacency pairs.

Adjacency Pairs and Preference Organization

A conversation analytic perspective on factual discourse will start by considering its role in actions which are, in turn, embedded in sequences. Thus before we continue on the topic of facts we will need something of a digression on the interaction sequences in which they occur. The point of this will be apparent shortly.

One of the simplest, but most fundamental, of these action sequences is what conversation analysts have called the adjacency pair. The observation here is that many actions come linked together in pairs; that is, when one specific action is done it is likely to lead to a second specific action. For example, a greeting is likely to lead to a return greeting, a question is likely to lead to an answer, an accusation is likely to lead to a denial. Note, it is not the brute empirical regularity that is interesting here but the subtle patterning of that regularity and what it can tell us about factual discourse. Conversation analysts are not trying to prove through research that questions tend to be followed by answers!

The first thing we must do is unpack these metaphors of 'linking together' and 'leading to'. What precisely is the relationship between the actions that make up an adjacency pair? One way of looking at the relationship is to say it is a *normative* one. When one of these first actions is produced there is an expectation that the second one will follow, or at least be relevant. Thus with greetings, when one party does a greeting they expect the recipient to greet them back. But this regularity is not causal – the recipient is not forced to say 'hello' or 'hi' back; nor is it purely statistical – there are all sorts of occasions when the greeting is not returned. Moreover, as John Heritage (1988) emphasizes, the absence of a return greeting is not an exception that undermines the expectation about the pairing of actions. The inference from a missed greeting is certainly not: 'oh, you don't need to return greetings after all!' Rather, such an absence is treated by participants as an event that can allow a rich set of inferences: 'she doesn't like me', 'she didn't hear', 'she's making a joke', and so on. From the recipients' point of view, if you ignore the greeting you have not abstained from interaction; quite the reverse.

There is a further complication here; with a number of actions there are alternative second actions that can follow. For example, although an offer may lead to an acceptance it is also quite likely to result in a refusal. However, these options are not symmetrical; in terms of interaction they are ranked. This is apparent in the very different ways in which these options are treated by participants in conversations. There are very strong regularities in the ways in which the two different possibilities are realized. Take the following extracts, the first of which is an offer and acceptance and the second an offer and a refusal or declination.

8 *Gladys*: I have the paper here I thought you might like to have it
  Emma: Thank you
(Simplified from a transcript by Gail Jefferson NB:IV:5:R: 1)

9 1 *B*: Uh if you'd care to come over and visit a little while
  2   this morning I'll give you a cup of *co*ffee.
  3 *A*: hehh
  4   Well
  5   that's awfully sweet of you,
  6   I don't think I can make it this morning .hh uhm
  7   I'm running an ad in the paper and-and uh I have to
  8   stay near the phone
(From Atkinson and Drew, 1979: 58)

I want to pick out three features of Extract 8 which are characteristic of invitation acceptances. First, the invitation is accepted immediately, without delay or inserted material. Second, the acceptance turn is brief, which means that the acceptance component is delivered straight away – no extraneous material is added beforehand. Third, there is no qualification of the acceptance – it is clear cut and positive.

Contrast this with Extract 9, which displays five features which are highly characteristic of invitation rejections (the lines are numbered for ease of reference). First, there is a delay before the turn proper starts, here filled with the particle *hehh* (line 3). Second, the turn is prefaced by the term *well* (4). This acts as a marker of the type of turn that is to follow (a rejection rather than an acceptance) and also increases the delay before rejection is broached. Third, we see an appreciation of the invitation (5). Fourth, is the rejection itself. Note the way it is 'softened' – we do not see a harsh, blunt 'no': instead there is the hedged 'I don't *think* I can make it' (6). The fifth component is an account – the speaker gives a reason for turning down the invitation – they have to stay near the phone because of people responding to a newspaper advert.

Conversation analysts refer to these sorts of regular differences in turn shapes as part of *preference organization*; for invitations the *preferred* option is acceptance and the *dispreferred* option is rejection. *Preference* is used as a general term to deal with cases where there are non-equivalent courses of action available, and the alternatives are ranked (Sacks and Schegloff, 1979). It is important to stress that the term *preference* refers to features of the actions themselves, not the psychological desires or motives of speakers. For example, even though a speaker may 'prefer', in the usual psychological sense, to turn down an invitation, they may opt for the 'preferred action', in the conversation analytic sense, of accepting it. The preference is part of conversation as an institution rather than of the psychology of individual speakers, although some researchers have argued that it is hard to keep these two things separate (Bilmes, 1987).

It is also important to emphasize that preference organization is not a set of templates that conversationalists use to generate coherent utterances. When introducing the notions of adjacency and preference the tendency is to use simple, clear examples which can easily make it seem as though there is a rigid form being adhered to. However, preference organization can best be thought of as a set of considerations which are likely to be attended to in the course of particular actions – although precisely how they do will vary from context to context. For example, there is often considerable elaboration of both the appreciation and account components, and the whole dispreferred action may be spread out over a number of turns. A range of studies have shown regular differences of this kind for a range of actions – see, for example, Drew (1984); Levinson (1983); Heritage (1984); Pomerantz (1984a). The preference organization for some of the most important actions is summarised in Table 2.1.

Accounts and Descriptions

The discussion may seem to have drifted away from the main theme of facts and fact construction. However, its relevance should become clear as we

Table 2.1 *Preference organization for some common adjacency pairs*

Action	Preferred response	Dispreferred response
Offer/invitation	Acceptance	Refusal
Request	Acceptance	Refusal
Accusation/blaming	Denial	Admission
Assessment	Agreement	Disagreement
Self-deprecation	Disagreement	Agreement

focus on a particular feature of adjacency pairs: the account. There has been quite a large amount of research on accounts which deals with them in a rather abstract manner as actions performing justifications or excuses (Scott and Lyman, 1968; Semin and Manstead, 1983 – see Antaki, 1994, for a critical overview). The advantage of the conversation analytic work is that it treats accounts in context, taking seriously the ethnomethodological stress on the importance of indexicality. That is, the work pays attention to the role of accounts as one part of a dispreferred action, and it also attends to the particular type of action that the account is a part of. For example, invitations and accusations *occasion* different sorts of accounts.

When we come to look closely at accounts, one feature that is striking is that they are typically made up of descriptions of one kind or another. Consider again part of the above example.

```
10        A:  Well
               that's awfully sweet of you,
               I don't think I can make it this morning .hh uhm
    →          I'm running an ad in the paper and-and uh I have to
               stay near the phone
(From Atkinson and Drew, 1979: 58)
```

Here the speaker, A, describes a state of affairs – running an advert in the paper (see arrow). This provides a *reason* for turning down the invitation, as well as formulating the *constraint* that the state of affairs places on the speaker – they have to stay near the phone in case of replies to the ad. In this way A can present herself as *wanting* to accept the coffee invitation, but *constrained* to turn it down. Paul Drew (1984) notes that in the context of refusals of invitations or offers accounts typically cluster around the issue of ability. Thus A could have given as a reason for refusal that B was boring, that there was something more interesting to be done, that chatting over coffee is a waste of time; and each of these might have been what A, in another context, would describe as their 'real reason'. However, by here emphasizing her *inability* to attend, the invitation is turned down without assigning blame to either party.

The beauty of the kind of account seen in Extract 10 is threefold. First, it avoids suggesting that the invitation was unwelcome or unattractive; this is obviously something important for maintaining positive social relationships. Second, it works on the basis of information that the recipient could not be

expected to know. There is no reason why B should know that A is running an
ad in the paper; indeed, this sort of *ad hoc*, rather uninteresting event is just
the sort of thing that B would *not* be expected to know. So B is not being
made to appear thoughtless or insensitive in the provision of this account
(compare 'I'm still preparing for Jack's funeral'). Third, precisely because B
would not be expected to know about the ad, it is not something that B can
easily dispute; the account will not be much use if it can be immediately
bypassed by the recipient. The general point, then, is that this account can be
seen to be a description that is exquisitely designed in such a way that it sat-
isfies these different requirements simultaneously.

What we see here, then, is that description has become an analytic topic in
its own right. We are starting to consider the way a description is put together
to provide important features that make it usable and effective: it attends to
the relationships between speakers and to the practical task of refusal; it is
also made appropriate to the particular action sequence of which it is a part.
In a small scale, this illustrates one of the basic aims of this book. It shows
how it is possible to take descriptions, reports, versions as a topic for study
and investigate how they are designed to perform particular actions (see also
Wooffitt, 1993). Let me take another example to develop these possibilities a
bit further.

Building a Successful Account

We have already noted that many sorts of sequences involving dispreferred
actions are more complex than Extract 9. The following example is considerably more elaborate. The feature to note here is that the recipient resists the
force of the account in the face of a number of reformulations. This presents
an opportunity to study the building of a successful description over the
course of an interaction. The two speakers are discussing a Thanksgiving
dinner; Emma's daughter (Barbara) and grandchildren were to have come to
stay.

```
11   1   Gladys:   Everything's okay for the weekend?
     2   Emma:     Ah:: I'm gonna cancel the kids. I just don't feel up to it
     3             Gladys
     4   Gladys:   Aw↓::::::::::
     5   Emma:     I just uh:: four days I of 'em I just I'm really kinda shot
     6             and Bud s- (.) Bud s-says cancel it so
     7   Gladys:   Well what about poor Barbara she's looking
     8             forward ┌to Thanks- Tha:nksgiving
     9   Emma:              └Well I don't know I just not up to- I'l I'm gonna
    10             talk to 'er I just don't feel up to it really to cook a big
    11             dinner: (0.2)┌En have 'em
    12   Gladys:               └Oh I don't know I think it would do you
    13             good dear (0.4) Ah rilly do::
    14   Emma:     Do you?
    15   Gladys:   En I think it would be good for for Bud to be with
    16             those boys (.) And see them and uh (0.3) play with 'em
```

17	*Emma*:	He: said to cancel it So I guess I should do what the great
18		whi:te father ⌈ says I don'know
20	*Gladys*:	⌊ We::ll hu dear of course you know
21		best about that dear

(Simplified from a transcript by Gail Jefferson – NB:IV:5:R:4–5)

This is a much more complex example than that in Extract 9. For one thing, it is not Gladys' *own* invitation (note the lack of an appreciation component in line 2). For another, Emma's account for her change in plans does not end the sequence. Instead Gladys shows disappointment about the cancellation. Without going too far into these complexities, what I wish to concentrate on are the different descriptions used by the two speakers.

First, note the change between Emma's description of her reason for cancelling in lines 2 and 5. In line 2, Emma gives tiredness as her reason, which she formulates as 'I just don't feel up to it'. However, after Gladys' expression of a disappointment/concern in line 4, Emma produces a more elaborate formulation: 'four days I of 'em I just I'm really kinda shot'. Here the significance of being 'kinda shot' is heightened by emphasizing the task involved: four days of dealing with children. Note also this description 'four days' is a contrastive one to Gladys' formulation 'the weekend': the longer time period displays the 'tiredness' as more significant.

What we see here, then, is a modification and strengthening of the account component of this sequence after the first formulation had failed to generate acknowledgement and sympathy (Gladys has not said: 'Oh, I'm sorry, yes I can see it would be a burden'). It is easy to miss the profound point here, as we are so familiar with mundane interactions of this kind. What is significant is how the description of mental states and circumstances is produced *precisely* to perform the particular action. No more detail about the mental/physical state is given than is necessary to show the problem with having the children visit. The time formulation used is a maximal one that emphasizes the long duration and therefore difficulty of the stay. This description is reflexive: it is undoubtedly *about* Emma's state, and *about* the length of the visit; but these particulars are formulated for what they *do*: accounting for the problem activity of cancelling the visit.

Let me briefly elaborate on this analysis by considering some other features of the descriptions used in the accounts. In line 6 Emma provides a new reason for cancelling: 'Bud [her partner] s-says cancel it'. This provides a different kind of constraint on Emma's actions. She might struggle through against her tiredness, but she is not responsible for Bud's view. This spreads responsibility for the cancellation, building up the strength of the account in the face of Gladys' lack of support.

As I noted above, in dispreferred seconds to invitations, speakers tend to produce accounts which invoke privileged knowledge. In this case, only Emma can pronounce with this authority on her own mental and physical condition. However, although Gladys does not question her status as 'shot', she turns its significance round: it is because she is shot that the children's visit will do her and Bud good. Emma fends this off by reiterating that Bud had told her to cancel – the external constraint – and this brings to a close Gladys' questioning of the decision. There is another fascinating feature of the ways descriptions are used in this interaction, and that is the difference between the rather colourless construction 'Bud says cancel' and the later vivid characterization 'I guess I should do what the great white father says'.

Without trying to provide an exhaustive discussion of it here, there are two things to note about this latter description which terminates the sequence. First, by using this idiomatic description (the sort of description the 'Indians' might use of the 'settlers'' leader in 1950s Western films) she simultaneously indicates her orientation to his authority and ironizes that authority. This is a complex piece of business. Building up the authority of *his* instruction by depicting him in this way provides an externalized account for *her* cancellation. But there could be a potential identity issue at stake for Emma here because of its implication about her deference. The potentially critical 'great white father' formulation distances her from appearing to be simply subservient. A second point to note is that idiomatic or formulaic expressions of this kind often appear in situations where a conversationalist is failing to get support in making some sort of complaint. Paul Drew and Elizabeth Holt (1989), in an analysis of such expressions, suggest that their figurative quality gives them a robustness that makes them hard to challenge – as such, conversationalists use them to finish off problem sequences. Again, the point to note here is not so much the specifics of this somewhat speculative analysis but the general point: we see a description built and used in a way that is precisely suited to the action that is being performed.

Intention and Truth

Before completing this discussion of conversation analysis, there are two important general issues to address, which come under the headings of intention and truth. The first – which I briefly addressed earlier in the chapter – is the notion that speakers of descriptive discourse are strategically and intentionally designing their talk to satisfy these varied concerns. I have used terms like 'design' and 'building' which often imply a lot of mental planning; what precisely is being suggested? This is a very tricky question, which depends on one's assumptions about speakers' planning, and their conscious representations of outcomes.

My suggestion, following Harvey Sacks (1992), is that it is most analytically fruitful to remain agnostic on this issue. It is not inconceivable that speakers may, on occasion, carefully plan out conversational effects, particularly where they are working from materials that have been developed or rehearsed prior to an interaction, such as the Prime Minister's performance at Question Time following prior briefing on ways to handle likely points (Edwards and Potter, 1992). However, it seems doubtful that this is happening the majority of the time, and, anyway, it is particularly difficult for an analyst to distinguish those occasions where there is strategic planning from those where there is none (Heritage, 1990/91; but see Pomerantz, 1990/91). And if we are concerned with the social analysis of people's practices rather than the cognitive psychology of language use, it may be of little importance whether an utterance was 'carefully planned' or was just said as 'obvious and natural'. People spend their whole lives becoming extremely well practised at all facets of talking, and it seems quite plausible that they develop very finely tuned practical skills that allow them delicately to produce descriptions appropriate to particular actions without having to consciously to plan or think through what they are doing.

The difficulty with the analytic language used is to depict talk-in-interaction. The options tend to be the sorts of strategic language common in one area of psychology or the sorts of mechanistic, cause–effect language common to another area. The, perhaps unsatisfactory, resolution to this dilemma I have taken is to combine more intentionalist, strategic language which talks of descriptions being *designed* to perform particular actions, or being constructed *in order to* produce particular effects, with disclaimers about what is being implied cognitively.

The second problem concerns truth, and it can be expressed in the following way. Surely, the question of the design of the accounts in Extract 12 is beside the point – either Emma is feeling bad or she is not, and either Bud told her to cancel the kids or not. She is, then, either merely describing the world, which is not very interesting, or she is lying, in which case she may or may not get caught out – and that is not all that interesting, either. Now one of the problems with formulating things in this way is that there is no 'merely' about describing. Describing involves a set of issues to do with categorizing into classes of things, formulating as something, providing detail or not, making judgements and so on. We encountered some of these issues in the previous chapter when we considered philosophy of science attacks on the traditional distinction between theory and data. And philosophers as different as Popper and Wittgenstein have raised important conceptual problems with 'simple' issues of describing, referring and naming.

From a conversation analytic perspective, this problem is addressed in terms of practices of description. Rather than ask what sort of thing description is in the abstract, the question is how descriptions are treated by participants in the course of activities. If we consider Extract 12, the difference between the descriptions 'Bud' and 'the great white father' is not an epistemological one; in this setting neither causes a problem with reference to an individual person. Gladys is not confused about who Emma is referring to, as her response shows. The significance is for the action they are used to perform. As Emanuel Schegloff (1972) has argued, virtually any scene or state of affairs can be formulated in a multitude of different ways, each of which can be correct by some logical or abstract criterion. Scenes do not determine their descriptions, and particular selections can be made which are both defensible as true and capable of suggesting varied upshots and evaluations.

The second difficulty with the 'simple-minded' formulation about Emma's truth telling is that it presupposes the analyst has access to some unproblematic truth against which the truth of participants' utterances can be tested. In this case, the analyst is as much in the dark about whether Bud has been issuing instructions about the thanksgiving as Gladys is. Yet, just as with the truth of scientific theories discussed in Chapter 1, the analysis can and should go on without trying to sort those truths out. It can make the same observations about the role in this interaction of Emma's utterances irrespective of what might or might not be the case elsewhere. That is, the analysis above follows the injunction to be symmetrical.

Ethnomethodology, Conversation Analysis and Factual Discourse

In this chapter I have introduced some of the basic notions of ethnomethodology and conversation analysis and their application to factual discourse. The three concepts reviewed (indexicality, reflexivity and the documentary method) all have important implications for the way factual discourse should be understood. An emphasis on indexicality leads us always to ask, when addressing some description or report, what is the *context* here? How is this description *occasioned*? An emphasis on reflexivity encourages us to consider reports and descriptions *both* in relation to the event or action they describe, *and* in relation to what they are doing. What *actions* are they are part of?

The documentary method of interpretation draws our attention to the sorts of practices for managing factuality people use, and in particular to the two-way relation between people's locally developed models of the world and the specific phenomena they encounter. This method permits considerable flexibility in dealing with any phenomena, not unlike the flexibility in scientific reasoning highlighted by the Quine–Duhem thesis where how an observation is dealt with depends on the whole system of beliefs. The documentary method highlights the way in which people continually revise past perceptions and future expectations in the light of their current understanding. History is being continually reworked on a large and small scale. Finally, these sorts of methods for making sense of the world are conventional: the world is continually remade as it is expected to be.

Some of these notions are illustrated in ethnomethodological studies of organized practices of fact making. These focus on the procedures through which particular records or statistics are produced. For example, I described Atkinson's work on the production of suicide statistics, and how those practices were themselves based on lay theories of suicide. Pollner's work on mundane reason took another tack in elucidating, through a study of reality disjunctures, some of the basic methods through which people sustain the idea of a solid and agreed-upon world to which all observers have access.

I introduced conversation analysis as a strongly analytically based exploration and development of some of the basic concepts of ethnomethodology in the context of conversation. One of the great virtues of conversation analysis is that it has tried to convert theoretical or philosophical issues of fact and description into questions that can be addressed analytically through studies of records of interaction. It leads us to look at the conversational sequences in which descriptions are used, the kinds of activities that descriptions are part of, and how they are modified or contested in the course of interaction. The topic of accounts was used as an example here – however, this general approach can be applied to many different elements of interaction.

One of the features of ethnomethodology and conversation analysis is their strong focus on what is there: on the specifics and details which are part of particular settings. For example, when dealing with Emma and Gail's interaction in Extract 11 there was no attempt to contextualize events in terms of the age, social class or cultural background of the speakers – none of the 'big' sociological variables was brought into play. Neither was the extract interpreted on the basis of psychological factors purportedly lying within the individuals: their attitudes, beliefs, motives or whatever. Conversation analysts such as Emanuel Schegloff (1991, 1992b) have argued that the relevance of these things cannot be taken for granted – after all, there are a range of possibly consequential 'variables' of this kind at work in most interactions – rather, they should be shown to be consequential for the interaction. They are there, in effect, when they are there for participants. In the next chapter we will look at the very different tradition of semiology, post-structuralism and postmodernism. This too has little time for traditional sociological and psychological 'variables'; however, it is very strongly concerned with absence. To understand the operation of some descriptive terms which are used, for example, it is necessary to understand what descriptive terms are not used.

3

Semiology – Post-structuralism – Postmodernism

The loose perspectives of semiology, post-structuralism and postmodernism provide an approach to fact construction very different from the positions discussed in the previous chapters. One of their major characteristics is a profound distrust of the idea that referential language works through mirroring or mapping reality. To consider facts to be guaranteed by inspecting some scene 'in the world' is to fail to recognize that they are dependent on something much broader. In semiotics this is a system of differences between signs; in much post-structuralism and postmodernism it is a discourse or a regime of truth. Researchers in these traditions have attempted to explore fact construction by bringing these production systems into the open. That is, they have tried to reveal the system, or the set of discourses, that are hidden behind the simple word-and-object story about facts and, by doing so, radically disturb common notions of fact and representation.

I will introduce some of the main features of these structuralist perspectives by making three contrasts to conversation analytic work. The first difference is between the materials that have been studied. While conversation analysts have focused largely (although not exclusively) on everyday talk, over the telephone or in work settings, structuralists have been concerned either with language considered as an abstract system (in semiology), or with literary and philosophical texts (in post-structuralism and postmodernism). As a consequence, structuralists have focused more directly on questions about the nature of representations. How are effects of realism produced in a short story? How does a political speech draw on ideas from the arena of sport to justify a military intervention? How is a system of metaphors mobilized to make a philosophical argument work? As we will see, this emphasis on formal texts highlights some features of fact construction which have received little attention from conversation analysts; yet it also has its drawbacks.

A second contrast is related to the first. Conversation analysts have been closely attentive to the way participants orientate to conversational phenomena. An invitation is not identified as such through the analyst's judgement; rather, this judgement is supplemented by attention to the participants' response. Does the recipient, for example, treat the prior piece of talk as an invitation or not? This concern has been largely absent from the structuralist tradition. There is no easily available turn-by-turn display of understanding when a person is reading *Madame Bovary* or listening to Björk. This means that there has been less to hold the process of interpretation in check.

A third contrast is between the moral and political stances of these traditions. With some notable exceptions, ethnomethodologists and conversation analysts have rejected the social critique common elsewhere in sociology as positively unhelpful (Coulter, 1982; Button and Sharrock, 1993). They have commonly drawn a distinction between showing how a particular fact is constructed – how a claim is made to appear stable, neutral and separate from the speaker – and criticizing that fact, or suggesting it ought to be understood differently. For example, John Heritage (1984) argues that an analysis of how a fact is constructed *as* a fact does not imply that there is anything less significant or valuable about it. Similar disclaimers are common in recent sociology of scientific knowledge (SSK), although often offered with less conviction. Whether this non-critical, non-ironizing line can be fully sustained will be a topic I will come back to. In comparison, many researchers in the structuralist tradition have developed an explicitly critical concern with fact construction: for them the *point* of looking at fact construction is to demonstrate the way particular representations of the world are partial, related to interests, or work to obscure the operation of power. Often the concern with fact construction comes from a broader concern with questions of ideology, most prominently: in what ways can a set of social relations be made to seem necessary, natural and timeless?

Post-structuralism and postmodernism are broad labels that have been used in varied ways to cover theoretically disparate bodies of work. Semiology is easier to specify, but even here there is a range of competing interpretations which do not always hang together. In this chapter the exposition will move from semiology to post-structuralism to postmodernism. My reading will be a selective one, concentrating only on areas which relate directly to issues of fact construction, and trying, as far as is possible, to ignore the many other complexities that can ensnare writers and readers alike. It should also be stressed that although there is some historical sense to this ordering, and it is a helpful way of introducing some of the major concepts, it is also misleading to consider these positions as a tradition. There is at least as much diversity amongst post-structuralist and postmodernist positions as there is between different approaches to SSK. So with the emphasis that, *of course*, this chapter is a story which involves a range of constructive work, sets of simplifications, categorizations and implicit rhetorical oppositions, let us move on to consider semiology.

Semiology

de Saussure and the Basic Argument

One of the principal ways in which semiology (or semiotics, as it is sometimes called) undermines conventional notions of facts is through its critique of traditional notions of word meaning and reference. Ferdinand de Saussure developed his general science of signs in the lectures presented at the turn of the twentieth century and subsequently published as a *Course in General*

Linguistics (1974). Famously, one of his targets was the idea that words derive their meaning by standing for things in the world. This is the notion that, for example, you understand the word *river* by relating an isolated sound 'river' with a specific object, a river. Against this view de Saussure argued that terms derive their sense from sets of relationships or contrasts. So the word *river* derives its sense partly from its use in contrast to alternatives such as *stream, canal, lake, ditch* and so on. Another part of its sense derives from the position it takes in utterances: it can be preceded by words such as *the* and followed by words such as *flows*. Semiologists suggest that these two sets of relationships make up a system of differences which underlies the meaning of any particular word. Indeed, for de Saussure this is the essence of language:

> Everything that has been said up to this point boils down to this: in language there are only differences. Even more important: a difference generally implies positive terms between which the difference is set up; but in language there are only differences without positive terms. (de Saussure, 1974: 120)

This sort of argument starts to eat away at the simple word–object view by emphasizing the importance of relations between words – the system of differences – over the relation between the word and object. Saussure argues that the set of concepts used by a culture are not determined by their world. Rather, different cultures may use quite different ranges of concepts. He is here resisting the idea that there are natural sets of things such as rivers and streams waiting to be named by any group of humans who happen to evolve language in their vicinity; rather, each language produces its own distinct conceptual world.

The sort of evidence that de Saussure uses to support this argument comes from comparing different languages. For example, in English there is a distinction made between 'river' and 'stream' which is largely to do with size: a stream is a small river, and vice versa. However, in French a rather different distinction is made by the words *rivière* and *fleuve* which is more to do with the destination of the water: a *fleuve* flows into the sea, while a *rivière* flows into a lake or a river (Culler, 1976). The point is that in any particular utterance involving reference to bodies of flowing water the sense depends on the appropriate set of distinctions; that is, the system of differences.

If we consider this more broadly, de Saussure's argument implies that descriptive language *of any kind* cannot be understood through a consideration of just the words that have been uttered, or written. Semiology is primarily concerned with understanding what is present through understanding what is *not* present. You need to understand the underlying system that gives the words their full sense, and this system is only realized through the whole set of *possible* utterances, it is never apparent in any one utterance. For de Saussure, then, the aim of semiology is to elucidate the underlying system of differences that gives sense to any domain of meaning, whether it is a language, fashion, architecture or road signs.

There are a number of crucial difficulties with these basic semiological arguments. However, before considering these we will consider one of the most important applications of these ideas, the work of the French semiologist Roland Barthes.

Barthes and Second-level Signification

One of the central elements of de Saussure's argument about the nature of language is the claim that meaningful units – signs – are produced by combining together concepts and 'sound images'. Thus the concept of tough denim trousers is combined with the 'sound image' of the word *jeans* to make up a meaningful linguistic sign: 'jeans'. The possession of signs like this allows people to communicate with one another: they can say things like 'I have spilt Pepsi down my jeans' and be understood; knowing the conventional signs allows the listener to know precisely what kind of garment has been despoiled by Pepsi.

Barthes's (1972) important argument is that in human cultures things do not stop here. In fact, they cannot stop here. The same sort of process that allowed the combination of the concept and sound image to produce the meaningful sign 'jeans' also allows the sign 'jeans' to be combined with a new concept at another level. This new concept can be produced by the sorts of associations that go with 'jeans'. With a deliberate nod in the direction of anthropology, he calls these sets of cultural associations myths. For example, if jeans are worn in tough work settings, seen particularly on ranch hands and construction workers in Hollywood movies, they can come to signify those things. Through their associations jeans can become a signifier of rugged open-air labour, of people who do physical work and are not fastidious about dirty jobs. Note, this is also a contrastive sense building: jeans are not the smart clothes worn by office workers and professionals. Once this association is established it opens up the possibility of jeans being worn not because they are hard-wearing work trousers, but because of what they signify at the second level: ruggedness, a lack of fastidiousness, independence perhaps (cf. Williamson, 1978).

The process does not simply stop here. As jeans are worn because of their signification of ruggedness, rather than actual needs of ruggedness, then they may develop a further signification: that the wearer is fashionable; and as fashions change for various reasons, they may, in turn, come to signify *un*fashionable. In this process jeans may come to signify discos and bars rather than ranches and construction sites; and the advertisers may need to build up those traditional associations by again showing jeans in tough work settings. For example, at the time of writing, Lee jeans are running a campaign in which a muscular cowboy swims a flooded river to rescue a steer which has been trapped. Another advert shows a 'cowgirl' using her Wranglers to put out a hay fire inadvertently started by some inept novice cowboys – a visual reference to the film *City Slickers* in which a group of office workers learn about the rigours of the wild. Some of the subtleties of this process are discussed in Barthes's extended study of fashion (1983) and his investigations of the significance of everyday cultural objects and symbols in his book *Mythologies* (1972). Barthes has been pivotal in opening up this topic, which he calls the 'doxa' – the untheorized common sense of a culture – for study.

The point is that this process of semiosis means that we cannot make a hard-and-fast distinction between the dictionary meanings of words and their cultural significance. The word *jeans* certainly refers to tough work trousers, but when *jeans* is used in some description or report its role may depend on what is conveyed on a second level. For example, police report that a suspect was wearing 'stonewashed' jeans. This may not be simply an indicator of what the suspect was wearing during the crime (and thus made irrelevant when they have changed into some other trousers); it may be used to indicate something about the suspect: it may be suggestive of age, for example, or social class. As we will discuss later in the chapter, in literary texts descriptive particulars of this kind can be used to convey a wide range of effects.

Some Problems with Semiology

There are a number of important problems with this perspective on fact construction, only some of which are relevant here. A first point to make is that the status of the system of differences is not clearly specified. In particular, it is not clear whether it is an analytic theorization of the distinctions available *in* a language, or an account of the *psychological* map of these distinctions that underlies the perception of word meaning. In de Saussure's own writing he tends to place this system in the minds of speakers (hence his rather clumsy focus on 'concepts' and 'sound images'). This can have important analytic consequences. For example, if we wished to consider the sorts of distinctions operating in a particular stretch of descriptive discourse, we might be encouraged to engage in some sort of cognitive psychological investigation of mental conceptual organization. Indeed, some of the passages in de Saussure's *Course in General Linguistics* bear a striking resemblance to work in contemporary cognitive science. There is a tendency in semiology to drift away from considering actual practices of language use to look for phenomena under the skulls of the actors (cf. Baker and Hacker, 1984; Harris, 1981). Some of the problems with this will be discussed in Chapter 4 (see also Edwards, 1996).

This failure to deal with participants' practices is built into the basic assumptions of semiology, not only with its cognitivist emphasis, but also in its conceptualization of problems of language in terms of the correlation between the world (or in this case conceptualizations of the world) and words (or, as de Saussure prefers, the sound images of words). As linguistic philosophers such as Ludwig Wittgenstein, and conversation analysts such as Harvey Sacks, have emphasized, when you consider things in this way it raises a host of confusions because it loses sight of the way language is orientated to activities: it obscures its *practical* nature.

A related problem to this is how an underlying structure can be investigated. There is an important difference between making the argument that the sense of descriptive terms is underpinned by a system of differences *in principle*, and analysing a set of differences *in practice*. If we take the linguistic example we started with, we can identify contrasts between the words *river*, *stream* and *ditch* from a dictionary; but it is much harder to show the practical management and consequentiality of *this* set of distinctions in any given case. For example, it might not capture the implications in a set of estate-agent particulars of describing a house as having a *stream* running through its garden, or the absence of descriptions of houses which have *ditches* running through their gardens. And it is notable that Barthes's analyses of second-order signification in *Mythologies* are not systematically conducted investigations using the categories of semiology; rather, they are (brilliant) interpretative exercises where Barthes draws heavily on his own subtle, members' understanding of French culture and its underlying assumptions. This problematic tension between the overt theoretical apparatus and the covert analytical procedure is commonplace in semiological work.

Within the structural tradition, however, it was not these sorts of criticisms that counted against semiology. The concern was with some of the phenomena that the basic distinctions of Saussurian semiology obscured. Saussure had argued that the proper topic of semiological study was the underlying system of differences (*la langue*) rather than the realization of this system in particular instances of language (*parole*); and he also argued that a coherent linguistics should look at the state of language at a particular time rather than be concerned with the historical development of word meanings. One of the features that broadly characterizes post-structuralist thinkers is that they accept the importance of some sort of system of differences underlying meaningful signs, but they reject the injunctions against looking at historical change and looking at actual language practice. There are a range of reasons for this, but one of the most important is political; de Saussure's original theory was viewed as ahistorical and idealist and (with the notable exception of Louis Althusser) as not meshing happily with Marxist social analysis.

Post-structuralism

There are a variety of strands of post-structuralist argument that relate to our concern with fact construction and, even with very selective coverage, it will not be possible to do justice to the many complex issues that separate them. We will start by considering Barthes's work on realism in literature. Barthes was a thinker who straddled the semiology post-structuralism divide, but in his later work he moved away from the aim of identifying an underlying system or structure to considering more fragmentary discourses or codes of understanding.

Barthes and the Construction of Realism

We have already examined some of Barthes's semiological work with implications for fact construction. One of the central concerns in his thinking is the idea of realism, particularly when applied to literary texts. Rather than treat realism as a consequence of discourse naïvely reflecting the world, he asks us to consider realism as an artful assemblage of language that creates the effect of naïve representation. Expressed another way, his argument is that realism is *itself* a beguiling story which has nature generating its own representations, untouched by human hands. But this story obscures the human work that goes into the production and understanding of representation. Like sociologists of scientific knowledge and conversation analysts, he is concerned to reveal that human work and explore its operation. As he put it in a general discussion of his project:

> The 'analogical' arts (cinema, photography), the 'analogical' methods (academic criticism) are discredited. Why? Because analogy implies an effect of Nature: it constitutes the 'natural' as a source of truth; and what adds to the curse of analogy is the fact that it is irrepressible: no sooner is a form seen than it *must* resemble something: humanity seems doomed to Analogy, i.e., in the long run, to Nature. (Barthes, 1977: 44)

The book *S/Z* (1974) is one of the works most relevant to considering the operation of descriptions and factual discourse. Here Barthes addresses the issue through discussing the distinction between denotation and connotation. He suggests that the traditional view has treated denotation (where a word stands for an object or concept) as primary and connotation (the sorts of second-order signification discussed above) as secondary. In opposition to this, he argues that such an emphasis on denotation is an ideological one; it is a fiction about the nature of factuality that is used in sustaining authoritative discourses of science, literary criticism and philosophy. It is a fiction which can do this because it makes things seem simple: 'here are some words and here is what the words stand for'. It draws attention away from much more subtle, open-ended effects of connotation.

This is best illustrated by considering Barthes's analysis of a short story by Balzac. He chose this because of its widely accepted status as a classic realist text – although his analysis makes problematic that status, and indeed the very category 'classic realist text'. The analysis involves breaking the story up into fragments – some a few sentences long, some only a few words – in a deliberate contrast to more traditional literary criticism which typically focused on *the* meaning of a text as a whole. He then attempted to show how each of these fragments drew upon at least one of five cultural codes which work via connotation. The central argument of *S/Z*, then, is that the sense of the text, including its 'realism', is produced by the operation of these basic codes.

These codes should not be understood like a Morse signal, where there is a simple correspondence between the dots and dashes and particular letters. Rather, they are pathways through the reverberations of past texts: 'the code is a perspective of quotations, a mirage of structures . . . each code is . . . one of the voices out of which the text is woven' (1974: 20–1). Decoding the text is therefore an operation of tracking the pathways through these quotations.

For the reader this will happen instantly and automatically; Barthes is trying to slow down the process and make it as explicit as possible.

Five codes are discussed in *S/Z*, although it is not clear whether Barthes considers these as sufficient and appropriate for dealing with all literary texts. The codes can be characterized as follows. The *'hermeneutic'* code is involved with the various enigmas in the text, and their gradually unfolding solutions. For example, the title of the story, 'Sarrasine', raises the question of what or who Sarrasine is; the text provides progressively more complete answers to this question as it unfolds. A second (*'semic'*) code operates to create characters and particular ambiences: masculinity, Italianness, femininity. A more traditional *'symbolic'* code draws on classical associations. For instance, Barthes suggests that the introductory words of the story, 'I was deep in one of those daydreams', introduces a basic antithesis – day-dream – which will be repeated and reworked in different ways in the course of the story. Of the final two codes, the *'cultural'* code involves knowledge of a broadly sociological kind. This covers such things as the expected psychological characteristics of social groups such as artists or the workings of mythological actors such as genies. The *'proairetic'* code is involved with the construction of action patterns in the text, things that might more traditionally be understood as plot. For example, Barthes suggests the narrator's 'deep daydream' is a form of scene setting for some event that will bring it to an end.

I have given only the broadest hint of some very rich and subtle ideas because the concern here is not with the details of the five codes as such. They have been criticized by numerous commentators for mixing very different features of story construction as well as leading to arbitrary analyses. In addition, the distinction between the different codes is not always easy to sustain (for example, Culler, 1975). The significance here is the general approach to the working of a literary text and the potential for using it to help understand the working of texts in other arenas. Despite some shortcomings, Barthes effectively shows the way codes of connotation are involved in generating the sense of a text. The raw referents of the words, even if it were possible to distinguish such things, are in no way sufficient to carry the story.

Take the second sentence of the Balzac story: 'Midnight had just sounded from the clock on the Elysée-Bourbon.' Barthes claims that there are three layers of connotation involved here, all of which derive from the specific geographical positioning of the clock. First, wealth is connoted, as the Elysée-Bourbon runs though a wealthy neighbourhood of Paris; second, the wealth is that of *nouveaux riches*, it is an area associated with 'new money'; third, it is an area of Paris linked to a specific historical era (the Bourbon Restoration) when sudden fortunes could be made. Whether less sophisticated (and perhaps less French) readers than Barthes would generate *all* these connotations may be open to doubt. However, in terms of the story these are the sorts of connoted elements which contribute to the sense, not the denotation of one specific clock.

We can see this if we consider the effect on the story of replacing the clock. On the one hand, another clock would do if it had the same connotations, as would an appropriate geographical reference of another kind, such as a street. On the other, this new, specific clock would not work if it failed to bring these connotations (say it was a well-known landmark in a working-class residential area). As Barthes puts it, 'denotation is not the first meaning, but pretends to be so; under this illusion, it is ultimately no more than the last of the connotations' (1974: 9). He is arguing, then, that denotation is a powerful image or story which misleads us about the way sense, and therefore factuality, is produced in descriptions. Its simplicity, its obviousness – 'there is the word, and there the thing' – beguile us into thinking that it is what guarantees realism.

Barthes, Balzac and Conversation Analysis

Barthes is keen to stress that the type of analysis he has performed is not a semiological one in its traditional sense. By this time he had rejected traditional semiological categories as too rigid. There is no comprehensive system of connotations that can be exhaustively characterized. Rather, the codes are an indeterminate set of reverberations 'whose origin is lost' (1974: 10). There is no possibility of making a complete tracing of their origins. He is also keen to head off the idea that his is a purely personal interpretation of the story based on his own private networks of textual connotations. He does this in an interesting way. Rather than deny its subjectivity, he reformulates the notion of subjectivity itself. Indeed, he suggests that his own subjectivity is constituted out of the same codes that constitute the sense of Balzac's story. For Barthes, then, a person is built out of the same stuff used to build a specific culture, so you are doing something rather similar if you analyse a culture, analyse a realist text and analyse a person's subjectivity.

It is open to question whether Barthes has succeeded in countering the problem of subjective interpretation. Even if the argument about the textual construction of subjectivity is successful (and a wealth of post-structuralist and feminist thinking has explored this idea – Hollway, 1989; Moi, 1985; Weedon, 1987), it is not clear that this should result in the sorts of uniform construction that would lead to agreement in interpretations. Part of the problem with using post-structuralism as the basis for a general theory of fact construction arises from the tendency to assume that interpretations of formal literary texts are the key to understanding the world. Against this it could be argued that stories and descriptions in more mundane, everyday settings are at least as fundamental. Furthermore, insights gained in informal or interactional settings might reveal important elements in the workings of more formal texts. For example, it would be possible to follow a more conversation analytic strategy and consider the ways stories and descriptions are offered in interactional settings – at family meal times, in schools, in court rooms. What this adds to post-structuralist research on formal texts is the possibility of studying how the various participants *orientate to* one another's descriptions. Instead of attempting to back up interpretations with the *idea* of a perspective of quotations, such an approach would consider the arrangement and appearance of *actual* quotations.

Take the clock on the Elysée-Bourbon again. Barthes notes how the connotations of this geographical reference are what is crucial to the sense of the story. References to places are by no means unique to literary contexts. A conversation analytic study by Paul Drew (1978) has looked at the use of geographical references in a tribunal investigating police reactions to violent events in Northern Ireland in 1969. In the following extract C, the Counsel, is reading sections from the police logbook; while W, the witness, is a senior police officer involved in the events under investigation.

1   C: So there you have 'Fighting in Percy Street – crowd out of control',
        'Crowd coming down Conway Street from Shankill Road' and 'Crowd on
        Donegal Road from Sandy Row'.
   W: Yes.
   C: All indicative of an invasion of Catholic areas by Protestants?
   W: I would say incensed at the shooting that was taking place – scared?
(Drew, 1978: 1–2)

Drew's point is that the use of place names is not merely a guide to where in the city violence was taking place. Rather, the geographical references are being used to indicate features about the *identities* of particular groups of people. Not only that, but the particular *ordering* of places is used to indicate a pattern of activity involving attack and invasion. And, unlike Barthes' Elysée-Bourbon example, we do not have to accept conjectures about what inferences potential readers *might* make about the nature of an area of Paris, because we see the *actual* inferences about the various Belfast locations spelled out in the passage. The Counsel formulates the geographical locations as pointing to the nature of the crowd and its activity ('attacking'), and the Witness does not disagree with the formulation; instead, he constructs a possibly less blameworthy motive for the attack.

Now I do not want to suggest that there is a simple, methodological divide here, that Drew has evidence and Barthes is speculating. On the one hand, Drew's analysis trades heavily on his knowledge of, among other things, tribunals and what sorts of things accusations are. On the other, Barthes is making a specific claim about the connotations of a particular area of Paris that readers knowledgeable about French culture are in a position to assess. However, Drew's analytic task is made much simpler because he is considering descriptions embedded in sequences of interaction. They are produced as part of the witness's cross examination which (it turns out) builds to an accusation: the police are accused of failing in their duty to stop the attack. Having access to the orientations of the participants displayed through the turn-by-turn nature of their interaction helps make sense of the particular connotations of this description as well as providing a means of justifying the analytic interpretation (Drew, 1995). This is a possibility not available to Barthes.

Intertextuality and War

Another notion Barthes explored in his work was that of intertextuality. This notion was developed by Julia Kristeva (1980) from the Soviet theorist and literary critic Mikhail Bakhtin's (1981; see also Volosinov, 1973) notion of 'heteroglossia'. There are a number of competing interpretations of this term and this is not the place to get to bogged down with exegesis, which would take us far from the topic of fact construction.

Intertextuality can be thought of as a consequence of the post-structuralist move away from looking at the underlying system of differences (*la langue*) to considering the realization of language in texts and discourse (*parole*). Having abandoned the abstract, idealized structures of semiology, analysis needs to address actual texts, actual discourse and actual relations between these things. For Barthes, the relation between texts is one of quotation: each text is, at least in part, a pastiche or set of quotations of past texts. And intertextuality means, for him, relationships of quotation. The various codes he discusses in *S/Z* are expressions of intertextual relations in this sense. However, as we will see, intertextuality can also be treated as a relation between genres or forms of representation; and taken to encompass situations where the central metaphors in one area of discourse are being used in another.

Some of these other senses of intertextuality can be illustrated by focusing on texts concerned with war and conflict. Take Stanley Kubrick's black comedy about the dangers of nuclear armageddon, *Dr Strangelove*. There is one section of the film which records an attack by American marines on one of their own airbases in which the crazed commander has ordered a nuclear attack. What is striking about this sequence is that it does not follow the conventional forms of representation of fictional war films of the 1950s. Nor does it follow the camera and editing style of the rest of the film. Instead it closely follows the style familiar from documentary films of military engagements, such as the D-Day landings and the Korean War. The camera is hand-held and jerky, and the film is shot as if the camera operator was part of the action, running with the soldiers, ducking bullets and so on. The film is blurred, grainy and poorly lit; the action is chaotic.

There is plenty of film criticism discussing the possible roles of this sequence in the film. However, one role it seems to have is to provide a contrast to the deliberate stylization elsewhere. This contrast is built in part through the sequence's appearance of realism; it mimics genuine documentary footage of war, rather than standard filmic recreations of war. The effect of this look depends on the audience's familiarity with the genuine footage. We can '*read*' the sequence in Kubrick's film text in this way because of our experience of other texts. Note, this is not intertextuality in Barthes's sense because there is no specific quotation. Instead a whole *style* of representation has been relocated in a different context.

In a discussion of the way people understand television news coverage of military action in Northern Ireland, John Fiske and John Hartley (1978) suggested that the reverse process is also at work. Viewers interpret documentary reportage in terms of the conventions of fictional depictions of war. For example, viewers make sense of camera shots of soldiers looking warily out from behind defensive positions in terms of the sorts of black and white logic in which the 'good guys' peer out from the trench, wagon train or blockhouse at an unseen and evil enemy. The style of shot encourages the viewer to see the soldiers as 'one of us'. Their claim, then, is that the intertextual references of the imagery provide a set of surreptitious moral categories for understanding good and bad, while the broadcasters appear to be doing no more than simply recording what is happening in front of the camera. Film, as with photography of all kinds, has a strongly established rhetorical aura which whispers 'it is just capturing what is there' (Barthes, 1981; Shapiro, 1988).

On the basis of these two examples, it is tempting to treat what is happening as a confusing together of artfully constructed fictional and naïvely recorded factual modes of representation. However, this is too simple. Documentary film, too, is a construction on a number of levels (see contributions to Crittenden and Potter, 1986; especially Kuehl, 1986). With war film shot in actual battle situations there are obvious and common constraints on what can and cannot be filmed, and how the filming is done. For example, it is difficult for the crew to avoid filming events from the point of view of their own side's troops. And there are many less obvious sorts of selection issues to do with what is interesting, filmic, news, and what sorts of narrative can be told. Images are put together into narratives in the editing suite – the narratives are not lying around in the world to be picked up. There is also another intertextual level relevant when dealing with human subjects such as soldiers. If, as ethnomethodologists stress, people are designing their conduct in ways that make it intelligible and accountable, they may draw on their understanding of various familiar texts to achieve this. For example, an ethnographic study of news reporting in the Vietnam War suggested that young soldiers were able to turn on a particular style of interaction when being filmed because they knew what was required from their experience with war films (cf. Krohn, 1992). This makes the point that it is important not to see conduct as somehow natural and only its representation as artificial. From another perspective, conduct is inseparable from its design and the way it is made intelligible (Garfinkel, 1967; Sacks, 1992).

Michael Shapiro (1989) has argued that it is not just the conduct of war, and interpretation of specific images, but the general understanding of the nature and reasons for war that is related to various intertexts. He was particularly interested in what he characterizes as the sport/war intertext in North American political discourse. Shapiro suggests that in North America the population are thoroughly familiar with sports discourse because they have wide experience of both participation and spectating. There is not the same doubt here as there is about whether the majority of the French population can connect the Elysée-Bourbon to the financial significance of the Bourbon Restoration.

The familiarity of sports discourse gives it a 'significant "figurability" as a representational practice' (Shapiro, 1989: 72); and this is a figurability that may be exploited by politicians. Sports discourse enables a wide range of distinctions to be drawn: winners and losers, natural ability versus hard training and so on. It also has a range of central metaphors associated with notions such as competition, fairness and spectacle. What sports discourse provides, then, is an elaborate set of building blocks for constructing versions of how things are; and these can be used to produce accounts of international relations which emphasize certain features and hide others. Describing a book by a recent US defence secretary, Shapiro argues:

> it shows a preoccupation with an image in which the United States and its adversary are involved in a contest that functions within a space emptied of any significant content . . . other than the kinds of strategic locations . . . one finds on a sporting field or arena. The sporting figuration articulates well with the kind of geopolitical imagery that has promoted a strategic and thereby mystifying mode of the effects of conflict and security policy. (1989: 89)

This brief account of intertextuality by no means exhausts the available senses in which the term has been used (for alternatives, see Worton and Still, 1990). The main point to emphasize is that the notion of intertextuality foregrounds the often hidden relations between texts, discourses or genres, while stressing the limitations of the simple word and object view of facts. Moreover, this notion encourages us to stop treating realism as a unitary, straightforward feature of texts, but to see it as itself fragmentary and varied (McCabe, 1974; Nichols, 1992). For an even more thoroughgoing repudiation of the word and object view, and its unitary story of realism, we now turn to Jacques Derrida and the notion of deconstruction.

Derrida and Deconstruction

Jacques Derrida's work has not been principally concerned with realism or with fact construction. His main target has been the central assumptions of a wide range of western traditions of knowing, from Greek philosophy onward (Derrida, 1976). However, in this sustained attack on western thought he develops notions about discourse, metaphor and rhetoric which have important implications for the way in which factuality should be understood. As far as possible the discussion of these contentious and convoluted ideas will be limited to those which are relevant here, noting at the same time that Derrida himself has claimed that his work resists systematization and summary (Bennington and Derrida, 1993). I believe him! (For accessible general discussions of Derrida's work, see Culler, 1983; Norris, 1987.)

Derrida has explored the way 'truth effects' are produced in philosophical discourse; that is, how an argument is sustained and made to appear logical or necessary. As the critic Christopher Norris puts it, for Derrida truth is a 'mobile marching army of metaphors, metonymies and anthropomorphisms . . . truths are illusions of which one has forgotten that they are illusions' (Norris, 1988: 14). This description itself illustrates a central theme in Derrida's work – for Norris is here citing as an illustration of Derrida's thought the cultural critic Gayatri Spivak, who is in turn citing the philosopher Friedrich Nietzsche. The quote is repeated as it is circulated across different texts; something Derrida treats as fundamental to language use.

As I indicated above, an approach of this kind does not necessarily have to be treated as critical. It can consider the production of truth without treating the truth as any less truthful for having its devices exposed to analytic scrutiny. However, Derrida is not trying simply to expose the machinery that makes philosophical arguments work in order to admire its elegance; his aim is to show that the working is precisely dependent on the machinery and, moreover, that the machinery is flawed. The aim of his programme of deconstruction is to dispel the fictions about language, truth and logic that philosophers peddle.

Derrida focuses his critique on two closely related assumptions that underpin much philosophical discourse. One is that philosophical arguments are under the intentional control of the great thinkers who develop them; the other is that their 'transcription' into written language is a secondary operation, a trivial but necessary part of the process of transmission of ideas. We will take the second assumption first.

Derrida argues that philosophical truths are dependent on their realization in discourse. Instead of having their truth generated by their abstract logical form, their effectiveness is a product of the language they are 'expressed' in. They depend on the mobilization of an army of metaphors and systems of oppositions. The specific task of Derrida's deconstruction is to explore and take apart this system, to expose its operations. For example, in a classic deconstruction-inspired analysis, Richard Rorty (1980) argues that the metaphor of mind as mirror – a 'glassy essence' within, on which are reflected representations of the world – has been central to the working of philosophical discourse. Far from being a mere rhetorical flourish floating on the surface of 'proper' argument, metaphor and the workings of language are actually responsible for the appearance of truth in this discourse.

Derrida's work develops a very wide notion of discourse and rhetoric, which has close links with the Saussurian notion of an underlying system that gives sense to individual lexical items. This semiological thinking is partly used to destabilize dominant traditions of philosophy which have emphasized what is present over what is absent. Yet it is not isolated lexical items that are being given sense, but whole arguments; and unlike semiology, the 'underlying system' is not made up merely of oppositions and sequential relations, but also of metaphors, figures of speech and large-scale organizing assumptions.

By foregrounding the role of systems of discourse – a role which has been unnoticed or repressed in traditional philosophy – Derrida highlights a major problem with the idea that arguments originate in, and must therefore be referred back to, the thoughts of individual people. For speakers do not invent these systems with their speech; rather, they have their own complex cultural histories. Speakers draw on the systems; but they are not in control of them. Philosophical texts are part of the public arena. They are read, interpreted, analysed, criticized, reworked. In just the way that writers such as Barthes and Foucault attacked the traditional idea that only authors provide the definitive interpretation of their novels, so Derrida questions the privilege of philosophers to govern the sense of their own arguments.

Signatures and Parasites

These basic themes in Derrida's work can be illustrated by considering his critique of John Austin's account of speech acts in *How to Do Things with Words* (Derrida, 1977a). I have discussed Austin's work briefly in the Introduction. which emphasized the importance of his treatment of language as a medium for action. Particularly relevant is Austin's rejection of the dominant idea that statements are a special class of utterances that must be understood through their abstract relation to reality and his attempt to emphasize the performance of an *act* of stating, similar to the performance involved in making a bet, marrying or naming a ship. In this, Austin had started to provide a theoretical apparatus for understanding descriptive discourse in pragmatic terms.

Derrida was attracted to Austin's argument for a number of reasons. It eats away at the traditional image of communication as the transportation of meanings from one speaker to another. Austin was concerned more with how things are made to happen than how information is exchanged. He also downgrades the importance of truth/falsity, emphasizing instead the notion that utterances are used with a particular force. Rather than consider an utterance such as 'the door is open' in terms of truth (is the door open or not?) the focus is shifted to whether it is said with the force of a request, an order, a complaint or whatever. (Derrida delights in drawing a parallel here with ideas of force in Nietzsche which Austin would probably have shuddered at!) A final attraction for Derrida was Austin's heightened awareness of the workings of language, dramatized by his frequent use of puns and neologisms in a way reminiscent of Derrida himself.

Derrida's main critique is that Austin's view of language privileges spoken discourse and takes its force to be under the intentional control of the speaker. He subjects *How to Do Things with Words* to a deconstructive analysis which, first, shows that Austin's text does privilege the spoken and the role of intentions and then, second, reveals the management techniques through which the text sustains an appearance of coherence in the face of threatening problems and complexities.

Let us focus on a specific example to clarify what is going on here. One of the features of discourse which is particularly apparent with writing, but often lost in descriptions of speech, is what Derrida calls its *iterability*. Discourse can be used in the absence of any referent it might have (we can talk about an open door when we are in another room or another continent) and it is not tied to the intention of a current speaker. This is most obvious in written discourse which is likely to be read well away from its author, but is also the case with talk. Iteration emphasizes the 'used again' quality of discourse; people are drawing on words, phrases and figures of speech which have been used and heard repeatedly. Talk may be quoting someone else, reading poetry or, indeed, being ironic or playful. Contrast this, for instance, with the linguist Noam Chomsky's (1966) claim that talk is unmanageably original and complex as each speaker creates potentially unique sentences.

It is not that Austin fails to notice the iterability of discourse – its presence troubles his text in various ways. He deals with it through making a distinction between *serious* and *parasitic* forms of talk. He focuses his theory on serious, authentically meant speech acts while deferring ironies, jokes, actors on stage and so on for later examination (which never arrives). In his text these become parasitic forms of language, which will be deferred for later examination. Derrida's point is that in the guise of an examination of the workings of ordinary language Austin is introducing an 'ethical determination' of what is, and is not, properly ordinary language.

Derrida develops his case by focusing on one of Austin's own favoured examples. Austin suggests that, in the case of written utterances that perform speech acts, the absence of the intending speaker as a source and guarantee is managed by the use of a signature. The signature underpins the textual performance. Derrida points out that there is a paradox here. Although signatures seem to underpin the textual performance by providing the unique mark of the author, they can only achieve this task because they are repeatable or iterable. 'In order to function, that is, in order to be legible, a signature must have a repeatable, iterable, imitable form; it must be able to detach itself from the present and singular intent of its production' (Derrida, 1977a: 193). In a cheque franking machine, for example, the signature may be printed and the person whose signature is printed may have no knowledge of the particular cheque, let alone have a specific intention which guarantees its authenticity.

Derrida goes to town on this point in a debate with the speech act theorist John Searle, generated by his original article on Austin. Searle (1977) had replied to Derrida's original article and had sent a manuscript copy of his article for Derrida to, in turn, write a reply to. Derrida illustrated a range of problems through an extraordinary and playful exploration of this manuscript. For example, the handwritten name John Searle appears at the end of the manuscript, next to a claim of copyright. That is, Searle's article itself provides a practical case to explore the role of signatures. Derrida wonders if the presence of this signature means that Searle is claiming to be the *origin* of the text, as the speech act account of signatures suggests? If so, what of the fulsome acknowledgements to others who helped him? Are they authors too? Moreover, Searle was Austin's student and claims to know and follow Austin's intentions in his reply – so should Austin too be credited as an author? And should unconscious intentions be taken into account, particularly given the potentially Oedipal nature of Searle's student/supervisor relationship with Austin? Does this mean that Searle himself does not have unitary intentions governing the text but both conscious and unconscious intentions (perhaps pulling in different directions)?

Following this line of argument, Derrida playfully proposes that the author of the article be called not Searle but Sarl, which is both a pun on his name and a reference to a French legal formulation ('"Société à responsabilité limitée" – literally, "Society with Limited Responsibility" (or Limited Liability)' – Derrida, 1977b: 170). In this way he opposes the speech act image of the single unitary origin of the discourse with the idea of a more or less anonymous society with limited responsibility. Derrida's move here is similar to that of Barthes, when he rejects the idea that he is producing a purely personal interpretation of the Balzac story by stressing that what he is as a reader is constituted out of socially distributed codes of sense making.

Derrida develops his critique by wondering whether Searle/Sarl will try to sue him for breach of copyright as, in the course of an extended response, he has quoted the reply in its entirety. This does three things. First, it provokes consideration of the way that intentions, means and origins might have to be resolved, not through abstract philosophical analysis but by the practical procedures of the law court. Second, it raises the question of whether Searle/Sarl's text is still governed by his unitary authorial intentions guaranteed by the signature as it is repeated in this new context. Third, it emphasizes another aspect to the iterability of writing, which is that each repetition involves addition and transformation – Searle's/Sarl's text takes on new meanings as it is turned back on itself in the reply. In this way, then, Derrida chisels away at the idea that there is a simple intentional authority of one individual – in this case Searle – over the text, and stresses the way texts constantly take on new meanings and are used in new ways.

Derrida, Factual Discourse and Conversation

All this may seem arcane, philosophical, and away from the central concern with factual discourse. However, this detour into Derrida's work is important because these arguments about language and intention do not switch off once we depart from the realm of philosophy. If these arguments work, they ought to apply equally to *all* descriptions and statements. For instance, they ought to apply to the sorts of scientific and mundane discourse that were the analytic topic in the last two chapters. Equally importantly, they ought to apply to the discourse of those sociologists and conversation analysts who have written *about* fact analysis. And they provide another reminder that the discourse of this current book is itself a work of fact construction. Derrida's texts are particularly attentive to their own operation, often to the frustration and confusion of Anglo-Saxon critics. As I have noted, this text has directed its gaze mainly outwards. It has not explored its own metaphors and oppositions; it has made little of its own varied constructive decisions about disciplines and figures; and it has drawn freely on varied devices and tropes to sustain its own authority. On the whole, I have opted to use the familiar and well-worn figuration of fact construction to formulate fact construction itself. This largely unreflexive voice helps to keep the text as simple as possible, particularly when dealing with literatures as complex as post-structuralism – however, post-structuralists caution that simplicity is often precisely a sign of shared but hidden assumptions. You have been warned.

One area of potential tension lies between deconstruction and conversation analysis. Derrida has campaigned ceaselessly against the unwarranted privileging of speech over writing in philosophy. In contrast, conversation analysis has raised the study of speech itself to a fine art. Given the importance of conversation analysis for my argument it is important to consider this. The first point to make is that this contrast may be more apparent than real. Like Derrida, conversation analysts have been unwilling to treat speech as simply under the intentional sovereign control of speakers (Heritage, 1990/91) and they have been nearly as critical as Derrida of speech act approaches to language (Levinson, 1983; Schegloff, 1988a). Indeed, conversation analysts have turned this issue around, treating people's own concerns about what meaning was intended and who was the precise origin of a spoken view as a research topic in its own right (Levinson, 1988; Clayman, 1992).

Another issue is the role of analysis in conversation analysis. The process of turning recorded talk into transcript is a crucial research preliminary. A transcript can be seen as a device which precisely emphasizes the iterability and textuality of talk. It allows patterning to be identified which is not connected to any individual speaker and to consider the regular properties of devices for fact construction. It detaches talk from the immediacy and presence of voice so that different sections of the same speaker's utterances can be seen side by side. It might be said that conversation analysis has raised lack of interest in individual governing intentions to a fine art.

These points emphasize some parallels between deconstruction and conversation analysis. However, there are still some major contrasts. Most notably, a deconstructive critique can bite into the basic conversation analytic opposition between mundane and institutional talk. Some conversation analysts have proposed that mundane talk is the primary, indeed the primordial, form of interaction, and that other forms of interaction and talk in institutional settings are a derivation from this core form (Heritage, 1984). This is just the sort of hierarchy that Derrida has deconstructed to such effect in Austin's work. And, indeed, David Bogen (1992) has argued in this vein that the primacy of mundane talk is not a *discovery* of conversation analysis but an analytic and theoretical presupposition. Furthermore, the very notion of mundane talk is open to critical examination, with its implication of a somewhat homogeneous realm, free from institutional concerns or structures.

Some of these issues will recur in a different form in later chapters. For the moment, the important point to take away from this section is that Derrida's arguments direct attention away from the intentions of the speaker or author and focus them on the organizations of discourse that make particular talk or writing seem plausible and natural. The arguments here demonstrate that a focus on absences and unstated oppositions can be fruitful, as can as a concern with the central systems of metaphors and figures of speech that are part of factual discourse: the metaphor of the mirror, say, or the image of an isolated word relating to a pre-existing object. Let us take a deep breath and move now to consider a final post-structuralist: Michel Foucault.

Foucault and the Construction of Objects and Subjects

As with Derrida, I am not going to attempt to systematize the ideas of as prolific and complex thinker as Michel Foucault, whose work has been characterized by important theoretical shifts and covered a wide range of topics (see Dreyfus and Rabinow, 1982). The concern is specifically with features of his theoretical system which relate to facts and fact construction, and with other elements only in so far as they are needed for clarity.

One way of classifying Foucault is as a sociologist and historian of knowledge: or, following the title of one of his most influential works, as an *archaeologist* of knowledge (1972). Although he comes from a very different tradition from most of the researchers discussed in Chapter 1, he makes a move similar to those sociologists with respect to truth. To avoid becoming ensnared by epistemological questions about the correctness, say, or adequacy of some realm of knowledge, he brackets these questions off. The benefit of this move is the same. He is free to focus on the production of knowledge through institutions such as psychiatry or criminology, and on what that knowledge is used for, without being side-tracked by the participants' concern as to whether the knowledge is true or not. To emphasize this he uses the striking metaphor of *regimes of truth*, which encourages us to see truth as related to a specific social organization, moreover one which is likely to be hierarchical, potentially oppressive, and subject to radical change in *coups d'état* and revolutions.

The success of Foucault's metaphor illustrates one of the central features of his thinking. In effect, he has brought a new object into the world: a regime of truth. That is, his discourse has produced a new thing, and this thing can be described and discussed. Foucault suggests that, as institutions such as psychiatry have developed, they have continually produced discourses that constitute new objects. For example, the notion of a homosexual can be traced as a particular category that emerges from the development of the disciplines of medicine and psychopathology. The homosexual is produced as an object that can be identified, counted, surveyed and contrasted to the 'normal'. Indeed, Foucault strongly emphasizes the role of developing administrative procedures for counting and classification in a way that is not dissimilar to the ethnomethodological arguments about the production of institutional facts, such as suicide statistics. In each case the image of a simple countable object is undermined by stressing the procedures and assumptions that go into its production, and how these are related to an institutional organization.

At the same time as producing objects, Foucault (1972) suggests that discourses can be seen to be producing subjects. What he means by this is that forms of speaking about objects relate closely to particular identities. For example, the medical discourse of examination, questioning, diagnosis, prescription and so on constitutes a range of objects. At times in the past these might have been invasion of spirits, vapours; more recently they are more likely to be Hodgkin's lymphoma and HIV+. However, that discourse also constitutes the doctor as a particular person. The doctor is produced as a subject with particular authority, knowledge, skills and so on. We should stress that Foucault is not making a psychological point here; he is not talking about the feelings of authority that the doctor might have, or the healing skills that doctors might possess. Rather, the doctor is brought into being as a particular subject through drawing on the varied discourses that make up medicine (cf. Harré and van Langenhove, 1991).

These points can be illustrated by a recent Foucault-inspired study of the history of twentieth century British psychology. Nicholas Rose (1989) argues that as psychology has developed it has produced successive regimes of truth which have entered new areas of people's lives. Within these regimes new psychological objects were fabricated: the satisfaction of workers, the aptitude of soldiers, the bonding of parents and children. These regimes brought into being 'new ways of saying plausible things about other human beings and ourselves . . . new ways for thinking about what might be done to them and to us' (1989: 4). Here the twin processes of producing objects and subjects are closely intertwined. As psychological discourses generate new entities, they also generate new positions from which to speak. The speaker can talk as an extrovert, as a borderline schizoid, as thoroughly repressed; in each case the discourses provide ways of speaking, particular channels and authorities.

Discourses and Limitations

In many ways this is a very attractive approach to the study of fact construction. The role of discourse in, broadly, the construction of objects and subjects will be an increasingly important theme in later chapters. Moreover, it links factuality to institutions and issues of power, on the one hand, and to individuals and their practices, on the other, thus making discourse the central dynamic of the system. Yet it has limitations. First of all, the relation of Foucault's notion of discourse to any particular instance of talk or writing is not always well specified. As it stands the notion of discourses producing objects has shortcomings both with its specification of discourse and its account of production.

By treating discourses themselves as objects he draws attention away from the practices and contexts in which they are embedded. Indeed, it is easy for those using Foucault's ideas to turn the notion into something akin to the geology of plate tectonics – great plates (discourses) on the Earth's crust circulate and clash together; some plates grind violently together; others slip quietly over the top of one another; volcanoes burst through while massive forces work unseen below. The limitation with this approach is that the discourses in this view become pre-formed coherent entities which act as causal agents. That is, the processes of interest are seen as those of an (abstract) discourse working on another (abstract) discourse. What the approach is not sensitive to is the way discourses operate in, say, any particular doctor's surgery; the sort of arena where conversation analysis has found purchase. Note, this is not a plea to abandon the big issues that Foucault was concerned with in favour of an examination of the minutiae of actual interaction, for if Foucault's account is to be convincing it should help account for actual interaction.

Foucault's description of the process through which objects are produced is not as developed as other areas of his thought. It is clear that he means more by production than merely the use of descriptive terms in discourse. As formulated by Shapiro, one of the features that makes a discourse able to produce an object is a historically developed familiarity: 'to the extent that a representation is regarded as realistic, it is because it is so familiar it operates transparently' (1988: xi). A second, and more implicit, element of the production seems to be the authority that accrues to institutions of knowledge creation. The knowledge of criminology, say, is treated as real because of its social status. While these elements are interesting and potentially important, they are rather abstract and ill specified. What Foucault's approach has not developed is what I am attempting in this book; that is, an account of the sorts of devices and procedure that contribute to the sense that a discourse is literally describing the world.

Postmodernism

Defining postmodernism is not easy – and it is probably not wise either. One way to think of the difference between modernism and postmodernism is as two of your friends. The modernist is well meaning and hard working, but she has not got much of a sense of humour: she is constantly struggling to get to the best understanding of what is going on in any situation. She knows what she is like: confident, honest and forthright. The postmodernist talks more about work than actually doing it; she is witty and ironic – you never know whether she is making fun of you or sending herself up. You would be hard put to say whether she has a particular personality or not; she is many things at once, and none of them seems more true than any other. Or, think back to the discussion of Austin and Derrida above. Austin's elevation of the serious, literal, intended speech act as the paradigm form of communication is modernist, while Derrida's refusal to privilege these things over the humorous, ironic and unintended is postmodernist.

Any definition of postmodernism is likely to provoke controversy, for it is characterized by challenges to received definitions and distinctions. For example, much postmodernist writing has worked critically on fundamental oppositions between fact and fiction, natural and artificial, literal and figurative. There are radically different views about what postmodernism is within different disciplines and in relation to different topics. It has been applied to certain kinds of architecture, to particular films and novels, and to whole societies. It has been seen as a condition and a problem, and as something to be either celebrated or attacked, or both. What is not in doubt is that any contemporary discussion of representation, truth and fact construction must address the debates in postmodernism. A number of the issues at the core of postmodernism have already been discussed in the previous section on poststructuralism, however, but here I will develop them with a particular inflexion. Postmodernism will be explored by way of three themes: postmodernism as a feature of society, postmodernism and theories of knowledge, postmodernism and description. Being postmodern, of course, these themes will blur into one another.

The Postmodern Society of Cyborgs

One approach to postmodernism is to treat it as a condition of contemporary western societies. Here postmodernism is not a philosophy or an aesthetic style but a state of social organization which may be investigated sociologically. This condition is said to have a wide range of features. For example, the postmodern society is characterized by time and space distortions which are the result of recent technologies of travel, telecommunication and information transfer; in a global postmodern culture financial markets can be open somewhere 24 hours a day, and people no longer have to live in the same location in which they work. They can communicate across time zones simultaneously in what William Gibson called the cyberspace of computer networks. In David Harvey's (1989) critical Marxist diagnosis of the postmodern condition, western capitalism has transcended the increasingly outmoded boundaries of the nation state, and processes of consumption and aesthetics combine to produce ever faster changes of design and fashion. Production is becoming reorganized away from the massive 'Fordist' factories which were the traditional site for mass production. Gone are the linear production lines and fixed work, and gone too is the organized mass resistance of workers.

There is plenty of sociological dispute about how far these phenomena should be treated as a profound break with earlier social forms, let alone whether there is an historical era that can be called modernist which has been overturned by postmodernism (Featherstone, 1992). Nevertheless, the phenomena themselves are profoundly involved with our concerns about factuality and representation. Let us take as an example one of the important distinctions bound up with the making of factual accounts; that is, the distinction between what is natural and what is social. It is common to treat a state of affairs which is part of nature as lying outside of the domain of moral or political dispute. Barthes talks of the 'doxa', or 'Voice of Nature', which appears to speak from a space outside of human influence (Barthes, 1977). To characterize something as natural can be a powerful way of legitimating it: take a violent incident involving police officers. They are described as 'lashing out' and 'cracking a few skulls', but that is *only natural* (given the provocation), it's what human beings do (Wetherell and Potter, 1989).

Donna Haraway has argued that one of the features of postmodern culture is that the distinction between the social and the natural has become increasingly porous. This is partly to do with the ever more invasive growth of technoscience, particularly in the areas of communication, computing and genetics. She starts one discussion with the striking example of an advert in a scientific magazine for a genetically engineered mouse that is guaranteed to develop cancer: OncoMouse™ – 'available to researchers only from DuPont, where better things for better living come from' (Haraway, 1992). She is not particularly interested in the *literal* status of this rodent, extraordinary though that is. Rather, her interest is in its *iconic* status as a form of life that is not only humanly produced, but owes its life (and death) to a complex interplay of the operation of capitalism and medical research. The OncoMouse™ represents for Haraway a 'cyborg', a compound of the organic, technical, mythic, textual and political.

Haraway's point is not directly a critical one; she is not simply recoiling in anti-scientific horror from the mouse programmed with its own cancerous destruction. Instead, she is suggesting that the image of the cyborg should be embraced as a rhetorical and political strategy, an argument she makes most powerfully in her feminist 'Cyborg Manifesto' (1991). Here the cyborg image is mobilized against notions which characterize woman as a part of nature and against the possibility of universal and correct theories of gender and gender relations. The cyborg is utilized as a rhetorical lever for unsettling established debates and opening up new possibilities. For example, Haraway uses it to breach taken-for-granted boundaries between human and animal, between animal-human and machine, and between the physical and the non-physical and to dispel the modernist dream of working towards a common language or forms of unalienated labour. In their place will be a more fragmentary emphasis on creating local fictions about gender relations and organizing politics around identities such as women of colour which are themselves defined oppositionally (cf. Sampson, 1993a).

What we see with Haraway's work, then, is a double movement. She is not only diagnosing features of our postmodern condition, but also reworking and developing those features as part of a political narrative. She is deliberately collapsing the distinction between factual and political accounts. This is most developed in her massive study of primatology: *Primate Visions* (1989). For her, the study of primates is both a fascinating field of investigation and also a space in which myths of human origin are constructed and reactionary stories about gender and race are inscribed. In telling her own story about these stories of primates, Haraway is keen not to restore the fact/politics distinction. Instead, she proposes that her study be treated as a form of science fiction; it is telling a story about primatology, but that story draws on, yet resists the temptations of, four primary narratives: sociology of scientific knowledge (SSK) of the kind discussed in Chapter 1, Marxism, the legitimating narrative of the scientists themselves, and finally histories of gender and race and their involvement with science. Why are these temptations? Because each risks taking over the account and turning it into the One True Story, a story that takes on the mantle of timeless and unimpeachable fact. Postmodernism involves living with the tensions between these narratives rather hiding them or forgetting them.

Stories of Knowledge

As can be seen in Haraway's work, concerns about the various ways in which contemporary society is postmodern can quickly blur into issues about the very nature of knowledge and facts. This is equally true of the work of another of postmodernism's key figures: Jean-François Lyotard. He too draws on observations about radical transformations in science, literature and art in contemporary western societies. However, his particular focus is on what he called the 'crisis of narratives', that is, a crisis in the grand stories or 'metanarratives' that we use for understanding the world and legitimating our versions of it. Indeed, Lyotard is willing to start from a simplifying definition of postmodernism as 'incredulity to metanarratives' (1984: xxiv). Lyotard uses narrative as a contrast term to the abstract or theoretical knowledge produced by science. Narrative knowing is a more traditional, or pre-scientific, form of knowing which is embedded within a culture.

The targets of his critique are grand narratives such as Marxism and, most importantly, the metanarratives that are used to legitimate the enterprise of science. By calling these things narratives he is deliberately placing them in the category of cultural myths and stories in contrast to accounts offered by science. We will not go into his critique here, for we have reviewed a number of critical approaches to science in Chapter 1, and Lyotard's own account seems rather simplistic when set beside recent work in SSK. In fact, his critique is directed mainly at broad stories about the progress of science and its role in society, and he seems to take on trust ideas about the workings of scientific practice in a way that constructionist studies of science do not. What I am more interested in is Lyotard's proposal for what replaces these metanarratives.

Lyotard looks to linguistic philosophy and particularly to Austin and Wittgenstein. He draws on the Wittgensteinian idea that language is made up of a large number of different 'language games', each bound to a particular domain of practice and having a particular logic. And he combines this with Austin's notion of performative discourse, speech used to perform actions rather than to state or describe. The crucial point of this is that, instead of overall narratives legitimating science, there is a constellation of evolving and fragmentary arguments that work in particular situations. Strangely, Lyotard sticks closely to the traditional philosophy of science task of attempting to provide a justification for science, although precisely how an emphasis on performativity and 'having ideas' provides such a justification is not clear. Moreover, there is a powerful reflexive tension between his attack on metanarratives and his own confident metanarrative which blends cultural, social and philosophical claims in a panoramic sweep.

One of the things that distinguishes Lyotard from Haraway, and also Derrida and Barthes, is his lack of attention to his own representational practices. For example, he displays little concern with the status of his own story about stories. In many ways, what he has produced is a traditional piece of social theory cum epistemology which happens to have extravagant conclusions. Contrast this to Haraway's work, where the representational practice and political claims are joined together in the writing. Thus the deliberate political framing of the 'manifesto' and its contribution of the troubling image of the cyborg which is intended to work not because it is an *accurate* or *correct* description of gender in western society, but because it opens up chains of connections and destabilizes the current conceptual *status quo*. Moreover, Haraway is not impressed by Lyotard's conclusion that big stories are bad and little stories are good. She is attracted by the radical possibilities opened up by bringing together contrasting discourses; yet, as we have seen, she also emphasizes the value of working with (but also resisting) grand narratives such as Marxism, feminism or constructionist sociology of science. One of the ironies here is that Lyotard's text is often taken to define postmodernism, and yet it is entirely without the reflexive exploration which is elsewhere one of postmodernism's most vivid characteristics.

Representation and Reflexivity

Postmodernism is often closely identified with particular developments in art, and especially with films and novels which are self-referential, ironic, involving pastiches or parodies of other forms – that is, with works which experiment with, and undercut, standard narrative forms. Let us concentrate on one example to illustrate this idea: David Byrne's film *True Stories*, subtitled *A Film about a Bunch of People in Virgil, Texas*.

The film follows a narrator figure, played by Byrne himself, who is exploring a fictional/mythical town in Texas which is preparing to celebrate the 150th anniversary of the founding of the state. The narration is ingenuous and without judgement, and the various characters and events that feature were developed from the sorts of extraordinary, but factually presented, stories that appear in magazines such as *National Enquirer* commonly sold at supermarket checkouts. For example, there is a worker on a microelectronics assembly line who can pick up radio in his head and a woman who has chosen to spend her life in bed. The film is packed with postmodern elements, but we will concentrate on the introductory sequence.

The film starts with a long shot of a young girl unselfconsciously chanting and dancing on an unfinished road that stretches to the horizon on a flat, featureless landscape. Then the narration starts:

> This is where the town begins. This part of the country has been through a lot of changes – not all of them small ones. I think they're in the process of going through another one.

The narrative continues through dinosaurs ('I used to be fascinated by dinosaurs when I was a kid – a lot of kids were'), early settlers ('a group of Spanish settlers offered the Indians the chance to be slaves; the Indians thought about it, decided it was not a good idea, and killed the Spaniards') and fighting ('the Spaniards were fighting the Mexicans; the Mexicans were fighting the Americans; the Americans were fighting the Wichitas'). As it does so, the road disappears and is replaced by grainy early photographs and familiar overacted sequences from silent black and white cowboy films. When the narration tells us that 'recently, the bones of a woman who lived twenty thousand years ago were found here' this is illustrated with a photograph of people staring at a rather rudimentary museum exhibit of the skeleton and then with the famous publicity still from the film *One Million Years BC* of Raquel Welch staring up at a dinosaur while wearing an animal-skin bikini. The narration ends with a sequence of familiar magazine-style pictures of silicon chips:

> And now – micro electronics – the silicon based transistor was first proposed here in 1949. In 1958 Mr Jack Kilby invented the integrated circuit. He was working at Texas Institutes then – he doesn't work there any more.

This is a classic postmodern sequence, telling history not in terms of processes or connections, but in terms of events which are memorable or striking to the narrator. More than this, however, the images suggest that the narrator's story about Texas is actually built up by way of cultural images and knowledge: the pictures of dinosaurs, childhood films, mythic ideas of recovering the land and contemporary news stories ('covert military operations to seize Texas for the US of A were begun in 1835' – suggesting the 1980s US of Oliver North and Iran Contra). These images make no conventional distinction between the factual and fictional: the ludicrous dinosaur epic *A Million Years BC* is as relevant to the understanding of events as the actual picture of the recovered skeleton. The historical story moves in a circle as it ends with the integrated circuit, itself a reverberation of Haraway's manifesto. The integrated circuit is also a basic part of the technology of contemporary mass communications through which the various myths of the past, 'factual' and 'fictional', are circulated. So the sequence is both telling the history of modern Texas and, simultaneously, undercutting that history, suggesting that the history is *itself* a construct put together out of cultural materials. Note that the point is not that history is irrelevant, but that its relevance is constructed and riven with fictions.

The critic Linda Hutcheon has suggested that this double property of both telling a story and undermining the basis of what is told is a characteristic feature of postmodern art and literature.

> It is rather like saying something whilst at the same time putting inverted commas around what is being said. The effect is to highlight, or 'highlight', and to subvert, or 'subvert', and the mode is therefore a 'knowing' and an ironic – or even 'ironic' – one. Postmodernism's distinctive character lies in this wholesale 'nudging' commitment to doubleness or duplicity. (Hutcheon, 1989: 1)

In terms of our interest in facts and representations, the sequence from *True Stories* is both providing a representation and providing a critical way of understanding how that representation is put together. Hutcheon suggests we think about this process in terms of Barthes's notion of the 'doxa' – the common-sense discourses that make up a culture. Postmodern texts work 'to 'de-doxify' our cultural representations and their undeniable political import' (1989: 3). Their political edge is to question the common-sense ways in which we make sense of the world.

As Hutcheon emphasizes, these issues are not restricted to fictions of history but are of acute and troubling concern for what might be called real, or 'real', historians. Indeed, Hayden White has argued in his influential *Tropics of Discourse* (1978) that writing history is itself a form of fiction making. Histories cannot be produced without drawing on the techniques of narrative and character construction which are so developed in the fictional domain. There is a paradox here which will recur in the course of our book; and that is that one of the best places to find the machinery of fact production at work is the domain of fiction. The procedures for painting a scene to make it seem vivid and alive, to sum up a person as though you actually know them, to explore emotions in a way that makes them palpable to the reader, are all hugely refined in great works of literature and Hollywood blockbusters.

There is a convergence here between the postmodernist concern with literary forms which draw attention to their own status and recent developments in SSK which emphasize reflexivity and new literary forms (Ashmore, 1989; Mulkay, 1985; Woolgar, 1988b). Both share a concern with 'de-doxification'. They work to question the assumptions about knowledge and representation built into the customary literary forms used in both fiction and social science.

Facts and the Structuralist Tradition

In this chapter I have tried to give an account of some strands of the structuralist tradition that are most relevant to the study of fact and representation. There is a vast body of work that could have been included, and I am very conscious of what was left out in the attempt to say something manageable in the course of a single chapter. Moreover, in telling the story in this way it has no doubt over-emphasized continuity and similarity at the expense of diversity and conflict.

Semiology, post-structuralism and postmodernism are all intimately involved with questions of representation and the way descriptions and arguments are produced. Semiology cuts away at the word-and-object story of descriptions by emphasizing the underlying system of oppositions that are implicit even in such a simple utterance as 'a small stream meanders through the back garden'. There are plenty of difficulties with sustaining the full semiological account. For example, the status of the underlying system is ambiguous: is it a metaphor, a cognitive structure, or what? And there are limitations in the way language *use* is theorized in semiology. Nevertheless, the basic insight that description must be understood by reference to sets of alternative possible terms and sequential arrangements is an important one, and is one we will take forward to later chapters. In addition, Barthes's observations about the process of semiosis are fundamental to our exploration of fact construction. In effect, Barthes is noting that symbol use is constantly in a process of promiscuous multiplication: any sign can act as the signifier for new signs. A new style of jeans is produced: are they going to signify fashionable or naff? Will they manage to conjure up images of cowboys and masculinity, or will they be redolent of lager and football terraces? How will their signification change as new fashions are introduced?

Post-structuralism contains a wide range of resources for considering facts and descriptions. Barthes's *S/Z* analysed the production of realism, the sense of having produced a solid and convincing world. Two points are worth emphasizing. First, realism is construed as the consequence of a number of cultural codes. Moreover, a literary scene makes sense to the reader because it is constructed using the very codes of sense making – sociological, symbolic, hermeneutic – that the reader uses. Second, this approach to realism provides a powerful critique of the idea that the sense of realist texts is produced by simple processes of labelling or denotation. A description of a clock has its place in the text because of what the clock signifies – socially, geographically, historically. Its specific 'clockness' is beside the point – it could equally well have been a fountain or some other Parisian landmark. Yet, Barthes argued, the *illusion* is that the text is realistic because it provides a simple description of things.

This idea of cultural codes took a further twist with the notion of intertextuality which can be understood as a set of relationships of quotation or as a relation between different genres or forms of discourse. The working of intertextuality was illustrated by considering representations of war. Intertextuality is relevant both to post-structuralism and postmodernism. For example, the postmodern condition can be partly understood as a consequence of the massive expansion of intertextual relations made possible by the pervasiveness of representational media in western lives. Our understanding of war undergoes a continual process of transformation as we watch news footage of the so-called Gulf War, and vicariously fly with Tom Cruise in *Top Gun*. *True Stories* emphasized the intertextual construction of Texan history with its pastiche or assembly of 'factual' and 'fictional' texts. Donna Haraway emphasized the value of *encouraging* novel intertextual relations because of the potentially radical consequences opened up. By reworking woman as a cyborg, for example, to bring together discourses of technology and nature, and of the natural and the social, Haraway wanted to move beyond notions of woman as Earth God and myths of a common language.

Jacques Derrida provided another development away from the semiological emphasis on a broad underlying system, stressing instead the way truth effects are produced in argument through a wide range of discursive features such as metaphors, general assumptions and more or less standard patterns of 'figuration'. For example, he deconstructed Austin's arguments about speech acts, revealing and interrupting the operation of a hierarchy between sincere, literal speech acts and parasites such as irony, poetry and quotation. Although Foucault's targets were somewhat different, we see in his work a similar move to treat discourses as fundamental for the construction of objects such as illnesses and categories of persons: the mad or homosexual. Both of these thinkers are central to accounts of postmodernism. Derrida has radically undermined the grand philosophical traditions and their notions of truth; Foucault has done the same for traditional, individualized notions of the human subject. They have driven out the modernist certainties, to replace them with uncertainties, but also with new possibilities.

With this chapter I have finished introducing the principal theoretical perspectives available for considering factuality and fact construction. In the next, we will be leaving the heady generalities and wide sweep of postmodernism to return to more tightly analytically based concerns with the way factual accounts can be warranted as such and what they are used to do. This will draw selectively on themes from the first three chapters as attempts to develop a systematic scheme for analysing factual materials.

4

Discourse and Construction

Although the traditions of work discussed in the last three chapters contain a wealth of material relevant to a systematic study of factual accounts, they each have their limitations and blind spots, as well as specific arenas of development and application – namely, science, everyday talk and literary texts. This chapter can be thought of as a crossroads in the book. It will start to lay out a scheme for understanding the operation of factual accounts, synthesize some of the features of the perspectives that were reviewed in the preceding chapters, and draw on a range of specific research studies which will be described in detail in later chapters. The chapter is intended to serve as both a frame and organizing introduction to the next three chapters. It will also introduce a range of more specific questions. Why do people use descriptions or factual accounts? What sorts of activities can they be used to achieve? How are accounts made to seem solid, factual and independent of the speaker? What procedures are used to undermine factual accounts? However, before we tackle these questions there are some fundamental theoretical and analytic precursors that must be addressed.

Some Stories of Construction

The Mirror and the Construction Yard

One way of conceiving the arguments of this book is as organized around the clash between two metaphors: the mirror and the construction yard. With the mirror metaphor there are a set of things in the world which are reflected onto a smooth surface, but in this case the surface is not glass but language. Language reflects how things are in its descriptions, representations and accounts. And as these are circulated in the world of human affairs they may be treated as accounts which are reliable, factual or literal, or, alternatively, the mirror may blur or distort in the case of confusions or lies. This metaphor is familiar in stories about science and a whole range of more 'mundane' human practices. It is a metaphor which makes descriptions passive: they merely mirror the world. Yet like a mirror image or a photograph, they can also stand in for that world and be as good as the world for many purposes.

The metaphor of construction works on two levels when applied to descriptions. The first is the idea that descriptions and accounts *construct the world*, or at least versions of the world. The second is the idea that these descriptions and accounts are *themselves* constructed. Construction here suggests the possibility of assembly, manufacture, the prospect of different structures as an end point, and the likelihood that different materials will be used in the fabrication. It emphasizes that descriptions are human practices, and that descriptions could have been otherwise. There is nothing much that can be done about the reflection in a mirror; you can clean the mirror, make sure it is flat and smooth, but that relates only to its ability to receive an image passively. Yet a house is built by people, and it could have three chimneys and lots of windows, or it might have no chimneys and a set of French doors. It might be built with concrete, mud bricks, or girders and glass, and it might be very strong or rather delicate.

How strong is construction in this metaphor? The strongest version of the metaphor would have the world literally springing into existence as it is talked or written about. Ridiculous, surely! Perhaps, but I want to opt for something nearly as strong. Reality enters into human practices by way of the categories and descriptions that are part of those practices. The world is not ready categorized by God or nature in ways that we are all forced to accept. It is *constituted* in one way or another as people talk it, write it and argue it.

Now there is no sense in trying to decide whether one of these metaphors is true and the other false. It is most unclear how such a judgement could be made – although that has not stopped considerable philosophical energy having been expended on the problem for a long time. The difficulty is in formulating the question. To judge whether a description was mirroring or constructing reality requires the description to be compared to the reality. Yet reality (or 'reality') cannot enter this debate except as another description, which would beg the question of whether this new description is *itself* descriptive or constructive.

I have chosen the construction metaphor on *pragmatic* grounds. It is the more productive of the two because it allows a set of questions to be asked that do not make sense if we accept the mirror metaphor. If we treat descriptions as constructions and constructive, we can ask how they are put together, what materials are used, what sorts of things or events are produced by them, and so on. I do not see the main issue here to be philosophical discussions of ontology; that is, discussions of what sorts of things exist and what their status is. Instead, these arguments about metaphors are intended to clear the way for a focus on practical and analytic issues. Indeed, the abstract formulation of this problem can be positively misleading because it focuses on the relation between a description and 'reality' in the abstract, rather than considering the sorts of practices in which descriptive discourse operates.

Another way of thinking about this problem of construction and reality is to apply the requirement of methodological relativism discussed in Chapter 1. Methodological relativism is the claim that scientists' assertions or judgements about what should be treated as true or not should not be the start point for social analysis. It allows researchers to avoid the kind of tangle that results in the social researcher needing to know more about science than the scientists themselves. Their science needed to be better so they could properly assess what was true and what not as a prelude to social analysis. Not surprisingly, social analysts are not better at physics, say, than fully trained physicists. The attempt to do social analysis of science without adopting methodological relativism often resulted in what Michael Mulkay (1981) dubbed 'vassalage'; the situation where the sociological conclusions became parasitic upon the claims of a dominant group of participants. The sociologist becomes the vassal or servant of this group.

These sorts of tangles that result in vassalage are not restricted to work on scientific facts, although they are vividly apparent with that topic. In any area where the factual versions of some group are taken as a start point for analysis the analyst may end up as a vassal. Take, for example, Paul Willis' (1977) classic study of the transition from school to work of a group of adolescent boys. Willis built his story partly through selectively privileging certain accounts of a group of pupils he calls 'the lads'. These participants took on a role like that of central characters in a realist novel; they are rich and rounded, capable of irony and self-critique, and ultimately not speaking just for themselves but on behalf of a social class. In contrast, the girl pupils enter the text only as objects of 'the lads'' discourse, they have no independent voice. Neither do the pupils who will go on to take exams and are more accepting of the school culture; Willis adopts in his text 'the lads'' sneering description of them as 'earoles' (see Atkinson, 1990; Marcus, 1986; Potter et al., 1984). The point, then, is that Willis' sociological text becomes a vassal to the perspective of a particular social group, taking their evaluative descriptive constructions and treating them as a factual version of their social world. This in itself is not the problem – it could be defended on the grounds that it gives voice to a subordinate group (see Sampson, 1993b). The problem is the realist treatment of their categories as a neutral and objective picture of this set of social relations, disengaged from any local interactional business.

Having established something of the general value of embracing a construction metaphor, we need to go beyond that to be more specific. What sort of building are we talking about here: houses or bridges? And what types of manufacture? It is helpful to distinguish five different lines of work which can be described as constructionist. The Introduction briefly discussed Berger and Luckmann's *Social Construction of Reality* (1966), and Chapter 1 gave a rather more elaborate discussion of constructionism in sociology of scientific knowledge (SSK) (for example, Latour and Woolgar, 1986; Knorr Cetina, 1995b). In this chapter I will discuss constructionist work in linguistics, as well as making more explicit the constructionist themes in ethnomethodology and post-structuralism. The object is not to produce watertight lines of demarcation but to indicate areas of overlap and tension between the different forms of constructionism.

Linguistic Construction

The best-known linguistic constructionist is undoubtedly Benjamin Whorf (1956), who contributed, with the linguist Edward Sapir, to what has come to be known as the 'Sapir–Whorf hypothesis'. In psychology a large amount of research has attempted to test the hypothesis that people's *perception* of the world is determined by the language they use. For example, Eskimo tribes (as they were then called) were claimed to be able to make very fine distinctions between different kinds of snow because of the wide range of different words they had available. They had separate terms for snow that has just fallen, for wet snow, for snow that has frozen hard and so on. Whorf worked for a company which assessed insurance risk, and he used his job to illustrate the hypothesis. He gave the example of employees of a firm who had described gasoline drums as 'empty' and therefore safe; yet the drums were actually full of highly inflammable vapour which had exploded and started a fire. If only they had described the drums as 'full' (of dangerous vapour) they would have seen how dangerous they were and taken more care when dealing them. In this constructionism, language constructs people's perception of the world.

According to Derek Edwards (1994b 1996) the problem with this idea is that it treats language as a system of classification lying between the static individual perceiver and the world. What it does not do is treat language as part of a set of social practices. For example, with the gasoline drums we can ask what the employees who talked to Whorf were *doing* with their descriptions? If we do so, another possibility becomes available. Perhaps the description 'they were empty' was not a simple report using language that influences perception, but an *account* offered in a situation where issues of blame ('who was responsible for the fire?') and its practical consequences ('should the insurers pay up?') are pressing? That is, what Whorf is not doing is examining the *reflexive* quality of descriptions which emphasizes their role in both describing the world and contributing to current activities.

Later linguistic work in this tradition is in some ways more sophisticated, as well as being more integrated with developments across the social sciences. Nevertheless, this kind of limitation is still apparent. For instance, we can see this same assumption at work in Roger Fowler's interesting study of language in news reporting:

> Language and other codes . . . have a cognitive role: they provide an organized mental representation for our experience. Whatever the 'natural' structure of the world . . . we handle it mentally, and in discourse, in terms of the conventional meaning-categories embodied in our society's codes. (1991: 3)

Again, the story is of an inchoate and unformed world which is crystallized out into entities and processes somewhere in the perceiver's mind by a suitable set of linguistic spectacles.

One of the most ambitious recent attempts to spell out the process of linguistic construction comes from the linguist George Grace (1987). He suggested that the linguistic construction of reality involved three distinct stages. The first stage involves the 'specification' of a 'conceptual event'. Each language includes sets of terms, tenses, grammatical forms and so on, which allows for a range of possible events to be specified. For example, modern English makes it very easy to distinguish something that happened yesterday from something that happened last week or last year, in a way that the language of the Hopi Indians does not (Whorf, 1956). The second stage of the constructive process involves this 'conceptual event' being set into an ongoing stream of talk – Grace is not very specific about how this should happen. The third stage involves what Grace calls 'modalization'; that is, the event is framed as something that is being asserted, questioned, denied or whatever. Overall, then, the account of construction is this: the lexical and grammatical resources of English allow an object to be specified as a 'conceptual event', such as 'open door'. This 'conceptual event' can then be fitted into a conversation about the door, where it might be modalized as a question ('is that door open?'), say, or a request ('please shut the door').

The virtue of this model is that it is an attempt to characterize explicitly what might be involved in processes of construction. It also highlights the way different languages may provide different resources for performing actions. Nevertheless, it shares the flaws of other linguistic constructionisms. In particular, it is not attentive to practices of actual language use; rather, it treats language as a whole system and asks how it constructs a world. For example, it starts with the specification of events and treats what is done with those events once they are specified as secondary. Yet in practice this process may work in the reverse direction. Consider the interrogation of a murder suspect. The suspect may give a variety of descriptions of their victim, but it would be misleading to suppose that the nature of the victim is specified first and then fitted into some utterance that performs an activity. It seems much more plausible that the nature of the activity drives the nature of the description. For example, the victim may be described precisely in a way that mitigates the act of killing (Watson, 1978; Wowk, 1984). Generally, it may be simpler to say that talk involves categorization of persons, objects and processes, it tends to occur in interaction sequences and it is used to perform actions. Separating these things out as distinct and sequential stages causes more confusion than clarity.

Construction in Post-structuralism and Conversation Analysis

In the previous two chapters I spent some time discussing the various ways in which post-structuralist and conversation analytic work treats the construction of facts or the establishment of descriptions as realistic. At this point I will concentrate on making clear their basic assumptions about processes of fact construction.

In semiology, the central argument is that descriptions require a whole system of distinctions to work. This shows the word-object picture of description to be too simple. However, there is little in semiology which addresses the question of *how* a description is made to seem more or less factual. Post-structuralists have been more concerned with fact construction in the guise of the nature of realist forms of representation, particularly in literature. Both Barthes and Foucault focus on the way discourses or interpretative codes produce objects or descriptions which seem solid and unproblematic. Yet they have paid little attention to how such codes have their effect, although they emphasize both their *familiarity* and their *authority;* that is, the codes have a taken-for-granted quality that makes their products seem natural or commonsensical and they are often associated with powerful and influential institutions such as medicine and educational psychology. Even Barthes's *S/Z*, for all the obsessional detail in its analysis of Balzac's text, describes the codes at work without saying why the use of any particular code will make the text seem more real. Derrida was certainly concerned with what might be called the textual mechanics through which arguments are made to seem obvious and effective. However, for the most part his arguments were directed at the truth or validity of philosophical arguments rather than at realism or factuality as such and, apart from a highly suggestive emphasis on the central role of tropes and metaphors, his approach is not easily applied to the construction of factual versions.

In contrast to the linguistic and post-structural stories of construction, conversation analysts treat reality construction as something that has to be *achieved* using some devices or techniques. That is, from a conversation analytic perspective the use of a particular descriptive term, or even a familiar discourse, may not be enough to construct a version of events which will be treated as real or factual. Rather, realism and factuality are worked up using a set of rhetorical devices and techniques which may be specific to particular settings. Moreover, these techniques do not guarantee that a version of an action or an event will be treated as factual. They can be deployed effectively or badly, and they can be undermined vigorously or accepted credulously.

Conversation analysis provides the final story of how fact construction gets done. It is particularly attractive because it opens up an area of research not strongly emphasized by the other approaches. The story of linguistic construction left little to explain; whenever words are uttered construction gets done. There is some value in this, as it is certainly the case that using descriptive language produces versions of the world. Yet it does not engage with the question of why some versions 'work' and some do not; that is, the question of why a version is treated as a factual depiction of how things are in some interaction, or why it is repudiated as biased, confused or self-serving. The post-structuralist story raises the important question of how particular interpretative codes or discourses came into being, and genealogical research in the Foucauldian tradition has attempted to provide answers to questions of this kind. Nevertheless, it too fails to open up the field of research on fact construction because it makes only general claims about familiarity and forms of understanding that have become habitual. It works less well when applied to the specifics of descriptions and to non-textual materials where the rigours of conversation analysis come into their own.

Let me assemble these different kinds of construction into an overall model. We can imagine the words and syntactical possibilities as the bricks and girders that are needed for any building. Post-structuralist discourses and codes can be thought of a prefabricated wall and ceiling sections that can be used as parts of very different buildings. The devices and procedures that are grist to the mill of conversation analysis make up the bolts and cement that hold the whole structure together. Nothing works without the stuff revealed by conversation analysis, but a study of fact construction will be limited without a close examination of bricks and prefabricated parts.

At the same time as elaborating this metaphor, let me briefly emphasize some problems. Its main shortcoming is that it treats the parts as solid prior to the building. What we actually need to imagine is that the bricks are soft and vague in outline, so that they only snap into shape as they are cemented into place. And the prefabricated sections must themselves be somewhat inchoate, with their solidity emerging as they are bolted together. Everything exists in a fuzzy and fluid state until crystallized in particular texts or particular interactions.

Discourse, Mental Furniture and Rhetoric

So far I have discussed a number of general features which characterize a constructionist approach to facts, starting from the traditions discussed in the earlier chapters. Before moving on it is necessary briefly to address three themes that have important implications for the understanding of facts and descriptions. The themes are anti-cognitivism, discourse and rhetoric; and they turn out to be closely bound together.

Anti-cognitivism

I have already discussed problems with cognitivist accounts of the operation of facts and descriptions in the context of de Saussure's semiology and other kinds of linguistic constructionism which see that what is constructed is inner pictures or representations of some kind. It is necessary to go into a bit more detail with the problems with cognitivist accounts to show why they are rejected here. There are now a range of general lines of criticism of cognitivism, mostly stimulated by Wittgenstein's later philosophy or by ethnomethodology (Costall and Still, 1991; Coulter, 1991; Edwards, 1996). Three problems are particularly pertinent here.

The first problem is with the notion of representations as 'inner' mental entities. Should they construed as concepts, or pictures, or what? The very coherence of the idea of inner representation is problematic (McKinlay and Potter, 1987). Moreover, inner representations are inferred from various representational practices involving talk and writing, and such inferences tend to circularity with the inner representations being used, in turn, to explain those representational practices. The straightforwardness of the notion of mental representations dissolves when it is examined closely, particularly in the context of actual interaction involving representations and descriptions.

A second problem with taking a cognitive focus is that representations become separated from the practices in which they are used and start to be conceptualized as static entities which individuals carry around with them. Put another way, the cognitive focus draws attention away from what is being *done* with representations and descriptions in the settings in which they are produced. It prevents their reflexive and indexical properties being explored analytically. In terms of the metaphor of construction, then, the concern will be with descriptions and representations as they are built in the course of interaction; it will not be addressed to notional, in-the-head entities such as perceptions or representations, along with the cognitive apparatus of scripts, schemas and so on that go with such explanations.

Third is the problem that cognition is often the *topic* of description. In everyday life people spend a lot of time talking about their 'inner life': their thoughts, feelings, attitudes, goals and so on. When dealing with natural discourse, it is very hard to distinguish this kind of talk from discussions about whether the National Health Service is being run down or whether there is an invitation due for Saturday's party. Take the following extract from a relationship counselling session (C is the Counsellor, W is the wife; she mentions Jimmy who is her husband).

1   C: So you- you <u>seem</u> to be saying you're recognizing some
          kind of <u>pattern</u> (0.6)
      W: But the pattern <u>I</u> recognize is not (0.8) the pattern (.) that Jimmy
          recognizes about the situation. Y'know? (.) I just (.) <u>feel</u> that
          (2.2) I feel (.) that (.) he didn't (0.4) he says he didn't leave <u>me:</u> (.)
          for another woman (.) but I f- (.) believe (.) that if she hadn't've
          been <u>there</u> (.) this wouldn't have happened [*Continues*]

(DE-JF/C2/S2:2)

The wife's talk here moves fluidly between descriptions and avowals of her own mental life ('the pattern I recognize', 'I feel', 'I believe'), that of her husband ('the pattern that Jimmy recognizes'), and descriptions of actions and events ('he says . . .'). Now it is certainly the case that these different elements may be treated differently by participants: the procedure someone uses to undermine another's claim about his own feelings, for example, may be different from the procedure for undermining a report of what happened in a past event. However, from an analytic point of view, to start with the assumption that cognitive descriptions have a different *status* will lead to all sorts of tensions and confusions.

The approach to fact construction developed will, therefore, be just as interested in the construction of descriptions of the world of cognition as with descriptions of the world of actions and events. Indeed, as we will see later, there are often complex patterns of inference between these realms in ordinary talk (Edwards, 1996; Edwards and Potter, 1992; Potter et al., 1993). This can work in both directions. On the one hand, people can construct a description of how the world is that will warrant some cognitive state or event; a description of an insult can be used to warrant and make believable feelings of anger. On the other, descriptions of mental life may be used to warrant the existence of events in the world; a claim about having seen a flying saucer may be buttressed by noting a long-standing scepticism about such things on the part of the observer.

Discourse

The arguments against attempting to treat the business of fact construction as the business of building mental versions of the world, when turned around, become arguments for focusing on discourse. Indeed, we have already seen a discourse focus to be central in ethnomethodology, conversation analysis and post-structuralism; although there are important differences in the way discourse is understood in these different fields. I am taking a focus on discourse to mean that the concern is with *talk and texts as parts of social practices*. This is somewhat broader than the conversation analytic concern with talk-in-interaction, but rather more focused on the specifics of people's practices than the Foucauldian notion of a discourse as a set of statements that formulate objects and subjects. This sense of discourse will be exemplified in the next three chapters where the focus will be on actual materials – transcripts of conversations in different settings, newspaper articles, formal texts of various kinds – and on what is done in and through these materials.

It is important to emphasize that I am not arguing that a focus on discourse in the specific sense developed here is a prerequisite for producing sophisticated research on fact construction. There is plenty of high-quality research in this area that uses other approaches, some of which was discussed in earlier chapters. For example, sociologists of scientific knowledge have conducted revealing ethnographic studies of laboratory work (for example, Knorr Cetina, 1995a; Traweek, 1988); I have already quoted Karin Knorr Cetina's claim that 'ethnography furnished the optics for viewing the process of knowledge production as "constructive" rather than descriptive' (1995b: 141). Nevertheless, there are reasons for a discourse focus being particularly apposite for studies of fact construction.

Take the difference between what an ethnographic observer and a discourse researcher might make of the interaction reproduced in Extract 1 above. In ethnography the researcher is typically using their own participation, either actual or vicarious, as a basis for building understanding, and this will be supplemented with field notes (Hammersley and Atkinson, 1983). The goal is typically to generate an account of the actions and events that happen in a setting. So the ethnographic observer might make a number of observations about the woman's feelings, those of her partner, past events that have happened and so on. In contrast to this, the discourse focus proposed here will be concerned with the way in which the woman's account is established as literal and objective, and what it is being used to do. This will involve attending to what is often thought of as the (mere) detail of interaction: the hesitations, repetitions, repairs and emphases. Conversation analysts have shown just how important these things are to interaction – and they are virtually impossible for an ethnographic observer without a tape recorder and high-quality transcript to capture adequately.

There is a final virtue of taking a discourse focus. If we have a transcribed record of discourse, rather than a set of formulations in note form, it places the reader of the research in a much stronger position to evaluate the claims and interpretations. Harvey Sacks' goal of producing a form of analysis 'where the reader has as much information as the author, and can reproduce the analysis' (1992: I, 27) may be impossible to realize in practice. Nevertheless, there is an important sense in which this approach democratizes academic interaction. For example, the reader does not have to take on trust the sensitivity or acuity of the ethnographer. In the end, however, it is the relative success of these different approaches that is important. Are analyses with a discourse focus productive and convincing? Perhaps the answer to that question will be a bit clearer by the end of the book.

Rhetoric

So far I have stressed the value of focusing on fact construction in public discourse rather than mental pictures or subjective feelings of certainty. I wish to combine this focus on discourse with a stress on rhetoric. Recent work on rhetoric by Michael Billig (1987) has maintained that rhetoric should not be confined to obviously argumentative or explicitly persuasive communication. Rather, rhetoric should be seen as a pervasive feature of the way people interact and arrive at understanding. For example, he suggests that the social psychological notion of attitude needs to be rethought in rhetorical terms. Attitudes have traditionally been treated as individuals' isolated cognitive evaluations of parts of the world. Billig argues that they should be seen as public positions that are inseparable from current controversy; indeed, there is no role for attitudes except in issues where there is conflict and dispute. The implication of this is that 'every attitude in favour of a position is also, implicitly but more often explicitly, also a stance against the counter position. Because attitudes are stances on matters of controversy, we can expect attitude holders to justify their position and to criticise the counter position' (Billig, 1991: 143). This same argument can be applied to factual accounts. Indeed, Herbert Simons has argued that that 'part of the job of the rhetorical analyst is to determine how constructions of "the real" are made persuasive' (1990: 11). The consequence of emphasizing rhetoric here will be that, when descriptions are analysed, part of the interest will be in what alternative claims or arguments are being undermined. Put at its simplest, one of the features of any description is that it counters – actually or potentially – a range of competing alternative descriptions (see also Dillon, 1991).

Lyotard suggested that a characteristic of the postmodern condition is its emphasis on local rhetorical wars:

> In the ordinary use of discourse – for example, in a discussion between two friends – the interlocutors use any available ammunition, changing [language] games from one utterance to the next: questions, requests, assertions, and narratives are launched pell-mell into battle. The war is not without rules, but the rules allow and encourage the greatest possibility of flexibility of utterance. (1984: 17)

Without wanting to accept the postmodern assumption that there is something historically new about such fragmentation and dispute, the metaphor of war is useful. In a war it is possible to consider offensive as well as defensive weaponry. Many weapons serve both purposes, of course. Following this through for factual accounts, we can consider how a factual account can be inspected for its *offensive* and its *defensive* rhetoric.

On the one hand, a description will work as *offensive rhetoric* in so far as it undermines alternative descriptions. It may be constructed precisely to rework, damage or reframe an alternative description. On the other, a description may provide *defensive rhetoric* depending on its capacity to resist discounting or undermining. A whole range of techniques may be used to protect descriptions in this way, and they will be an important topic of later chapters of the book. The point, then, is that this rhetorical emphasis can serve as a counter to the more familiar approach to descriptions as primarily about the relationship between a particular set of words and a particular part of reality. Instead, it emphasizes the relation between a description and alternative descriptions, and the way such relationships may be worked up in argument.

The distinction between offensive and defensive rhetoric also emphasizes the value of taking a double analytic focus. Studies should look both at the procedures through which factual versions are built up, and the ones by which they are undermined. As we will see, these things are closely related. There is some terminology that will be useful here. I will refer to discourse which is constructing versions of the world as solid and factual as *reifying* discourse. *Reifying* means to turn something abstract into a material thing; and this is the sense I wish to emphasize, although material should be understood very widely. These are accounts which are producing something as an object, be it an event, a thought or a set of circumstances. In contrast, we will refer to discourse which is undermining versions as *ironizing*. The standard meaning of irony is to use words in the opposite way to their literal meaning. However, irony has come to have a more specific sense in SSK as an approach to discourse which treats it not as literal but as a product of interests or strategy (Woolgar, 1983). Falling somewhere in between these senses, I will treat ironizing discourse as talk or writing which undermines the literal descriptiveness of versions. It is the opposite of reifying discourse: it turns the material thing back into talk which is motivated, distorted or erroneous in some way.

Let us illustrate this by returning to Extract 1:

1a *C*: So you- you <u>seem</u> to be saying you're recognizing some
          kind of <u>pat</u>tern (0.6)
    W: But the pattern <u>I</u> recognize is not (0.8) the pattern (.) that Jimmy
          recognizes about the situation. Y'know? (.) I just (.) <u>feel</u> that
          (2.2) I feel (.) that (.) he didn't (0.4) he says he didn't leave <u>me:</u> (.)
          for another woman (.) but I f- (.) believe (.) that if she hadn't've
          been <u>there</u> (.) this wouldn't have happened [*Continues*]
(DE-JF/C2/S2:2)

The wife's talk is organized to reify a particular object: 'the pattern I recognize'. That is, it presents this as something that is actually the case. At the same time it ironizes another object: 'the pattern that Jimmy recognizes'. It presents this as a version claimed ('he says'), and even perhaps believed ('recognized'), by Jimmy – but nevertheless implausible because of the pattern of the events (which is itself a version that is reified in this talk).

There is a final point to note about rhetoric. Often rhetoric is treated as virtually synonymous with persuasion (Cockcroft and Cockcroft, 1992). However, this can easily turn the study of rhetoric into an exercise in cognitive psychology. It will treat the answer to the question of whether rhetoric is effective as dependent on an assessment of whether there has been a change in mental state in the audience. The way rhetoric is used here will not depend on psychological judgements of this kind. Instead, rhetoric will be treated as a feature of the antagonistic relationship between versions: how a description counters an alternative description, and how it is organized, in turn, to resist being countered. This conception of rhetoric meshes much better with the general approach to discourse introduced above. It is close to the traditional notion of 'suasive' rhetoric, which is discourse designed to elicit expressions of agreement from an audience.

The remainder of the chapter will introduce a scheme for understanding descriptive and factual discourse which will be elaborated on in the next three chapters. The basic argument will be that factual accounts have a double orientation. They have an *action orientation* and an *epistemological orientation*. On the one hand, a description will be orientated to action. That is, it will be used to accomplish an action, and it can be analysed to see how it is constructed so as to accomplish that action. On the other, a description will build its own status as a factual version. For the most part, the concern is to produce descriptions which will be treated as *mere* descriptions, reports which *tell it how it is*.

It is important to emphasize that the perspective developed here treats the epistemological orientation of accounts as *itself* a form of action; it is something built by speakers or writers – although it does not assume that this building is necessarily, even often, conscious or strategic. This quality is a *constructed* element to descriptions rather than something they either possess or not. The study of the epistemological orientation of accounts is the study of this building process.

The Action Orientation of Description

Why Descriptions Are Used

The idea that people can and do use descriptions to perform actions, or as part of actions, is not novel, and it can be easily illustrated. Take the following extract, in which some students are discussing a noise outside their flat.

```
2        Becky:   oi (.) sh shh (.) it could have been that
         Neil:    NO┌ that's not making a noise
         Alan:       └ no (.) something outside (0.4) it was
                  definitely outside
    →    Diane:   Neil you've got shoes on
      (DSS-K:94:1)
```

At the end of the extract Diane addresses Neil with the utterance 'Neil you've got shoes on'. Now as competent conversationalists, and people familiar with cultures where shoes may be taken off indoors but are required out of doors, we do not have any trouble hearing the arrowed utterance as a request for Neil to investigate the noise. Crucially, the participants clearly treat it in this way; for the extract is followed by a slightly jokey conversation about the danger of meeting a burglar and the risk that they might be carrying a weapon.

My concern is not so much with the specifics of this example. It has two features that are interesting because they are characteristic of the use of descriptions in performing actions. The first is that there is no *explicit* formulation of the request. Diane does not say 'please investigate that noise, Neil' or 'can you see what is going on?' Instead, a description is offered ('Neil you've got shoes on') from which a request may be *inferred*. In this context, the description of Neil's shoes identifies him as someone who can most easily investigate.

The second feature is connected to the first. The action being done by the description is a somewhat *sensitive* one. Diane is requesting Neil to do something that involves effort and perhaps even risk. The sensitivity here is not just about the pressure it puts on Neil. There is also an issue about the identity that is displayed by Diane, the person doing the requesting. By asking that Neil investigate the noise, Diane opens herself to being seen as 'lazy' or even 'cowardly'. That is, the focus on shoes displaces attention from these troubling interpretations by focusing on the topic of who has shoes on, and therefore *can* go out, rather than who can be bothered to or who is not scared (see also Pomerantz, 1980).

It is no coincidence that this sensitive action is done indirectly. Quite the reverse. One of the principal reasons for doing actions indirectly by way of descriptions is that the actions are sensitive or difficult in some way. Commonly, they will involve a potentially undesirable or problematic identity; that is, they may be actions which display the speaker as selfish, cowardly, insensitive, racist, stupid, flirty, pushy or one of a whole range of possibilities which are negative in the relevant context. This may seem like something of a paradox at first, for descriptions are commonly associated with coldness, objectivity and neutrality. However, it is not a paradox if we consider that it is precisely this feature that makes factual versions so suitable when there is a conflict or sensitive issue. For example, Bruno Latour noted that when dispute between different groups of scientists gets vigorous, description gets more and more technical (1987); and Anita Pomerantz notes that in everyday settings it is precisely when there is some dispute that people start to provide detailed warrants for their claims (1984b). Or, to give a final illustration, take Extract 1 again.

1b   C: So you- you <u>seem</u> to be saying you're recognizing some
           kind of <u>pattern</u> (0.6)
      W: But the pattern <u>I</u> recognize is not (0.8) the pattern (.) that Jimmy
           recognizes about the situation. Y'know? (.) I just (.) <u>feel</u> that
           (2.2) I feel (.) that (.) he didn't (0.4) he says he didn't leave <u>me:</u> (.)

for another woman (.) but I f- (.) believe (.) that if she hadn't 've
been <u>there</u> (.) this wouldn't have happened [*Continues*]
(DE-JF/C2/S2:2)

Note the way the wife accompanies her contradiction of her husband's
version – which treats his affair as not relevant to their marital difficulties –
with a description which links the affair and the difficulties together.

The Dilemma of Stake

One way of understanding these features to the production of descriptions is
to see them as a way of managing what Derek Edwards and I (1992) called the
dilemma of stake. The dilemma is that anything that a person (or group) says
or does may be discounted as a product of stake or interest. The referencing
of such a stake is one principal way of discounting the significance of an
action, or reworking its nature. For example, a blaming can be discounted as
merely a product of spite; an offer may be discounted as an attempt to influence. The Prime Minister's claim that tax cuts are needed to stimulate the
economy can be discounted as an attempt to make people feel good just
before an election. In the case of Extract 2 above, Diane's request that Neil
should investigate the suspicious noise could be discounted as a product of
her not wanting to do it herself. Diane resists this danger by making the
request implicitly via a description.

It is important to emphasise what I am *not* claiming here. The argument is
not that social researchers should interpret people's discourse in terms of
their individual or group interests. There are all sorts of difficulties with such
an analytic programme, not least of which is that it is very difficult to identify
interests in a way that is separable from the sorts of occasioned interest attribution that participants use when in debate with one another (see, for
example, Woolgar, 1981; Yearley, 1982; and the discussion of interest theory
in Chapter 1). The argument here is that people *treat one another in this way*.
They treat reports and descriptions *as if* they come from groups and individuals with interests, desires, ambitions and stake in some versions of what the
world is like. Interests are a participant's concern, and that is how they can
enter analysis.

Take this extract from an account of the deliberations of a jury:

3 It wasn't, in truth, much of a case. The only defence witness was a cousin of one
   of the defendants and she got her story muddled up anyway; and the prosecution witnesses, many of them passers-by with no conceivable axe to grind, were
   articulate and plausible. (*Independent on Sunday*, 15 May 1994)

The author's explanation of why the defence case was treated as uncon-
vincing by the jury relies heavily on judgements about the stake of the
different witnesses. By naming the defence witness as a *cousin* of the defendant, he provides information from which readers (and jurors) can infer a
motive for her to lie on the defendant's behalf. In contrast, the prosecution
witnesses are described as *passers-by*, and the implication of this is spelled out

by stating that they have 'no conceivable axe to grind'; that is, they have no prior relationship or stake in the fate of the defendant. As we will see, the management of stake is one of the central features in the production of factual discourse.

There are two final cautions to make. I have started with rather simple examples to make the argument as clear as possible, but such examples may not be characteristic of the sorts of cases we will consider later. The first problem is the nature of the agent who is assumed to have stake and interest. So far we have considered cases where stake is treated as a feature of individuals. Yet, stake attribution is by no means restricted to such cases; it is regularly attributed to social groups, nations, ethnic groups, on the one hand, and to parts of persons such as their unconscious, or ideal, self, on the other. Accounts can move fluidly between attributing stake at these different levels. Second, descriptions are bound up with the performance of actions in all sorts of complex ways. Sometimes a description is used *alone* to perform an action, as in Extract 2; at other times descriptions have a standardized role as *part* of an action, as is the case with the way accounts play a role in turning down requests and invitations (see pages 60–4).

How Descriptions Are Used

So far, then, I have argued that factual or descriptive discourse may be drawn on to manage issues of stake, in particular where the speaker or writer may be treated as having a negative or problematic identity. However, this only gives an account for *why* descriptive discourse may be used. This must be complemented by an account of *how* particular actions are performed by descriptions. In other words, how is a particular description constructed to perform a specific action? This question will be the focus of Chapter 7. For the moment I will just note some of the considerations which such an account will need to address.

Potentially, there are a huge number of ways in which the production of descriptions is involved with actions. Descriptions are closely bound up with the idiosyncratic particulars of settings. In Extract 2 there are references to Neil and shoes which are crucial to the workings of this account, but are likely to be irrelevant in almost every other piece of discourse it is possible to imagine. At first sight this might well make us sceptical about the very possibility of making general claims about the procedures through which factual accounts are used in actions. Nevertheless, when we start to study the describing it becomes possible to make some general observations.

A central feature of any description is its role in categorization; a description formulates some object or event as something; it constitutes it as a thing, and a thing with specific qualities. The description presents something as good or bad, big or small, more violent or less violent, although often with more subtle options. Another common role of descriptions is to present some action as routine or, conversely, exceptional. Sometimes, the success of a description in action will depend on its selective management of the realm of objects and events that are to be considered. The point, then, is that although the details of what is talked about may be endlessly varied, the sorts of procedures for constructing and managing descriptions may be much more regular, and therefore tractable in analysis. We have already seen an example of this with the discussion of accounts in Chapter 2, where we noted the way that accounts for turning down invitations and offers have a highly regular overall structure.

The Epistemological Orientation of Description

Referential talk on its own carries no guarantee that it will be treated as factual; producing a text with descriptions in it does not, on its own, constrain the reader to treat those descriptions as literal. This is particularly true in situations of conflict, or where there are delicate issues of identity, where descriptive discourse is common. People have a wide range of resources that they can use for ironizing descriptions, including notions of lies, delusions, mistakes, flattery, deceptions and misrepresentations, all of which can be drawn on to undermine the adequacy of a description. Given that there are these resources for undermining factual versions, it is not surprising that there are a developed set of counter-resources that are used to work up the facticity of a version and make it difficult to undermine. These are the resources that are used to construct a description as a factual account.

Bruno Latour and Steve Woolgar conceptualize this process in terms of a hierarchy of modalization (Latour, 1987; Latour and Woolgar, 1986 Woolgar, 1988b). This is illustrated in Table 4.1. At one end of the hierarchy there are descriptions whose status is considered highly suspect or provisional and may be treated as the lies or confusions of the speaker; at the other end, there are descriptions which are treated as solid and unproblematic, and quite separate from the speaker. At this end, some statements may be treated as so unproblematic that they do not even need to be explicitly formulated; they can be presupposed.

Table 4.1   *A hierarchy of modalization*

[...]
X
X is a fact
I know that X
I claim that X
I believe that X
I hypothesize that X
I think that X
I guess that X
X is possible

The process of fact construction is one of attempting to reify descriptions as solid and literal. The opposite process of destruction is one of attempting to ironize descriptions as partial, interested, or defective in some other way. Often, of course, these things are combined as one version is established at the expense of another, as in Extract 1, for example. If we think of the hierarchy as a ratchet, processes of reification attempt to ratchet the description up through the hierarchy; processes of ironizing attempt to ratchet it back down.

The brief overview that follows is intended to illustrate the issues rather than deal with their complexities. It will divide processes of fact construction into two. On the one hand, there are resources that work on the identity of the describer; their descriptions may be undermined by reference to stake and they may be built up by reference to knowledge entitlements. This will be the topic of Chapter 5. On the other hand, there are a range of resources that contribute to the independence of the speaker from the description. These will be the topic of Chapter 6.

Interest Management

Interest management is one of the most fundamental approaches to fact construction. In Gaye Tuchman's well-known ethnographic study of newspaper reporting, she lists attention to interests as the first thing a reporter will note when assessing a source: 'Most individuals, as news sources, have an axe to grind. To be believed, an individual must prove his or her reliability as a news source.'(1978: 93). I have already noted some of the discounting through interest imputation in the discussion of the dilemma of stake. Indeed, one of the basic arguments here is that descriptions are often used *precisely* because they manage issues of interest. This point can be developed by returning to the two examples we used previously. By describing Neil's state of dress ('Neil you've got your shoes on'), Diane in Extract 2 provides a reason for him to investigate the suspicious noise which focuses attention on Neil – it does not involve Diane addressing any of her own possible reasons (fear, laziness) for Neil going. Put simply, a description like this can attempt to take the sensitive concern away from the speaker and make it a part of what is described.

The report of a jury deliberation in Extract 3 shows the writer reporting a pattern of stake to represent one side of a case as strong and the other weak. The defence witness is suspect because she is a relative of the accused; the prosecution witnesses' accounts are likely to be accurate because they have no stake in the outcome: they are mere passers-by. Just mentioning these particulars is treated as sufficient to cast doubt on the claims of the defendant. This again illustrates the power that interest invoking can have.

Extract 3 also illustrates a more general feature of fact construction. Claims about stake are *themselves* descriptions, and as such they are subject to the same concerns about fact construction. People may need to work up the factual nature of the elements in the accounts that are used, in turn, to work up the factual nature of what is being described. Put another way, the resources for reifying descriptions can work recursively. Just as much effort may be needed to construct the facticity of the resource as goes into using the resource to construct the facticity of what is at issue.

My overall argument is that stake is both a potential problem for those wishing to establish the facticity of accounts and a resource for those wishing to undermine it. I have deliberately left the specific nature of stake and interest vague. Stake is a participants' issue which may be constructed in many different ways. It may be treated as something to do with features of a specific individual, or as something to do with their broader group allegiances; it may be as 'trivial' as a concern not to look foolish, or as 'important' as a desire not to be identified as a murderer. The role of analysis is not to assess whether these are right or not, but to explore the practices through which stake is established and discounted. A range of these practices will be explored in the next chapter.

Category Entitlements

If interest management is generally involved with the problems of accounts being undermined, category entitlements are the other side of the coin. Knowledge is culturally and normatively linked to categories of actors in a variety of different ways. Certain categories of actors are treated as entitled to know particular sorts of things, and their reports and descriptions may thus be given special credence. At its simplest, a person visits the doctor because she is expected to know something about illness. She is in a category of people who are treated as *entitled* to have such knowledge; she knows about illness *by virtue of the fact that* she is a doctor. That is, we assume that her category membership is a product of training, knowledge and so on.

The role of category entitlements can be seen in materials from a study by Jack Whalen and Don Zimmerman (1990). They analysed calls to an emergency switchboard of a large North American city and noted the ways in which different kinds of caller were treated. Some sorts of caller were asked about how they knew about what they were calling in, and others were not. Take two examples. The call in Extract 4 comes from an 'ordinary caller', an unknown member of the public (CT stands for Call Taker, C for Caller):

```
4   CT:   Mid-City emergency
    C:    Would you send thuh police to eleven six oh Arvin Avenue North?
    CT:   Eleven six oh Arving Avenue north?
    C:    Yes there's been raping goin' on
    CT:   WHERE
    C:    Eleven si⌈x oh
    CT:        ⌊Inside ur outside?
    C:    Inside thee house.
    CT:   There's somebody being RAPED?
    C:    Yup=
    CT:   =How do you know this?
    C:    I live next door. Two ladies bein raped, eleven six oh=
    CT:   = Di- How do you know they're Being raped inside that house.
    C:    Because . . . [Call continues for 15 more lines]
```
(Whalen and Zimmerman, 1990: 473)

In this call we see the caller being questioned in some detail about their grounds for the claim that someone is being raped and the police should attend. Now contrast this to the brief and smoothly managed call in Extract 5:

5   *CT*: .hh Mid-City emergency
     C: Hi .hh This iz General – there's been an over dose (.) twenty-six twenty-six .hh Columbia: hh upstairs apartment num:::ber two: .hh
    CT: O:kay thank you
     C: umhm bye
Whalen and Zimmerman, 1990: 483)

In this case the caller from the hospital is treated as someone entitled to know about drug over-doses and their location. They are not asked how they know.

Now it is tempting to think that these categories are merely a feature of the world, and that speakers and writers will be assessed according to their membership in a straightforward way. However, this is too simple. As we have noted, fact construction processes need not just work on the facts, they can also work on the resources that build up the facts. Thus participants can work up their category entitlements in a variety of ways. And conversely, of course, they can undermine the entitlements of others. We can speculate, for example, about the way the caller in Extract 5 builds up his or her category entitlement, not just by naming ('This iz General'), but also by the familiar greeting at the start and the air of routine ('General' rather than 'the General Hospital'). Interests and category entitlements, then, are pervasive participants' concerns as they work up, and undermine, factual accounts.

Interest management and the building of category entitlement both involve constructions of the person who is making the report. That is, they are not focused on the content of what is being reported, but on the status of the reporter. In effect, they are addressing two relevant questions that can be asked when descriptions are offered. Does the person making the report have an *interest* that discounts the report? Does the person have an *entitlement* that increases its plausibility? These are not the only sorts of constructions that can help ratchet descriptions up or down through the hierarchy of modalization. Other approaches can involve the way the topic of the report is described (empiricist discourse, detail and narrative) and also the relationship between different reports of the same event (consensus and corroboration).

Empiricist Discourse

In Chapter 1, I discussed a range of sociological approaches to science. However, discussion of the strand of this work that has focused on scientists' discourse was postponed until later because of its direct relevance to issues of fact construction. One of the main conclusions of work on scientific discourse is that scientists draw on different vocabularies or 'interpretative repertoires' when they are describing their work. Interpretative repertoires are systematically related sets of terms, often used with stylistic and grammatical coherence, and often organized around one or more central metaphors. They are one of the major resources that scientists use when constructing versions of their worlds. Nigel Gilbert and Michael Mulkay (1984) call the repertoire that predominates when scientists are describing their own work, and work that they take to be true, the 'empiricist repertoire'. Discourse of this kind treats data as primary and provides only generalized, inexplicit formulations of the actions and beliefs of the scientist. When the scientist does appear he or she is depicted as forced to undertake actions by the demands of natural phenomena or the constraints of rules.

> 6   A long held assumption concerning oxidative phosphorylation has been that the energy available from oxidation-reduction reactions is used to drive the formation of the terminal covalent anhydride bond in ATP. Contrary to this view, recent results from several laboratories suggest that energy is used primarily to promote the binding of ADP and phosphate in a catalytically competent mode and to facilitate the release of bound ATP. (Gilbert and Mulkay, 1984: 41)

We will explore this discourse in more detail later. For the moment there are two points to note. First, although this discourse is characteristic of formal science writing, many of its features are familiar in other settings, including everyday conversations. Second, we can make sense of some of the features of this kind of discourse by considering the general role of fact construction and its relation to dilemmas of stake. Although science, as I have already noted, tends to be taken as an arena where there is disinterested discussion of pure facts, a whole variety of interests are potentially invokable to discount a scientist's claims (Gilbert and Mulkay, 1984, ch. 4; Potter and Wetherell, 1987: 151–2). Empiricist discourse manages the dilemma of stake by directing attention away from the scientist and on to what is being reported, in much the same way that we saw Diane in Extract 2 focus on Neil's shoes rather than her own reasons for not investigating the potential burglar. Indeed, the empiricist repertoire takes this to extremes by not merely focusing on the data, but also by constructing the data as having its own agency. The reporter becomes a passive responder to the requirements of the facts.

Constructing Corroboration and Consensus

Notions of corroboration (is there another witness to this event?) and consensus (do the different witnesses agree?) are familiar in legal settings. However, they have a much wider currency. As with category entitlements, it is tempting to think of these things merely as straightforward and sensible features of reasoning. Independent witnesses, particularly if they are all saying the same thing, make an account more credible. The argument here is not that this intuition is a mistaken one. Rather, it is that it is too simple on its own because it ignores the way that witnesses can be *constructed as* independent and the way that their versions can be *constructed as* the same. And this is not simply a technical, analytic observation. This is also a participant's concern. That is, participants orientate to both corroboration and its construction as they build and undercut such accounts.

For example, in a study of arguments about what went on at an off-the-record press briefing (Potter and Edwards, 1990), we found examples of the press's case being bolstered by emphasizing the consensus of a set of different reports. The following is from an MP's question posed as part of a parliamentary debate to do with the content of the briefing; it comes from *Hansard*, which is the official parliamentary record:

7 *Mr David Winnick (Walsall, North)*:   As all the Sunday newspapers carried *virtually the same story*, is the Chancellor saying that *every journalist* who came to the briefing – he has not denied that there was one – misunderstood what he said?

(*Hansard*, 7 November: 26, emphasis added)

Here the consensus across the range of different stories is invoked as a warrant for their truth in a setting where the truth of an account has been challenged. However, our emphasis on rhetoric and the constructed nature of versions leads us to expect that there can be commonplace counters to such forms of warranting. One such counter is to suggest that the consensus across a set of accounts is a product of collusion rather than a set of people independently witnessing the same thing, and thus providing the same description. The following extract is from shortly after in the same parliamentary debate. The speaker, Chancellor Lawson, has attempted to deny the newspaper stories.

8 *Mr Lawson*:   [. . .] the statements that appeared in the press on Sunday bore no relation whatever to what I in fact said. [. . .] they will have their shorthand notes and they will know it, and they will know *they went behind afterwards* and *they thought there was not a good enough story and so they produced that.*

(*Hansard*, 7 November: 26, emphasis added)

The minister discounts the idea that the reports are the same because they are true by introducing the notion that they are the same because the reporters made them up to be the same. Note, also, that this claim about collusion is itself a description which is open to dispute, and the minister warrants it by reference to the *interests* of the reporters. Their story was not good enough so they made one up. This reminds us that these procedures of fact construction are not working in isolation. They are equally likely to be drawn on together, as in this case.

Detail and Narrative

The *detail*, the *specifics* of a description, are crucial for the activity that the description is used to do. However, vivid detailed descriptions can also be used to build up the facticity of an account. They can provide an impression of being there by sketching features which, although not substantial to the claim or argument, would have been apparent to someone who actually witnessed some event. Again, to treat this as a rhetorical construction is not to argue that detail is not an important element in fact construction; rather, it is to note that such detail can be produced and worked up for its fact-constructional properties. After all, this is one of the primary skills of novelists as they tell a story in a believable way.

Take the dispute about what went on in the controversial off-the-record press briefing I have just discussed. As the dispute continued, with further questions being posed about the news reports of the briefing, several of the papers responded with lengthy articles which included detailed descriptions of the briefing, containing much contextual detail.

> 9   Mr Lawson sat in an armchair in one corner, next to a window looking out over
>   the garden of No 11 Downing Street. The Press Secretary, Mr John Gieve, hov-
>   ered by the door. The rest of us, notebooks on our laps, perched on chairs and
>   sofas in a circle around the Chancellor. It was 10.15 on the morning of Friday,
>   4 November. . . .
> (*Observer*, 13 November)

Few of the details in this account are directly relevant to the substantive issue of dispute which was focused on potential change in the government's arrangements for the payment of benefits. Neither the armchair, the garden, the hovering by the door of Mr Gieve, or the perching on chairs is consequential for the benefits change and none of these particulars had been denied, or even commented on, by Chancellor Lawson. However, such descriptive features are characteristic of the way scenes are built in novels (Fowler, 1977). They work to make what is described graphic and believable by warranting the speaker or writer as a proper witness.

It is here that a concern with detail blurs into a concern with narrative and narrative organization. Details of this kind can be organized to provide narrative structure to an account; the order of events, who the characters are and so on. Narrative organization can be used to increase the plausibility of a particular description by embedding it in a sequence where what is described becomes expected or even necessary.

Although detail can be used in this way, there are times when detail can be ineffectual and descriptions that are vague or global can be the preferred pathway to a sustainable account. One of the problems with providing rich detail is that it may be undermined in various ways: details may be picked apart, or inconsistencies identified which cast doubt on the credibility of the speaker. The use of vague or formulaic descriptions may provide just enough material to sustain some action without providing descriptive claims that can open it to undermining.

Combining Action and Epistemology

So far, for the purposes of this initial exposition, I have separated out the action and epistemological orientations of descriptions, as well as treating the various styles of epistemological warranting as themselves separable from one another. However, in actual situations these different types of warranting are generally blended more or less seamlessly together and bound up with the action itself. It is important to stress again that these styles of fact construction do not work in a mechanical way. Rather, they have to be worked up and fitted to the specifics of the situations they are used in and there is always the potential for their being undermined.

To end this chapter, I will devote a bit more time to a single example to show how the various elements and considerations I have introduced can be meshed together. The following extract comes from the first five minutes of the initial relationship counselling session involving a couple whom we will call Connie and Jimmy. We have already met them briefly in Extract 1, which was taken from their second session. One of the points of contention in this first session is precisely what the couple's relationship problems are. The Counsellor asks about the sequence of events that led up to an abortive move to start counselling.

```
10   1   C:   Wha- (.) what happened at that point.
     2   W:   At that poi:nt, (0.6) Jimmy ha- (.) my- Jimmy is
     3        extremely jealous. Ex- extremely jealous per:son.
     4        Has a:lways ↓been, from the da:y we met. Y'know?
     5        An' at that point in time, there was an episo:de,
     6        with (.) a bloke, (.) in a pub, y'know?
     7        And me: having a few drinks and messin'. (0.8)
     8        That was it. (0.4) Right? And this (0.4)
     9        got all out of hand to Jimmy according to Jimmy
    10        I was a:lways doin' it and .hhh y'know a:lways aggravating him.
    11        He was a jealous person I: aggravated the situation. .h
    12        And he walked out that ti:me. To me it was (.)
    13        totally ridiculous the way he (.) goes o:n (.)
    14        through this problem that he ha:s.
```
(DE-JF/C2/S1:4)

There are a lot of fascinating features of this account, but I will concentrate especially on Connie's description of Jimmy, and her description of the events that preceded his 'walking out' (for analyses that deals with these materials in more detail, see Edwards, 1995, 1996). Note first the way Connie breaks off a direct response to the Counsellor's question to insert a description of Jimmy (2–3). She describes Jimmy as an 'extremely jealous person'. The specifics of the description are crucial here. Jealousy can be something to do with the person who is jealous, or it can be caused by someone else. Connie's description paints Jimmy's jealousy firmly as something to do with him: he is an extremely jealous *person* and he had been like that 'from the day we met'. This description counters the possibility that the jealousy was caused by something that Connie did – flirting with men in pubs for example, as Jimmy later claims. The description of Jimmy does two things. In terms of the dispute over why Jimmy left her, it counters the inference that he left because of her actions. In terms of epistemological entitlements, it provides a sceptical frame for hearing Jimmy's subsequent version of the same event. A pathologically jealous man's description of his wife's good time in a pub is unlikely to be fully objective.

Now take Connie's construction of the event itself (5–8). One of the notable features of this description is its lack of detail. *Episode* here is the sort of term that can be used to remain neutral to issues of cause and effect; critical linguists have identified language use of this kind as characteristic of newspaper reports where causality is being questioned or recast (Fowler, 1991; Hodge and Kress, 1993). 'Bloke' and 'pub' specify minimum particulars. And in line 7 Connie characterizes her activity in a minimal fashion. In this speech community 'messin' is part of a familiar idiom, 'just messing'; that is, being playful or non-serious. And even this is further mitigated by noting that she had had a 'few drinks'. What one does after 'having a few drinks' is often (although not always – the rhetoric can be worked either way) less criticizable than what one does when sober.

Having strongly built up Jimmy's jealousy as a feature of his personality, and provided a description of an event which downplays its seriousness, Connie is in a position to disparage his (reported) claim that he left her because of the event as 'totally ridiculous'. It is particularly important to see just how subtle and sophisticated what is going on here is. It is easy to think this sort of discourse, full of hesitations and repairs as it is, is an example of poor argument or general clumsiness of expression where inarticulate people are stumbling over their words. Yet it becomes apparent when examining examples of this kind how the different features contribute to the task at hand. For example, the global formulations Connie uses in her descriptions of the event are robust against undermining. Some of the effort Jimmy puts in shortly afterwards is shown by the way his description of the evening extends to 130 lines of transcript compared with the 3 that Connie devotes to it (some of his version will be discussed in Chapter 7). The general point, then, is that descriptions are closely fitted to particular activities, and their epistemological basis is attended to in a variety of different ways.

Overall, this chapter is intended to prepare the ground for a more systematic and elaborate discussion of procedures for fact construction in the two chapters that follow. It started by arguing that exploration of the manufacture of factuality will be facilitated by pressing the metaphor of construction to its limits, and by selectively combining elements from the constructionism in linguistics, conversation analysis and post-structuralism. Such a constructionist approach will be facilitated by three analytic emphases. First, it is anti-cognitivist. Its concern is not with construction understood as a mental process, involving the cognitivist apparatus of schemas, memory stores and social representations. There are a variety of reasons for eschewing such a perspective. However, one of the principal ones is that it draws attention away from how factual accounts are organized and how they are fitted into particular interactions. Whether derived from cognitive psychology (Neisser, 1976), social representations theory (Moscovici, 1984) or critical linguistics (Hodge and Kress, 1993), cognitive theorizing tends towards an individualistic perspective and away from the human practices in which fact construction are embedded. The second emphasis is on discourse; that is, talk and texts as social practices, rather than, say, ethnographic reconstructions of these things. The focus on discourse makes it more straightforward to retain the order of detail that is involved in establishing factuality. The third emphasis is on fact construction as rhetorically organized. That is, analysis will work on two closely related dimensions. It will be concerned not only with fact construction (*reification*) but also with fact destruction (*ironization*); and it will be dealing with both the *defensive rhetoric* through which an account is protected against attack, and also the *offensive rhetoric* through which a contrasting description is undermined.

Following these preliminaries, I developed a distinction between the *action orientation* and the *epistemological orientation* of descriptions. The point here was to show that descriptions can be analysed both in terms of the sorts of actions that they are performing or contributing to, and in terms of fact construction; that is, the process by which description is built up into accepted fact. Different features of descriptions may be involved in each of these things. It should be emphasized, however, that this distinction is more heuristic than actual. After all, in many cases it is precisely through fact construction that actions get done. The epistemological orientation is not an abstract, philosophical concern with truth; it is a practical, situated concern with making a description credible.

Finally, a number of different elements that can contribute to fact construction were broken down into two clusters. On the one hand, there are practices which involve different constructions of the agent, such as constructions of interest and disinterest and the building of category entitlements. On the other, there are practices that make descriptions separate and external to the actor, such as the use of empiricist discourse, the manufacture of corroboration, and the organization of descriptions into narrative. These will be the topic of the next two chapters.

5

Interests and Category Entitlements

This chapter will pick up and develop some of the ideas from the previous chapter on the ways in which the identity of the agents who produce descriptions can be worked on to effect their credibility. In terms of the broad distinction introduced between the action and epistemological orientation of descriptive accounts, it will concentrate primarily on the epistemological business being done. In the first place, it will focus on the way issues of the stake or interest are drawn on in an attempt to undermine claims and accounts, and the way such attempts are resisted. In the second place, it will focus on the way descriptions can be given authority by emphasizing or building up category memberships which imply particular knowledge entitlements, and the way these too may be undermined. The twin themes of stake and category entitlement are pervasive features of everyday reasoning about facts and descriptions. The facticity of an account can be enhanced through working up category entitlements; it can be weakened by emphasizing the personal or institutional stake of the account's author.

Although the management of stake and epistemological entitlement will be central themes in the chapter, there is a further significant consideration which arises when considering the relation between the identity of the speaker/writer and the facticity of the version they produce, and that consideration is what Goffman (1981) calls 'footing'. This refers to the range of relationships that speakers and writers have to the descriptions they report. For example, people may make their own claims, or they may report claims of others; and when they report claims they can display various degrees of distance from what they are reporting. Just as there is a central concern with stake and interest, so there is a concern with neutrality; that is, how the *absence* of such stake is displayed. Footing is central when dealing with factual reports, because it is through the paraphernalia of footing that speakers manage their personal or institutional accountability for such reports. As we will see, footing provides a set of distinctions that guide the assignment of blame, compliments, scepticism or whatever.

It is simplifying massively, but still – I hope –heuristically useful, to present these concerns in terms of a diagram (Figure 5.1). This indicates some of the most important relationships between category entitlement, interest formulation and footing, and their consequences for facticity and speaker accountability. Category entitlements can be used to build up the facticity of accounts; interests can be formulated to undermine them. As we will see, however, when we get to look at some of the detail of practices of interest invocation and claims for category entitlement this pattern becomes rather less neat. As factual accounts, diagrams have a range of virtues and pitfalls (Gilbert and Mulkay, 1984: ch. 7; Myers, 1990).

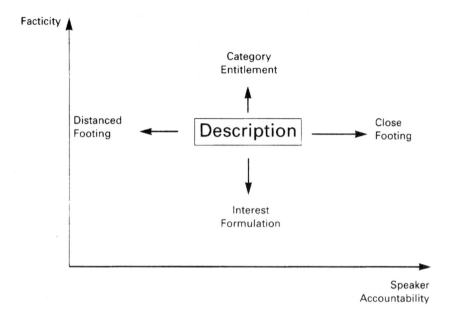

Figure 5.1 *Relations between category entitlement, interest formulation and footing*

Before starting to consider stake and interest in a bit more depth, it is important to reiterate some of the warnings from the previous chapter. First, it is important to remember that the enterprise of this book is not one of attempting to assess the adequacy of factual accounts. The goal is not to be better able to say that some claim or description is true or false. Instead, it is focused on the way people *themselves* manage and understand descriptions and their facticity. Thus it is particularly important to distinguish this enterprise from the social scientific literatures whose goal is to explain the nature of claims and arguments in terms of the interests of their producers; that is, the sort of interest theory discussed in Chapter 1. Taking its lead from the ethnomethodological theorizing discussed in Chapter 2, interests here will be a *topic* of analysis. That is, there will not be an attempt to produce an analytic account of how descriptions are determined by interests; instead, the aim is to produce an account of how *people themselves* undermine descriptions through invoking interests, and how, in turn, they design descriptions to attend to such undermining. The same goes for footing. There will be an exploration of how people mark distinctions between, say, who is the origin of a particular description and who is simply relaying it. But that will not involve a commitment to either a general account of the relation between being origin and relayer of views, nor to which agent is actually origin or relayer in any specific context.

The second warning concerns how the agent – the speaker or writer – is construed. Much of the work discussed in this chapter and elsewhere has a conversation analytic inspiration and works with transcripts of talk using individual speakers. Because of this, it is all too easy to fall into thinking that the basic units of such analysis are individual persons. However, following the emphasis on participants' own constructions, it is important to resist this assumption. Descriptions may be treated as the product of individuals, but also of collectivities of various kinds: '*The Times*' leader stated', 'the Government claimed today', 'the judge summarized the report's findings'. As Jenny Mandelbaum has neatly illustrated in a number of studies, stories and versions are often worked up collaboratively (Mandelbaum, 1987, 1993). Looked at another way, the nature of the agent who is speaking or writing is *itself* established through processes of fact construction and may well become the contentious point in an interaction.

A third warning is about the necessarily limited ambitions of this chapter. Stake, entitlement and footing are each huge topics. It is not hard to imagine whole books devoted to each. The coverage here will not be skimming the surface, but it will swim near to it. However, I hope that this coverage will show, first, just how important these concerns are in the building of factuality and, second, some of the basic procedures through which they may be drawn on to build and destroy factual versions.

Finally, although much of the research discussed in this chapter was conducted within a broadly conversation analytic tradition, that does not mean I have abandoned the important insights from the sociology of science and post-structuralist work. The reason for this is that conversation analysis, with its detailed attention to actual interaction sequences, has most fully developed the idea that descriptions have to be worked at and worked up, and that there are various devices and procedures that can be used to do this. It captures precisely the level of consequential detail that often falls through the cracks between the big ideas in sociology of scientific knowledge and post-structuralism.

Stake and Interest

I have been using the general terms *stake* and *interest* as emblematic of a whole range of considerations that people may use to discount descriptions. At their strongest, these notions are used to suggest that the description's speaker, or the institution responsible for the description, has something to gain or lose; that they are not *dis*interested. They have a stake in some course of actions which the description relates to, or there are personal, financial or power considerations that come into play. Descriptions may be broadly inspected in relation to a backdrop of competences, projects, allegiances, motives and values. People may be constructed as having an 'axe to grind', an ingrained set of prejudices, or as being simply too stupid to properly see what is going on (although discounting a description does not always depend on showing that the speaker has something to directly gain or lose).

Here is an example where stake is explicitly formulated. It is taken from an interview with the author Salman Rushdie by David Frost. The topic is the so-called *fatwah*, the religious death sentence on Rushdie.

1	*Frost*:	And how could they cancel it now? Can they cancel it – they say they can't.
	Rushdie:	Yeah, but you know, *they would, wouldn't they,* as somebody once said. The thing is, without going into the kind of arcana of theology, there is no technical problem. The problem is not technical. The problem is that they don't want to.

(*Public Broadcasting Service*, 26 November 1993, emphasis added)

Rushdie's first response to the claim that the *fatwah* cannot be cancelled is to treat the claim as motivated. The expression 'they would, wouldn't they' refers back to a famous British political scandal. In that context it was used in court in response to the denial of sexual relations by a member of the aristocracy by a woman accused of prostitution. The phrase has a number of interesting design features that makes it particularly fitted for interest invocation. Notably, it treats what was said as something to be expected: it is the sort of thing that people with that background, those interests, this set of attitudes *would* say, and it formulates this predictability as shared knowledge: they would say that, *wouldn't they* (see also Edwards and Potter, 1992: 117–18). That is, it does not have to specify or elaborate on the nature of the interests.

This example involves a forthright, almost stereotyped form of interest invocation. It illustrates the phenomenon clearly, but is probably not characteristic. The invocation of stake and interest is often much less explicit. My concern here, however, is not in how interest attributions are constructed but in how they are resisted. Given the pervasive possibility that descriptions may be undermined in this way, explicitly or otherwise, it is not surprising that a range of approaches to head off or minimize such discounting have been developed. I will focus on approaches that make explicit reference to interests as these provide a relatively clear start point.

Stake Inoculation

The pervasiveness of stake and interest as a consideration where descriptions are used is shown both by the way interests may be invoked in undermining versions and by the way versions are fashioned to head off such undermining. Let me start by considering some examples where descriptions are constructed to head off the imputation of stake or interest. Taking a medical analogy, we can refer to these as attempts at *stake inoculation*.

The first example is the simplest. The following passage comes from a newspaper article headlined 'Psychiatrist reveals the agony and the lunacy of great artists'.

2   The stereotype of the tortured genius suffering for his art and losing his
         mind in a sea of depression, sexual problems and drink turns out to be
         largely true, a psychiatrist says today.
            While scientists, philosophers and politicians can all suffer from the odd
         personality defect, for real mental instability you need to look at writers
         and painters, says Felix Post.
    →   Dr Post was initially sceptical, but having looked at the lives of nearly 300
         famous men he believes exceptional creativity and psychiatric problems
         are intertwined. In some way, mental ill health may fuel some forms of cre-
         ativity, he concludes. (*Guardian*, 30 June 1994)

What is particularly interesting in this extract is the arrowed description of Dr
Post as 'initially sceptical'. Why is this here? The first thing to note is that its
presence shows that the article is orientated to the possibility that the claims
of Dr Post might be treated as motivated, in this case by his failure to transcend familiar stereotypes. The inoculation works by countering the potential
criticism that Dr Post is simply perpetrating common stereotypes of madness
and creativity. Note that we do not have to invent analytic speculation about
the relevance of this stereotype because the article itself starts with it. Indeed,
part of the 'story' of the article is that this is a stereotype that 'turns out' to
be right. The point, then, is that the stake inoculation encourages us not to
treat this claim as a product of some *expectation* that Dr Post has, but a
product of the facts themselves. The implication is that the facts are so strong
that they can overcome the scepticism.

   Here is another example showing the same procedure used in an interactional setting. It comes from a study of youth subculture members talking
about their lives and identities by Sue Widdicombe and Robin Wooffitt
(1995). These researchers note that for members of such subcultures there
may be problems in displaying authenticity – that is, showing that they are
making considered choices rather than just following a fashion or caving
in to peer-group pressures. In the extract, the speaker provides an account
of how he developed a particular musical taste characteristic of his subculture:

3   *I:*   When and how did you get inta being a rocker?
         R: it must have been when I was about fourteen or fifteen (.)
                some friends at school were (.)
         I: mmhm
    →   *R:*   an they- an I said oh heavy metal's rubbish, they said nah it's not
    →   an they gave me some tapes to listen to an I did enjoy it,
                did ⌈like it
         I: ⌊mmhm
         R: and that's when I s-sort of started getting into it (.)
                before I sort of liked things like Duran Duran and Spandau Ballet
                (.) huh ˙hh
         I: mmhm and then I ⌈mean how-
         R: ⌊but that's cos I hadn't heard heavy metal you see
(Widdicombe and Wooffitt, 1995: 140–1).

One way of understanding what is going on here is to consider the respondent to be solving a problem: how can he provide a description of how he became a rocker without it becoming the sort of story of social pressures which will threaten his *authentic* rocker identity. This problem becomes particularly acute early in the extract where the role of school friends – the peers who might exert the pressure – is introduced. It is notable at this point that the speaker hesitates and breaks off to provide a description which constructs his initial view of heavy metal: 'I said oh heavy metal's ru<u>bb</u>ish'. It is against this initial expectation that he comes to see how enjoyable heavy metal is. He had not liked it before because he 'hadn't <u>hear</u>d heavy metal you see'. It is here that the stake inoculation is operating.

This descriptive sequence is rather more complex than Extract 1, for the constructive work is being done both on the quality of heavy metal music (enjoyable if you listen to it) and on the sequence of events. The interactionally significant feature is that the narrative presents the development of the rocker identity as a thoughtful product of musical appreciation. Crucially, the speaker did not take on the identity merely to follow his friends, but because of the quality of the music itself. That is, he was not merely copying what they were doing, but making a considered judgement that went against his own prior prejudices.

As a third example of stake inoculation I will discuss some elements from Dorothy Smith's classic study of fact construction: K is mentally ill (Smith, 1978; 1990). Smith analysed the way an account of a 'girl's' descent into mental illness is constructed to make the illness appear a neutral fact in the world. The full details of this study are not relevant here at this point (see Potter et al., 1984; Wooffitt, 1992, for more detailed discussion); I will concentrate on the opening sequence of the account which includes the interviewer's gloss on some of the events, and then the initial part of her description of what the interviewee – Angela – said about K.

4   Angela met K about 4 years ago, during her first
     year at university. Angela had been to the same school
     but in a grade below K and when introduced to K felt full of
     admiration. Here was a girl, a year older, of such a
     good family, a good student, so nice, so friendly, so
     very athletic, who was willing to befriend her. K suggested outings, and they went skiing, swimming, playing
     tennis together. In the fall they shared in a car-pool, so that
     more people were immediately involved in the contact. [...]
Angela: My recognition that there might be something
            wrong was very gradual, and I was actually the last of
            her close friends who was openly willing to admit that
            she was becoming mentally ill.
(Smith, 1990: 17–18)

One of the features of the account of K's illness is that it includes much that could be treated as critical of K. And of course, the description *mentally ill* is often used negatively. Because of this, the account has the potential to be treated as motivated; in other words, it could be a product of dislike, jealousy or whatever. One of the tasks performed in the opening section of the account is to provide a stake inoculation against such an interpretation. The inoculation here is even more complex than in Extract 2 and involves a number of features combined together.

First, it constructs Angela as K's friend, indeed, her close friend. One of the features of the everyday use of the category 'friend' is its implications of positive feelings and loyalty; friends are people you stick by. What they are not are people to be attacked and criticized. A second feature is that the account provides a series of particulars from which Angela's status as K's friend can be inferred. There are a series of positive assessments ('such a good family, a good student, so nice, so friendly'); there is the report that she had been befriended by K; and there is the description of shared sporting outings. Third, Angela's recognition of K's problem is constructed as *reluctant*; it is not something she wanted. As Smith puts it:

> Since the 'fact' to be realized or established is a negative one and the structural frame declares for only positive motives toward K, there are no grounds for suspecting Angela's motives. The rhetoric of the fact is here that Angela is constrained to recognize it. It is a fact independently of her wish; she does not wish it and yet she is 'forced to face' it. (1990: 27–8)

Just as with Dr Post's early scepticism about madness and creativity and the rocker's initial negative expectations about heavy metal, the stake inoculation works to build up the credibility or factuality of the description by heading off the discounting work of stake attribution. In situations where descriptions might be undermined as interested, stake inoculation presents a counter-interest: in Extract 1 credulity is countered with scepticism; in Extract 2 blind imitation is countered by prior negative views along with careful evaluation; in 3 hostility is countered by friendship.

Stake, Facts, Attitudes and Attributions

It is useful to clarify what is distinctive about this approach to fact construction by comparing it with some social psychological research in the mainstream 'social cognition' tradition (see Augoustinos and Walker, 1995, for an overview). One of the questions addressed in that tradition is how the process of attribution leads to changes in attitudes. In particular, do certain sorts of attributions lead people to discount claims and others lead to their enhanced credibility?

A study by Wendy Wood and Alice Eagly (1981), for example, explored this issue in an experiment concerned with the credibility of arguments about pornography. Participants in the study were provided with a pack of materials relating to a person called Jim. These included a set of arguments for the restriction of pornography which were made by Jim in an interview and various snippets of information about what Jim had said at times in the past, whether he was a practising Catholic and so on. The researchers went to some trouble building up Jim as a real, believable person – although he was entirely their invention. The crucial feature of the study lay in how Jim's past views on pornography were represented. For half the participants he was described as having a history of supporting freedom of speech and the availability of pornography; for the other half, he was described as being anti-freedom of speech and pornography.

When the participants were asked how important the factual evidence had been in Jim's arguments against pornography, the ratings were highest for the participants for whom Jim had been described as having previously been a supporter of freedom of speech and pornography. Wood and Eagly's interpretation of this finding was that, in the condition where Jim was consistent in his anti-pornography position, the participants simply attributed the arguments to what he was like as a person. Yet, when he was presented as previously pro-pornography, this attribution was not possible: he was not a pro-pornography person, so the participants had to find something else to which they could attribute the cause of his change of mind, and the obvious thing was the factual nature of the arguments themselves.

Now, superficially this research chimes in with the examples described in this section: Jim's credibility is advanced by his change of mind just as Dr Post's is. It is not news that someone with long-standing anti-pornography feelings argues against pornography; nor that someone who believes the stereotype that madness and creativity go together reproduces this in his research. Yet there is a fundamental difference in the way what is going on is understood. For Wood and Eagly, attribution is a cognitive process driven by perception of the world, and the world is populated with entities: Jims who have their minds changed, and Jims who don't. In contrast, the argument here is that these things are constructed and reworked in interaction. People *construct themselves* as having had particular views or expectations, and they do so as needed and in a way that is closely fitted to the current interaction.

There is another crucial difference. Wood and Eagly's participants are expected to treat the materials relating to Jim as simply factual, as windows on what Jim is really like (or what he would be like if he existed). If they accept the experimenters' cover story, they have little choice but to treat the arguments about pornography as actually credible enough to win over a sceptic. There is no other explanation easily available to them. However, outside of the specialized environment of the social psychological laboratory, people have no such strictures. For example, unlike the case with Jim and his views on pornography, listeners can inspect Angela's claims about her friendship with K and doubt them, rework them or even argue against them. The rhetorical skills that allow people to do stake inoculation also allow them to combat it. The social psychology laboratory is a bastion well-defended against that kind of open rhetoric.

Stake Confession

Although inoculation is one common approach to managing the dilemma of stake another common approach is confession. On the face of it, this is hardly a technique of fact construction. In the abstract, it might seem as if the confession of an interest in this way is giving in, or providing ammunition, to critics, whether in the course of an argument with an opposing political leader or with one's partner in a relationship. However, in some kinds of interactions issues of stake may be so salient that inoculating against them may be difficult and ignoring them unlikely to be effective. If stake considerations are unavoidable, perhaps the best thing to do is confess them.

Here is a simple example. The author is a theatre critic writing in his newspaper column about the role played by critics, and about a fellow critic who had been strongly attacked in an open letter by a group of artists. The critic concludes his column with a familiar form of stake discounting, although, here, it is turned round as a stake confession.

5   My own feeling is that the British theatre critics are a kindly and perpetually
      hopeful bunch, and that if we have a fault it is that we tend to praise shows
  →   too much. But then I would say that, wouldn't I?
(*Daily Telegraph*, 8 January 1994)

It is notable that the stake confession here comes after a highly positive assessment of theatre critics, the category of people he is strongly and visibly affiliated with, and this itself comes after the main body of the column which is mainly defending critics. The stake here is particularly obvious; here is someone explicitly and elaborately praising members of the social category of which he is writing as an explicit member. It is virtually unmissable. In this situation, confessing stake shows that the writer is live to its relevance and is not trying to dupe the readership. It may also work as a display of honesty and objectivity: the author is someone who can stand outside his interests and is well aware of their distorting potential. In this sense it is disarming. Also it puts potential objectors in the interactional position of making a point that has already been conceded and the objection that this critic praises too much would simply prove the critic's point! They will be bringing up old news. Such a stake confession may not wipe out the sorts of interest discounting that readers make, but it may be more effective than simply allowing them to do their own stake discounting.

The following example is rather more complicated. It comes from a newspaper article which includes a discussion of the cruelty involved in making fur coats and it quotes from a representative of the British Fur Trade Association on a decision by a charity to accept donated fur coats.

6   'Years ago, everyone who could afford it had a fur coat because we were all
      blissfully ignorant of the cruelty involved in their making. Today we do not
      have that excuse. What has changed?' Not much, according to Valerie
      Brooke of the British Fur Trade Association who,
  →   while she obviously has a vested interest, makes a telling and poignant
      point. 'Oxfam's decision to accept fur coats for sending to Bosnia is a
      belated and partial triumph for common sense over political correctness.'
(*The Observer*, 2 January 1994)

The role of paid representatives of organizations is precisely to make arguments in favour of what they represent. We would be amazed if such a representative started to attack their own product, and would expect them to be sacked immediately. Such people are definitively and officially interested. To quote the arguments of such a representative in an article, then, risks the immediate thought that, indeed, they would say that, wouldn't they. As with the last example, here 'confessing' the role of interest may be the most effective response. The extract starts with a quotation from a letter. The role of interests is clearly and explicitly formulated, but treated as not sufficient to discount the description of Oxfam's decision and its general significance. The stake confession here shows that the writer has not been duped, or failed to miss the obvious stake inferences that are available; rather, the point is strong enough to work *even* after taking stake into account.

There is another interesting and important feature of Extract 6 which is worth mentioning. The article is describing a pattern of stake with respect to the arguments about fur coats. The stake is formulated as lying 'out-there': it is a feature of the world but not something relevant to the current writer. By focusing on the stake of the fur trade representative, in this way the author is rather neatly able to deflect the focus from the potential question of her *own* stake. For example, is she a fur-coat wearer/defender who is constructing an argument in their favour?

Stake and Subtlety

These examples of interest inoculation and interest confession are not necessarily representative of patterns of interaction in other settings or other cultures – although I suspect that readers will find them familiar. They are examples where stake is formulated in rather explicit ways using well-known idioms and phrases: 'axe to grind', 'vested interest', 'they would, wouldn't they'. The very existence of such a variety of phrases shows the importance of stake as an issue. Such examples give an indication of some of the ways in which stake can be managed, built up and discounted, and they emphasize the potential significance of stake in participants' understanding of facts and descriptions. Their role here is to open up the issue of stake as a central one, as well as giving some pointers to how it might be analysed in other settings. Stake may be managed in rather more subtle ways in the course of relationship disputes, say, or business meetings.

I will take just one pair of extracts to indicate briefly something of this potential subtlety. The first comes from the same relationship counselling session that was quoted in earlier chapters. This extract comes right at the start of a long narrative where Jimmy describes a difficult evening with his partner. The second comes from a speaker who is being interviewed about race and race-related issues in New Zealand. He is responding to a question about crime. The important segments have been italicized.

7   *Jimmy*:   Connie had a short skirt on *I don't know*
(DE-JF:C2:S1:10 – emphasis added)

8 *Jones*: There have been a lot of ideas put out, *what is it*,
             that the majority of rapes are committed by
             Islanders or Mäoris and . . .
(Wetherell and Potter, 1992: 96 – emphasis added)

Both of these descriptions are especially delicate ones, where the speaker's interest is likely to be of particular concern. Extract 7 is part of a dispute where Jimmy is complaining that his partner, Connie, flirts with other men, and at the same time dealing with the accusation that he is pathologically jealous and prone to seeing harmless sociability as sexual suggestion (see Extract 2 in Chapter 4 and Edwards, 1995, 1996). Extract 8 comes from a long passage of talk where he had made a number of highly blaming descriptions of minority groups living in New Zealand. In each case, the speakers qualify their descriptions.

In Extract 7 the qualification displays uncertainty. Such a display works against the implication that Jimmy was jealously inspecting his partner's clothing, already concerned about it before the evening was under way. We might, of course, wonder whether this is simply a statement of Jimmy's actual uncertainty; yet elsewhere in the same narrative Jimmy does not seem to be in any doubt at all about the length of Connie's skirt (see Extract 16 in Chapter 6 below). In Extract 8 the qualification is slightly more complex: the display is not so much of uncertainty but of searching ('grasping') for someone else's formulation. The 'what is it' displays the 'ideas' as both not the speaker's own and ones that he has not quite remembered; that is, he is not the kind of (racist, hostile) person who actively notes down negative items about minority groups, let alone produces them himself. The point, then, is that each speaker subtly displays their disinterestedness precisely at a point where it could be a particular issue.

A final comment is that it would, no doubt, have been possible to build up this chapter entirely from examples from my own everyday talk or even with extracts from this manuscript. A whole range of interest stories, positive and negative, are available for discounting academic work. And, just as with the fur-trade representative, a 'disinterested' account of interest can be a powerful rhetorical device both there and here.

Category Entitlement

When Harvey Sacks introduced the notion of entitlements in his lectures he was particularly concerned with entitlements to *experience*. He discusses a story told about coming across a horrific auto-accident ('people laid out and covered over on the pavement'). One of the features that concerned Sacks was the differential 'rights' to feelings about the accident that the teller and the recipient of the story have. He argues that the teller has a specific *entitlement* to feel awful, to cry, to have their day ruined in a way that the recipient does not:

if you call up a friend of yours who is unaffiliated with the event you're reporting, i.e. someone who doesn't turn out to be the cousin of, the aunt of, the person who was killed in the accident, but just a somebody you call up and tell about an awful experience, then if they become as disturbed as you, or more, something peculiar is going on, and you might even feel wronged – though that might seem to be an odd thing to feel. (1992: I, 242–8)

It is the *witness* who has the entitlement. These sorts of issues have been developed with more of a focus on knowledge than experience by Whalen and Zimmerman (1990), as I noted in the previous chapter. Their enterprise of 'practical epistemology' is similar to that being developed in this book, although they have a narrower focus on how knowledge and knowledgeability are treated in the specific setting of calls to emergency services.

I want to pick up the idea of *category* entitlement; that is, the idea that certain categories of people, in certain contexts, are treated as knowledgeable. In practice, category entitlement obviates the need to ask how the person knows; instead, simply being a member of some category – doctor, hockey player, hospital worker – is treated as sufficient to account for, and warrant, their knowledge of a specific domain. Yet, as the Widdicombe and Wooffitt (1995) study discussed earlier indicated, 'being a member' is not so simple as it might appear. Membership can be achieved or worked up; people can fail to be treated as having certain memberships. The nature, boundaries and implication of both categories and their entitlements can be reworked in a whole range of ways (Gilbert and Mulkay, 1984: ch. 6; Potter, 1988; Shuman, 1992; Yearley, 1984). And while some categories are especially visible, or given official credentials, others are highly localized and negotiable (Jayyusi, 1984).

Take, for example, the study Derek Edwards and I (1992) did of a disputed press briefing. One of the things we noted were differences in the way the 'newspaper reporters' were described (note, by the way, the problem I am having giving a 'neutral' description of the 'thing' that is subject to competing description). In one sense the people doing the reporting for the papers were simply journalists; no party to the controversy argued that they were impostors, or that there is no such thing as journalists (although these kinds of arguments are not impossible). However, this is a category that can be constructed in different ways. Take these two examples drawn from two different articles in the same newspaper on the same day, and describing the same set of people.

9   10 fully trained shorthand-writing *journalists*

10   So the *hacks'* notebooks contain only a sketchy summary . . .
(Both cited in Edwards and Potter, 1992: 63, emphasis added)

The point is that being a journalist does not *in itself* carry a ready-made and mechanical set of entitlements. Such entitlements can be built up or undermined in various ways. For example, Extract 9 comes from an article where the accuracy of the reporter's stories is being established. In this context, their special skills and entitlements are built up. In contrast, Extract 10 comes from an article which is criticizing the system of off-the-record briefings (of which the specific briefing was a part) as open to exploitation and corruption. Here limitations on the skills of the reporters are emphasized along with a categorization – hacks – which suggests cynical interests. Indeed, the word *hack* comes from 'hackney carriage' – and is a reference to the cabs reporters used to race from the scene to the newspaper so they could be first to sell their story. The point, then, is that category entitlements should be treated as things that can be built up or undermined, rather than frozen parts of a social system. Reporters can be tired old functionaries, gutter manipulators slavering after sleazy stories with their chequebooks, or heroic fighters after truth.

Entitlements, Friends and Urban Myths

Let us develop the idea of category entitlements, taking the case of so-called urban myths as an example. These are stories told about shocking events such as picking up a 'little old granny' hitchhiker who turns out to be an escaped axe murderer (the driver spots the hairy hands, gets 'her' to check the indicators are working, and then drives off – only later to find the axe in her handbag). Many people have told, and been told, such stories which have an international circulation. A newspaper series of such urban myths (albeit presented in a somewhat humorous context) allows us to examine some of their features. One striking thing is that they almost invariably start in the same way. This one is typical.

> 11   *A friend of a friend* was driving home when she noticed a strange object in the
>   road. Closer up it appeared to be a small child lying in the gutter. So she
>   slammed on the anchors and ran over. [The narrative continues to the denoue-
>   ment which involves discovering a sinister-looking man had hidden in the
>   back of the car.]
> (*Guardian*, 16 July 1994 – emphasis added)

Of course, the entire content of stories of this kind is fascinating, and academic studies have been done on the standardized narrative structures that they use. However, the interesting point here is how urban myths are introduced. Why the standardized opening: 'a friend of a friend'? We are used to thinking of 'friend' as a descriptive category from the domain of psychology: we have 'close friends', 'boyfriends', people we know who are 'not friends but merely acquaintances', we are 'just getting friendly'. Yet it is also possible to think of this category in epistemic terms.

Consider the difference between 'a friend told me that X' and 'somebody told me that X'. I take it that the former is a construction that is more likely to be used to warrant the factuality of X. Friends are people whom one knows well enough to make judgements about them, including judgements about potential stake; they are also people with whom you are in a relationship. You are displaying an investment in the claim. Friendship is taken to involve trust and sincerity rather than lying and deception. For reasons of this kind, friend is a category that can have epistemological implications.

However, in the urban myth example, the construction is not simply 'a friend was driving home', but 'a friend *of a friend* was driving home'. So why the extra friend?

One feature of these stories is that they are surprising or shocking – and as such they raise a host of questions: 'tell me about the person it happened to'?; 'why didn't she'?; 'how is she now'?; and so on. These are precisely the sorts of detailed questions that might get the teller of such an unlikely tale into difficulties, or even make it unravel altogether as they try to deal with them. It will be hard for the teller to maintain both that this event happened to a friend, and that they do not know how the friend is feeling now, say. A friend of a friend is different. It is a construction which neatly circumvents these difficulties. It is still a connection which trades on some of the positive epistemological implications of the category 'friend'; yet with this construction the teller need not be expected to know any further, potentially troubling, details.

The 'friend of a friend' construction, then, provides some category entitlement but, at the same time, means the teller is not accountable for gaps, questions and issues with respect to the story: it was just what they heard. What it provides is trade-off between factuality and deniability. This draws attention to one of the common features of factual discourse of this kind. Not only must it be attentive to the fact construction, but also to the sorts of comeback that others may have; that is, the questions that are asked and criticisms proffered of the particular factual formulation. Looked at another way, this is just what is to be expected when we consider factual accounts of this kind to have a rhetorical design; they are prepared for various kinds of undermining. In fact, the 'friend of a friend' construction has been so repeated that it has almost become emblematic of unlikely stories. It can itself be drawn on for undercutting – just as with 'one of my friends has got this nasty problem' said to the doctor. The general point to stress is that a comeback is always possible; inoculations and entitlements do not guarantee success.

Community Leaders

When Quentin Halliday and I (Potter and Halliday, 1990) were building an archive of newspaper accounts of a particular crowd event (an 'inner city riot' in the mid-1980s), we were struck by how commonly 'community leaders' were quoted. Community leaders seemed to figure in almost every article or news bulletin as claiming one thing or accusing the police of doing another. In these materials community leaders were treated as valuable informants about the events. Indeed, one of the features that seemed to define such people was that they were knowledgeable about their communities. In terms of our discussion of the relation between category memberships and knowledge entitlements, community leaders are people who know about their communities. When their claims are reported or when they are interviewed on television, they are not asked how they know. Like the caller from the General

Hospital we met in the previous chapter, they were treated as having special knowledge entitlements.

However, when we compared different stories about the same event we found that there were striking differences in the way it was described, and in particular there were differences in the claims attributed to community leaders. For example, some newspapers made claims such as the following:

> 12 local community leaders had warned that there would be a repetition if the area's problems were not tackled. (Potter and Halliday, 1990: 910)

while others offered a rather different version:

> 13 the explosion of violence which shocked the nation has baffled both police and community leaders. (Potter and Halliday, 1990: 909)

We suggested that two sorts of things were going on here. In the first place, newspapers and reporters have a central task, which is to be able to tell an authoritative account of events. They need to 'get the story'. This is so whether we treat them as disinterested organs of truth or outlets for the political views of media moguls. It is often particularly difficult to provide authoritative accounts of crowd events because they tend to happen without clear advanced warning, and are often geographically spread and highly confusing to outsiders (Reicher, 1987). This means that telling the story is often particularly hard, and local informants especially important. This may lead to difficulties in achieving an authoritative account.

This is where the second suggestion comes in. One of the features of the category 'community leader' is that the criteria for who counts as a 'community leader' are particularly complex. Lena Jayyusi (1984) has listed five commonly used criteria for deciding a person's category incumbency. These are: (1) perceptual availability (what they look like); (2) behavioural availability (they act in particular ways); (3) first-person avowal (they claim to be in X category); (4) third-person declaration (others claim they are in X category); and credential presentation (official badges or documents). Now one of the interesting things about the category 'community leader' is that the criteria are very diffuse: they cannot be identified from appearance; there are no official credentials and it is unlikely that simply avowing 'I am a community leader' will be treated as sufficient. What seems to be crucial is how the person acts and what other people say about them, neither of which is easy to check.

The point of this, then, is that 'community leader' is a category which combines a strong knowledge entitlement with weak incumbency criteria, or at least incumbency criteria which are hard for outsiders to apply. This means that they are ideally suited to be used to warrant journalistic claims. On the one hand, community leaders are people who are expected to know; on the other, it is hard for readers or other journalists to dispute their adequacy as informants because the membership criteria are so diffuse. Indeed, it is made even more difficult to dispute membership because overwhelmingly in the materials we examined 'community leaders' is used as an anonymous plural description (as in Extracts 12 and 13 above). As with 'a friend of a friend . . .', the combination of strong entitlement and obstacles to criticism seems to be a robust one. That is, this is an example where offensive and defensive rhetoric are working in consort.

Building Entitlements on Television and in the Field

One of the arguments I have made in this section is that category entitlement is not a fact of nature. It is not simply the case that some people are members of categories with knowledge entitlements, and some are not. Instead, such entitlements are worked up, and they also may need to be insulated against lines of rebuttal. Most of the time, this working-up is apparent only from the delivery of the talk, or from considering the way the discourse might have been different; for example, with the 'community leaders' categorization, considering why the plural anonymous form was used so commonly. However, there are occasions when we can study some of the reasoning that goes into the building of category entitlements. One of these is where we have a team of people working together in building a text such as a television pro-gramme. The teamwork necessitates considerations about fact construction being made publicly and explicitly whereas they might otherwise have remained tacit. Let us consider some materials of this kind.

Television workers often work to a punishing schedule. The example repro-duced here comes from the making of a current affairs programme about the misuse of cancer charity money to fund pure research (see Potter et al., 1991, for details). All the extracts are taken from a long conversation between three of the programme makers, who are sitting, having lunch, in the buffet of a large London railway station. They are planning an interview they will be filming that afternoon as well as discussing the programme in general. You have to imagine the sounds of crockery and eating, and the occasional train announcement, in the background.

The following extract comes from a discussion of a list of questions that the director has supplied. She is not present, and the people who are there seem to be rather cross with her. Chitty is reading the list out, and they talk about them in turn.

14	*Chitty*:	<u>Lin</u>ks between (0.8) ↑ehr::m cancer charities
		and the drug companies?
		(0.6)
	Finnis:	Does'e know anything about that.
	Chitty:	°↑ohhah° I think he may well sus<u>pe</u>ct.
		(.) I think what (.)
→		she's <u>hop</u>ing is that he'll ⌈give you
	Finnis:	⌊yeah
→	*Chitty*:	(a guy that) having <u>doct</u>or in front of his name
		any opinion that- (0.2) <u>extre</u>me opinion
		that's not <u>supp</u>ortable (.) that he <u>ma</u>kes
		(0.2) we can use (.) in lieu of the fact that

> we've lost the two people who were
> going to say those things from the programme

(Tape 5: 3)

The issue of links between drug companies and cancer charities is a sensitive one. In response to Finnis's question about whether this interviewee knows anything about the topic, Chitty is only cautiously positive, but explains its importance in terms of the problem of having someone who is entitled to speak on the topic because of his title (having doctor in front of his name). This is a simple example, then, illustrating their explicit orientation to the potential importance of category entitlement.

Later in the discussion they return to this issue, and it becomes clear that they do not think that merely having the interviewee categorized as a doctor ('any old GP') will be sufficient.

15   *Finnis*:   To set up an interview we need
                 to establish (.) him as being more credible than
                 (.) a doctor speaks. (0.6)
     Chitty: Yes I now- now Caroline why? is he more
                 credible than just any old- any old GP
                 [*20 lines omitted*]
     Finnis: S'we we ↑want (.) some general
                 statement from him ⌐about
     Chitty: ⌊Umm (0.6)
     Finnis: how many ((*laughing*)) cancer patients
                 he's seen over the last ten years?=
     Chitty: =Yeah well we can- we can do that
                 in commentary can't we?

(Tape 5: 11–12)

There is no immediate answer to Chitty's question as to why their interviewee has any more credibility than anyone who is a doctor. In their search for further category entitlement they propose to emphasize his *experience* of treating cancer. Finnis's laughter may well indicate some doubt about whether this is sufficient to establish his entitlement to speak authoritatively on the topic. Yet the joking element is not picked up – Chitty goes on to propose how the interviewee's experience can be built into the voice-over when he is introduced. As it turns out, in the finished film this interviewee is introduced in the voice-over as *both* a doctor and as founder of an organization: 'Dr Aubrey Hill is a homoeopathic physician and founder of New Approaches to Cancer' (Film: 26). Perhaps it was decided that these items were sufficient to provide an entitlement to appropriate expertise and insight – while even a large number of treated patients does not differentiate him from many other medical workers.

The first two examples deal with the fairly straightforward issue of how the interviewee can be categorized in a way that gives them credibility on the topic. The next example is more subtle. Again, my point is that these subtle, less explicit, cases are probably more usual, but we can start to understand them by considering the issues highlighted by the more explicit cases. The issue described here is not how the interviewee can be categorized, but how he should *act* if he is to be treated as a member of the appropriate category. Chitty tells the others about an incident in filming another interview. The interviewee had started to use the word *punter*, which had been in the questions, when describing the sorts of people who contribute to cancer charities. The director, Vivienne, had asked him to avoid the word.

16	*Chitty*:	So then they're askin (.) you know saying
		<u>Jim</u> what do you think the average punter thinks
		and he comes out with
→		↑o::h punters think this, and punters think that,
→		you know, poor old punters sort of line. (.)
		Vivienne told him he- could he mind <u>not</u> using the
		word punter.
	Finnis:	Why?
	Lasko:	Why::?
	Chitty:	((*laughingly*)) Because its a ↑<u>televi</u>sion term.

(Tape 5: 38–9)

The point here is that the interviewee's credibility is seen as reflected, at least in part, through his using the sorts of words appropriate to a cancer specialist. If he starts to use 'television terms' this may raise problems for his category membership; and this category membership is crucial for his entitlement to speak with expertise on this topic. The story here, then, is of an interviewee being coached by the television director to produce his talk in a way that is consistent with the categorization needed for the programme. This is a different kind of working up than the previous ones, but the effect is the same: to build factuality of a version through managing the categorization of the informant and, at the same time, to manage the accountability of the programme makers as having interviewed the right people.

It might be objected that television workers, even working in documentary arenas, are pressed by their deadlines, and by the requirements of making exciting and controversial television, to distort the category memberships of their interviewees. However, it is not clear that the sorts of examples in Extracts 13–16 are distortions. They *could* be treated in this way; but, equally, they could be treated as examples where the programme makers are doing their best to present informants clearly and indicate why their views should be taken seriously.

Moreover, it is not hard to find examples from arenas much closer to home of similar work on category entitlements. For example, Paul Atkinson (1990) provides a detailed discussion of the way that ethnographers construct versions both of themselves and their informants (see also Bal, 1993). He notes the presence of certain standard features in the way the character of the ethnographer is built up, and the way these contribute to the credibility of accounts. For example, narrative descriptions of the process of ethnography often present the researcher as initially callow and naïve, suffering many confusions and misunderstandings. They only gradually come to understand, often through reflecting on their initial difficulties. As Atkinson puts it:

> The retrospective account of failures resolved and troubles survived thus vouches for the authenticity of the author's experience. He or she claims uniquely to have gone through that baptism of fire in order to achieve the close acquaintance that is the foundation of ethnographic knowledge. (1990: 110)

Atkinson's argument is not that the accounts of ethnographers should be treated as merely got up, or that we should necessarily be more sceptical of them because of this; rather, it is that there are certain sorts of standard description used to build up the entitlement of the category 'ethnographer'. Ethnography writers, like TV programme makers, and like everyday story-tellers, and scientists too, are attentive to the epistemological entitlements of the categories they use. Category entitlement is a pervasive concern.

Stake, Category Entitlement and the Paranormal

So far in this chapter I have focused mainly on examples where the stake or category entitlements are being explicitly formulated. This makes the point clearly and is an easy way into analysis. However, given the importance and availability of stake and category entitlement, it should be expected that people can formulate and resist inferences about such things in inexplicit ways. It may even be that inexplicit uses are more prevalent because they are likely to be harder to identify and undermine and easier to deny. A study by Robin Wooffitt (1992) of the way people produce accounts of paranormal experiences provides an example of this.

Wooffitt put adverts in the local paper to track down people who claimed to have had paranormal experiences and he conducted open-ended interviews with them about their experiences of ghosts, poltergeists, psychokinesis, and so on. He suggested that when telling stories of this kind people have two closely related tasks to attend to. On the one hand, they have to demonstrate the *factual* nature of their paranormal experience. That is, they need to accomplish it as something out-there, as existing in the world rather than a mere product of fantasy or imagination. On the other hand, they have to show that they are sane, rational, *normal* people. For when reporting experiences like this there is a danger of being written off as a crank or mad person. This can be seen as a problem of managing the two available categories, *normal* and *crank*. The speaker must construct his or her account so it will be heard as coming from someone in the category normal and not the category crank. Actually, the category problem is not independent of the fact problem, for it is, in part, by appearing in the category normal that people are entitled to be a credible witness of the extraordinary event; once having been categorized as a crank (or similar) the category entitlement will be all but lost.

To help understand how this is accomplished, Wooffitt drew on some of Sacks' work on the way people report extraordinary experiences – such as hijackings, shootings and plane crashes (1984; 1992, vol. 2: 215–21). Sacks noted that there is a regular pattern used when making such reports. Typically they take the form 'at first I thought, but then I realized' or alternatively 'I was just [doing a very mundane thing], when [a very exceptional thing happened]'. Thus you get examples like 'at first I thought it was a car backfiring, but then I realized that the president had been shot'; alternatively: 'I was just chatting to Emily on the telephone when this great fireball erupted in the field outside.' Sacks suggests that descriptions of extraordinary events are organized in this way to present the speaker's first assumption as being an innocuous or ordinary one; that is, this speaker is presented as having the kind of first thoughts that any normal person would have. In effect, Sacks is suggesting that these descriptions work to present the speaker as falling into the category ordinary/rational and discount potential alternatives such as crank or mad person.

Wooffitt suggested that this issue is a particularly acute one for people reporting parapsychological experiences, especially as there may be no independent corroboration to their reports (as there is with assassinations and plane crashes) and, because of this, their accounts tend to be produced in what he calls the X/Y format, where X is a very mundane thing and Y is the extraordinary thing. Take the following example:

```
17        an I went in there (.) er:m: w-with my mother in law
          and uhm: (.4) friends that were with me
          (1.3) .hhh (.)
X→        and I was just looking at the coffin
Y→        and there was David standing there (.3)
          he was in Blues (1.0) .hh he wasn't wearing his hat
          his hat was on the coffin and he was there
(1992: 123-4)
```

The mundane context here is 'just looking at the coffin', and it is only after establishing this that the speaker goes on to describe the paranormal event (the vision of the speaker's recently dead husband). Now we might think that Wooffitt has overdone the interpretation here. Surely, it could be argued, this pattern of description is just what you would expect from someone simply reporting the events as remembered; doing what cognitive psychologists might call 'doing a dump' of the contents of the relevant long-term memory store. That is, people are 'playing back' their memories into talk much as a set of computer files in memory are 'dumped' onto a floppy disk. Cognitive psychologists might also point to the phenomenon of so called 'flashbulb memories'. This is the idea that people have vivid memories of what they were doing, or what the setting was, when they witnessed shocking or wonderful things such as the assassination of President Kennedy or the resignation of Mrs Thatcher. Could it be that the 'I was just looking at the coffin' part of the talk was the flashbulb part of this memory dump; the mental recording at the moment of the shocking event?

Wooffitt considered this argument in some detail and suggested that we turn it on its head. Far from this material being explained in terms of flashbulb memories, his interactional and fact constructional explanation of what is going on here might itself be a better and, what is more, a non-cognitive account of the flashbulb memory phenomenon (see Wooffitt, 1991). Indeed, the flashbulb memory phenomena might turn out to be nothing to do with cognitive psychology and the activation of neuronal networks, or whatever, and instead be a feature of the pragmatics of reporting extraordinary experiences.

One of the main lines of argument in favour of seeing these descriptions as worked up, rather than simply memory dumps, concentrates on the detailed way in which these accounts are put together. Take the following:

18   I was thinkin' well (0.4) ( ) on the lines of it (.3) i(t)- i- must
        be very easy to be Saint Paul because yuh get yer blindin'
        light on the Road to Damascus sort u(v) thing un eh .hh (0.6)
        you've no problems (so you) yo:u: know as far as you're concerned
        you measure all things according to that experience the experience
        was exterior to yourself an' so therefore (1.3) you viewed it (0.7)
        as a star:t (.5) (>yu know<) yeah
  X→ I were just thinkin'
        (.3) er:m:
  Y→ and then suddenly (.) I was aware of (.7) almost (.)
        the sensation was almost as if a veil was lifted
(1992: 129)

The thing to note about this description is that before the report of the paranormal experience there is an extended description of some things that the speaker had been thinking about. These concern his faith and the nature of extraordinary experiences, and are hardly ordinary or everyday thoughts. Moreover, they provide a strong indication of the potential interestedness of this speaker in having experiences of this kind or, at least, a degree of credulity about such experiences. Now, if we were just to consider this report as a memory dump none of this should matter. The downloading should take place irrespective of the potential problems that the account generates. However, this is not what happens. After the report of these extraordinary thoughts they are repackaged in the mundane form, 'I were just thinkin''. Thus we can see here the mundane context being built (in rather unpromising circumstances); it is not simply there. Again, the speaker is building for the entitlements endowed by the category 'normal person' and avoiding the epistemological precipice that beckons with the category 'mad person' or 'fantasist'.

Footing, Neutrality and Alignment

In the final section of this chapter I want to cover the closely related topics of footing, or the different participant roles that people may have in conversation, and neutrality. They can be understood as part of a more general issue of alignment; that is, how far speakers are presenting some factual account as their own or distancing themselves from it. The notion of footing was developed by Erving Goffman, particularly in his paper of that name (1979, 1981). This paper did a number of things, but the most relevant here involved its building up of a distinction between various kinds of role that transcend the rather limited distinction between speaker and listener. In particular, he distinguishes three different roles that are available for the production of speech and a number of different reception roles. Thus, he argues that for a particular piece of speech it may be necessary to distinguish the *principal*, whose position the talk is meant to represent, the *author*, who does the scripting, and the *animator*, who says the words.

Imagine a situation where a shy boy wants to ask a girl out. He may get a friend to think of some phrase that he can use to represent his feelings, and possibly another friend to pass them to the girl. The hopeful boy in love would be the principal, the friend who composed what to say the author, and the other friend who passed it on the animator. Then, if we imagine the scene of telling, the loved girl would be the *addressed recipient*, her friend who is standing next to her might be an *over-hearer*, while another girl, sitting discreetly at a nearby table, might be an *eavesdropper*.

Now these distinctions have implications for accountability. The animator should be treated as 'just passing something on' – the girl is not expected to respond to the amorous advances as his but as those of the principal (of course, the potential tensions that arise in such situations have been deliciously exploited in fictions such as *Cyrano de Bergerac* and *Roxanne*, where the reluctant animator of romantic advances ends up being a competing principal). In terms of factuality, there are obvious differences between making a description or factual claim yourself, and reporting that of someone else. You are not generally accountable for factual claims that are merely reported (although messengers do get shot!). One place where this sort of distinction has been exploited is in news interviewing on television and radio.

Achieving Neutrality in News-interviews

A feature of both British and North American news programmes is that there are legal and quasi-legal requirements that the news be neutral or impartial. Much research in media studies has been devoted to arguments about whether the news is actually biased or not (for example, Glasgow Media Group, 1982). However, conversation analysts have taken a rather different approach, asking how an *appearance* of neutrality is managed in practice, particularly given the emphasis placed in modern news programmes on asking tough questions and putting politicians and others on the spot. The goal of producing good, stimulating television may compete with the stress on impartiality.

Steven Clayman (1992) has researched the way footing shifts are used in the achievement of neutrality. His argument is that when interviewers confront an interviewee with a contentious description of some state of affairs, they tend to produce it as a quote from a particular speaker, or even treat it as what people in general have claimed. That is, they draw on the distinction between animator and principal, and construct their points within the ostensibly neutral role of animator.

Here is one of Clayman's examples from a television broadcast. IR is the interviewer, IE is the interviewee. The topic is the management of nuclear waste.

> 19 *IR*: You heard what Doctor Yalow said earlier in
>   this broadcast she'll have an opportunity to
>   express her own opinions again but she seems
>   to feel that it is an EMinently soluble problem,
>   and that ultimately that radioactive material
>   can be reduced, to manageable quantities,
>   'n put in thuh bottom of a salt mine.
>   *IE*: Thuh p- thuh point that she was making earlier
>   about (.) reprocessing of: thuh fuel rods goes
>   right to thuh heart (.) of thuh way a lotta
>   people look at this particular issue . . .
> (Nightline 6/6/85: 19–20 in Clayman, 1992: 168)

The interviewer's turn here is constructed by producing an assertion about the manageability of nuclear waste which is attributed to a third party – 'Dr Yalow'. The claim about waste management, then, is not the interviewer's own but 'belongs' to the third party. Moreover, the interviewee treats it in this way too, by arguing with it as Dr Yalow's point rather than treating the interviewer as himself accountable for it.

As with the Wooffitt analysis discussed above, confirmation of this claim about the role of footing in news interviews can be found by considering in detail the manner and placement of footing shifts. For example, footing shifts tend to appear when more contentious factual claims are made, or even when contentious words are used. In the following example, the relatively uncontroversial fact that President Reagan won a big election victory is merely asserted as common knowledge; however, the controversial description that his programmes are in trouble is introduced with a footing shift:

> 20 *IE*: Senator, (0.5) uh: President Reagan's elected
>   thirteen months ago an enormous landslide.
>   (0.8)
>   It is s::aid that his programs are in trouble . . .
> (Clayman, 1992: 169)

Clayman emphasizes something important here. Whether a description is controversial or not is itself a potentially controversial issue over which there may be no consensus. He draws on the ethnomethodological notion of reflexivity to stress that the familiarity of this practice of footing shifting means that it serves, in part, to *constitute* the item as sensitive or controversial. Put another way, a display of neutrality through shifting footing is, at the same time, and ironically, an indication that the news interviewer is treating something as controversial or sensitive.

Another line of evidence that footing shifts are actively managed comes from the detail of participants' practices of self-repair. For example, in the following extract the interviewer seems to be about to make a controversial assertion, but breaks off and changes footing.

21   *IE*:   But isn't this- uh::: critics uh on thuh
                conservative- side of thuh political argument
                have argued thet this is:. abiding by thuh
                treaty is:. unilateral (.) observance. (.)
                uh:: or compliance. (.) by thuh United States.
(Clayman, 1992: 171)

Again, the point is that the change of footing displays neutrality, and avoids the possibility that the news interviewer will be treated as accountable for the contentious description of US policy. Note, of course, that there are many other ways in which quotation can be used in news reports (Zelizer, 1989).

Footing and Stake

Exceptionally there can be breakdowns in the standard pattern of footing shifts and neutral accountability. And when they happen they can be very revealing. After the recent death of a well-known British radio interviewer, Brian Redhead, a number of obituaries in newspapers and on the radio quoted a well remembered moment when the normal interview etiquette broke down. The sequence starts with the end of a turn from Chancellor Lawson, who is boasting about the government's effectiveness in reducing unemployment.

22   *Lawson*:   . . . Unemployment will go on falling throughout the
                       course of this year.
         Redhead: But much of that fall is in the creation of special
  1→   measures. You may have heard ↑mister Hattersley
                       talking about .hh young people being invited to job clubs,
                       to play games under the supervision of nursery school
                       teachers. .hh Creation of- two thirds of the new jobs are
                       low paid part time jobs. These aren't the real jobs that you
                       used to talk about way back in nineteen seventy nine and
                       eighty.
  2→   *Lawson*:   .hhh Well you've been a supporter of the Labour Party all your
                       life Brian .hh so I I expect you to say something like that
                       but you ↑really shouldn't sneer at these job clubs which are
                       giving (.) real hope to the long term .hh unemployed. Getting
                       them into the- .hh getting them out their depressed state of
                       mind many of them are in, and they are going on .hh to get
                       real jobs. (.)
  3→   *Redhead*:   Do you think we should have a one minutes silence
                       ((*laughing*)) now in this interview. One for you to apologize
                       for daring to suggest that you know how I vote, and secondly
                       perhaps in memory of monetarism which you've discarded.

Lawson: Ehhehh I see no cause for (.) er: a one minutes silence,
              monetarism (.) as you call it is not discarded, what is- what 'as
              happened is that, er:: the- we have <u>li</u>berated the financial
              markets to a great extent. . . .
(*Today Programme*: 12 April 1994)

The first thing to note about this extract is that it provides another example of the way interviewers shift footing when dealing with controversial
topics. At arrow one Redhead attributes the much more negative version of
unemployment to a Labour shadow minister. We might also note, however,
that the footing shift is not as inclusive as many of Clayman's examples. The
opening and closing parts of this turn can easily be heard as the views of the
interviewer. Redhead seems to have become too animated to be an effective
animator! Even so, other work on news interview shows that interviewees generally tend to avoid treating interviewers as accountable for claims and
descriptions (Heritage and Greatbatch, 1991).

What Chancellor Lawson does in response at arrow two, then, is most
unusual. Not only does he treat the version of unemployment as Redhead's
own version, he also identifies it as a version in which Redhead has a stake
because of a long-standing political affiliation. We can now recognize this as
a familiar form of discounting using interest invocation. At arrow three
Redhead responds strongly and critically to this highly unusual breach of
interview etiquette. The sorts of problems illustrated in this interaction show
precisely why interviewers may engage in careful footing shifts, and why interviewees may prefer to treat interviewers as if they were neutral or
disinterested, even if they believe otherwise.

Neutrality, Footing and Descriptions

Stephen Levinson (1988) has attempted to provide a comprehensive systematization of Goffman's distinctions between the different possible participant
roles. On the basis of an analysis of the different elements that go to make up
producer and receiver roles, he identifies ten separate production roles and
seven reception roles. Some of these have familiar English equivalents, such as
spokesman, while others, such as 'targeted overhearer', are more esoteric. One
of the issues that this enterprise throws up is the status of these different
kinds of footing. Should they be seen as categories that allow improved linguistic analysis and conversation analysis, or should they be seen as
distinctions that participants make in the course of different kinds of activities? When we are concerned with an analysis of fact construction there are
good reasons for treating them as primarily participants' distinctions.

In the first place, we should be wary of taking on board a set of distinctions
that are made in a variety of settings and treating them as an adequate and
coherent analytic scheme. Furthermore, the distinction between principal
and animator looks decidedly problematic from the sorts of post-structuralist perspectives on subjectivity explored in Chapter 3. More importantly for
the enterprise of studying fact construction, a study such as Clayman's of

what is being done with displays of footing should not commit the analyst to treating them as either correct or incorrect. The management of the distinction between animator and principal can be a very delicate affair, as Amy Shuman (1992) has shown in her study of teenagers' fight stories, where the teller risks the story turning from a mere report into a challenge for a fresh fight. Alison Young (1990) provides a very different example in her discussion of the use of quotation marks to manage objectivity and subjectivity in newspaper reporting of anti-nuclear peace protests (or 'peace' protests). A search for the genuine principal or the pure animator, then, is likely to be an analytic cul-de-sac (see Leudar and Antaki, 1996; Potter, 1996a). For this book, then, the various kinds of footing will be a topic for analysis and not a system for classifying factual discourse.

Another feature brought out in Levinson's chapter is that some languages provide grammatical marking of certain footing shifts in a way which is highly pertinent for a concern with factuality. He cites, for example, work on the Hidatsa people, who have a language which embodies within its grammar a number of distinctions which explicitly mark out the speaker's orientation to the factuality of the utterance (Mathews, 1965). The Hidatsa can add an ending to a sentence that tells the listener that the speaker sincerely believes what is said to be true, although it might turn out not to be. This is the most used form of speaking. Another type of ending is used to indicate that what is said in the utterance is a quotation, but not of any specific individual; it is just something that people say. This is used particularly for stories. This contrasts with another way of ending sentences which Hidatsa speakers use to report something that was told them as true by another person, but for which they have no independent evidence.

Cross-cultural linguistic evidence of this kind is fascinating and potentially important. However, it is limited if it sticks to *linguistic* phenomena. More recent anthropological work has been starting to show the way that the different footing and grammatical categories are exploited and managed in a range of different ways. The grammatical distinctions provide a resource, but that resource can be used flexibly and creatively (see especially papers in Hill and Irvine, 1992). Work by Levinson and others shows that English speakers themselves have many ways of displaying footing and, in addition, of displaying their alignment with, or scepticism about, reported claims and descriptions (for example, Peräkylä, 1993). Sacks (1992, vol 2: 309) too discusses the way footing and fact considerations become intertwined. Take the difference between these two (invented) utterances: 'Karen can't come down the pub because she's revising' and 'Karen said she can't come down the pub because she's revising'. In the first example, the speaker is aligning herself with Karen's explanation; it is treated as *the* explanation. However, in the second example the speaker is avoiding this alignment; by reporting it as Karen's reason, she is not committed to it being her reason too.

Stake, Entitlement and Footing

This chapter has explored three closely related dimensions which relate the identity of the speaker to the factuality of the claims they produce. Referring back to Figure 5.1 as a rough, broad-brushed summary, we see the formulation and invocation of interests as something that eats away at the factuality of claims. The potential for such invocation can be undermined by stake inoculation or, where this is hard to sustain, a stake confession may disarm criticism by turning it into old news and treating the speaker as having already taken his or her own interests into account. I speculated that effective stake management is probably best done implicitly rather than explicitly, because this makes it both harder to undermine and allows the speaker the possibility of denying that this is what they were doing.

In contrast to interest formulation, category entitlements could be built up to establish the facticity of a description. This discussion focused particularly on the categories friend, community leader, doctor and normal person. One theme that was highlighted was the way category entitlements may also orientate to issues of accountability and deniability. Thus the 'friend of a friend' construction provides some entitlement to knowledge, but also a degree of accountability: it allows the speaker credibly *not* to know all sorts of details that might be expected of such a story from another source. Likewise, anonymous, plural community leaders provide strong warrants for the facticity of stories about crowd violence and its context without being sources that are easy directly to contradict or undermine.

The final part of the chapter concentrated on the notion of footing. This is implicated in fact construction in a number of ways. The most researched issue has been that of neutrality, and the way footing practices are used to work up an appearance of neutrality in news interviews. In this case, the concern is not so much how the speaker establishes the description as more or less factual, but how they manage their accountability *vis-à-vis* the description. As expressed in terms of Figure 5.1, distanced footing – careful quotation, making the description a report from others – decreases the speaker's accountability, while footing practices that present the speaker as both animator and origin increase the potential accountability. Footing issues are by no means separate from issues of fact construction, however, as a cursory look through the examples used in this chapter will show. Well over half use some kind of animator/origin distinction as a major part of building up the credibility of a description. Consider again the subtle way in which a distanced footing is produced by 'there have been a lot of ideas put out, *what is it*' (Extract 8). Although in themselves different footing positions are not necessarily bound up with increased or decreased facticity, the paraphernalia of footing is often a major resource in building factual versions. The relation between footing and fact construction is plainly an interesting and fruitful arena for research.

One final point before moving on to look at a rather different range of techniques for working up the facticity of descriptions. There is a tension in this chapter between its analytic focus and the conclusions drawn. On the one hand, the emphasis has been on studying the building of factual discourse in specific, often interactional situations. Such an approach is highly sensitive to what is unique in any setting. On the other hand, the aim has been to propose some principles of fact construction which are relevant across a range of situations. My aim is not to attempt a resolution but to treat the combined attempts at specificity and generality as analytically productive.

6

Constructing Out-there-ness

This chapter continues the focus developed in the last of the devices that are used to construct descriptions as factual. While the previous chapter concentrated on the way in which the nature of the producer of the description could be managed by discounting any potential stake they might have in it and building their category entitlement to be a competent describer, this chapter will concentrate on procedures which, for the most part, draw emphasis away from the nature or identity of the producer. These are procedures designed to provide a quality of what might be called *out-there-ness*. In other words, they construct the description as independent of the agent doing the production. More specifically, these procedures draw attention away from concerns with the producer's *stake* in the description – what they might gain or lose – and their *accountability*, or responsibility, for it.

One of the most basic and familiar forms of *out-there-ness* construction involves the use of what Nigel Gilbert and Michael Mulkay called empiricist discourse. This eschews constructions such as 'I found that . . .' in favour of 'it was found that . . .'. These are descriptions in a grammatical form that delete the description's producer. Another approach to producing *out-there-ness* involves constructing consensus and corroboration by presenting a description as shared across different producers, rather than being unique to one. Descriptions of this kind undercut attempts to discount them as the product of a particular person's stake or concerns. Detail and narrative work rather differently. They are involved in producing a version which is 'real' and vivid; they paint a scene as it might have been observed. One way to think of this is that they work to put the recipient of the description in the place of its producer. Indeed, one way of thinking about such descriptions is as providing an impression of remote sensing; they pull the recipient into the scene in the manner of a telescope viewer.

Steve Woolgar calls approaches to fact construction such as these *externalizing devices*. As he puts it, the 'externalizing device provides for the reading that the phenomenon described has an existence by virtue of actions beyond the realm of human agency' (1988b: 75). In effect, the description is of a thing (or action or whatever), and that thing exists, as described, without the describer's having any influence on it. Expectations about agency are moved from the producer of the factual account to the entity that is being constituted (see Figure 6.1). Let me emphasize strongly at this point that I am not assuming that people simply have agency and that they work to conceal it by various techniques. My concern with agency is as a participants' notion which may be understood and reworked in a very wide range of different ways appropriate to particular settings (see Ashmore et al., 1994; Callon and Law, 1995).

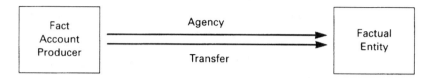

Figure 6.1 *Externalizing devices*

To illustrate this, let me turn Woolgar's idea of externalizing devices around and apply it to itself. In this text I am formulating [externalizing devices] as pre-existing objects. (The descriptive word *device* helps here, of course, as it is commonly used for physical gadgets that can be picked up, or put together.) As I describe this chapter as a *survey* of [externalizing devices], their treatment is made equivalent to doing a survey of the numbers and types of cars in a parking lot, say, or of the range of different uses of some farm land. It is dealing with pre-existing things that the surveyor just comes across. In these ways [externalizing devices] are being produced in this text as not something made up, or constituted, or argued for; not something which might be controversial, confused, a daft idea or simply non-existent; they are just there. They are, as it were, constructed as not being constructed. So, on with the device survey. . . .

Empiricist Discourse

The notion that there is a specific set of tropes, grammatical forms and argumentative styles that hang together comes originally from a sustained study of the discourse of a group of biochemists who were researching the way body cells store energy by Nigel Gilbert and Michael Mulkay (1984). They called this type of fact construction 'empiricist discourse' because many of its features are characteristic of traditional empiricism. Gilbert and Mulkay conducted, jointly, extended interviews with 34 members of this group. These interviews were conversational in the sense that they ranged across a set of topics in a fluid and informal manner. The main focus of study was transcripts of these interviews along with the scientists' research papers and letters.

Gilbert and Mulkay's work contrasts markedly with most of the studies of scientific knowledge discussed in Chapter 1. Unlike empirical relativists and social interest researchers, their aim was not to provide an account of what science is really like. For example, Gilbert and Mulkay did not try to decide on the best model for how scientists select between different theories. Instead, they were concerned with how scientists constructed *accounts* of theory choice and, in particular, in the variations between such accounts. They noted, for example, that scientists typically offered one version of theory choice when describing their own theory selections, but a rather different one when criticizing as misguided choices the theory choices of competing scientists (Mulkay, 1991: ch. 10; Potter, 1984).

In effect, Gilbert and Mulkay's analysis extended the general emphasis on methodological relativism in sociology of scientific knowledge (SSK) to scientists' accounts of their actions and beliefs. Just as empirical relativists did not attempt to decide, say, which theory of neutrino production was correct (Pinch, 1986), discourse analysts of science did not attempt to judge which description that a scientist gave of theory choice was correct. They were not looking at accounts of choice in research papers, interviews or even scientific jokes, for their truth; the interest instead was in how that account was constructed and how it was used to manage specific interactional tasks.

The Empiricist Repertoire

The broadest level of analysis Gilbert and Mulkay carried out compared the way scientists described their actions, theories and experimental procedures in informal interviews with what they wrote in more formal contexts of research papers. They found systematic and widespread differences between the versions produced in these two settings, and they suggested that these differences are a consequence of scientists using two contrasting vocabularies or 'interpretative repertoires'. In this chapter the focus will be primarily on the empiricist repertoire.

Take the following examples. The first comes from the introduction to a research paper and the second from a methods section. Note that the technical details here are, well, technical – luckily it is not necessary to have a full understanding of them to get Gilbert and Mulkay's point.

1   The chemiosmotic hypothesis (1) proposed, inter alia, that each span of mitochondrial respiratory carriers and enzymes covering a so-called energy-conservation site (2) is so arranged that 2H are translocated across the mitochondrial inner membrane for each pair of reducing equivalents transferred across that span. Evidence in favour of this value of 2.0 for the ratio of protons translocated to reducing-equivalent pairs transferred (i.e. $\rightarrow H^+/2e^-$ ratio) has come mainly from one type of experiment.
(Gilbert and Mulkay, 1984: 44)

2   Heavy beef heart mitochondria were prepared by the method of Wong and stored in liquid nitrogen. Well coupled mitochrondrial particles were prepared by a modification of the procedures of Madden. These particles were used to prepare inhibitor-protein-depleted particles by centrifuging under energised conditions according to the method of Gale.
(Gilbert and Mulkay, 1984: 51)

Gilbert and Mulkay proposed that scientific papers have a coherent and distinctive set of linguistic and rhetorical features. These are clustered around three broad themes. First of all, papers draw on a grammatical form which minimizes the involvements or actions of the authors. The style is impersonal, using constructions such as 'the hypothesis proposed' or 'evidence has come mainly' which make no explicit mention of the authors' actions, interpretations and commitments. Second, data are treated as primary, both in the logical sense of forming the foundations of any theoretical ideas, and in the chronological sense of being identified before theory was developed from them. Indeed, verbs that might be expected to be applied to the actions of humans are often applied to data in this form of discourse: constructions such as 'these data suggest . . .' and 'the findings point to . . .' abound. Third, laboratory work is characterized in a strongly conventional manner as being constrained by rules which have a clear-cut and universal application. Methods sections construct a world of standard routines and analytic procedures ('centrifuging under energised conditions', 'the method of Gale').

These three features (grammatical impersonality, data primacy and universal procedural rules) are by no means restricted to 'hard' sciences. The biochemists studied by Gilbert and Mulkay seem to be doing science which is pretty hard when compared to social psychology, for example, but both disciplines share a widespread utilization of the empiricist repertoire, as a quick perusal of the mainstream journals will confirm.

Why does the formal writing of science use the empiricist repertoire? From the point of view of the smooth operation of science these sorts of constructions may have a positive consequence. Science is an institution where dispute is commonplace, and often a requirement of successful work. The pervasive use of the impersonal constructions of the empiricist repertoire may dampen this conflict down and reduce the possibility of the journals ending up full of personal attacks. Yet empiricist discourse is also bound up with the business of fact construction. The empiricist repertoire provides for descriptions of scientists' actions and beliefs which minimize the involvement of the scientist in constructing and interpreting what is studied. The scientist becomes passive, virtually a bystander, or evaporates altogether; while simultaneously the data take on a life of their own. They become rhetorically live actors, who can do suggesting, pointing, showing and implying. The empiricist repertoire is a standard device for constructing the out-there-ness of scientific phenomena.

Empiricist Discourse Beyond Science

One of the important questions for a project concerned with fact construction in general, rather than with construction only in science, is whether there are similar features to empiricist discourse outside of science. Are Gilbert and Mulkay documenting something specific to science? Or does empiricist discourse have a more widespread currency? To address these questions we need to look for other situations where this transfer of agency from author to phenomenon takes place.

First note, however, that even within science the empiricist repertoire only appears in its fully fledged form in research papers and formal publications. Although Gilbert and Mulkay found a number of elements of the empiricist repertoire in their interviews, the grammatical impersonality – which is perhaps its most striking characteristic – was not widespread. The biochemists did not lace their interview talk with phrases such as 'it is believed that' or 'a study was conducted'. Such impersonal constructions might well have sounded peculiar in a situation where the speaker is physically and vividly present; although that is not to claim that such constructions will not appear when certain sorts of actions are performed or in certain sorts of face-to-face settings. For example, think of the formal speech associated with the British upper classes: 'one finds that the servants don't respect one as they used to'. However, Gilbert and Mulkay's analysis did not explore this level of specificity.

When considering whether the empiricist repertoire can be found in non-scientific situations two considerations are helpful. First, we can ask whether the different elements of the empiricist repertoire necessarily hang together outside of the domain of formal scientific writing. Second, we can ask whether some features of the empiricist repertoire mark out the institutional specificity of science. That is, do elements of the repertoire have a role in constituting what it is to do science (Drew and Heritage, 1992; Schegloff, 1991)?

Take the question of whether the empiricist repertoire is a coherent entity first. When Gilbert and Mulkay considered its role in scientific discourse, they did so in rather general terms, suggesting that it plays a central part in warranting scientific belief through giving primacy to the role of experimental findings and omitting references to personal or unique features of the scientists' beliefs or actions. As they put it, the 'great advantage of this form of account is that it makes the speaker's scientific conclusions appear entirely unproblematic and in need of no further support' (Gilbert and Mulkay, 1982: 400). There is a limitation in this style of argument, however, as Robin Wooffitt (1992) has pointed out. It tends to treat the empiricist repertoire as working both as a seamless whole, and at a level which is separable from individual instances of use. As we will see in a moment, it is possible to ask how specific elements of the repertoire are working in particular settings.

The second consideration is the question of the institutional specificity of science discourse. I will explore it by comparing Gilbert and Mulkay's work on science with a set of records of North American broadcast television and radio news. Transcripts of CNN, National Public Radio and so on are available on CD-ROM. This allows them to be searched for particular strings of words. This is a great help for doing large-scale searches for the prevalence of the sorts of constructions characteristic of the empiricist repertoire. A search through one year's output on CD-ROM came up with no examples of the sorts of present-tense impersonal formulations common in scientific writing: 'it is believed that', 'it is claimed that'. We can perhaps see why this is if we consider the difference between broadcast news and science with respect to the footing categories introduced in Chapter 5.

Scientific authors are in a complex and potentially tricky footing situation.

On the one hand, *they* have written the scientific articles which are presenting *their* research, *their* theories, *their* claims and so on. It is *they* who will be presented with the Nobel Prize, or perhaps accused of fraud; *they* are accountable for the contents of their papers as both principal and author. On the other hand, the empiricist repertoire is constructing the experimental data as an agent; *it* points in particular directions, *it* shows things, *it* leads to conclusions. Here the researcher maintains the role of author; but at the same time the data start to take on the role of principal. There is a potential tension, then, between these two tendencies, and impersonal constructions such as 'it is claimed that' may be a way of managing this tension. This is a construction which both implicates a responsible agent (the person or group who does the claiming) while avoiding a *direct* identification of the current writer or writers with that agent. The contrast will become clearer in the next section when I consider similar constructions in media contexts.

Constructions of Impersonality

News interview talk has a rather different pattern of footing from that in scientific papers. News interviewers are typically constructed as, and treated as, animators who are merely reporting the claims and views of others (Clayman, 1992; Heritage and Greatbatch, 1991). In general, broadcast news presenters do not get Pulitzer prizes and their everyday views and character can be at odds with their news persona – a theme played upon in the British comedy about a satellite news programme *Drop the Dead Donkey*, in which on-screen gravitas is contrasted with off-screen frivolity and slobbishness. Talk of this kind does not have the same requirement for impersonal present-tense constructions such as 'it is thought that'. And even where such constructions are used it is not likely that the news reader will be treated as the agent doing the believing. Past-tense empiricist constructions are much more common (see also Roeh and Nir, 1990).

Here is a specimen, with the empiricist construction highlighted. The context is the report of an attack on a 'tavern' in Cape Town prior to South Africa's first multi-ethnic election.

3   A caller has claimed responsibility on behalf of UPLAR, the military wing of the radical Pan Africanist Congress, but UPLAR's headquarters hasn't confirmed this. The weapons and tactics used are very similar to previous racially directed attacks. In July, five gunmen used grenades and [inaudible] rifles to attack a church service in a white suburb of Cape Town; 11 people were killed. That attack *was believed to be* the work of the UPLAR.

(*National Public Radio*: 12 December 1993 – emphasis added)

This extract is part of a complex news story. However, it is not an unusual one; readers of this book will no doubt be familiar with news reporting of this kind. What I want to pick out particularly are the sorts of pragmatic considerations that occasion the empiricist construction 'was believed to be'.

The first thing to note is a similarity between news reports and scientific articles. Just as in science data are given meaning by theories, so news 'events' are given meaning by interpreting them in frameworks of other events and embedding them in narratives (Tuchman, 1978). In this case, an attack on a tavern in South Africa, even with its details of death and drama, is only partial news. We expect stories to provide motive and background: who planted the bomb and why, and what is the response? With this story, the event has been linked to a previous attack, and this attack is linked to a political organization: the UPLAR. So one of the fact construction issues for this story to attend to is how these links are produced. The connection to the UPLAR is particularly interesting because it is not managed through citing evidence but through reporting a belief.

It is here that the report draws on an empiricist construction, for the belief is not attached to an agent or collective ('Kerry believed in discipline', 'Christians believed in God'). Instead it is free floating: 'that attack *was believed*'. In some ways it is rather odd to have a belief referenced without its 'owner'; we might think that it would be hard to recognize such a disembodied entity! However, this would be to try to understand beliefs within the rhetoric of cognitivism as objects with specific locations and therefore to miss the practical, interactional roles that such constructions serve (cf. Coulter, 1979).

One role for constructions of this kind is to avoid dealing with issues to do with the status of the claims made by news organizations. The official rhetoric of such organizations stresses both neutrality and an emphasis on reporting facts. As Gaye Tuchman (1978) documents in some detail, news organizations profess not to have beliefs and opinions; rather, they report facts, including facts about the beliefs and opinions of others.

This 'official story' about facts is *itself* a construction. For example, one of the common preoccupations of the television current-affairs film makers which we met over lunch in the last chapter was finding a set of informants for the film which would fit the pre-planned argument. The following extract displays this concern.

```
4   Thompson:   So w- we know what he's going to do (.) in questions
                 one to nine, we don't know what he's going to do in
                 ten and eleven.
                 (1.8)
                 And that's the bits that we most (.) ┌need him to be good on.
     Chitty:                                          └Right.
     (Tape 5: 2)
```

The point is that this careful procedure of selection and encouragement provides a finished film which appears to do the film maker's job of merely reporting on views rather than having views. The narrative appears to originate with the interviewees rather than the film makers.

Now, coming back to our current example, if we assume that the same sorts of considerations apply with National Provincial Radio's report of the tavern attack, we can see that reporting the involvement of the UPLAR as something believed by the news reporters or presenters will be problematic. Officially at least, it is not their job to be having beliefs.

Another way for the newscasters to deal with the issue of belief about UPLAR involvement is to attribute it to some individuals or organizations. This is what Clayman's work on footing might lead us to expect. However, there are two potential problems here. First, some of the relevant parties might well be seen, by newscasters and listeners, as having a stake in claiming UPLAR involvement. For example, the South African police are an obvious source of information about violence of this kind, but were widely felt (!) to be discredited as a source. And the official white politicians and officials who could have been quoted might have been seen to be making inferences based on stereotypes or simply as wishing to smear the Pan African Congress in a period leading up to an election. Second, the news sources might be fragile or limited in a whole range of ways: news reports rarely carry claims attributed to 'what another reporter told me in a bar', or 'something I rather indistinctly overheard'.

In the light of these considerations, we can see the potential value of the construction 'was believed to be'. For it reports the belief, which is needed to build the general news narrative, while avoiding the potentially problematic attributions either to the news organization or to interested or limited parties in South Africa. Without wanting to labour it further, the point is that the empiricist construction 'was believed to be' can be understood as more than just an element in a general vocabulary used to warrant facts. Rather, it can be seen as a specific design solution to a range of fact construction and warranting problems. It is not the only solution, of course – it is easy to imagine the news story in Extract 3 constructed in different ways – but it is one neat way of managing the combined concerns of factuality and accountability.

Agency and Evidence

In addition to grammatical impersonality, a cardinal feature of the empiricist repertoire is its attribution of agency to experimental data: 'the results show', 'the data support' and so on. A further search through a recent broadcast news CD-ROM was able to find recurrent constructions of a similar nature such as 'the record shows', 'the facts lead' and 'the evidence shows'. Here are three examples with the 'facts show' construction emphasized:

5 *Facts show that* there's no increase in drug use related to [needle-exchange] pro-
    grammes and there will likely be a decrease in HIV infection because of them.
    Anybody who looks at these facts as objectively as we have, I think, will come to
    the same conclusions.
(CNN: 30 September 1993)

6 [Governor of Florida responding to the death of a British tourist] I think *the
    facts show very clearly* that this year we've had much less crime against tourists
    than we had the year before, than we had the year before that. Every- any act is
    an act too many.
(CNN: 18 September 1993)

7 [Responding to claims that 'Gangsta Rap' is anti-social] And why should we tell,
    you know, young youth that, well, you should go to school, and [success] is

what's going to happen, when *facts show that* that's not what's going to happen. (CNN: 27 January 1994)

I have reproduced three examples here because they illustrate some shared characteristics in the use of this construction. It is notable that they do not come from the newscaster's own discourse; that is, they are not from news reports or from the newscaster's own contribution to discussion. In addition, they are from settings where there is a controversial issue, and where the speaker is potentially in a weak or minority opinion. The doctor talking about the virtue of needle-exchange schemes in Extract 5 is presented in the context of official condemnation of the policy. In Extract 6 the Governor of Florida is responding to questions about the well-publicized death of a British tourist in the state. In Extract 7 the speaker is defending the values of his brand of music, 'gangster rap', in the face of critical points from callers to a phone-in programme.

I have already noted that in situations of conflict in both scientific and everyday settings people will provide increasingly technical support for positions and be increasingly concerned with giving a basis to their claims (Latour, 1987; Pomerantz, 1984b). This form of empiricist discourse can be understood as an extension of this process. The support is built up by constructing the facts, the record, the evidence, as having its own agency. Such constructions obscure the work of interpretation and construction done by the description's producer: 'the facts' are, first, not being constructed as facts and, second, their significance is not being generated by their producer, it is provided by the facts themselves. They do their own showing.

The general point here, then, is that the empiricist repertoire embodies features of fact construction that are found beyond scientific settings. The sociologist Seven Yearley (1985) has made a similar argument about other features of the empiricist repertoire and the social psychologist Nigel Edley (1993) has provided a fascinating analysis of its use in news reporting concerning British royalty. Particular elements of the repertoire that have more general currency are constructions of impersonality ('it was believed') and fact agency ('facts show'). Rather than see these constructions as embedded in a repertoire that is used as a whole and with general consequences, as Gilbert and Mulkay (1984) argue is the case with science, I suggest that they are better thought of as having discrete uses with respect to practices of fact construction involving warranting and accountability. It will be interesting to investigate such uses further as well as to go on to explore the epistemic use of these forms in everyday discourse. In the meantime, the empiricist repertoire can be considered as a set of resources that may be drawn on when externalizing facts by *divesting* agency from fact constructors and *investing* it in facts.

Consensus and Corroboration

Quite a lot of space was devoted to technical issues related to the empiricist repertoire. However, the transfer of explicitly formulated agency from the speaker to the facts by broadly grammatical means is only one of a number of externalizing devices. Constructions of consensus and corroboration are two further, and closely related, externalizing devices.

One way of transforming a description into a fact is to produce the assent of reliable witnesses. Note that this is quite different from the superficially similar argument that some belief is true or justified because it is endorsed by many people, or the claim that some activity is acceptable because many people do it (cf. Hilton et al., 1988). The crucial feature of this kind of everyday reasoning about facts is that consensus in reports provides *corroboration* of the factuality of a version – if one witness to a car accident claims the driver was going too fast they may be discounted; however, if most or all witnesses claim this they are likely to be more convincing.

There are potential problems with consensus warranting of this kind, however, which may require the use of a second form of everyday warranting. Although witnesses to an event may agree because they all saw the same thing, the agreement may be produced in other ways. For example, they may have cooked up a story together or, more innocently, interacting with one another may have resulted in a common but flawed understanding of the event. This places a premium on finding witnesses who have not communicated with one another, or who are independent because their versions cannot be cross-contaminated. Thus this second form of fact construction stresses the *independence* of the holders of the consensual view.

The question, then, is how can consensus and corroboration be constructed? How can they be deployed as resources for fact building? I will focus particularly on two studies that we have encountered already from Dorothy Smith and Robin Wooffitt. They address this question in some detail.

Smith and Henny-penny

We have already considered features of Smith's study of an account which establishes the facticity of a girl's mental illness which relate to issues of interest management. Smith also discussed the construction of the account's objectivity via the use of independent witnesses. Indeed, the narrative structure of Angela's account of K's decline cumulatively adds a series of witnesses to her mental health problem in a way that Smith equates with children's stories such as Henny-penny, where an increasingly large band of people go to tell the king that the sky is falling. Some extracts will give a feel of this. Note the way the descriptions of K's (supposedly) problem behaviour are produced as coming from each of the witnesses.

First there is Angela, the teller of the tale:

8   We would go to the beach or pool on a hot day, and I would sort of dip in and
    lie in the sun, while K insisted that she had to swim 30 lengths.
(Smith 1990: 18)

And then there is Angela and Trudi:

9   . . . a mutual friend, Trudi who was majoring in English, had looked over one of
    her essays, and told me afterward: She writes like a 12 year old – I think there is
    something wrong with her.
(Smith 1990: 18)

And then there is Angela, Trudi and Angela's mother:

10 At that time Angela's mother thought, well she misunderstood me. But later she
    noticed that K was unable to put on a teapot cover correctly, she would not
    reverse the position to make it fit, but would simply keep slamming it down on
    the pot.
(Smith 1990: 19)

The cumulative adding in goes on through the narrative with the addition of
Betty and a woman friend of the family.

As Smith notes, the effect here is of each of these witnesses coming *independently* to inspect K's behaviour, and each *independently* coming to the
conclusion that K is not well. The consensual judgement that K is mentally ill
is given independent corroboration. Of course, it might be objected to Smith's
analysis that she is merely picking out features of a perfectly straightforward
descriptive text. What is wrong with the claim that this account is a simple
description which colourlessly reports various people's independent discovery
of K's mental illness?

The first response to this is that, hopefully, at this stage in this book it
should be clear that description is anything but simple and straightforward.
However, Smith goes further than making the sorts of general claim that
descriptions are selective, and involve categorization, that we saw in earlier
chapters. She suggests that the independence of the various witnesses is carefully managed by the organization of the narrative, which cuts across a
number of other, rather downplayed elements. For example, there are parts of
the account which suggest that Angela and Trudi and others are in fact good
friends, and may have been in regular contact with one another. Such features
could be used to build alternative narratives in which K is not actually mentally ill, but instead her mental illness is a shared fiction which develops
among the group of friends in the course of conflicts and jealousies. Indeed,
Smith puts some effort into building up the plausibility of this alternative version of events. The point here is that the consensus and corroboration are
being worked up to have their effect.

Wooffitt and Active Voicing

It is worth repeating that Robin Wooffitt's study of accounts of the paranormal trades on the scepticism with which they are commonly greeted.
Because of this scepticism such accounts are likely to be designed to resist
undermining, and this is why they can be such a revealing topic for study
when the concern is with fact construction. One of Wooffitt's observations is
that when people produce accounts of extraordinary events they often
include sections of quoted speech. These are commonly marked out as such

by shifts in intonation although they are not always explicitly named as such ('he said . . .'). For reasons that will become clear, he calls this *active voicing*.

Wooffitt identifies a number of specific uses of active voicing in establishing the factuality of some claim. The first is through providing corroboration. Take the following extract which follows a story about a strange experience the speaker's husband had with a particular hut while living abroad.

> 11   And, well, what is even more fascinating about the story is,
>   that he's telling the experience to other people and they said
> →   'Oh, that wasn't too strange an experience'
>   because they had heard it before from this particular hut.
> (Wooffitt, 1992: 158)

This general way of establishing objectivity works by showing that different people have had the same experience or seen the same thing. Here this is constructed by providing a quotation which supposedly comes from a group of witnesses. The active voicing here confirms that there was something present in the situation which could also be experienced by other people. Moreover, it is not just the speaker's judgements that other people had experienced something from the hut – we have their own words to prove it. This is the beauty of active voicing – it brings into being separate corroborating actors who, like ventriloquist's dummies, seem to have life, opinions and personality of their own.

This extract also illustrates why Wooffitt wants to call this active voicing. Here the quote is not claimed to come from an individual; it is what *they* said. Unless we are to imagine a chorus of synchronized speaking, this makes its status as an actual quote unlikely. Rather, it may be taken to be emblematic, as the *kind* of thing that people said, or what they *would* have said, or a shortened version that is true to the *gist* or *spirit*. This shows that it is actively worked up as the voice of speakers. Although this is clear in the case of Extract 11, Wooffitt proposes that analysts should make the assumption that *all* such quotes are actively voiced or, looked at the other way round, that the analyst should not assume that words presented as quotes actually are quotes. As he puts it, it is 'useful to begin with the assumption that the speakers are designing certain utterances to be heard *as if* they were said at the time (1992: 161). If we think back to the discussion of footing in the previous chapter, Wooffitt can be seen to be exploring the rhetorical deployment of the animator/origin distinction.

There is another point worth noting about the construction in this extract. The voicing is plural: '*they* said'. This makes it easy to hear it as reporting a *general* experience of a *range* of people. (Remember, this is delivered in the fast and fluid flow of a conversation; everyday interaction does not work in the slow-motion manner of transcript that can be inspected and re-read at leisure.) However, without any details we do not know that it was not something said by only a small number of people – perhaps just two – and we don't know if they were independent; were they asked about the hut on separate occasions, or could some people be merely, and politely, backing up a single speaker? (*We* don't, of course, know if there were *any* speakers!) The point is that the non-specific plural avoids these troubling difficulties with the account. It allows the inferences that there are both wide consensus and independence; but the speaker has not actually or explicitly claimed that many people heard the sound, nor that they are independent. She is not accountable, then, for others' creative inferences.

The general point is that, although the account is making these inferences available, they are not explicitly stated, and are therefore deniable. This is a common feature of factual account construction. For example, if we look back to Extract 3 – the news report on a South African attack – we can see that the anonymous formulation 'it was believed that' allows the inference that the belief is widespread, which contributes to its fact constructional role, without being explicitly committed to the existence of more than one believer.

Wooffitt's work on active voicing shows the broader significance of footing and the way various features of footing may be constructed to service the task of fact building. It also shows that the 'seeing the same thing', which is basic to this kind of lay reasoning about consensus and corroboration, is not something simple; rather, it can be managed and worked up. In fact, one example which vividly illustrates this point is the sociological work on replication in science discussed in Chapter 1. Replication can be thought of as an institutionalized forum for independent witnessing. As Harry Collins and others have demonstrated, what counts as a proper or competent replication often becomes as contentious as the finding that is to be replicated. If Wooffitt had been a parapsychological sceptic rather than a conversation researcher he would have questioned participants about the number and status of the witnesses to the noise. The ventriloquized witnesses would themselves have become a focus for dispute and come to need their own procedures of fact management.

Detail and Narrative

Back in Chapter 3 I discussed post-structuralist work on realist discourse, particularly Barthes's study of the operations of Balzac's 'realist' short story in *S/Z*. One of the main roles of this work was to show up the limitations of simple ideas about realist discourse and, in particular, the idea that realist discourse derives its sense from a simple sequence of descriptions of objects and events. What Barthes was less interested in was the role of descriptive prose in establishing the factuality of a text. Issues of factuality do not immediately come to mind when dealing with literature, which is a paradigm fictional form – although it turns out to be quite difficult to make clear-cut distinctions between truth in literature and other realms (Whiteside and Issacharoff, 1987; Searle, 1975). Nevertheless, a number of literary theorists have been interested in the way particular literary effects are generated and, more specifically, in the way a vivid realistic world is created. One of the central concerns here is the role of detailed descriptions and their placement in narratives. For our purposes, what is interesting is how such effects can be generalized to other texts and to talk.

Detail and Focalization

The first thing to consider here is what is meant when talking about detail. Clearly, this is a contrastive category. What is detailed from one perspective might be gross and vague from another. The sort of detail given about the structure of a steel girder by a nuclear physicist is of quite a different order from the sorts of detail given by an engineer. Moreover, the term *detail* is often used with pejorative overtones for relatively unimportant things; there is the big picture and the details. However, I will use the notion of detail in its dictionary sense of 'treating something in its individual particulars' (*OED*). Specifically, I want to contrast descriptions which gloss general processes and categories with descriptions that capture the particulars of scenes or events as they might be seen by an observer.

Take, for example, the extracts from scientific papers reproduced earlier (1 and 2). They drew on general sorts of descriptions of the actions of scientists. Yet even in the procedure sections of scientific papers, which are often claimed to provide a description of the actions of experimenters, the descriptions are of *generic* practices ('mitochrondrial particles were prepared by a modification of the procedures of Madden'); that is, they are 'anybody's' descriptions. We are not told whether the test tubes were cracked, whether it was raining outside, or whether the stalls in the lab toilet had doors. Their point is to show that something standard or universal was done; any individual or unique features were unimportant, and therefore not described. Contrast this with an extract of counselling talk where Jimmy the 'jealous husband', whom we met briefly at the end of Chapter 4, is talking about an evening in a pub. This is just a small part of a long passage.

12   *Jimmy*:   U:m (.) whe:n these people came in. (.) >It was:< (.)
                John and Caroline. (1.0) And then they <u>had</u>- (.)
                this <u>other</u> fella <u>Da</u>ve. °With them as well.°
                [...]
                U:m. (1.2) He c- he came- (.) they <u>all</u> came in the pub anyway.
                (1.0) Well (.) Connie sat beside (0.6) Caroline. And I sat
                (further back). So you was (.) you was split between us.
                They <u>sat</u> in- on the <u>other</u> side. (1.0) The <u>only words</u> Connie
                spoke to me (1.0) for the rest of the eve:ning (0.8) was (.)
                <u>get</u> another drink. °Get another drink.°
(DE-JF:C2:S1:10)

In contrast to the extracts from the scientific paper, what is striking about this description is that it is full of specific references. These are not formulations of generic features of going to pubs, although a proper understanding of the extract might draw on knowledge of such features. Rather, it is full of definite characters (Caroline, Dave), indexicals ('you was split between us'), and active voicing ('get another drink').

To tease out some of the fact constructional issues in descriptions of this kind I want to draw on a concept from narratology known as *focalization*. This was developed in the work of Gerard Genette (1980) and Mieke Bal

(1985). The simplest way to think about focalization is in terms of the *point of view* which a narrative presents. For example, in some narratives there is an omniscient, God-like narrator who can peer round the back of any of the characters and swoop between scenes and into their thoughts. Genette calls this, perhaps confusingly, *zero* focalization. In other narratives the narrator views scenes, but has no access to the thoughts or feelings of individual characters; this is *external* focalization. The discourse in the extract above more closely corresponds to what Genette calls *internal* focalization. That is, the narrative is constructed from the point of view of an individual character – it accesses that character's thoughts and feelings, but not those of other characters except through inference. For example, here is an extract from later in Jimmy's account of the pub evening:

13   *Jimmy*:   Uh: I was (.) boiling at this stage and I was real angry
              with Connie (.) And uh went up to bed 'n (.)
              I lay on the bed. (0.7) °got into bed.° (0.6)
              I- uh (.) could hear giggling ('n all that) downstairs
              and then (.) the music changed (.) slow records.
   (DE-JF:C2:S1:11)

Jimmy describes his own feelings as with a simple report which requires no inference. In contrast, this description allows the actions and feelings of others to be only indirectly inferred. He describes the sounds which are available to him from his bedroom. These reports of sounds are not meaningless behavioural particulars. They allow precise inferences to be made about the activities downstairs. Even without the rich contextual detailing that has gone on in the prior 80 or so lines of the account, I imagine that it is hard to resist the implication that something intimate and potentially sexual is being overheard. Even if we do not know the etymological association of giggle ('a lewd wanton woman; a giddy romping girl' – *OED*), giggling is not a characteristic of interaction between strangers or in formal situations; it signals a certain informality, shared jokes. The change to slow records is, of course, associated with a shift to close, intimate dancing such as might happen when people pair off at the end of a disco; or, from a slightly earlier era Chuck Berry sang 'but when the sun went down the rapid tempo of the music fell, c'est la vie say the old folks it goes to show you never can tell'.

   The point, then, is that internal focalization is a narrative style which presents what goes on from what might loosely be called the perceptual field of an individual participant. In these extracts we can see it attending to both the position of the perceiver ('and I sat . . . so you was split between us', 'I lay on the bed') and what is perceived ('get a drink', the giggling). Such narratives allow the listener, or reader, to take on the position of the perceiver. They can understand things through the eyes or ears of the central character. In her discussion of focalization Bal indicates the link to issues of fact construction: 'If the focalizor coincides with a character, *that character will have a technical advantage over the other characters*. The reader watches with the character's eyes and will, in principle, *be inclined to accept* the vision presented by that character (Bal, 1985: 104 – emphasis added). Away from the purely literary arena, this kind of focalization goes with a special kind of category entitlement. The person is entitled to provide an authoritative description of a scene or event because he or she is a *witness*.

Witness as a Category Entitlement

As with other category entitlements, we can ask how the category entitlement of witness is built up and how it is undermined. What is its defensive and offensive rhetoric? One way in which the category 'witness' is established is to provide graphic, vivid descriptions. These are the sorts of descriptions that might be derived from a careful viewing of a scene, and they may have features that might seem hard to make up because of their specificity, perhaps, or their oddness. For example, direct quotation is the kind of thing that only a witness can properly report. It not only shows that the witness was present, but that they have powers of observation. Take 'get a drink' in Extract 12. It certainly does some business with respect to the moral identities of the parties to counselling, perhaps displaying Connie as insensitive or engrossed in her interaction with the other man. Yet it also displays Jimmy as a witness who is reporting an actual event rather than inventing or speculating, and, moreover, a witness who can report precise details (see also Juhila, 1995).

Another feature of establishing an identity as a witness involves establishing access to the witnessed scene. This both authorizes the presence of the witness and also aligns the reader or listener with the witness for the narrative. Paul Atkinson (1990) has explored this rather neatly in his study of the construction of social science ethnographies. He compared the introductory paragraph of a short story by Hemingway and a well-known ethnography about the life of cocktail waitresses. And he suggests that they bring the reader into the story in much the same way, by providing the sorts of external, as-perceived description that we saw in Jimmy's narrative above, and by building up a contrast between the inside and outside through apparently gratuitous references to the weather ('outside it was getting dark', 'outside a light rain gives softness to the night air of the city'). This kind of description, Atkinson suggests, 'furnishes the "guarantee" of an eyewitness report, couched in terms of the dispassionate observer, using the conventional style of the realist writer of fiction, or documentary reporter' (1990: 70). Jimmy's narrative does not have any references to the weather in it, but it does spend some time establishing why they went to the pub, who was there and where they were sitting.

One of the effective features of witnessing as an identity is that the witnesses' description is a report of the scene as perceived as opposed to being a broad formulation or interpretation of events. It provides the details that were seen or heard and allows the recipient of the description to make the inferences. The role of judging and evaluating is seemingly passed on to the recipient. For example, in Extract 13 Jimmy does not directly accuse Connie of being unfaithful to him – but his description is organized to make that inference hard to resist. In this way the category witness works as an externalizing device.

For most of this chapter I have considered externalizing devices which draw attention *away* from the producer of the description, and therefore their potentially problematic stake and interest in events, either by using impersonal empiricist discourse or by emphasizing corroboration and consensus across observers. In the case of the category witness, however, the externalizing is done by working with an implied distinction between doing observation and evaluation; describing the facts and saying what they mean.

The importance of the everyday distinction between describing and inferring is shown in Dorothy Smith's study of the mental illness account, and the way it is organized to allow recipients to make up their own minds. Maria Wowk's (1984) study of a murder confession makes a similar point. In the example she studied, the assailant did not make a direct accusation that the victim was a prostitute rather than an 'innocent victim'. Such a direct claim might well have been treated as interested, and as an attempt to mitigate the crime. Instead, he constructs a description from which the category 'prostitute' can be inferred.

This lay distinction between witnessing and inferring may be what came into play in a study by Kim Scheppele (1994), who noted particular difficulties for women victims of rape and sexual abuse who revise their stories over a period of time. Such revisions are exploited by the prosecution, who trade on the assumption that initial versions are likely to be accurate, witnessed descriptions while later changes are likely to be distorted or motivated in some way. In contrast to this, Scheppele suggested that the standard expectations can be inverted in such cases because of the sorts of psychological strategies of denial and self-blame that victims of sexual violence engage in which involve an initial avoidance of the reality of abuse. On this topic, and its relation to fact construction more generally, see Michele Davies' (1995) study of fact construction in an autobiography concerning repressed memories of child sexual abuse. This considers both the issue of witness and memory, and the more general notion of legitimating knowledge via experience (cf. Kitzinger, 1994; Manzo 1993).

Undermining Detail and Turning to Vagueness

Although the detailed description of particulars can be used to build up a category entitlement as a witness, it can be countered in a variety of ways. Indeed, any established approach to fact construction may be expected to have its established counters. The use of offensive rhetorics stimulates the development of defensive rhetorics and vice versa. One feature of detail is that it can be inspected for contradictions and confusions or provide material that can be reworked into a different kind of narrative entirely. For example, the fact that Smith can re-read Angela's account of K's mental illness and rebuild the supposedly independent witnesses as a connected group, who may have their own interests in painting K as ill, depends on her reworking of the provided detail. Although the rich detail allows the reader to 'make up her own mind', it also allows her to intervene in the story actively and invert its moral force, leaving K a victim of persecution rather than a psychiatric case.

This procedure of unravelling details has a distinguished past. James Herrick studied the rhetorical approach used by eighteenth-century Deists when criticizing Christian accounts of miracles. He suggested that the principal form of attack was a form of ridicule, which worked through a close reading of Christian texts searching for elements that were problematic, unclear or 'laughable'. These became the focus of an intensive, often exaggerated discussion, which typically removed the details from their original context. For example, Herrick quotes an attack which concentrates on the phrase 'flow of blood' in a description of Jesus healing a bleeding woman.

> Neither one nor the other of the Evangelists signify of what degree her haemorrhage was, nor from what part of her body it proceeded, nor how often or seldom she was addicted to it. It might be, for aught we know, only a little bleeding of the nose, that now and then she was subject to: Or it might be an obnoxiousness to an evacuation of blood by siege of urine: Or it was, not improbably, of the menstrous kind. Any of these might be the case of this woman for what's written; and I don't find any of our divines have determined of what sort it was. But a great miracle is wrought, they think, in her cure, without knowing the disease. (Cited in Herrick, 1989: 322–3)

The approach, then, was to work with potentially minor problems or details, and build them up so that they raised questions with the whole account. From a rather different perspective Malcolm Ashmore (1993) has shown how a combination of narrative detail and ridicule can be used to undermine an established scientific theory.

Let us now return to Jimmy's narrative of the traumatic evening in the pub. We can see the process of undermining at work in Connie's immediate response. (Remember, this is a counselling session, and both Connie and the counsellor are present to hear Jimmy's narrative.) Connie's immediate reply emphasizes the flexibility in the production of versions of events, and how they can be produced to show different things (cf. Simons, 1989).

14 *Connie*: I'd just like to say: when I te:ll that sa:me story (.)
             that same story sounds very very different.
(DE-JF:C2:S1:11)

And she goes on to rework details of Jimmy's account; for example, recharacterizing an event that Jimmy has presented as her pulling her skirt up to display her legs to a boy, Dave.

15 *Connie*: My skirt probably went up to about there.
             ((*Jimmy gives a sharp intake of breath.*))
             Maybe a bit shorter. It was done for no- I never looked at
             that particular bloke when I did it it was my friend commented
             Oh you're showing o:ff a lot o' leg tonight.
(DE-JF:C2:S1:11)

Detail of this kind, then, is a double-edged rhetorical weapon. It can be used to build up a category entitlement as witness, as well as do a range of specific actions, but it can also be reworked, undermined and ridiculed. In effect, the same story can be retold to sound different. For this reason, factual accounts may be constructed using vague or global formulations. Global formulations may be an important element in the armoury of defensive rhetoric.

One example of the rhetorical use of vagueness is provided by Paul Drew and Elizabeth Holt's (1989) study of the use of 'idiomatic expressions'; that is, clichéd or proverbial expressions such as 'it takes two to tango' or 'between a rock and a hard place'. They suggest that such expressions are not sprinkled randomly through conversations. Rather, they tend to crop up at specific junctures. For instance, one common situation in which they appear is where someone is complaining about something to a friend or relative, and that person is withholding support or agreement. This is illustrated in the following extract, in which Ilene is complaining about the actions of a company:

16   *Ilene*:   .hhh We've checked now on all the papers 'e has an' Moss'n
                    Comp'ny said they were sent through the post we have had
                    n:nothing from Moss'n Comp'ny through the post.
                    (0.3)
        Ilene: Anyway. (.) Tha:t's th- uh you know you can't (.) argue ih it's like (.)
                    uh: ⌈m
        Shirley: ⌊Well
                    (.)
        Ilene: banging yer head against a brick wa:ll
(Drew and Holt, 1989: 508)

If Shirley had been supporting Ilene's complaint we would have expected her to express that support at various points in this interaction. However, her only interjection here is 'well', which, as we saw in Chapter 3, is typically an indication that some dispreferred or disaffiliative action is likely to be produced (Levinson, 1983; Nofsinger, 1991; Shiffrin, 1987). It is at this point that Ilene produces the idiomatic expression 'banging yer head against a brick wall'. Drew and Holt suggest that such expressions have two roles. First, they tend to terminate or round off the sequence, and possibly change topic (cf. Drew and Holt, forthcoming). Second, because of their figurative or formulaic quality they are robust. In other words, they are not easy to challenge with specific facts or information. That means they are suited to situations where there is conflict, or at least lack of support. The vagueness here is not a weakness; it is a virtue. Banging yer head against a brick wall can be 'right', or descriptive, in all sorts of situations and in all sorts of ways. It takes work to undermine.

Vague or broad glosses do not have to be idiomatic, of course. For example, I spent some time discussing Connie's version of the evening in the pub at the end of Chapter 4. She formulated it as 'an episode, with a bloke, in a pub, y'know? And me having a few drinks and messin'.' This description does not have the internal focalization of Jimmy's narrative. It has no narrative point of view, it reports no individual perceptions or emotions; instead it provides a broad categorization of the event. The innocence of messin' contrasts with, and works against, what is implied by the giggles and slow music from downstairs in Extract 13. This example, then, shows a clash of two rather different fact constructional practices, each with its own strengths and shortcomings.

Hayden White, Oliver North and Narrative Warranting

The notion of narrative has become increasingly prominent in the social sciences in the past few years. It has been proposed as a central organizing concept for psychology (Bruner, 1990; Gergen, 1994; Polkinghorne, 1988; Sarbin, 1986) and is seen as central in ethnography (Atkinson, 1990; Clifford and Marcus, 1986), and other areas. As we saw in Chapter 3, narrative is treated as epistemologically central in some postmodernist arguments, particularly those of Jean-François Lyotard concerning the breakdown of grand narratives of legitimation. All of this has led to narrative being used in a range of often rather loose senses. Sometimes it becomes difficult to see what is *not* narrative. Nevertheless, there are important strands of work here related to fact construction, and the thinker who has probably done most to address them is the history theorist Hayden White.

White is an ambitious and subtle theorist; yet, the central theme in his work can be easily stated. His argument is that it is a mistake to see history making as the collection of facts about the past. Rather, history making is a combination of fact finding and producing narratives that give those facts sense. It is about producing coherence as well as correspondence. As he put it:

> Every history must meet standards of coherence no less than correspondence if it is to pass as a plausible account of 'the way things really were'. [. . .] A mere list of confirmable singular existential statements does not add up to an account of reality if there is not some coherence, logical or aesthetic, connecting them to one another. (White, 1978: 122)

The argument, then, is that plausible, believable accounts of the past are produced by placing facts within a narrative. White's (1973) major work was an attempt to characterize the major historians of the nineteenth century according to the style of narrative they favoured (romantic, tragic, comic, satirical), their basic modes of argument (contextualist, mechanistic) and the ideological implications that are drawn from their histories (radical, conservative). The narrative forms of history were treated as lying underneath the surface of historical texts as a 'deep structure'.

The analogy with the Chomskyan linguistics that was dominant at the time is very clear. In Chomsky's work utterances were taken to follow grammatical forms as a consequence of an underlying 'deep structure' which is 'hard wired' in to human beings. Both Chomsky and White characterize these deep structures as part of the psychological endowment of members of a culture.

> The historian shares with his audience *general notions* of the forms that significant human situations must take by virtue of his participation in the specific process of

sense making which identify him as a member of one cultural endowment rather than another.[. . .] The original strangeness, mystery, or exoticism of the events is dispelled and they take on a familiar aspect, not in their details, but in their functions as elements of a familiar kind of configuration.[. . .] They are familiarized, not only because the reader now has more *information* about the events, but also because he has been shown how the data conform to an *icon* of a comprehensible finished process, a plot structure with which he is familiar as a part of his cultural endowment. (White, 1978: 86)

White is writing more about understanding than fact construction, but the argument extends easily enough. An account of the past comes to seem factual as it draws on a narrative form that is part of the reader's cultural competence. She reads the history and experiences it as factual, because it conforms to her narrative expectations. It seems 'right', 'well formed', 'coherent'.

This argument has some plausibility to it. Or, as White might say, it provides an initially credible narrative of the workings of historical understanding. There is even some experimental research that broadly supports it (Bennet and Feldman, 1981). However, it also has some potential problems. Apart from the now well-established difficulties with the cognitivist deep structural notions about understanding (what is the status of this deep structure?; how does it work?), White has developed the argument rather more in the abstract than through detailed analyses of particular examples. Specific studies have attempted to apply this general idea about narrative to sets of texts. For example, Moya Ann Ball (1991) explored the narrative construction of 'the Gulf of Tonkin incident', arguing that it was framed as a specific and familiar narrative to justify increased US involvement in the Vietnam War. And John Sorenson (1991) studied media constructions of famine in the Horn of Africa suggesting that a familiar ideological parable was reproduced in reports. Yet, neither the presence of a single, coherent narrative, nor its role in fact construction is well established in these and similar studies.

Another difficulty with White's account is that it seems to depend on a distinction between the historical facts and the narratives they are woven into. I write 'seems' here because at times White offers a more constitutive account which has 'the facts' being constituted by the narrative rather than being pre-existing objects which are subsequently organized into narratives. Here is White at one of his more constitutive moments: 'tropics is the process by which all discourse constitutes the objects which it pretends only to describe realistically and to analyze objectively' (1978: 2). Any one of a range of the theoretical perspectives discussed in the first three chapters of this book could be used to raise searching questions with the facts/narratives distinction.

A further twist to arguments about historical facts and narrative interpretations is given by Michael Lynch and David Bogen in a study of Oliver North and his testimony to the Iran-Contra hearings. They were particularly interested in the policy of generating 'plausible deniability', which was the objective of a range of practices in the US intelligence community. The point of this policy was to be able to conduct covert operations in such a way that the sediment of documents and official recordings left by the operation would allow it to be officially denied and, moreover, that the denial would be plausible because it would mesh with the records. For example, Admiral Poindexter cited the policy of plausible deniability as the rationale for taking full responsibility for diverting money from covert arms sales to Iran to the Contras; by taking responsibility he protected the President. Lynch and Bogen claim that 'in his testimony before the committee, he asserted that he specifically withheld the authorizing documents from the President in order to give Reagan "deniability" in case the diversion should become public' (Lynch and Bogen, 1996: ms. 8; see also Bogen and Lynch, 1989).

Lynch and Bogen use the Iran-Contra hearings to make a point about interpreting historical records. They suggest that the way historical records were practically reconstructed in the hearings provides a broader lesson about history and interpretation.

> Over the course of these hearings it became clear that the historical archive was itself a product of organizational work – of collecting, assembling and deleting files, retrieving documents or shredding them, coding and recoding messages, and the like. This circumstance suggests, in turn, the following as a general, rather diabolical property of the historical imagination: that it not only involves interpretations of evidence, but that the evidence itself is suffused with the workings of an historical sensibility. (1996)

Rather than there being neutral, historical facts which historians organize into narratives, here the picture is of the documents that supposedly record historical facts being generated and selected precisely to sustain particular (fictional) narratives. Indeed, for Lynch and Bogen there is something fundamentally postmodern about North's approach to history. In working closely and practically with historical materials he blurs distinctions between the straightforwardly factual and the artfully fictional, and between the literal and the ironic. He has moved – for quite different purposes – into the kind of historical terrain populated by David Byrne and his 'history' of Virgil Texas in *True Stories*.

Lynch and Bogen draw heavily on ethnomethodological thinking, and their study of the Iran-Contra hearings fits closely in with the tradition of work I discussed in Chapter 2 on organizational practices of fact making. Their caution about the historical archive being designed to fit particular narrative reconstructions parallels Max Atkinson's (1978) argument about the embedding of theories of suicide in the operation of coroners' courts and their construction of suicide statistics.

General Narratives and Specific Descriptions

The discussion above leaves rather tarnished the originally simple picture of factual accounts being warranted by placing them in a set of fundamental or familiar narrative forms. However, it does not show that narrative is irrelevant to issues of fact construction; far from it. One of the difficulties is with the different senses in which the notion of narrative is used. It is useful to contrast narrative in the sense of broad literary forms or genres (comedy, detective story and so on) with the idea that versions of events can be produced using different kinds of narrative conventions (such as zero versus internal focalization) and in ways that relate to issues of motive and character. Producing narratives involves choices also of where to start and where to finish, what to include and what to leave out, what to put next to what, and so on.

This raises a range of general issues concerning the importance of the control and management of versions. For example, one of the most significant features of Smith's study of Angela's narrative construction of K's mental illness is that K is not present to intervene in the account, to provide alternative versions, to add other things that happened which provide a new context to events, or to simply deny that some of the claimed events took place. Studies of interaction in official hearings and courtrooms emphasize the importance of controlling where an answer starts and stops and what counts as a complete answer (Molotch and Boden, 1985). For example, in another study of Oliver North's testimony in the Iran-Contra hearing, Tim Halkowski (1992) showed how the Committee counsel effectively managed the witness's version by treating some of his answers as incomplete and in need of elaboration, and cutting off some attempts at elaboration.

Anita Pomerantz (1988/89) provides another example of the narrative management of versions in a study of a news report of President George Bush's involvement with smuggling aid to the Contras using laundered drug money. (The Contras may have been politically poisonous, but they have inadvertently been a boon to social research on fact construction!) The report details a minor Bush associate's CIA involvement using 'documentary evidence' and then shows a clip of this person denying any connection to the CIA. Pomerantz argues that the audience is primed to be sceptical by the report's factual assertion of the man's CIA involvement – and the immediately subsequent denial becomes further evidence of guilt. The effect of this report is to show up the man as not only part of the covert CIA operation but also a barefaced liar. Part of the effectiveness here is that the news team are in full control of their material, so they can juxtapose the contrasting versions as well as assembling a display of evidence in support of one of them. The point may seem obvious, but this is an important facet of fact construction which is well worth explicating.

To end this discussion of narrative and fact construction, let us return to Connie and Jimmy and their disputed evening in the pub. One of the important points to remember is that, like Balzac's clock on the Elysée-Bourbon, it is not the empirical particulars that are important. In this case, the point of the narrative is what it shows about the nature of the parties, and particularly their moral identities. Is Connie a hopeless flirt who would drive any partner to distraction? Or is Jimmy painfully and pathologically jealous and likely to blow up any incident out of all proportion? Jimmy's elaborate narrative, with its inexorable build of leg displaying, wilful ignoring, insensitive drink scrounging, and finally intimate slow dancing with another man, builds a powerful warrant for the version that has Connie as a hopeless flirt or worse.

In terms of counselling, Jimmy is trying to single her out as the one with the problem (for a fuller account, see Edwards, 1995).

The point I wish to emphasize is that Jimmy's work of identifying Connie in this way is a narrative construction. Yet it is not the sort of basic narrative genre discussed by Hayden White and others (see Gergen, 1994). It is not particularly comic nor is it especially tragic, despite a description of an abortive attempt at suicide towards its end. Rather, it is an organized and cumulative set of descriptions which focalize Jimmy and make his construction of events believable and understandable. Put another way, I am suggesting here that its status as a narrative of a particular genre is not, in itself, crucial for either the fact constructional role of this discourse or its specific action orientation. Instead, I suggest that 'narrative' should be thought of as a rather loose preliminary category that usefully collects together a range of disparate but important discursive phenomena.

Truth Is Stranger than Fiction

The well-known cliché has it that truth is stranger than fiction. However, the sorts of issues raised in this chapter suggest that there is no neat separation between the tropes of fact and fiction. Often, the resources for building vivid and plausible fictions are precisely the same resources that are used for building credible facts. This raises many interesting questions about relations between literary representations and representational practices in realms such as courtrooms and everyday talk. Is one parasitic upon the other, for example? Are the sorts of historical changes in conceptions of the real in literary texts documented by Erich Auerbach (1957) related to changes in other institutional forms, or perhaps to changing conceptions of self? These are hard questions to address, and up to now there has been very little work on the poetic and narratological features of everyday talk that could be used to even start to make sensible comparisons with literary studies (although Harvey Sacks, 1992, makes a range of rich and suggestive observations on this topic). For example, a more systematic study of the kinds of focalization that occur in everyday talk and news interview talk could be particularly revealing. Jimmy's story was internally focalized; in what sort of situations are narratives with zero focalization using an omniscient, God-like point of view used?

Despite some limitations in Hayden White's account of narrative, his emphasis on the dual importance of the correspondence and coherence of historical accounts has a wider currency. It is not difficult, for example, to find cases where 'getting things wrong' leads to an account being treated as *more* rather than less plausible; that is, where coherence, in some broad sense, triumphs over correspondence. In some recent cases of wrongful imprisonment in Britain the 'uncanny' similarity of different police versions of what happened in the cells was used as evidence that they were carefully rehearsed confabulations. The argument was that 'real testimony' has contradictions and confusions; all the officers describing events in the same way was 'too good to be true', much more likely to be the rehearsed outcome of conspiracy than spontaneous personal remembering (cf. Chancellor Lawson's discounting of consensual newspaper reports – pages 116–18 above).

A newspaper article about the poet Philip Larkin's meeting with Prime Minister Thatcher illustrates a more complex use of the same idea:

> He had been introduced to her once before, at a reception in Downing Street in 1980, and liked to tell the story that as she welcomed him she said: 'Oh, Dr Larkin, I am great admirer of your poems.' 'Quote me a line, then,' [. . .] Larkin says that Mrs Thatcher misquoted the line: 'Her mind was full of knives' 'I took that as a great compliment' [. . .]. '*I thought if it weren't spontaneous, she'd have got it right.* I also thought she might think a mind full of knives rather along her own lines, not that I don't kiss the ground she treads.' (*Independent on Sunday*, 3 July, 1994 – emphasis added)

Note the way that Larkin is reported to have used Mrs Thatcher's failure to get the quote precisely right as an indication that she actually knew the poem, but was having to recover it from memory. That is, her mistake was treated as evidence of genuine recall rather than the sort of too pat correctness which would go with a recent briefing (cf. Lynch and Bogen, 1996; Edwards and Potter, 1992).

This raises the theme of lay notions of memory and their relation to fact construction. For detailed descriptions to work as mere rememberings, and thus as externalizing devices, an image of memory as a neutral storage space from which memories can be dumped is most effective. The facts are loaded into memory via eyes and ears and dumped back at a later time untouched by interest, expectation or desire. The conversation analytic account of the way talk is constructed undermines this image. Rather than being passively dumped, it suggests that versions are highly patterned in their detail for the performance of action. Take Jimmy's narrative, for instance. At a superficial hearing it might seem like a simple record of the events of the evening: a dump. Yet, as we start to examine the detail that is placed in this narrative we can see that it is highly selective and carefully organized. What is in the narrative is there for its role in building a moral identity for himself and Connie.

I started the chapter with a discussion of Gilbert and Mulkay's notion of an empiricist repertoire. In their original conception, the empiricist repertoire is an integrated vocabulary of terms, explanatory moves, and metaphors, all used with a consistent grammatical style such that the author's involvement in the research paper is minimized and the data themselves are given maximum power over their own interpretation. The empiricist repertoire, then, is a systematic accounting procedure for externalizing. I considered the question of how general the empiricist repertoire is by examining empiricist tropes in news broadcasts. In this setting they do not cohere together into a full repertoire but are embedded in a range of other kinds of discourse where they perform specific tasks such as making assertions without being explicit about their sources or generality, or emphasizing the credibility of claims. This opens up a potentially fruitful avenue of study which would consider the use of empiricist tropes in a whole range of non-scientific settings.

The next theme in the chapter was consensus and corroboration. The centrality of corroboration in the appraisal of factuality is well established, and embedded in institutional procedures for factual evaluation such as the use of multiple witnesses in court cases and the emphasis on replication in discussions of scientific research methods. The emphasis here was on the way consensus and corroboration can be worked up in particular settings. There are a wide range of ways in which corroboration can be built; some more explicit; some less so. I concentrated on Smith's study of the construction of independent witnessing in her paper on K's putative illness and Wooffitt's analysis of the use of active voicing to ventriloquize a range of corroborating personages. Manufacturing consensus and corroboration is potentially a particularly strong form of externalizing as it shares responsibility for the factual account with other agents.

The final part of the paper focused on detail and narrative. Detail works on a number of levels. At its simplest, the provision of detail can offer a vivid representation of a scene or event; one which will perhaps be seen as unlikely to have been invented. Detail may be organized into an internally focalized narrative to present events from the point of view of a participant and thereby to build a special category entitlement of the speaker as a witness. Moreover, detail could be organized in ways that mirror literary techniques for drawing the listener or reader into the narrative. The rest of this section concentrated on some of the issues raised in relating narratives to fact construction and some of the vulnerabilities which arise when providing rich detail in accounts.

So where are we? At this point in the book we have finished our exploration of what I have called the epistemological orientation of factual accounts; the ways in which they are built as credible and factual. Given that an account has been established as factual by the appropriate management of interests and entitlements, combined with relevant externalizing techniques, how are such accounts designed to perform particular actions? Are there regular procedures for doing common actions? In the next chapter I want to move on to the complicated but fascinating topic of the action orientation of factual accounts.

7

Working up Representations

In Chapter 4 I introduced the distinction between the *epistemological orientation* and the *action orientation* of descriptions. This was meant to capture the difference between elements in a description which work to establish it as factual or neutral and elements that are orientated to some action or range of actions. One of the themes of this book has been to show that the epistemological orientation is not an abstract feature of descriptions decided by their relationship to some reality, but is a practical and rhetorical accomplishment. It is an order of activity in itself. I have now discussed a range of procedures through which the factual status of descriptions can be built up or undermined; that is, how descriptions are reified and ironized. However, it is important that these procedures are not seen as an isolated dimension of interaction; descriptions are not being worked up as factual just for the sake of it. Rather, descriptions are built in this way because of their role in activities. Some of the ways that descriptions can be part of people's practices will be the topic of this chapter.

It should be emphasized at the outset that this is a enormous topic. There are many different ways in which descriptions can be a vehicle for actions, and many of these in turn are likely to be specific to cultures and settings within cultures. For this reason the ambitions of this single chapter are relatively modest. The aim is to explore certain general features of the action orientation of descriptions as a way of showing how this analytic topic might be tackled and to start to identify some common questions and issues. The discussion will be organized around three, partially overlapping themes.

The first theme is that of categorization and ontological gerrymandering. This is concerned with the categorization and formulating of practices that are used to constitute an action, object, event, person or group as having a specific and distinctive character suitable for some action. This in itself is a major theme, with concerns ranging from the selection of individual words through to the use of alternative discourses or interpretative repertoires. In addition to this selection of words or repertoires, there are questions concerning the way particular realms of entities, or terrains of argument, are made relevant and ignored. This is what is highlighted in the notion of ontological gerrymandering.

The second theme is that of extrematization and minimization. The importance of this is that in many situations the business done by descriptions is a contrastive one: to show how large something is, or how good, how serious and so on. The work done by the description is to build up this goodness or seriousness. Such descriptions, I suggest, are a central feature of rhetoric.

The final theme is that of normalization and (for want of a happier word) abnormalization. This theme is to do with the way accounts of individuals and groups are recurrently concerned with presenting their own and others' actions as normal and natural, or as unwarranted, deviant or problematic in some way. If accountability is one of the central features of people's conduct, it is not surprising that there will be highly developed ways in which this accountability can be displayed or undermined via descriptions.

Categorization and Ontological Gerrymandering

When social psychologists have approached categorization they have generally focused on the way individuals are assigned to social groups of various kinds. In contrast, conversation analysts have concentrated on the way categorizations of persons and groups have a range of different inferential and organizational properties. Although both of these approaches are important, linguists, particularly those with a critical focus, have emphasized a more widespread kind of categorization that takes place whenever descriptions are used (Hodge and Kress, 1993; Lakoff, 1987). They have pointed out that the use of any descriptive word involves a categorization; some thing or entity is specified (Grace, 1987). There are different ways in which this specification can be understood. In realist discourse, where language is the mirror of nature, categorization is understood as a rather banal naming process; the right word is assigned to the thing that has the appropriate properties. In contrast, in the discourse of the construction yard that I have been elaborating, categorization is much more consequential. It is through categorization that the specific sense of something is *constituted*.

Images of Reality Constitution

It is easy to be misled into seeing constitution as a rather mystical process if we think about this in the abstract. For those trapped with the metaphor of reality and its mirror for understanding description, the constructionist alternative appears to come from a different metaphorical space altogether; a space from which reality is produced from the workings of isolated words like egg coagulating in boiling water (I imagine an out-take from David Lynch's *Eraserhead*). The way to rescue constructionism from this metaphor system is to emphasize that the reality constituting work of descriptive language is operating in the context of specific practices.

Formulating *as* something brings the thing into being only in so far as it is understood or treated as such in a particular interaction. What exists is the description – no mysterious entity is brought into being – and this description may be understood in various ways, or as having various implications and consequences. Of course, what follows from the last two chapters exploring fact constructional devices is that the participants in an interaction may well have the sense of a thing standing apart from, and producing, the description. However, I do not think it helpful to assume that people are necessarily registering such constructed objects. To become concerned with that can easily lead away from questions of rhetoric and practice into a realm of speculative cognitive psychology. Equally, I do not think that analysts of fact construction need do more than consider reality constitution a feature of descriptive practices; the concern is with interaction, such that philosophical questions of ontology can be left to the appropriate experts.

Take as an example the two descriptions of newspaper reporters that I discussed in Chapter 5 in the context of category entitlements:

1   10 fully trained shorthand-writing *journalists*

2   So the *hacks'* notebooks contain only a sketchy summary.
(Both Edwards and Potter, 1992: 62 – emphasis added)

It is possible to imagine a social cognition experiment where people were asked to sketch a brief vignette of a *journalist* and a *hack*. They might come up with a rather seedy, shabbily dressed tabloid reporter hunting for a steamy sex scandal for *hack*; while *journalist* might evoke a rather more courageous figure, Redford and Hoffman as Bernstein and Woodward investigating Watergate, perhaps. However, the fact construction questions do not require us to sort out this cognitive psychology before addressing them; instead, the fact construction role of the categories *journalist* and *hack* in a particular dispute can be understood, as they are in Edwards and Potter (1992), through a rhetorical analysis. Note that this does not mean that there is just rhetoric and no differences in word meaning. It is just a reminder of the point emphasized by conversation analysts that the flexible, open meanings of words are made concrete and particular in specific contexts.

Categories and Counselling

Virtually any of the pieces of analysis in the last three chapters could be used to illustrate the way the choice of words is bound up with specific activities. However, let me take a new example from the relationship-counselling materials to keep things interesting. I will start with a fragment from the counselling session with Connie and Jimmy which follows Extract 9 in Chapter 4. Connie had been responding to a question about how they came to request counselling with a account of an 'episode' in a pub. The Counsellor picks up from this to ask about its relation to the couple's first period of separation.

3   C: Was that the time that you left?=
     W: =He left the:n that was- [nearl]y two years ago.
     C: [°Yeh.°]
     W: He walked out then. Just (.) literally walked out.
          (0.8)
     C: ↑Oka↓y. So, (0.5) for me list↓enin:g, (.) you've
  →   got (0.5) rich an:d, (.) complicated lives,
          I nee:d to get some his [tory to put-   ]
     W: [Yyeh. mmm,=]

[Mmm. (.) Ye:h. (.) Oh ye:h.　]
　H:　[=Yeh. (.) that's (.) exactly wha]t ih °um°
(DE-JF/C2/S1:4)

I am particularly interested in the counsellor's global formulation that the clients have got 'rich and complicated lives'. I am sure that we do not have any trouble recognizing this as a characteristic piece of 'therapy' or 'counselling' talk. Yet, what is it that allows us to do this recognition? I take it that one of its central features is something very hearable; it is a formulation that converts a rather painful account of trouble and conflict into something positive or at the very least interesting. Note the care that is displayed in the selection of the terms, with the pauses before both the descriptive terms *'rich'* and *'complicated'*, combined with emphasized delivery in each case.

Without attempting a systematic study of formulations in counselling talk (for more on which see Buttny and Jensen, 1995), let me suggest a few of the things that this description could be doing. First, it serves as a contrast to the strongly critical or anxious responses to relationship troubles that the couple may have expected or had from friends and relatives; unlike them, the counsellor is not judging, nor is he made anxious by talk about difficult relationship problems. Quite the reverse, things that are rich and complicated may be interesting and rewarding to study; indeed, it is a formulation that looks forward to the exploration of these complexities.

Second, it is an impartial formulation. It neither criticizes nor praises either party more than the other. This, of course, is a delicate issue in relationship counselling where trust might easily be broken if the counsellor is seen as aligning with one party against the other. In its particular sequential placing, following the wife's criticisms of her husband, this turn neither disagrees nor agrees with the criticisms. They are left on the table, as it were, for possible later discussion. The success of this can be seen from the couple's simultaneous and emphasized agreement with the formulation.

Third, and less obviously perhaps, this avoidance of taking sides, and the treatment of the events as neither bad or worrying, can be part of a broader emphasis on how the couple can constructively work towards repairing their relationship. One step will be to become more relaxed about the problems and less fearful of their consequences. In Lawrence Wieder's (1974) ethnomethodological terms, such characterizations are multiformulative and multiconsequential; they formulate the world in a range of different ways, and they have a range of practical upshots.

A final thought about the word *complicated*. One of the things that this descriptive term does is characterize the relationship problems as a kind of puzzle that can be unravelled via counselling. That is, it makes counselling seem a sensible option where the technical skills will be put to enthusiastic work sorting out complications.

The point, then, is that if we wish to understand the selection of the terms *rich* and *complicated* we would not get very far if we saw the issue to be one of checking whether they are accurate or true. Nor do we need to carry out a cognitive psychological study of the mental images evoked by *rich* and *complicated* as individual words. To do either of these things would be to miss the business done by the local deployment of these descriptive categories. To understand this we need to consider their deployment in specific interactions and the nature of those interactions.

Categories and Metaphors

One of the most developed literatures concerned with the use of descriptive categories is that concerned with metaphor, and in particular the work of George Lakoff (Lakoff and Johnson, 1980; Lakoff, 1987). I do not want to devote a lot of space to metaphor here, but certain issues are particularly relevant to issues of factuality and categorization. Also, metaphor is often considered as an area where descriptions are being used performatively. Literal descriptions may be just telling it how it is, while metaphorical ones are doing something sneaky.

The first thing to note is that the distinction between metaphorical and non-metaphorical is far from clear-cut for historical, philosophical and practical reasons. Historically, metaphorical uses of language often come to be seen as increasingly literal, such that a person using a term may be quite unaware of its metaphorical root (Cooper, 1986). In conceptual terms, it is very hard to sustain a clear and reliable distinction between metaphorical and literal uses of language. As the philosopher and historian of psychology John Soyland (1994) makes clear in a thoughtful discussion of the issue, the central problem is that attempts to distinguish metaphorical from literal discourse *themselves* depend on metaphors to make them work. Note that I have already drawn heavily on metaphors in this paragraph about metaphor; *clear*, *clear-cut*, *root*, *reliable*, *work* and *heavy*. These are all terms from one field being used in another. The search for a non-metaphorical language within which to discuss metaphor is futile, or, at the very least, it begs the question of what literal uses of language would be. Is there an arena of language use which is literal and immune from the effects of figuration which Derrida and other post-structuralists identify as characteristic of language use? It is looking increasingly unlikely. One of the main themes of the current book is precisely how complex and subtle supposedly literal descriptions are.

In practice it is often hard to decide what is metaphorical and what is not. Take our counsellor's formulation of Connie and Jimmy's relationship as *rich* and *complicated*. I can think of various senses of *rich*: a person can be rich (wealthy), a cake can be rich (full of fruit and spice), a complaint can be a bit rich (cheeky and unwarranted). Yet as a mundane language user, the root meaning is by no means self-evident. I can look up the etymology of *rich* in a dictionary, and if I do I discover that it is defined as wealthy or having abundance, or being amply provided with, and it has been used in a variety of figurative (that is, metaphorical) senses. For example, Robert Boyle (whom we met recruiting observations for experiments in Chapter 1) is quoted from 1692 as writing 'Nature is much more rich in things, than our dictionaries in words' (*OED*). But obviously there is no sense in attempting to account for the workings of factual discourse in a way which requires participants to do a full etymological analysis, or even its mental equivalent.

As a response to these difficulties and issues I suggest that the metaphorical/literal distinction should not be treated as something that needs sorting out before the operation of descriptive discourse can be studied. Instead, all discourse can be studied for its rhetorical and constructive work. Thus, the observations I made about 'rich and complicated' above are unaffected by any technical decision about whether the words *rich* and *complicated* are metaphorical or literal.

There are two qualifications to this argument, however. First, to claim that the distinction is not a prerequisite for studying fact construction does not mean that it may not figure as an important *participants'* distinction on occasion. Someone may discount a description as 'only a metaphor'; or build it up as 'quite literally' the case; and this can be an important topic for study. Indeed, the literal–metaphorical distinction is hard to keep separate from the factual–fictional distinction.

Second, attention to the systematic properties of different sorts of metaphorical systems can be highly revealing, as George Lakoff (1991) has shown with his analysis of the different systems of metaphors used in the United States to justify their role in the Gulf War of 1990. For example, he shows the significance of understanding war as a kind of politics, and politics, in turn, as a form of business. His point is that what public debate there was did not focus on whether it was appropriate to view war as a form of politics and therefore a form of a business 'but only over how various analysts calculated the relative gains and losses' (1991: 3). From the standpoint argued here, the disagreement is not with Lakoff's revealing analysis but with the idea (not pressed by Lakoff) that such an analysis must be restricted to metaphorical constructions.

This point can be illustrated by way of two complementary analyses of descriptions of rape and sexual assault; Linda Coates and her colleagues (1994) focused on trial judgments, and Linda Wood and Heather Rennie (1994) focused on the accounts of self-identified rape victims. What both sets of researchers argued is that it is difficult to formulate the nature of the violent events in an appropriate way because of inadequacies in the two main repertoires of descriptive terms that are available. On the one hand, there is what Wood and Rennie call *the Hollywood rape construction* in which the rapist is typically an anonymous, jobless, itinerant who rapes and kills; on the other, there is consensual/affectionate and erotic sex between friends. Coates et al. show that for the much more common case of rape between acquaintances, judges tend to draw on the repertoire of terms associated with erotic consensual sex, while Wood and Rennie show that for the victims of such attacks there are considerable problems in constructing their own coherent narratives and understandings of the event. Undoubtedly, some of the terms in these descriptions could have been characterized as metaphorical, but none of the conclusions of these studies hinges on such an identification.

Categories and Agency Management

There are a large number of ways in which categories become used and usable for action. Some of these are very likely to be very domain-specific, but others may fall into broader patterns. To illustrate some of the ways that regularities in the use of categories might be studied I will take two examples where categories are related to inferences about agency: the use of 'nominalizations', which may obscure agency, and the use of 'intention-promoting' verbs, which may imply undue agency.

Critical linguists such as Roger Fowler, Gunter Kress and Robert Hodge have been particularly concerned with processes of transformation, where particular syntactical structures are modified to generate particular effects (Fowler, 1991; Hodge and Kress, 1993). One of these transformations takes place in the process of nominalization, where a verb is transformed into a noun. For example, the verb *kill* in 'police *kill* rioters' can be transformed into a nominal 'killing' as in 'the repercussions of yesterday's *killing* have been severe' (Trew, 1979). Critical linguists argue that such transformations obscure patterns of agency. Thus, in the case of 'police kill rioters' the reader will have no trouble in telling who the agent of the killing is, while in the case of 'yesterday's killing' the agent of the killing is not directly available.

Nominalization is a technique for categorizing actions and processes that allows the speaker or writer to avoid endorsing a particular story about responsibility. It may have an ideological role in managing the news reporting of actions which question the legitimacy of dominant assumptions. That is, state repression can be mystified behind agency-draining nominals. But nominalization may also be a consequence of the complex simultaneous tasks of reporting news and attending to concerns with bias and neutrality. Like the use of footing in news interviews described in Chapter 5, nominalization may be a device for displaying neutrality (which is not, I should emphasize, the same as actual neutrality).

While critical linguists have been primarily concerned with nominalization as a technique for obscuring agency, other kinds of descriptions build an impression of agency. One approach is to use what Randal Marlin (1984) calls 'intention-promoting' verbs. He gave the example of a newspaper headline: Pope Fouls Up Bar Mitzvah'. The story itself concerned the knock-on effect of the crowds that would inevitably assemble to see the Pope. Marlin suggested that while it is strictly true that it is the visit of the Pope that has caused the problem, this particular description implies something stronger, that the Pope had intended this consequence, and indeed that he may be malevolently disposed towards bar mitzvahs.

Marlin argues that different verbs have a different degree of 'opacity' with respect to the way they make explicit agency and intention (see also Coulter, 1983; Davies, 1995). For example, he suggests the utterance 'James defaulted, so that John lost' does not imply that James intended John to lose', although it may barely suggest that. However, 'James helped John lose' implies the presence of an intention, which may be further emphasized in constructions such as 'James brought about John's loss'. Marlin's argument is restricted to conceptual analysis and newspaper reports, but it seems likely that the relative opacity of different verbs may be exploited in a range of other situations. What he does not explore are the sorts of accountability concerns that such descriptions may orientate to in more interactional settings where they may combine agency promotion with a degree of deniability; after all, the report did not *explicitly claim* that the Pope wanted to stop the bar mitzvah! How, that is, do intention-promoting descriptions fare in everyday conversation?

The general point I want to conclude with is that the use of descriptive categories is an essential part of doing just about anything. Although some general features of categorization such as metaphor, nominalization and opacity may be of particular interest for the way they can be used to promote particular kinds of explanation or manage inferences about agency, the most important feature in an analysis will be the specific sequence of talk or writing that the categorization is embedded in as well as the rhetorical alternatives that it may be directed at. To understand the words *rich* and *complicated* in Extract 3 we need to consider their deployment in this particular sequence in this particular manner.

This way of understanding categorization is in stark contrast to the standard social science word-and-object concern with truth and factuality underpinned by what Steve Woolgar (1988b) talks of as the 'ideology of representation'. Although I want to argue that issues of descriptive categorization are fundamental to any discussion of reality construction, there is one way in which it can be potentially misleading. For it can focus too much attention on the descriptive language that is used, while directing attention away from that which is *not* used. If we heed the sorts of post-structuralist cautions against an overwhelming emphasis on presence discussed in Chapter 3, we will want some way of considering the sorts of things which are, significantly and relevantly, not there. One idea that can help with this concern is that of 'ontological gerrymandering'.

Categorization and Ontological Gerrymandering

When Steve Woolgar and Dorothy Pawluch (1985) introduced the notion of ontological gerrymandering they had a very specific target. They were concerned with the way explanations were used in social constructionist research on social problems. For example, Joseph Gusfield (1989) comments on the difference between constituting a problem as 'child abuse' or 'child neglect', suggesting that the latter is a more 'political' definition which focuses attention on issues such as poverty, homelessness and malnutrition, while the former draws attention to problems with individual families and procedures for their management.

What Woolgar and Pawluch objected to in this kind of explanation is not the constructionist analysis of 'the' problem, and certainly not the political critique that is its analytic goal, but the way it is combined with a realist account of the social system that the problem is part of. For example, the claim that the 'child abuse' definition is fostered because it is in the interests of governments and reforming individuals to do so given the expense and intractability of dealing with the poverty that causes it, is a relatively straightforward realist analysis. It treats some objects as unproblematically there – 'interests', 'governments', 'reform' and so on. The problem is that this realist ontology is *itself* amenable to constructionist analysis; yet such an analysis is avoided because it would undermine the overall explanation. This is ontological gerrymandering. As Woolgar and Pawluch put it:

> the successful social problems explanation depends upon making problematic the truth status of certain states of affairs selected for analysis and explanation, while backgrounding or minimising the possibility that the same problems apply to the assumptions upon which the analysis depends. By means of ontological gerrymandering, proponents of definitional explanations place a boundary between assumptions which are to be understood as (ostensibly) problematic and those which are not. (1985: 216)

Although Woolgar and Pawluch restrict this notion to specific manipulations where parts of an argument are protected from constructionist analysis, I want to use it in a more general sense here because it so nicely captures some of the central business done when using descriptions.

One of the aspects of making any description is that it will pick out a particular range of phenomena as relevant and ignore other potential ones. This is the extended sense of ontological gerrymandering; one realm of entities is constituted in the description while another is avoided. I will take three examples to flesh out this idea a bit more.

The first comes from a tribunal investigating the failure of members of the RUC (Royal Ulster Constabulary) to arrest rioters and protect property during crowd attacks in Northern Ireland. Here the Council (C) is examining the RUC police witness (W).

4   C: You saw this newspaper shop being petrol bombed on the front of Disvis Street?
     W: Yes.
     C: How many petrol bombs were thrown into it?
     W: Only a couple. I felt that the window was already broken and that there was part of it burning and this was a rekindling of the flames.
(from Atkinson and Drew, 1979: 137)

In their analysis of this material, Atkinson and Drew suggest that there are at least two issues of blame at work here. One is the failure to protect property that is being damaged; the other is the failure to arrest those people who are throwing petrol bombs. By concentrating on the issue of property the police Witness here selects a potentially less blameworthy issue on which to mount the defence. So, in terms of ontological gerrymandering, the witness' description selects one realm of entities (the nature of the property damage) and ignores another (the sanctions on the petrol bombers). Just as in electoral gerrymandering, where the vote is biased by drawing boundaries in the most efficacious way, the defence is shored up by drawing the rhetorical boundary around the most advantageous issues.

We can return to the Jimmy and Connie dispute for a second example of ontological gerrymandering. This practice is involved in their competing descriptions of the contentious pub evening. One of the features that distinguishes their versions is the boundaries of the described events. Connie's version formulates the event as having taken place in a pub:

5   *W*:   An' at <u>that</u> point in time, there was an episo:de,
→   with (.) a <u>bloke</u>, (.) in a pub, y'know?
         And <u>me:</u> having a few drinks and <u>messin'</u>.
(DE-JF/C2/S1:4)

I have already discussed some of the work done by the vague descriptive categories *episode* and *bloke*. The thing to note now is the way the description selects a terrain as relevant to the dispute; the episode is described as 'in' the pub, not *including* events in the pub.

The significance of this selection becomes clearer when we compare Connie's version to Jimmy's. He selects the terrain rather differently. His version also constructs events that went on in the pub (although using much more detail than Connie), but continues with a narrative that climaxes at Connie and Jimmy's home with a suspected tryst, emotional outbursts and an aborted attempt at suicide. His broad sweep is intrinsic to showing just how far he has been provoked by Connie. The piquancy of the event is heightened by its culmination for Jimmy while he was lying in bed listening to the activities downstairs (see Extract 13 in Chapter 6). Bed is a prototypical private and safe space, while Connie's more delimited *pub* version works to downplay the event and suggest Jimmy's over-reaction.

We have already seen in Chapter 3 that location categorizations can be particularly important. The location category *pub* does a lot of work here (Edwards, 1995; cf. Drew, 1992; Widdicombe and Wooffitt, 1995). In Britain and Ireland (where Connie and Jimmy lived and originate from) the pub is widely known as a major site of many people's social life. It is public and familiar. 'Messin'' in a pub is strongly contrastive to implied sexual intimacy heard from a bed in one's own home.

The third example comes from the study by Margaret Wetherell, Andrew Chitty and myself of the making and reception of a 'current affairs' television programme (Potter et al., 1991). The programme argued that people donating to cancer charities were being deceived because much of their money went to basic biochemical research which had little to do with fighting cancer. The disputes in and around the programme included a range of different ways in which cancer was being fought: for example, it could be made an issue of cure, of improved survival, of improving the quality of life of sufferers, and of prevention. So a first gerrymandering issue concerns the way an argumentative case could be made by selecting one of these ways and avoiding others.

When the issue of cancer research failure was dealt with in the television programme it focused exclusively on cure as the appropriate criterion for the success of cancer research. However, even the notion of 'cure' was understood in different ways in these materials. The programme makers adopted a stringent criterion (although one commonplace in medical settings) that required a high (80 per cent) five-year survival rate for the cancer to count as curable. Much of the subsequent argument revolved around the terrain selected for this claim about research failure. For example, when interviewed about the programme, the Public Relations Officer (PRO) of Britain's largest cancer charity (along with her Personal Assistant – PA) complained vehemently about the sense in which the notion of cure was used, and particularly about a table displaying a long list of cancers that picked out 'curable' ones in yellow (see Table 7.1 below).

> 6 *PRO*: I'm very very angry about [the table]. Well there isn't a form of cancer (0.2) for which (.) no one gets cured. Now if you were sitting at home with breast cancer with about (.) what's the cure rate (1.0) six- (*PA*: Fifty per cent) fifty per cent and you saw (0.2) that the only curable cancer was in yellow but breast cancer was in white you'd think your doctors had been lying to you and (0.2) I th- I thought it was totally irresponsible
>
> *PA*: Even the most intractable cancers, (.) say like lung cancer with an under ten per cent survival rate after five years, (.) there are people if you spot early enough who are cured.

(Wilkins interview: 5, slightly simplified)

In this passage the notion of cure is made to depend on the broad criterion that if some people can survive a cancer (even if it is only 10 per cent of sufferers) then it is wrong to avoid counting that cancer as curable. So while the programme makers are using a 'technical' definition which minimizes the success of cancer research in finding a cure, the more 'common-sense' notion used by the cancer charity representatives paints a much more optimistic picture of success. Note, however, that just because the programme makers and charity representatives use these versions of cure on this occasion does not mean that on others it will not be more suitable for them to characterize cure very differently, or to emphasize prevention, say, as the crucial index of success.

In each of the three examples discussed above a major part of the work of the descriptions comes from gerrymandering the terrain: selecting and formulating an area which is advantageous and ignoring others. In the first example, the RUC witness focuses on the issue of failing to protect property rather than the concern with arresting rioters. In the second, Connie formulates the problem event as having taken place inside a pub, while Jimmy provides a more extended narrative which sites much of the worst actions in their home. In the third example there is nested gerrymandering, with the programme makers initially selecting the terrain of cure (rather than, say, pain reduction) and then selecting a particular notion of cure to work with.

Before moving on to consider extrematization and minimization, there is an important analytic issue to address concerning ontological gerrymandering. The argument here is that one of the powers of descriptions often lies in what they *fail* to describe, what is ignored or left out. However, for any description an infinite number of things is inevitably left out, which makes the analytic identification of things that are significantly left out potentially difficult and contentious. In the three examples above this identification is done in different ways. In the police and rioters example there are two grounds for identifying the failure to arrest or stop rioters as significantly missing. On the one hand, it trades on shared general expectations about what police do and what they should do; on the other, it uses displays of what is important which appear elsewhere in the examination. The lines of questioning highlight what is and is not considered blameworthy in a way that aids analysis. In both the Connie and Jimmy and cancer deaths examples, the identification of significant absence can be done more directly as there are immediately competing versions which highlight potentially troubling issues that have not been described.

In fact, as semiologists in particular have emphasized, one of the features of using any descriptive categorization is the terms that are *not* used. So in effect there are two kinds of relevant absences that are of interest: particular descriptive terms and particular argumentative arenas. If we combine the role of descriptive categories in constituting actions and events with the potential for selectively gerrymandering what is to be formulated and what ignored we can see that there is an immensely powerful system for producing versions designed to do particular things. The choice of boundaries and the huge range of descriptive terms available mean that highly contrasting versions of the 'same thing' can be produced while resisting criticisms of inaccuracy, falsehood or active confabulation. We can see again that in these practical situations questions of *referential* adequacy may be of little importance.

Extrematization and Minimization

Anita Pomerantz (1986) has suggested that when people are attempting to justify, accuse or argue some conclusions they often draw on 'extreme-case' formulations. The use of such formulations is a common descriptive practice that involves using the extreme points on relevant descriptive dimensions. So, for example, a dress that is claimed to be damaged by dry cleaners is not just new, it is *'brand new'*; a person proposed as a potential friend is not just likeable, *'everybody* who meets him likes him'. These descriptions work persuasively to strengthen the case; they maximize the value of the dress and the likeability of the potential friend.

This practice is very familiar. Here is an example we have seen already:

```
7  W:  At that poi:nt, (0.6) Jimmy ha- (.) my-
    →  Jimmy is extremely jealous. Ex- extremely jealous per:son.
       Has a:lways ↓been, from the da:y we met. Y'know?
[DE-JF/C2/S1:4]
```

Here Jimmy is not described as merely a jealous person – he is an extremely jealous person. And note that this description is part of a dispute;

it is rhetorically designed to counter the kind of alternative that Jimmy might (and indeed does) produce.

In Pomerantz's article she concentrates on modalizing terms (for example, *every*, *completely*, *never*) or similar words which modify descriptions: the accused is not just innocent but '*completely* innocent'. However, there are other ways in which descriptions can manipulate quantity to make something seem extreme or minimal, or to build something as good or bad. I will use two examples to illustrate different procedures for maximization and minimization, the first using quantification, the second using particular styles of reference.

Maximizing and Minimizing Cancer Death Statistics

I have already discussed our study of the making and reception of a film about the failure of cancer research in the context of ontological gerrymandering. This work also illustrates some of the ways in which quantification can be used to maximize and minimize. Take the following two extracts which both formulate the success of cancer research, along with Table 7.1. The commentary in Extract 8 is from the transmitted programme and was accompanied by Table 7.1 which is a scrolling table of types of cancer used in the programme. Extract 9 is an untransmitted segment from the programme makers' interview with Jeremy Kemp, the head of Britain's second largest cancer charity.

    8   *Commentary*:   But those three curable types are amongst the rarest
                         cancers – they represent around 1 per cent of a quarter of a
                         million cases of cancers diagnosed each year. Most deaths are
                         caused by a small number of very common cancers.
    (From Potter et al., 1991: 339)

    9   *Kemp*:   Er, one way that I find useful to look at this is that er,
                         each year in the United Kingdom two, roughly two hundred and
                         forty thousand people get cancer. Each year er, roughly a
                         hundred and sixty thousand people die from cancer, so there's a
                         difference of eighty thousand, and eighty thousand is one third
                         of two hundred and forty thousand which is the number of
                         people who get the disease, so one could say that one's a sort of
                         third of the way there. It's not a totally useless way of looking
                         at it and sometimes quite helpful. So there has been progress
                         but we're probably not half way there yet.
    (From Potter et al., 1991: 349 – note that this is the programme maker's own transcript)

Extract 8 follows a quote from cancer charity head Kemp (the speaker in Extract 9), in which he provided an upbeat account of success against cancer, using three instances. The commentary counters this assessment and minimizes success in a number of ways. First, it uses two sorts of counting – *types* of cancer and *cases* of cancer – and formulates both as small. Second, it gives a quantitative characterization of the fraction of cancers that are 'curable':

Table 7.1   *Scrolling table of cancer incidence*

Annual incidence of cancer	
Placenta	20
Childhood leukaemia	350*
Eye	400
Small intestine	400
Pleura	500
Bone	550
Mouth	900
Connective tissue	900
Thyroid	950
Testis	1000*
Pharynx	1000
Liver	1200
Gall bladder	1300
Hodgkin's disease	1400*
Larynx	2000
Myeloma	2300
Melanoma	2600
Brain	3200
Kidney	3500
Uterus	3700
Cervix	4400
Leukaemia	4400
Hodgkin's lymphoma	4600
Oesophagus	4800
Ovary	5100
Pancreas	6400
Prostate	10,400
Bladder	10,500
Rectum	10,600
Stomach	13,100
Colon	16,800
Breast	24,600
Skin	25,000
Lung	41,400
Total	243,000

*Asterisked lines appear in yellow (in contrast to white) on screen to mark curable cancers. The figures are said to denote cases of cancer diagnosed in a single year.

'around 1 per cent of a quarter of a million cases'. This characterization is interesting because it mixes a relational quantity (the percentage) with an absolute quantity (X many cases). Why is there this mixture? One reason for this mix – as opposed to, say, giving two absolute figures – seems to be the effectiveness of the contrast: '1 per cent' has an almost definitive smallness to it, while 'a quarter of a million' is a different order of number altogether; it is 'millions talk', not 'thousands talk'. Third, the stress on deaths being caused by 'a small number of common cancers' is interesting because it introduces yet another dimension of quantification, rare/common, claiming success with rare cancers but not with common. This places progress in the category of cancers that are, perhaps, uncharacteristic or esoteric, which may have unusual properties that make them more tractable but perhaps of less interest to a public concerned with fighting major killers such as breast and lung cancer.

These features of the commentary are combined by a visual representation which is summarized in Table 7.1. All through the commentary section in Extract 8 a list of cancers scrolls down the screen along with a figure said to be the diagnosed cases of that kind of cancer in a year. Most of the cancers are presented in white, while the three that had been previously named as curable are picked out in yellow. This visual display reinforces the commentary and makes vivid the contrast between curable and incurable, as well as between common and rare. One way of thinking about the operation of this table is to consider the way a market trader builds the contrast between the value of goods and the selling price (Pinch and Clark, 1986). A common approach is to build the worth of goods by selling them as a collection (a pen is sold with a pencil, a fibre tip, a case and so on). In the sales patter these can be listed exhaustively to make it seem a big collection relative to the small price. In the film, the exhaustive listing of 'incurable cancers' helps to build a contrast with the few 'curable cancers' and, in combination with the contrastive work in the commentary, helps sell the message of cancer charity failure that is intrinsic to the film's main argument (see also Orcutt and Turner, 1993).

There is always a temptation to see these sorts of calculation and representational practices as simply clear and obvious ways to capture what is there; that is, to see them as merely descriptive rather than rhetorically constructive. To counter that temptation it is useful to look at contrasting versions, in this case Extract 9, which illustrates the use of very different calculation practices to different effect. While the commentary compares the total for the three 'curable' cancers to the total of diagnosed cancers, Kemp takes a figure for deaths each year ('a hundred and sixty thousand') and then subtracts the deaths from the figure for those diagnosed ('there's a difference of about eighty thousand'). He then expresses this difference as a fraction of the total ('one third') and this is glossed: 'so one could say that one's a sort of a third of the way there'. This is finally glossed again: 'we're probably not half way there yet'.

What we see in these extracts are two different calculation practices which are able to formulate a bottom-line figure for progress as either 'about 1 per cent' or approaching 'half way there'. Note that they are able to come to these different conclusions despite using the same set of basic figures as a start point – this is not a simple question of different ways of collecting statistics for death and diagnosis. Nor is there a straightforward way in which one of these versions is wrong and the other right – although proponents of each were highly critical of the other.

More generally, here is an example where a particular set of descriptive categories and calculation practices are used to produce a maximized and minimized version. Also, quantification is often thought of as an especially precise and clear-cut form of description which is contrasted to value judgements and vague qualitative assessments; however, here we see that there are a wide variety of mathematical procedures which allow a considerable flexibility in versions. And this conclusion meshes with a range of studies that have started to consider the rhetorical construction of quantity (Ashmore 1995; Ashmore et al., 1989; McCloskey, 1985; Porter, 1992).

Describing Violence

For a second example of maximizing and minimizing descriptions I want to consider accounts of violence. How are descriptions constructed to maximize and, more interestingly, to minimize the violence? Put another way, how can a description of a violent act make it seem shocking, bad or damnable; or, alternatively, how can it be softened or made to seem acceptable? For the purposes of this discussion I will concentrate on the production of minimized or softened versions.

One way of starting to consider this topic is by considering the sorts of terminology that can be used for acts of physical violence. Consider the difference between 'punch' and 'biff', for example, or between 'kick' and 'boot'. Taken in the abstract, the latter term in each pair is the more softened. And these are the terms more likely to appear in the descriptions in children's comics, say, or as captions flashed on the screen when Batman and Robin fought the Joker and his henchmen in the old television series (but missed from the movie versions).

Here is a rather more complex example that comes from an article following a well-publicized attack by a Manchester United footballer on a crowd member who had been taunting him with racist abuse (and note the way even this minimal description sets up a range of expectations about the nature of the action as well as potential accounts). The article was explicitly written to counter strong newspaper criticism of the footballer, and is concerned with the brittle psychology of sporting geniuses and contains a number of illustrations including the following about Hughie Gallacher ('Ah, Hughie Gallacher . . . alcoholic and genius'):

10   He [Gallacher] once said to the eminent referee Bert Fogg that the latter's surname reflected the state he had been in all afternoon. Hughie went to apologise to Mr Fogg after the match and, on entering the dressing room, saw him standing with his back to the door naked. He could not resist the temptation and *booted* the referee's bare backside, sending him flying into the bath.
(*New Zealand Herald*, February 1995 – emphasis added)

Here the softening of the term *booted* is combined with a number of different features into a narrative that paints this as a moment of jovial excess (cf. Squire, 1994). Note the repetition of the referee's vaguely humorous name, and the general scenario which is reminiscent of slapstick comedy or *Carry On* films. Note also how the temptation is treated as an intrinsic and understandable part of the situation; this is temptation that anyone might be expected to have just as they would if faced with a bank note lying on the pavement. This is not a brutal, unprovoked and surprise attack on a man in a vulnerable state of undress (a narrative which could easily have been constructed with the same materials); it is the understandable and rather engaging act of a larger-than-life individual. The description softens the violence. Similar points are made in Adams et al. (1995) concerning men talking about their violence towards women and by Auburn et al. (1995) in the context of police interrogations.

For many of us, our main exposure to violence is through media reporting and fictional constructions in novels, television and films. However, there are situations where violence, directly or indirectly, is something practical to be dealt with. One of these confronts social workers who are dealing with the parents of children who have been taken 'into care' because of physical or sexual abuse. The following extract comes from a corpus of social work materials collected by Mick Roffe (see Roffe, in preparation). It comes near the start of an 'assessment interview', where the social worker (SW) is talking to a couple ('Lucy' and 'Mark') whose two children are currently with foster parents. Mark has a court case for alleged violence to one of the children pending.

```
11  SW:    Going through the files, which obviously I had to,
    Lucy:  [Ye↓a:h   ]
    SW:    [to get the] court thing together (0.2) y'know it was that you too had
           had difficulties arou:nd (.) uncontrolled responses, towards the children
    Lucy:  Ye↓a:h
    SW:    Y'know this is how I feel that it is. My assessment is that (.) you two:,
           (0.4) a- aren't systematically injuring the children. I mean some people (.)
           do do that, some forms of child abuse entail that.=
    Lucy:  =°Umhm° (0.2)
    SW:    For you two it's like an uncontrolled response. Y'know, the kids are
           too much, th- the world's too much, and so (.) you lash out, hh
           at a moment where you just can't control it. .hhh Now it'sa- its-
           because of that, and because I feel that that's (.) possibly workable with
    Lucy:  Um↓hmm (.)
    SW:    that (.) we want to place as much support into the family to reduce
           the levels of stress you're experiencing, and work with both you ↑and
           Mark
    Lucy:  °umhmm°
    SW:    to (continues with proposal)
(MR-SW/TE:4-5, slightly modified)
```

Let us start by considering the two descriptive categorizations of actions: 'uncontrolled response' (used twice) and 'lash out'.

By using the phrase 'uncontrolled response' the social worker presents the violence as something elicited or provoked, with the problem being lack of subsequent control. This is underscored by characterizing this as 'difficulties you had'; that is, the violence is described not in actional vocabulary, but as an affliction; something happening to Lucy and Mark. And this non-agentive, 'happening to' character is further emphasized by the contrast with the 'systematic injury' of other kinds of 'child abuse'.

There are two things I particularly want to pick out here. First, this is a description at a level of abstraction which avoids any 'witness' style depiction of actions: 'uncontrolled responses' could involve kicking, hitting, screaming – or indeed, biffing, booting and yelling. Nor does it present any consequences of actions, something which is commonplace in violence descriptions: 'laid him out', 'slashed his face', 'broke his arms'. Second, 'uncontrolled response' is a description which has accountability built into it. That is, unlike, say, 'kick', the explanation of the violence is started, at least minimally, in the description: the problem here is with responses that are not being controlled properly. This is probably reinforced by the technical/psychological connotations of the phrase.

The other phrase, 'lashed out', is interesting because it initially might seem to be a more direct action description than 'uncontrolled responses'. Yet I suggest that it too has a generic quality and it also provides its own accountability. One feature of 'lashing out' is that it is not premeditated or planned; it is an immediate and angry or emotional reaction to some provocation. It is the kind of description used for the actions of a cornered animal. Here is another example where an interviewee is rebutting claims of police brutality:

12 I think the police acted very well. They're only human, if they *lashed out* and
    cracked a skull occasionally, it was, hah, only a very human action I'm sure.
(From Potter and Wetherell, 1987: 112)

This constructs 'lashing out' as something that anybody might do in the appropriate circumstances. Note the way it is not used to refer to a specific action such as hitting someone with a truncheon; rather, a range of different actions might be collected under the category.

It is important to be aware that these phrases are not working in Extract 11 on their own. Their sense is being hardened up through their organization within turns of talk. Thus 'uncontrolled response' is contrasted with 'systematically injuring the children', something more intentional and premeditated and, presumably, more culpable. And the sense of 'lashing out' is carefully built by listing features that might be the provocation: 'the kids are too much', 'the world's too much'. As the social worker says a few moments later, 'it's like a volcano', to which Lucy continues, 'an' it erupts'.

What we can see, then, is that this descriptive passage provides a specific kind of minimization. It provides relatively abstract descriptions of the violent events, it does not formulate any of their consequences, and it provides both motive and mechanism (build-up of pressures, uncontrolled responses). We can make sense of this by considering the sorts of specific practices of which this violence description is part.

The first thing to note here is that the practice of social work, in this case, is orientated to the future: working with this couple, perhaps building to the return of their children. This is quite different from the retrospective orientation of, say, Mark's court case, where what is at stake is his past guilt. In addition, social work involves a much more personal interaction than what happens in courts; social workers often talk about building trust or partnership with clients. This will be a problem in a situation where it is necessary to refer to the violence repeatedly. The danger is that the conversation will become embroiled in moral issues of blame and admonishment which would disrupt the interaction and undermine trust. At the same time, a total denial of the significance of the violence might discourage the clients from taking the session seriously, or turn the issue into one of injustice rather than self-improvement. Thus we can see that the specific ways in which these violence descriptions are built are perfectly suited to the various local issues facing the social worker.

What I have argued in this section, then, is that there is a range of techniques that can be used to maximize or minimize some quality of an action or some feature of the world. This kind of descriptive work focuses on dimensions such as big versus small, violent versus non-violent, and what often amounts to the same thing, good versus bad. However, there is a further recurrent feature of descriptions, and that is the way they construct actions or events as normal or abnormal.

Normalization and Abnormalization

The issue of how a description can present some actions as abnormal was addressed in Dorothy Smith's 'K is mentally ill', the study which, probably more than any other, established fact construction as an analytic topic rather than a rather abstract philosophical or theoretical thesis. The central concern here was the way in which Angela (supposedly K's friend) described K's actions as systematically bizarre and problematic. One of the points that Smith makes is that what counts as normal is indexical. In other words, it is not sufficient simply to describe an action which will be consensually recognized as abnormal or weird; rather, that abnormality has to be constructed in discourse.

In the tale on which Smith focuses, abnormality is worked up principally through the use of a particular descriptive device that Smith calls a contrast structure. This is a discursive organization which both describes the activity and provides cues to understand it as abnormal or bizarre. For example:

13 When asked casually to help in a friend's garden.
    she went at it for hours, never stopping, barely looking up. (Smith, 1990: 18)

Smith notes that it would not be hard to recharacterize what is going on here as something virtuous; the actions of someone conscientiously and energetically doing their friend a favour. It would surely be a boon to have someone helping you with your garden like this! However, as described here the actions are not conscientious but peculiar. There is a contrast between the 'casual' request and the massive compliance. And K's actions are presented in a way that makes them seem driven or obsessive, particularly in the context of a whole spate of such contrast structures (Smith identifies 24 in 138 lines of transcript).

Sometimes there are particular difficulties in presenting K's behaviour as problematic. Take the description: 'she would go to the beach or pool and swim on a hot day'. It is hard to see this as anything other than entirely normal or even enviable, especially in someone who has been characterized as 'so very athletic'. How can this description be reworked to achieve a sense of K's oddness? The description is produced like this in Angela's account:

14   We would go to the beach or pool on a hot day.
     I would sort of just dip in and just lie in the sun
     while K insisted that she had to swim 30 lengths. (Smith, 1990: 18)

There are a number of features at work here that build K's abnormality. Smith emphasizes the role of Angela's description of what she would do: dipping in and lying in the sun are presented as appropriate in contrast to K's swimming. However, as Robin Wooffitt (1992) notes, the contrastive work alone is probably not sufficient to produce the effect. It is the introduction of 'insisted', which characterizes K as acting in a compulsive rather than leisurely manner, and the precise specification '30 lengths', which can be heard as an obsessional target. Compare Extract 14 to the following version, which I have modified to take out the term *insisted* and the precise specification of lengths:

15   We would go to the beach or pool on a hot day.
     I would sort of just dip in and just lie in the sun
     while K practised her swimming.

Here the contrast does not work to present K's actions as abnormal, let alone bizarre.

There is another notable feature of Extract 14. The repeated use of the word *would* ('we *would* go . . .', 'I *would* sort of . . .') presents this not as a one-off, but as something that happens generally. This is a major feature in the construction of K as someone with a problem because it presents actions as generic or representative rather than merely one-off oddities or misunderstandings. Wooffitt also emphasizes that the repetition of *would* has a fact constructional role: Angela is not extrapolating from a single case but has made repeated observations, observations which allow her to provide such rich detail as the precise number of lengths that K swam.

This last observation reminds us that the issue of normality is closely connected to the issue of regularity. Indeed, it is often hard to distinguish these two things. So one issue is how descriptions are produced that justify a characterization of something as normal or regular. And one approach to this is seen with Gail Jefferson's work on listing.

Jefferson and Three-part Lists

In studying transcripts of everyday conversation, Gail Jefferson (1990) noted that it was very common for lists to be delivered with three parts or items. For example:

16   *Matt*:   The good actors are dyin out.
     Tony: They're all- they're <u>all</u> dyin out ⌈yeah
     Matt: ⌊Tyrone Po-wuh. Clark

                        Gable, Gary Cooper,]
            Tony: Now all of 'em are dyin.
        (Jefferson, 1990: 74)

In this case Matt lists three examples to agree with the claim that all the good actors are dying out.

There are various features of the delivery of lists that indicate that three-partedness may often have a conventional or normative status. For example, people are rarely interrupted after the second part of such a list, even where there is plenty of opportunity presented by their groping for a suitable term for the third part. And they often draw on 'generalized list completers' such as 'etcetera' or 'and that kind of thing'.

Now Jefferson's point is not that lists of all kinds are not properly formed unless they have three parts – after all, shopping lists, lists of items to take on holiday, and so on appropriately have widely varying numbers. Her point is that specifically three-part lists are frequently used to summarize some general class of things. Three parts are sufficient to indicate that we have more than individual instances on their own but instances standing for something more general. For example, in Extract 16 the listing of three actors is used to support the general claim that good actors are dying out; note also the way my listing of specific kinds of lists earlier in this paragraph indicates the class of lists in general.

Here is an example from a study of political argument. The then Prime Minister, Margaret Thatcher, is being pressed by a television interviewer about whether she precipitated the resignation of her Chancellor.

17   *Interviewer*: but you are not claiming that there <u>was</u> seen to be full agreement
                     between yourself and the Chancellor are ↑you
      Thatcher: .hhh I am claiming that I <u>fully</u> backed and supported the
                     Chancellor (.) of course we discuss things
      1→   >we discuss things in Cabinet
      2→   we discuss things in the economic committee .hh
      3→   we discuss things with <u>many</u> advisers<
      (Edwards and Potter, 1992: 143)

There is a lot of complexity here (see Edwards and Potter, 1992). However, note the combination of categorization and listing. Mrs Thatcher does not use the interviewer's term *agreement* (with its implied opposite, *disagreement*) but replaces it with *discussion*. This is a term that can include disagreement, so it does not directly contradict the interviewer, and yet it suggests a more constructive and co-operative process. To emphasize the contrast between *agreement/disagreement* and *discussion* it is packaged in a three-part list, which specifies different kinds of 'discussion' that can take place. It characterizes *discussion* as happening routinely in a range of different settings. 'Discussion' – which might involve 'disagreement', or which others might mistake for 'disagreement' – is normal.

As a final example, consider the following relationship counselling materials. Here Connie is responding to a question about trust from the Counsellor.

18   *W*:   <u>Yeh</u> <u>def</u>initely (.) my trust has been broken altogether (.)
          I just feel now that I couldn't trust him again (0.4) not now (0.2) I- (.)
          ninety five percent believe (0.2) what he has told me is true (0.2)
          but as I said there's just a lot of coincidences (.) that I feel (0.4)
          well (.) if it was only a one night thing (.)
     1→   well how come he was on the phone to her one night (.)
     2→   my friend saw him sitting in a pub another night with her,
     3→   my other friend saw him in a <u>nigh</u>tclub another nigh- (.)
          it's just (0.2) to me: too <u>many</u>.(.)
(DE-JF/C2/S2:3)

Again the listing (which is picked out by a range of intonational cues in the spoken delivery) serves to emphasize the generality of something. In this case the three instances are taken as sufficient to display Jimmy's assurances about his affair being over as untrustworthy.

The general point here is that three-part listing can be drawn on to construct some events or actions as commonplace or normal. Of course, this is just one technique that can be used to this end. These concerns have been developed by Derek Edwards, and I am going to focus on his studies of script formulations in the final part of this chapter.

Script and Breach Formulations

Edwards introduces the notion of script and breach formulations as a direct contrast to the cognitive psychological notion of script (Edwards, 1994a, 1995, 1996). The idea behind classic script theory is that people negotiate routine, everyday situations by way of mentally encoded scripts. The analogy with a playscript should be obvious. Just as the play script guides the actors through a scene, determining which lines to speak at what point, the cognitive script lays down the instructions for dealing with a commonplace situation such as going to eat at a restaurant. The ultimate goal was to work back from such supposedly straightforward cases to explicate the scripted nature of more personal and idiosyncratic activities (Schank and Abelson, 1977).

Edwards took this notion and considered how it might be reworked as a concern not to psychologists but to people having a conversation, say, or the reader of a newspaper article. Cognitive psychologists have started with regularity as an unproblematic phenomenon and asked what cognitive apparatus can explain it; however, it is possible to treat regularity as something constructed and potentially disputed rather than a natural feature of the world. That is, rather than consider what orderly mental organization is responsible for a person's orderly conduct, Edwards asks how, in description, can that person's conduct be *made out* as orderly or not? How can an action be described in a way that constitutes it as orderly or commonplace? Or how can a description constitute it as a deviation from such an order, as in the way that K is made out to be deviant through constructing her as doing obsessional swimming rather than appropriate lazing?

Here is a relatively simple example that Edwards takes from the Connie and

Jimmy materials. Both respond to a question from the Counsellor about their marriage.

```
19  C:   Wh:en: (.) before you moved over here hhow was
         the marriage.
         (0.4)
    W:   ↑O↓h. (0.2) I- (.) to me: all alo:ng, (.) right
         up to now, (0.2) my marriage was rock solid.
         (0.8) Rock solid.= We had arguments like
         everybody else had arguments, (0.4) buthh (0.2)
         to me there was no major problems. Y'know?
         That's (0.2) my way of thinking but (0.4)
         Jimmy's thinking is ve[ry very different.]
    H:                         [Well (1.0)        ] Bein: (0.8)
         a jealous person, (0.8) u:m, (0.6) we go back- (.)
         back to: (0.6) when we were datin' (1.0) when we were
         dating first (0.8) well we met in this: particular pub.
         (1.0) >When we start'd datin' we was in there,< <EV'ry
         single week> we'd fight. (0.2) We were at each other
         the who:le time.
```
(DE-JF/C2/S1:7)

One of the contentious issues in this session is what the problem with Connie and Jimmy's relationship is which, in turn, is inextricably bound up with who is to blame for their current difficulties. For example, has their relationship been undermined by a recent affair had by Jimmy (a claim made directly elsewhere in the session), or does the problem date back from the relationship's inception? These concerns are played out in the contrasting versions provided in Extract 19.

Connie builds up a description of strong and enduring marital stability – it has been 'rock solid' up to the present time; that is, up to their current relationship problems. Note in particular the descriptive work done in the characterization of the 'arguments'. These are depicted as of a routine kind; the sort of argument that everybody has. In Edwards' terms, the arguments are script-formulated. We might, of course, wonder why Connie should bring up the issue of arguments at all in a version establishing the solidity of the relationship. Why not simply gerrymander the relevant actions and events in a way that best establishes the version? However, this would be to fail to recognize the rhetorical complexity of the situation with three participants.

Consider Dorothy Smith's mental illness materials. K was not present to counter Angela's claims. She could not develop a description of the routine or virtuous nature of her swimming at the pool, let alone chastise Angela for just lazing around. Here things are different, because Jimmy is sitting right next to Connie, and has the opportunity to speak next. He can cause difficulties for the 'rock-solid' version by constructing an alternative which references repeated arguments; something he has very likely done in the past. We can see, then, that when Connie makes reference to arguments, but characterizing them as the kind of *routine* arguments that relationships *generally* have, it works to head off this counter. The description is rhetorically organized to rebut a potential alternative.

Jimmy, as we can see from the extract, does respond with an immediate counter. This contrasts the version of the relationship as rock solid combined with routine arguments with a version stressing endemic and deep-seated conflict. Note the emphatic delivery and extreme case formulations: '<EV'ry single week>' and 'the who:le time'. In addition, Jimmy replaces Connie's term 'argument' with the stronger, more negative term 'fight'. It is a script formulation, but here the script for the relationship is one of severe and problematic conflict, as Edwards puts it, 'a marriage more rocky than rock solid' (1995: 328). This script formulation directs attention away from the potential role of his own extramarital actions and focuses attention on the relationship itself.

The general point, then, is that there is a range of descriptive approaches that can be used to make out activities as routine or exceptional, and to tie such activities to an individual's enduring dispositions, or to characterize them as a product of some feature of a situation or some unusual circumstance. Edwards cautions against the idea that it would be possible to provide an exhaustive list of techniques or devices through which 'script-and-disposition work' may be accomplished. However, he notes certain constructions that are recurrent in the relationship counselling materials.

Such constructions may draw on modals and verbs with an iterative aspect ('I *would* sort of just dip in', 'he *gets* so mad at me') which imply something regular or enduring. They may use event pluralization ('we had *arguments* . . .') and temporal adverbs (*always, usually*) to the same end, or explicitly characterize something as an instance from a pattern ('I'll tell you just a quick *instance* now . . .'). Alternatively, if-then structures ('*if* someone came up . . .') display a patterning to activity which blurs the distinction between what is actual and what hypothetical (see also Widdicombe and Wooffitt, 1995: 120). This is part of an array of discursive resources which can be used to constitute patterning in activity. Actions in relationships and political disputes can be established as ordinary and unproblematic, or undermined as weird and deviant.

Representations in Action

At the start of this chapter I stressed the enormity of the task of considering how representations are used to perform particular actions. There is a wide range of different levels at which such an analysis can be conducted and different topic areas that could be a focus for study. Nevertheless, what I have tried to do in this chapter is indicate at least the possibility that there may be general themes that recur across a whole range of settings.

The first main topic was the central role of basic categorizations where descriptions are constructed to perform actions. It is through categorization that an entity, action or event is formulated as having a particular quality or set of qualities. Describing a reporter as a *hack* may serve one kind of activity, while describing the same person as a *journalist* may serve another. Through using particular categorizations, speakers and writers may sustain or undermine particular inferences about *themselves*; for example, a counsellor can display both neutrality and enthusiasm by categorizing a relationship problem, which has been characterized as more the fault of one partner, as 'rich and complicated'.

The argument stressed the importance of being attentive to the sorts of metaphorical systems that may be involved in descriptions. There was a discussion of war as politics in this chapter, while war as sport figured in Chapter 3. However, I cautioned against starting from the expectation that non-metaphorical discourse is somehow less interesting, or less likely to be orientated to action, as well as against expecting there to be a straightforward analysts' distinction between metaphorical and literal discourse.

Although I stressed the huge variety of ways in which categorizations can be involved in action, I picked as particularly interesting the example of the way verbs may be agency-obscuring when nominalized, or how they can be agency-promoting when non-transparent. Thus the nominalization *killing* in the report of a violent crowd event may avoid the need to make an explicit judgement about who is doing the killing and who being killed, while *James helped John lose* may imply intentions yet does not explicitly claim them.

One of the features of these kinds of arguments is that they focus on descriptions that are actually made. Yet it is interesting to consider categorization as a process both of selecting some descriptions and rejecting others. Woolgar and Pawluch's notion of ontological gerrymandering is one way of conceptualizing this. It shows the way claims and arguments may be made effective by selecting particular sets of entities for decomposition while treating others as unproblematic. Treating this notion more broadly, it can be applied to any situation in which a particular argumentative terrain is selected out of the available options.

In addition to basic processes of categorization and gerrymandering I emphasized two constructive dimensions of descriptions: extrematization and minimization, normalization and abnormalization. There are many occasions where the business of description is to display something as very good or very bad, very big or very small, to show an offence was extremely severe or perhaps too trivial to be worth worrying about. Anita Pomerantz emphasized the specific phenomenon of explicit extreme case formulations ('brand new', 'everybody breaks the speed limit'), and concerns with extremity have a more general currency. I focused in particular on the way some different calculation and fractionation practices can be used to maximize or minimize progress in the medical fight against cancer, and the way violent actions can be formulated in a minimizing and indirect way to facilitate a particular kind of interaction.

The issue of what is normal and routine is a fundamental one in human affairs as it is so bound up with which actions should be treated as accountable and which not. It is not surprising, then, that there should be a wide range of ways in which activities can be made out as routine or as breaches of standard patterns. Dorothy Smith emphasized the role of contrast structures through which events are made out as abnormal or problematic by contrasting them to characterizations of what is appropriate ('just lazing around' versus 'swimming 30 lengths'). Derek Edwards developed the notion of script and breach formulations, and has shown how these enable particular actions to be made out as one-off occurrences or alternatively as instances of generalized patterns. Such formulations provide a basis for accountability and provide a technique for making an action description provide evidence of a person's 'dispositional state': their character, personality or state of mind. Thus Jimmy's actions may be made out as the perfectly routine and understandable consequence of being driven to desperation by his wife's flirting with another man, or they may be formulated as an irrational over-reaction to commonplace pub sociability by a husband who is endemically and pathologically jealous.

8

Criticizing Facts

So where are we now? So far I have focused on some of the principal ways in which descriptions are established as neutral, factual and independent of the speaker. I have considered how they are hiked up the hierarchy of modalization and pushed back down again. I have also studied some of the tasks done by factual discourse and the way specific discourse constructions contribute to their achievement. In this final chapter I will try to tease out some of the implications of the arguments and analyses presented above.

To start with I will return to consider the implications of this work for how we should understand the nature of descriptions and, more broadly, for the theoretical perspective of constructionism. After that I will focus on social research. Descriptions enter into social research at a variety of levels. There are the interactions on which most research is based, the theoretical descriptions of activities and structures that social researchers offer, and there is the language of academic writing and speaking itself. Description has rarely been problematized in social science, nor have the consequences of doing so been often addressed. The book will end by considering the important issue of criticism. In what sense do the analyses and perspective developed here give grounds for criticizing facts? Can such analyses be coherently linked to a political programme, for example, or is the notion of constructionist social critique incoherent?

Facts, Speech Acts and Constructionism

Speech Acts and Descriptions

One way of explicating the nature of the perspective on facts and descriptions developed in this book is in its relation to the speech act theory of the philosopher John Austin. As we saw in the Introduction, in *How to Do Things with Words*, Austin introduced a distinction between two sorts of utterances (Austin, 1962). On the one hand, there are utterances which *state* things – 'the cat is on the mat', 'Jimmy is extremely jealous' – and, on the other, there are utterances which *do* things – 'shut the door', 'would you send thuh police to eleven six oh Arvin Avenue North'. According to Austin we can distinguish these types of utterance by considering the way they go wrong. The first kind of utterance can get into difficulty in terms of its truth or falsity: the cat might be nowhere near the mat; Jimmy might be caring and open-minded rather than extremely jealous. In contrast, utterances of the second kind are not assessed for their truth. 'Shut the door' is neither true or false; yet it can 'misfire', as Austin called it, in other ways. Imagine how odd 'shut the door' would be when said by the patient to the surgeon just prior to an operation; we might wonder about hallucinations or anaesthetic failure, but not about whether the utterance is true. Or imagine 'would you send thuh police to eleven six oh Arvin Avenue North' as part of a hoax call to the police; the issue at stake would be sincerity, not accuracy.

Now Austin's aim in introducing this distinction was to combat approaches which treated language as an abstract system of representation. Having established a beachhead with the notion that *certain* utterances perform actions, he went on to suggest that performing actions is actually a *general* feature of utterances. In effect, what he did was drag philosophers' attention from the nouns in language and assert the equal importance of the verbs. No longer should philosophers exclusively concentrate on the relation between 'cat' the noun and the actual furry pussy that drinks milk; instead they should consider what makes an utterance such as 'I promise' a proper action (cf. Searle, 1969).

Austin produced a 'test' for whether an utterance is a 'performative' speech act or not, which requires it to be translated into the first-person singular present indicative form. Utterances that can be translated into this form are speech acts. Thus saying 'shut the door' becomes a shorthand way of saying 'I hereby request you to shut the door'. What is interesting to us is how Austin deals with descriptions, utterances that state things. For he noted that, far from being a contrast category to speech acts, statements can easily pass the speech act test. For example, 'the cat is on the mat' can be translated into the speech act form: 'I hereby state that the cat is on the mat', where the action done is that of stating. This argument served as a powerful critique of the then dominant approaches to language that treated it as an abstract system. Stating is made an element in human affairs.

This is a good start point. The problem is that, having focused attention on the practical role of language, Austin was satisfied to treat the action done by descriptions as one of stating. This is relatively persuasive in the case of made up examples such as 'the cat is on the mat', which are required to do nothing much more than illustrate philosophical arguments. When we take actual examples, however, the paraphrase into speech act form is not so straightforward. The status of 'Jimmy is extremely jealous' as a statement may be precisely what is at stake in a dispute; 'I'm not complaining, I'm just stating' is a commonplace attempt to manage the issue. For the participants in an interaction, then, whether some utterance is actually (merely, just) a statement, rather than a complaint, a compliment, a flirt or whatever, is not a question of its grammatical form. As we saw with the Jimmy and Connie dispute, parties treat each other as performing a range of complex actions through utterances that have the grammatical form of descriptions. The notion of a simple translation test may make sense in the domain of philosophy where the target is an even more abstract theory of language, but it is patently inadequate in the contested realm of situated human descriptive practices.

The point, then, is not that Austin was wrong to argue that making a statement is a form of activity, it is that working from invented examples of
individual utterances taken out of context, and considering the paraphrase
test to be something that could be performed by an uninvolved analyst,
misses precisely what is crucial in actual interaction. As I have been trying to
illustrate with a wide range of different examples, and drawing on a number
of different research traditions, descriptions are *established* as mere descriptions by the use of a range of procedures, which in turn may be *undermined* as
descriptions are made out as partial, interested, strategic or whatever. There
is an epistemological orientation to descriptions, and this can become the
focus of research. As it becomes such a focus, the distinction between issues
of truth and issues of practice becomes much more problematic. It is not just,
as Austin has it, that stating is an action; stating can do a *range* of actions,
and bringing off an utterance as factual is *itself* an activity.

Some of the actions performed by descriptions can easily be characterized
using 'speech act' verbs such as *inviting, blaming, complimenting* (as well as
more obscure examples discussed by Austin). However, many actions done
via descriptions are not easily specified using a single verb. For example,
there is no readily available verb in English for characterizing the complex
business done by Connie and Jimmy's Counsellor when he says 'you've got
(0.5) rich an:d (.) complicated lives' (see pages 178–80); although it is possible to imagine a form of life where such an action was commonplace and
explicit enough to acquire its own term. It is for this reason that I have followed the conversation analytic lead and written of the *action orientation* of
descriptions. Descriptions are bound up with people's practices, and the verbs
in a language are one important resource for characterizing those practices,
but there is no necessary correspondence between them.

This focus on descriptions as parts of practices cuts across the word and
object picture that has been so central to the way facts and descriptions have
been construed in the twentieth century. The question whether the words
rich and *complicated* in the Counsellor's phrase are accurate or truthful is virtually the least interesting issue about them. It certainly is not the issue taken
up by the participants in the subsequent interaction. Or take *hacks* and *journalists* as competing category descriptions (see pages 133–4). They are
commonplace alternatives where the crucial issue for participants is unlikely
to be whether they are truthful but what is being done with them in a particular interaction.

Systematic Constructionism

There is a wide range of work across the social sciences that can be, or has
been, dubbed constructionist. Some of this work was reviewed in the first
three chapters of this book, and I do not want to spend time here attempting
to specify in what sense it is, or is not, constructionist, *let alone* in trying to
produce some definition of constructionism. Constructionism has meant different things in different disciplines, and has often been used as a blanket

term for a swathe of broadly 'radical' perspectives without too much attention being paid to the analytic and epistemological issue of what construction is and what is constructed (Potter, 1996b). However, one thing is striking about a wide range of constructionist research, good and bad, and that is how little it has taken the processes of construction *per se* as a research topic. Construction has more often been the presupposition of such work than the topic.

One of the central aims of this book has been to show what might be involved in focusing systematically on the procedures through which descriptions are constructed as factual. A first requirement I argued for is a symmetrical stance to descriptions which participants consider to be true and false. This should be supplemented by a recognition of the distinction between the action orientation and epistemological orientation of descriptions. In analytic and theoretical terms, the focus should be on discourse and rhetoric rather than cognition.

I have identified a range of themes in the study of fact construction on the basis of a review and development of the existing literatures in sociology of science, ethnomethodology and conversation analysis, post-structuralism and postmodernism. Some of these were developed with analytic examples in subsequent chapters.

One major theme is the way in which the credibility of the producer of the description is built up or undermined by constructing a category entitlement and through invoking stake and interest. In effect, this theme concerns the fundamental participants' issues of how the producer knows and what motivates their descriptions.

A second major theme is the way speakers and writers manage issues of accountability when they produce descriptions as quotations, positions, ideas or their own personal views. This is the business of footing. Although footing is bound up with all kinds of practices, it is particularly important when the focus is on the epistemological orientation of descriptions.

A third major theme is the way descriptions are produced as external and independent of the speaker or writer. Various techniques for doing this include empiricist discourse, consensus and corroboration, narrative constructions of various kinds, and manipulations of levels of detail and vagueness.

These themes by no means exhaust the means for stabilizing and reifying versions, but they are nevertheless pervasive and recurrent. They are intended as a start point for a systematic examination of the way descriptions are turned into facts and how versions of the world are stabilized and reified as just how things are. They can be considered as a set of concerns attended to when producing and undermining factual descriptions.

Fact construction and stabilization are not abstract concerns focused on truth and falsity but are bound up with, and inseparable from, practices of all sorts. Descriptive categories formulate the world in specific ways which are relevant to, and usable in, current activities. Describing and formulating are implicated in activities in many different ways. I discussed examples where formulations could display neutrality ('rich and complicated'), obscure agency ('the killing') or promote it ('Pope Fouls up Bar Mitzvah'), and how a categorization that is actually used can draw attention away from rhetorically relevant alternative categorizations ('there was an episo:de, with (.) a bloke, (.) in a pub'). Descriptions can be built to make something extreme or large or, in contrast, to make it small or minimize it; likewise descriptions can be used to display an action as normal or routine, or to display it as abnormal or problematic. For instance, a description of violence can be built to emphasize its severity and badness, or can soften it to make it excusable or even playful. A description of swimming at the beach can treat it as expected and unproblematic, the kind of routine thing which is done in that setting; but it can also present it as obsessional and bizarre.

It is undoubtedly the case that these themes and distinctions have limitations, and work at different levels of generality. For example, while categorization is an inescapable feature of descriptive discourse, invoking consensus and corroboration is only one of a range of rhetorical possibilities. I have been struck repeatedly by both the subtlety and pervasiveness of the epistemological orientation of people's descriptive practices, and by its implications for a range of different research areas. Although I have picked out a particular set of themes to concentrate on, part of the aim is simply to show that this is an important issue which researchers with a variety of different interests might find beneficial to consider. My hope is that these themes will provide an analytic start point and stimulus for researchers to take the topic of descriptions further, and to see its implications in a range of settings where it was not previously noted. The general conclusion, therefore, is that constructionist social science would benefit from taking seriously the issue of construction. Rather than treat construction as a taken-for-granted start point, it should consider construction and deconstruction as a central and researchable feature of human affairs.

Social Science and Fact Construction

Social science draws on descriptive and factual discourse in a range of ways. For convenience a distinction can be made among three spheres of descriptive discourse in social science. There are descriptions involved in the interactions that take place during research; there is specific descriptive language of social science (most directly, terms such as *role*, *personality*, and *family*); and finally there is the general discourse of science writing: reports, articles, books (such as this one). I will concentrate on the first two spheres here and defer most discussion of the general nature of social science writing until later, where it will be considered as part of a broader discussion of fact construction and criticism.

The first sphere of social research discourse is generated at the point where materials ('data') are generated. Social research commonly requires participants to provide descriptions, whether in responding to questionnaires, tests and polls, filling in of experimental protocols or talking to interviewers and ethnographers. In turn, social researchers themselves produce a wide variety of descriptions when eliciting the discourse of questionnaire items, experimental instructions, and in the sorts of conversational interactions that take place in ethnography and open-ended interviewing.

This raises the issue, then, of what consequences there are for social science research for considering descriptions as active constructions orientated to action. I will concentrate on two contrasting examples to illustrate how our understanding might be changed by taking this perspective: public opinion polling and social representations.

Descriptions in the Research Process: Public Opinion Polling

Public opinion research is one of the most heavily funded areas of modern social science. Vast sums are spent on collecting people's views on presidents, products and political changes. Descriptions in poll questions are typically treated as straightforward stand-ins for some bit of reality. You cannot set the National Health Service before someone to ask their opinion of it, but including the words *National Health Service* in a poll question is considered to be just as good. The opinions themselves are treated as mental entities which have a sense independent of any particular context of expression; any fluctuation in opinion is treated as a consequence of one of a range of social influence processes. Work from a discourse and rhetorical perspective has criticized this picture for some time now (Billig, 1987, 1991; Potter and Wetherell, 1987, 1988). The argument developed here further refines this critique. In particular, it highlights the issue of how the descriptions in opinion poll questions construct versions that are potentially aligned with activities of, say, criticism or compliment.

The issue of 'question wording' traditionally focused on how far the poll question was neutral or biased; was its formulation colourless, or did it nudge people in a particular direction? The problem is that constructing the problem in this way presupposes that there is a neutral, factual form of description which captures reality in contrast to a distorting form that biases it. Even sophisticated critics of public opinion work have drawn on this simple notion of biased and unbiased questions, as the following example illustrates.

> Psychologists have written extensively on the elimination of bias from questionnaires. But one poll asked, 'Do you believe that British troops should be withdrawn from Northern Ireland even if, as seems likely in the opinion of many people, it led to civil war?' (*Daily Telegraph*, 13.2.72) This question, asked in the Irish Republic, obtained 45 per cent agreement. The unbiased question, 'Should British troops be withdrawn from Northern Ireland?' has consistently obtained over 50 per cent agreement when asked in the UK mainland, suggesting that the biased wording had some considerable effect. (Roiser, 1983: 159)

There is a simple sense in which the first question Roiser quotes includes a threat of dire consequences which the second one does not. However, to claim, as Roiser does, that the first question is biased compared to the other

is not merely to make a judgement about the question, it is to make a judgement about the world. The claim trades on being able to identify a disparity
between the words and the world. Let us see how far we can eat away at this
simple notion of bias. The first question treats the withdrawal of troops as
something distinct from any violence that is occasioned by that withdrawal.
If violence is the probable consequence, then, it could be argued, the second
question is doing a lot of implicit business by separating it from withdrawal.

Here is another issue. The first question presents withdrawal in a concrete
scenario; it places the issue in a practical context of events and consequences.
In the second question, withdrawal can be understood more abstractly. One
of the features noted by a range of analyses of argumentation is the way
people's discourse is organized around dilemmas over practice and principle
(Billig et al., 1988; Wetherell and Potter, 1992; Wetherell et al., 1987). People
can make strong statements about what should or ought to be the case in
principle, while still accepting that this is unrealistic in practice. In this case,
it is not hard to imagine someone arguing that British troops *should not* be in
Northern Ireland, but accepting that they *have to be* there because in their
view the alternative is the awful reality of sectarian conflict. Looked at in this
way, the second question allows the answerer the easy option of displaying
principles, while the first foregrounds what might be seen as the complicated
and painful practicality of putting those principles into practice.

Now, I do not want to go to the other extreme of suggesting that these
questions are equally good, or invert Roiser's claim to say that the second is
biased and the first is not. The point is that *both* of them are constructions of
events, and those constructions are related to broader judgements, and are
likely to be used in a range of different ways in argumentative settings. The
questions should be evaluated in terms of the versions of the world they construct and the practices of which they are part.

Let us follow up this idea more thoroughly with a second example. One
thing that troubles public opinion pollsters is variability between the findings
of different polls using different questions. They typically treat such variation
as irritating and anomalous, to be eliminated, if at all possible – certainly not
something interesting in its own right. The example I am using here is particularly dramatic, and will allow us to explore some of the ways in which the
descriptions involved in the questions work to generate different outcomes.
The following two opinion questions were asked in the space of a month by
the poll organization EMNID in the then Federal Republic of Germany
(FRG). They are both related to the highly controversial deployment of
Pershing and Cruise nuclear missiles in Europe in the early 1980s.

It is perhaps dangerous to speculate *post hoc* about what generated the difference between 58 per cent in favour of deployment in the one poll and only
16 per cent in the other. But let us take the plunge anyway. I will start from
the assumption that these different outcomes are related to the way the issue
is constructed in the question. What might it be about the different descriptions of choices and circumstances that led to these different outcomes?
Here I am not concerned with the epistemological orientation of these

Question One

Here is a list of statements. For each one, please tell me whether you tend to agree or disagree with it.

The West must remain sufficiently strong with regard to the Soviet Union. It is, therefore, necessary to deploy modern nuclear weapons in Western Europe if the Soviet Union does not dismantle its new intermediate-range weapons.
(Favour = agree; Oppose = disagree)

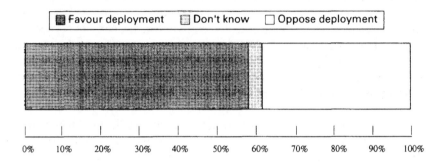

Question Two

In the event that the negotiations between the United States and the Soviet Union should not bring any results, new missiles are then supposed to be deployed; here in the Federal Republic as well. Are you in favour or opposed to the deployment of new missiles? What if you had to make a choice?
(Favour = deployment of new missiles; Oppose = oppose)

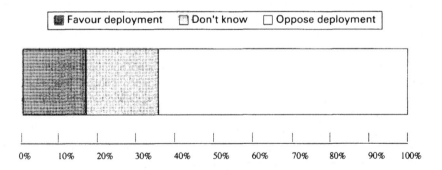

Source: Opinion Roundup (1984) Question Wording Makes a Difference: German Public Attitudes to Deployment, *Public Opinion* (December/January), 38–9.
Note: the translation here was in the original *Opinion Roundup* article.

Figure 8.1 *Variable answers to opinion poll questions*

descriptions, but with their action orientation; what are they doing? There is a range of contrasts between the two questions that are potentially relevant to increasing support for deployment in the first question and decreasing it in the second. I will concentrate on just three to illustrate the kinds of consideration that the arguments of this book highlight.

The first, and probably most important, contrast is between descriptions of where the missiles will be sited. In the first question the site is '*Western Europe*', in the second it is '*here in the Federal Republic*'. What this means is that the second question is asking not just for abstract support for siting missiles but for siting them in the respondent's own country, locally ('*here*'). 'Here' at this time was also the potential front line in any conflict between the west and the Soviet Union. Again, this shows the importance of the way participants rhetorically construct issues of principle and practice. Approving of something in principle (universal nursery education) can be treated as quite different from accepting the practicalities of achieving the outcome (higher taxes).

The second thing to note is that the actors in the conflict are formulated in very different ways. In the first question they are the '*West*' and the '*Soviet Union*'. One of the features of using this inclusive category description is that it implies membership of the persons responding to the poll; it is painted as 'our' conflict, something that 'we' are potentially involved in and have some responsibility for. In the second question, the actors are the '*United States*' and the '*Soviet Union*'. Not only is the United States not 'us', it is a nation which might well invoke ambivalent feelings for respondents in the FRG.

The third difference is in the descriptions of the weapons. In question one the west should deploy '*modern nuclear weapons*'. The description '*modern*' is potentially effective in two ways. On the one hand, in political discourse modern is often simply a good thing which should be supported (for example, Wetherell and Potter, 1992: ch. 7). On the other, '*modern*' is often a contrast term to old-fashioned and outdated; so the implication is that these new weapons are there to replace outdated ones. In contrast to this, Soviet nuclear weapons are described as '*new*', which suggests additional weapons rather than merely the replacement of old-fashioned ones. Deploying nuclear weapons can in this way be justified as a way of both keeping up to date and matching Soviet deployment. In question two, however, it is the US weapons that are constructed as the '*new missiles*' (a phrase repeated twice) while no mention is made of Soviet deployment. Deploying nuclear weapons here is not something obviously required by Soviet actions.

This discussion only starts to get at the complex differences between the descriptive language of these two questions. Nevertheless, it throws up some of the kinds of fact constructional considerations that arise even when we have rather simple opinion statements for respondents to express agreement and disagreement with. It is important to emphasize that I am not claiming that opinion researchers are unaware of these issues; indeed, they spend considerable effort worrying about them. And it is likely that when formulating questions researchers draw heavily on considerations of this kind, albeit in a less explicit way than I have done here. The point is that they are treated as question wording effects; that is, as something to do with the biasing effects of language, as if some more careful linguistic selection could produce a neutral and unbiased outcome. What is missing is a thoroughgoing constructionist perspective which will treat these phenomena as an endemic feature of the way descriptions are bound up with action and evaluation.

There is a research corollary to this. My discussion of these opinion items drew heavily on my own linguistic and cultural intuitions about, for example, the particular sense that the words *new* and *modern* – or more precisely their German equivalents – would have had for people living in the FRG late in the Cold War. However, these terms come to be understood with these senses when used in particular discursive contexts, by writers in the political columns of newspapers, say, or between friends in supermarket check-out queues. A better, more analytically nuanced understanding of the systematic role of these constructions will be gained through researching the way people construct their social worlds in these settings, in the way that Michael Billig (1992) has done with talk about the Royal Family, and Margaret Wetherell and I (1992) did with discourse about 'race' and politics. Perhaps it is unlikely that opinion poll organizations will be keen to sponsor research of this kind which undermines some common poll assumptions. However, it may be that in the future a new style of polling might actually benefit from abandoning the assumption that the world is populated by objects and policies which are neutrally describable, and that people carry around with them opinions of these things independent of the occasion of expression and separable from more general political, factual and moral arguments. While at first sight the study of descriptions and opinions might seem quite separate, my conclusion is that the study of descriptions has important implications for the study of opinions.

Descriptions in the Research Process: Social Representations

The second example comes from a very different research tradition. Serge Moscovici's (1984) social representations theory is a sophisticated constructionist approach which is focused on the psychological role of people's shared representations of the world. Despite placing more emphasis on representation than virtually any other approach in the social sciences, the theory does not deal with representation as a practice; that is, it deals neither with how representations are *built* and made factual nor with what is being *done* with representations (see McKinlay et al., 1993). Instead, its overwhelming focus has been on the role of social representations in helping people to perceive their world as safe and orderly, and in promoting communication between people. Work on social representations has utilized a range of quantitative and qualitative research techniques. Here I want to concentrate on a well-known example of work done using qualitative analysis of open-ended interviews. Again, my aim is to show how issues of fact construction come to the fore when we carefully examine such materials and the inferences that social scientists have made from them.

In her study of 'madness' and social representations, Denise Jodelet (1991) was interested in the representations of mental patients in a pioneer community care scheme in the French town of Ainay-le-Château, and particularly in how specific representations were used to classify the patients, to make their actions intelligible, and to manage feelings of fear or anxiety that they might provoke in others. Jodelet's book is dense and complex, and contains a mass of interpretation of open-ended interviews. I have chosen to focus on just one extract, which is the first in the book from which Jodelet draws substantive conclusions about social representations. She uses it as an example of the way that local people cannot fully rid themselves of consciousness of 'the silent and close menace of insanity'. Here is Jodelet quoting from one of the local people:

> I get the impression some people are going to raise objections because they're afraid. Because you do see it, you know! I always wait for my little girl when she leaves school, in a square with a bus stop. I wait there along with lots of other mothers, in the car. Some of them come up to talk to you, to joke with you because you're a woman. All the same, I don't think some of them are very good for the community. Some of them you don't notice, but there are others . . . There's one of them, on the road up towards Saint-Mamet, one of them who I don't like one little bit. If I went out by bike I know I would meet him. Perhaps he's quite harmless. I don't know. It's just the way he looks. He makes an impression on me. He walks a bit like a dancer, and he's got a black face, and his eyes . . . he stares at you. It's really dreadful and it scares me. There's something about him which frightens me. His face is . . . I don't know how to describe it but it worries me. His eyes stare at you. He stares at you when he looks at you. That's all. I can't describe the effect it has on me. It upsets me. (1991: 54)

Jodelet goes on to provide the following analysis of the quote and what it reveals:

> In the face of this multiform, incessant presence of insanity a subtle knowledge evolves, one which makes it possible to stifle the onset of this obscure apprehension, transformed into the terse *leitmotif* 'he frightens you', and which sometimes overwhelms its victim with a specific illness: the 'attack of fright'. Seen from this viewpoint, the smoothing away of emotional reasons seems to result from a collective technique of maintaining a calm, harmonious social façade. (1991: 54–5)

As her analytic comments indicate, Jodelet is not concerned with what is being *done* in this extract, she is not considering it as a description organized to perform particular activities. Instead, her stress is on how the participant's anxieties are controlled by the use of a particular representation of madness. There are a number of obstacles to developing an alternative to Jodelet's account which is attentive to the fact construction that is going on. She does not provide information about the sequence that the extract is embedded in; notably, what the interviewer said just prior to this extract can only be guessed at. Moreover, it is a cleaned-up transcript which has transformed the participant's talk into the sorts of orderly sentences that are characteristic of playscript. It is also a translation, which might miss idiomatic nuances that were significant in the original French (Jodelet worked with the French, of course). Nevertheless, even with the materials as they stand it is possible to start to develop an alternative.

From what is said at the start of the extract, the issue at stake seems to be people's actual or potential objections to the community care scheme. This is the kind of sensitive topic where a speaker may be concerned to avoid sounding prejudiced against a minority group, in this case 'mentally ill people'. Note, then, that although the speaker does not align herself directly with the people who may raise objections to the care scheme, she spends some time elaborating the kind of reason ('fear') that could be used as a basis for raising objections. This interpretation is at odds with Jodelet's. For her fear is something that shows through the extract; indeed, it is mainly *stifled* or *smoothed away* to lie below the surface, while I am suggesting that fear is being *highlighted* precisely because it makes accountable a reaction that may otherwise be heard as prejudiced.

Other features of the passage fit with this interpretation. Note that immediately after introducing the issue of fear, the speaker 'script formulates' a picture of regular joking conversations with some 'mental patients' which occur while waiting for her daughter to come out of school. Note the modal 'always' and the present tense, both of which work up the routine nature of what is described. This is a neat way of showing that the speaker does not have a *general* prejudice against mentally ill people; rather, she is scared by some of them who look and act in frightening ways, but is happy to share a joke with others. And note how carefully this judgement is managed. She displays her rationality by indicating that she could be wrong ('perhaps he's quite harmless') and, perhaps, her disinterested status ('I don't know' – cf. pages 131–2 above). It is not a fear based on blind prejudice; she presents herself as an open-minded women who encounters some disturbing people (cf. Wetherell and Potter, 1992: ch. 8). So what Jodelet treats as the disturbingly 'multiform' expression of mental illness can be seen as a particularization into different kinds of patient to display her non-prejudice. She jokes with some and is scared by others – she does not have a general (prejudiced) response.

I am not suggesting that Jodelet's claims about what is going on are simply mistaken. She presents a rich and thoughtful account which works with a variety of materials in addition to interviews. What I am arguing is that attention to the fact constructional and action orientated nature of talk raised major problems with at least some of her interpretations, and at the same time it throws interesting light on some of the things that might be going on in those materials. More generally, I want to use it as an illustration of how fact construction is not merely a supplementary issue that social researchers can attend to if they wish; fact construction is inseparable from the activity that is being done in talk and texts. As such, attention to fact construction is an essential part of any high-quality analysis. Note also that, although I have chosen to focus on opinion polls and open-ended interviews, I could equally have taken examples from questionnaire research (Cicourel, 1974) or ethnography

(Atkinson, 1990; Clifford and Marcus, 1986) or some other social science field.

The Descriptive Language of Social Science

Each of the three traditions discussed in the starting chapters of this book has thrown up arguments that are consequential for the way the descriptive language of social science is conceptualized. In the sociology of scientific knowledge (SSK) there is the argument concerning *vassalage*. Michael Mulkay (1981) argued from a discourse analytic perspective that as social researchers construct definitive versions of scientists' actions and beliefs from their talk and texts they may enter a relationship of vassalage where the analyst's 'technical' description is implicitly furthering the business done by the participant's everyday description. In ethnomethodology concern focused on the way social researchers drew in unexplicated ways on everyday notions as resources in their analysis rather than taking them as a topic of research in their own right (Zimmerman and Pollner, 1971). And in post-structuralist thinking, and particularly work inspired by Michel Foucault, there has been a sustained concern with the way social research constitutes the very thing it is studying in its varying practices of surveillance, counting and classification.

In this section I want to illustrate briefly the consequences of this set of issues using some of the analytic studies which have focused on various key social science notions. These are all studies which take notions that have become established parts of the technical terminology of social science – motive, role and so on – and it considers their practical use in everyday or institutional settings. The point here is both simple, and one that has been made before – although its implications have been rarely taken seriously. It is that the descriptive language of social science provides a set of constructions of the social world that can be, and are, orientated to action. Put another way, if these notions have been locally developed to constitute particular objects and generate particular effects, social science work which ignores this constitution and these effects may end up with flaws and confusions. Whole areas of work may have drifted unnoticed into a relation of vassalage to the projects of groups of participants.

Dorothy Smith formulates this point succinctly:

> a major methodological problem for social science is its practice of making use of the language of naturally occurring social processes by extracting terms from their contexts of use and incorporating them into the social scientific discourse as theoretical concepts or categories identifying features of the social world. . . . In this process they enter into the theoretical relations of the discourse, becoming the objects and instruments of theorizing. In so doing, their connection, their meaning and usage in the social relations in which they originate is attenuated and occluded. The major methodological problem has become a motive to the construction of a methodological edifice concerned with finding the phenomena in the actuality of which we think we speak. (1983: 309–10)

Now, I do not take this argument to prove that such terms *cannot* be usefully descriptive. To do so would be to make a powerful assumption about what is factual and what is not, and would be a major departure from the symmetry principle. Instead, the argument here is for the virtue of studying, first, the way the terminology of social science is used in a range of non-technical contexts, and, second, going on to consider the implications for the use of that terminology in technical settings.

There are a wide range of revealing studies which show the ways the descriptive terminology and concepts of social science are drawn on in everyday and institutional settings, although they are not all characterized in this way. These are studies that take social science categories as a research topic rather than assuming it as an unproblematic resource. That is, instead of using the notion of role, say, to understand and explain people's behaviour, the way people *themselves* use the notion becomes the research topic. Here I want to review them briefly with the aim of showing their broad scope. They cover a rough continuum from intrapsychic objects and processes that are the common topic of psychology, descriptions of persons and their actions, small collectivities, general social processes that shade into sociology and finally to the collectivities that are the topic of political science and studies of international relations. I will take them in this order.

Motives   Some of the studies of 'inner' psychological notions in practice are particularly interesting because of their epistemological role. We have already explored the way the notion of motivation can be drawn on for discounting in Chapter 5, where we looked at the management of interest in producing versions as neutral, factual and disinterested, or building them up as biased or distorted. The psychological language of motives is a resource for constructing a wide range of stories about interest. Producing the appropriate versions of motives is an important way of producing a description as factual. For example, Dr Post's findings about madness stimulating creativity were established as objective, in part, through the explicit claim that his motive in doing the research was to find precisely the reverse ('Dr Post was initially sceptical'). In a rather more complex example, Derek Edwards and I (1992, ch. 6) studied the descriptions used by a British cabinet minister to present his motive for resignation as appropriate and virtuous. Finally, a range of studies of murder interrogation have shown the way particular descriptions of the crime and circumstances by the suspect were constructed to suggest less culpable motives; provoked anger rather than greed, say (Watson, 1983; Watson and Weinberg, 1982; Wowk, 1984). The simple point here is that the language of motives is closely bound up with constituting acts in particular ways and building and undermining the legitimacy of actions. Social scientists bypass this to build their own colourless, unmotivated motive stories at their peril. As the sociologist C. Wright Mills famously argued, 'the different reasons that men give for their actions are not themselves without reasons' (1940: 904).

This discussion of motive also illustrates a more general point. In people's interaction there is a circular relationship between versions of the world and versions of inner life. Participants give descriptions which construct their motivations as appropriate to build up their factual versions, and they provide factual descriptions of some pattern of events in the world which can warrant the existence of a particular motive. The point, then, is that the processes of building factual versions of the world and the mind are bound up together (Potter et al., 1993). There is a complex, and largely undocumented, interplay between cognitive construction and fact construction. This is explored in more detail in Edwards (1996: ch. 2).

Memory   The notion of memory also has an important epistemological role. Rather than see memories as mental objects which can be tested for their accuracy by psychologists, remembering can be seen as a set of social practices related to a range of actions and providing particular kinds of accountability (Middleton and Edwards, 1990). At its simplest, remembering can be a charged and highly contested issue in contexts as varied as court cases and relationship disputes. Not remembering can be a powerful device for managing delicate or incriminating issues, or accounting for the withholding of some description or knowledge (Goodwin, 1987). One of the most elaborate studies of this is reported in Michael Lynch and David Bogen's (1996) book on Oliver North's testimony, where they document a range of ways in which North uses disavowals of recall to manage accusations.

Role and Personality   The notions of role and personality appear as rhetorical opposites in a variety of everyday settings. A person's actions can be a natural consequence of their nature as a person, their personality, or they can be determined more institutionally by their job or lifestyle. For example, the dilemma is played out with the minister's resignation; is it a consequence of some fundamental *personality* clash with a political adviser or is it the legitimate and principled action of someone following the requirements of their job (*role*)? The discourse of role and personality can be used to construct events in ways that justify or undermine (Edwards and Potter, 1992). Margaret Wetherell and I (1989) illustrated something similar to this when studying the way police actions, elsewhere described as brutal and unprovoked, could be mitigated using *personality* descriptions (they were 'only human' in their violent actions) or role descriptions (they were 'doing the job' required of them by superiors; cf. Halkowski, 1990; Mehan, 1986).

Social Influence   The sorts of descriptions of social influence processes that figure in social scientists' accounts can also be studied in their non-technical settings for what they may be used to do. For example, Peter Stringer considered the well-known social psychological analysis of 'groupthink', which is the idea that a constellation of different psychological processes can come together in pressured decision-making groups with irrational and potentially disastrous consequence (Potter et al., 1984). This notion was developed in a set of studies of American international fiascos such as the abortive 'Bay of Pigs' CIA-sponsored invasion of Cuba in the early 1960s. Stringer argued that groupthink is not an abstract, neutral description of what went on. Rather, it is a piece of technical jargon built from the descriptions of various parties involved in the fiasco which attempt to mitigate both their own actions and those of President Kennedy. Groupthink is perfect for this because it is a general process not initiated by any of the parties involved; it is the social psychological equivalent of a tornado: nasty, destructive, but really no one's fault.

Wetherell and Potter (1992) provide another example in our study of the way two of the principal accounts of social influence ('normative' influence, and 'informational' influence) are deployed in people's everyday accounts of social conflict. Rather than seeing these technical accounts as acting entirely separately from what happens outside the world of textbooks and journal articles, the technical and everyday blend into each other. In interview talk about political disturbances, the normative account – which is not distilled into a single word, but represented in a constellation of terms or tropes – was used to undermine actions as influenced by a range of irrational factors, while the informational one – likewise not a single word – could make those actions rational, considered and legitimate. In fact, the interviewees in this study painted complex scenarios of influence which were populated by a florid thesaurus of social groups: stirrers, hysterical extremists, the susceptible masses. Social science ideas and terminology provided a wide range of resources for constructing versions of their world – but not versions with a merely abstract goal of representing, but versions which engage with that world, evaluate it, support some changes and undermine others.

Social Categories   The various categories used by social scientists for social collectivities are a hugely fertile area for studying the performative use of descriptions. On the small scale, the notions of 'family' and 'community' have received particular attention for the kinds of rhetorical work they can do in simultaneously constituting and legitimating some actions and social arrangements (Gubrium and Holstein, 1990; Holstein and Gubrium, 1994; Potter and Halliday, 1990; Mulkay, 1994). For example, characterizing a riot/disturbance as a 'community relations' problem can be part of a version of events consonant with promoting interpersonal policies to deal with its causes, such as increased sensitivity and 'community policing'; while characterizing it as a 'conflict between the community and the police' paves the way for a more structural critique of police racism and structural unemployment (Potter and Reicher, 1987).

It is important to emphasize that notions such as these do not have a static and consensual meaning. For example, 'family' tends to be used as an unproblematically good thing in contemporary political debate in the United Kingdom. Politicians claim to espouse policies which support 'family life' while accusing opposing parties of undermining 'the family'. Yet, in their speeches, politicians rebuild the notion of 'family' in accordance with current versions of party ideology (Gill et al., 1995).

On a larger scale, the language of 'regions', 'countries' and 'nation states' has been a particular focus of critical study (Anderson, 1993; Billig, 1995;

Shapiro, 1988; Todorov, 1985). Michael Shapiro notes that the region known as 'Southeast Asia' is not a natural consequence of the physical organization of landmasses. A historical study of mapping reveals that the region was constituted in this way as map makers followed Allied military movements during the Second World War: the way the map encloses territory is not a natural fact of spatial organization (if such a thing were conceivable) but a consequence of unfolding military strategy. As Shapiro puts it:

> this representational practice is so familiar it seems natural (i.e., not a practice), but this representation of bounded areas partakes of a venerable rhetorical gesture: the map is a spatial trope which, far from simply representing (natural) boundaries, is an aggressive practice, delivering up the discursive territory within which legitimate speech about bounded areas can occur. (1988: 93)

Moreover the 'nation state' has been the largely taken-for-granted currency of the discipline of 'International Relations'; yet the nation state is a relatively recent entity in historical terms, and one which foregrounds certain features of modern politics (national economics, citizenship), but sidelines others (multinational economics, gender politics).

The point, then, is that the factual discourse of social science is also a performative discourse; it is everywhere involved in versions which relate to evaluation and action. The danger is that the technical versions may unwittingly support the world view of certain groups of participants and obscure the views of others. And it is also rhetorical discourse in Michael Billig's (1987) sense. Each time one of these descriptive categories is drawn on it not only engages a particular form of understanding, constituting the world in a particular way, it also counters opposing descriptions and forms of understanding.

What is the implication of this rather breathless jog through studies of social science and everyday practice? The conclusion is not that social science as an enterprise is untenable because its descriptive categories are bound up in a range of practices across different social settings – although Schegloff (1988b) comes close to that conclusion; rather, it is that work of this kind should encourage social researchers to attend to two things. First, they should consider the theoretical baggage, loosely speaking, that commonly taken-for-granted social science descriptive categories may carry with them. Second, they should attend to the complex two-way relations between these theoretical categories and the kinds of everyday practices of fact construction, evaluation and outcome that take place elsewhere. These studies highlight the potential for social science vassalage and sketch out the sorts of social objects that are constituted by social science. Their challenge is to follow through the consequences of this performative conception of social science categories in research practice.

Criticizing Facts

To end this book, I want to consider the implications of the arguments I have been developing for criticizing facts. The concern is with the broader implications and issues raised by the arguments in this book, and the various literatures and projects on fact construction which it reviews. Can it, and should it, be a help, say, to the examining barrister in a fraud trial? Would Connie and Jimmy's Counsellor have benefited from a more theorized understanding of the way descriptions are related to actions prior to his sessions? Does it have more general implications for arguments about the objectivity of the media or the status of everyday knowledge? Can this kind of examination of fact construction be linked to more general traditions of ideological critique? These are big and complex questions, and definitive answers are neither possible nor desirable – however, their very importance makes them worth considering.

As a way of building up to these issues I will take as a start point two strong positions which take contrasting stances on the role of facts and criticism. In the blue corner sit Graham Button and Wes Sharrock (1993) with their anti-constructionism inspired by ethnomethodology and linguistic philosophy; while in the red corner sit fighters on behalf of Critical Discourse Analysis such as Robert Hodge and Gunther Kress (1993), Norman Fairclough (1992, 1993) and Roger Fowler (1991). Put simply, the blue position is that any generalized fact criticism is incoherent because it is not possible to transcend the agreed ways of establishing objectivity that are embodied in human practices; in contrast, the red position takes descriptions in newspaper articles and other texts to be ideological in the sense that they construct a version that mystifies relations of power and obscures agency. The red position, therefore, is that criticism of factual versions is one of the most important roles of social scientists. Having raised some cautions about these two positions, I will explore a range of other ways in which fact criticism can be productively conceptualized.

Button and Sharrock's Anti-constructionist Anti-criticism

The ethnomethodologists Graham Button and Wes Sharrock's (1993) specific target was the constructionist sociologists of scientific knowledge whom we met in Chapter 1 (and particularly Harry Collins, Nigel Gilbert and Michael Mulkay, and Steve Woolgar). But their sophisticated arguments in defence of scientists' notions of objectivity and empirical testing pose a challenge for any constructionist approach to facts. Indeed, they threaten to show that constructionist reworking of the way facts are established is both misguided and irrelevant. For this reason they are worth spending a bit of time on, even if we have to struggle a bit with their complexities.

There are various steps to Button and Sharrock's argument. The first is to claim that constructionists have misconceived the nature of human practices. In particular, they are stuck with a version of cognitivism that has been shown to be flawed by Garfinkel and Wittgenstein. Constructionism is cognitivist in its treatment of social practices as a product of people's knowledge and beliefs: that is, their cognitions: '[cognitivists] think that action is grounded in knowledge and/or belief, [while] the proper Wittgensteinian and

Garfinkelian position is exactly the other way around: that activities come first, and that knowledge and agreement arise within the space the organisation of action opens up.' (1993: 3).

The problem with this cognitivism is that it fails to address the way representations are part of practices and comes to focus instead on the abstract relation between descriptions and the world. The only thing that distinguishes the new constructionists from the old-fashioned empiricists, according to Button and Sharrock, is the direction of causality. Empiricists saw representations as a product of objects, while constructionists see objects as produced by representations.

The second step in the argument is to specify what they see as the constructionist notion of objectivity. According to Button and Sharrock, where scientists treat objectivity as a consequence of the application of standardized methods and formal criteria for truth testing, for constructionists what scientists call objectivity is actually a consequence of *agreement* between different scientists produced by the deployment of rhetorical devices. The traditional picture of science's objectivity 'is deprecated by constructionist accounts to the effect that scientists' methods for establishing objective findings actually consist of *the employment of rhetorical techniques for persuading others to agree and rhetorical techniques for displaying consensus*' (Button and Sharrock, 1993: 5 – emphasis in original).

The third step is to note a distinction between two kinds of agreement. There is a (cognitivist) notion of consensus which involves agreement in their representations and beliefs, and there is also a more fundamental notion of consensus, inspired by Garfinkel and Wittgenstein, which considers consensus as agreement in actions. Agreement in this latter form of consensus is derived from shared practices such as running scientific experiments or judging the quality of different beers.

The fourth and final step is to suggest that constructionist research on science has shown an absence of consensus at the level of belief, but failed to show an absence of a more fundamental consensus in practices, and it is at this more fundamental level that scientific (and, presumably, everyday) notions of objectivity operate. Thus two scientists may disagree radically over the quality of a set of experimental findings, but they would endorse the use of the same sorts of practices to resolve their disagreement.

Problems with Button and Sharrock

There are problems at each of the steps in Button and Sharrock's argument. There is plenty to disagree with in their characterization of constructionism; for example, it is not clear to me that any of their central sociology of science targets – Collins, Gilbert and Mulkay, Woolgar – treat representations in the way that is claimed or fail to consider the practical nature of science; although there might well be scope for arguing about what is practical in this context. However, I will restrict myself to addressing Button and Sharrock's most important, and potentially damaging, point, that objectivity comes from fundamental agreement in practices and thus is not threatened by constructionist analyses.

Button and Sharrock illustrate agreement in practices using the example of beer tasting. They ask us to imagine two hypothetical drinkers visiting Manchester pubs and arguing over whether Boddingtons or Marstons is the better-tasting beer. They suggest that underlying this surface disagreement over taste is a more fundamental agreement on what counts as taste. The drinkers will agree, for example, on 'what is bitter, what is sweet' (1993: 16). A constructionist critique of objectivity will be harmless if it notes only the surface disagreement and fails to tackle the more fundamental agreement in practices.

The problem is that their argument about basic taste practices is not hard to challenge. I have in front of me an article from the wine column of today's paper. It reports a clash between two different camps of wine tasters in how they understand and describe tastes.

> The old-timers seek to convey the structure of a wine; the modernisers are more interested in specific flavours. So while the former camp will talk about 'breed', 'class', 'balance', 'harmony' and 'vigour', the latter favours peaches, cream, melons pencil shavings and, for good measure, the odd hamster cage. (*Observer Life*, 18 June 1995: 53)

Note that it is not just the descriptive terms that are at stake here, but the very taste framework used for evaluating wine ('flavours' versus 'structure'). Both groups, presumably, still swill wine around in their mouths and spit it out; but the basic categories they use to describe and evaluate the sensations are different. I do not know if arguments of this kind have broken out during the research for the *Good Beer Guide*, but it seems perfectly possible; certainly as plausible as Button and Sharrock's anecdotal bibulous trip round Boddingtons and Marstons pubs. Indeed, taste may be understood differently in different cultures (and perhaps there is no simple, natural category 'taste' which we can translate to show its different understanding).

My point, then, is that there are research questions which can be sensibly asked; it is not satisfactory to take taste agreement as a purely conceptual matter, let alone something given by common sense. The same argument can be applied to Button and Sharrock's defence of scientific objectivity. Although they do not discuss it, debate of precisely this kind was generated by Thomas Kuhn's theory of scientific progress (see Chapter 1, pages 23–4). Philosophers found Kuhn's account of progress wanting because his story of sciences developing through cycles of revolution and normal science seemed to provide no criteria to judge whether the science after the revolution was better than that before. The problem was that a Kuhnian revolution involved overthrowing not just the agreed findings in any particular scientific field but the very methods and standard forms of research. In Button and Sharrock's terms, it is not just the (cognitive) beliefs that change but a large part of the practices that underpin them. Changing this fundamental left it unclear what could provide a neutral arbiter of progress (cf. Lakatos and Musgrave, 1970).

Kuhn himself later came to fret about this problem, and he produced a modified account of scientific progress based around the existence of certain basic values that lay outside of any particular scientific field, and so could provide that crucial arbiter of progress (1977: ch. 13). He picked accuracy, consistency, simplicity, fruitfulness and scope as particularly important. If we follow Button and Sharrock's arguments we should see these values not as beliefs or descriptions but as formulations of the basic *practical* agreement that scientists express in their *activities*. It is this which is keeping science on the straight and narrow.

The problem with this account is this: how would we judge whether there is agreement in overarching values? It is a quite different thing to claim that these values are important from showing that they are actually impacting on scientific progress. It is no simple matter to check whether scientists' actions conform to these values. Consistency, say, is a technical matter which involves a range of scientific judgements. One approach is to study scientists' constructions of consistency; that is, to focus on what scientists themselves treat as consistent in a set of findings (Mulkay, 1991: ch. 10; Potter, 1984). This approach finds considerable variation in such descriptions. Button and Sharrock might object that such studies are considering representations rather than practices, but this would leave them in the anomalous situation of claiming consensus in notions of, say, consistency in the face of scientists' own disagreements. More fundamentally, the distinction between the representational and the practical breaks down once we start to focus on representations *as* parts of practices in the way I have been doing in this book.

Button and Sharrock's argument, then, starts to creak when it is moved from the conceptual realm of imaginary examples to the practical realm of research. In fact, they are not specific about the practices that scientists agree in that provide for objectivity; they simply share the confidence of many philosophers and scientists that such practices exist. I will take pain as a final example from their paper, as it seems to present most problems for a constructionist approach.

Drawing heavily on Wittgenstein, Button and Sharrock treat pain as part of a 'natural practice' prior to knowledge or belief about it. Yet even if pain *were* such a practice, this would not show that constructionist analysis would be irrelevant. Even as a 'natural reaction' pain is susceptible to what Sacks (1992: 120) calls 'subversion'. That is, people can mimic being in pain by displaying the sorts of behaviours of people in pain; likewise they can mimic not being in pain. The authenticity of pain in everyday settings such as when parents are dealing with children, doctors with patients, lawyers in compensation cases, is not guaranteed by any putative status as a natural reaction. One of Roland Barthes's (1972) most famous essays highlighted the difference between pain displays in wrestling, with its elaborate grimaces and anguished howls, and boxing, with its cold indifference to punishment from the opposition. Think of the World Wrestling Federation's Hulk Hogan and then think of boxer Mike Tyson. Pain display is an appropriate, and indeed fascinating, arena for analysis of fact construction.

Button and Sharrock's arguments may bite more effectively into some other forms of constructionism, particularly the varieties which treat an analysis of construction to be equivalent to a discovery of falsity (see Anderson, 1994, for example). However, the variant of constructionism that I have been developing in this book does not propose this, nor does it depend on analysts' judgements about consensus. As argued in Chapter 6, consensus is an important participants' concern when building and undermining the objectivity of versions, and it can be studied as such. Such a study does not require the analyst to produce a technical account of whether there is *actual* consensus or not: consensus is being studied as a move in a rhetorical struggle. Moreover, the constructionism developed here is specifically non-cognitive. Rather than be concerned with fact construction in terms of cognitive machineries of knowledge and belief, the concern has been with the way descriptions are used in parts of practices, and the way those descriptions are built up as factual or undermined as interested, false or whatever.

Button and Sharrock claim ethnomethodological support for their case against constructionism; yet, it is important to stress that ethnomethodologists are by no means lined up shoulder to shoulder with them against constructionist social critique. There are varying degrees of acceptance of the involvement of ethnomethodology in social critique. At its weakest, Lena Jayyusi (1991) by no means advocates a critical stance, but she does suggest that it is incoherent for ethnomethodologists to attempt a principled stance of 'cultural disengagement' because members of a culture will always have the option of treating their analysis as both relevant and partisan. More strongly, both Dorothy Smith (1990) and Alex McHoul (1988) have attempted to tie ethnomethodological concerns to a more directly critical enterprise. And, in the work of Paul Jalbert (1992, 1995), ethnomethodological analysis is drawn to a position very close to Critical Discourse Analysis, which is the topic of the next section.

It is hard to avoid the conclusion that Button and Sharrock have ended up with a conservative position which protects participants' notions of objectivity from proper scrutiny by assuming that they depend on consensual and natural practices. Their account treats practices as consensual and, for all intents and purposes, timeless and culture-free, and allows little space for talk of social change.

Critical Discourse Analysis

If the version of ethnomethodology developed by Button and Sharrock involved a principled anti-criticism, Critical Discourse Analysis is the opposite. It treats criticism as an intrinsic element of analysis. Critical Discourse Analysis is a broad label that covers a mixed field of research variously inspired by Foucault, Halliday and Chomsky and blending into linguistics at one extreme (indeed, much of this work was originally called Critical Linguistics) and semiotics and cultural studies at the other (Fairclough, 1992; Fowler, 1991; Fowler et al., 1979; Hodge and Kress, 1993; Martin, 1989). As a field of research it includes some penetrating and insightful analyses that highlight the workings of features of description that were previously overlooked. Indeed, it is a rich resource for anyone interested in fact construction and the relation between versions and actions. Yet, from the perspective I have developed here there are problems with some of the standard ways in which fact criticism is done.

Two issues in particular are worth highlighting. Critical Discourse Analysts commonly focus on the reality construction of a stretch of discourse, but draw on their own (often implicit) understanding of the 'actual' reality to ground their analyses. Thus studies of the news reporting of labour disputes often trade on implicit assumptions of who actually initiated the dispute, who is in the wrong and who is in the right, and so on. Critical Discourse Analysts also have difficulties with the pragmatics of language use: the involvement of talk and texts in activities. This is partly a consequence of its origins in the traditional linguistic perspectives of Noam Chomsky and Michael Halliday, who either ignored language pragmatics or treated it in a limited fashion. My discussion will focus on Robert Hodge and Gunther Kress' (1993) classic *Language as Ideology*, as it is the defining text in the field.

The notion of language transformation is central to Critical Discourse Analysis. In its original form in the work of Chomsky (1957), transformation referred to the possible modifications of a kernel sentence. Thus (simplifying wildly!) the fundamental ('deep structure') sentence, *'the cat sat on the mat'* can be transformed into the superficial ('surface structure') sentences *'did the cat sit on the mat?'* or *'the mat was sat on by the cat'*. In Chomsky's work this topic was central both to explaining grammatical form and, ultimately, to the sorts of cognitive processes through which language is produced. Hodge and Kress wanted to apply these ideas to issues with a more interactional and ideological focus. They argue that transformations work by deleting, joining or reordering 'elements which are in the underlying structures' (1993: 34) and that this has the consequence of 'suppression', 'distortion' or 'mystification' and can involve the masking of contradictions and confusions or the imposition of 'an unexamined consensus' (1993: 35).

The following is from their introduction to the notion of transformation.

> Imagine a situation where some job was to be done by someone, and someone else asks whether it has been done: it might be the emptying of the garbage can. The wife might ask *Has the garbage been emptied?* to which she gets the enraged response *You know bloody well I've been out all day, how could I have emptied the garbage can?* (or some version of this). We can ask: Why did the husband get angry? and how did he know that his wife has been aiming this at him? After all, he had not been mentioned. The answers lie in the fact that the wife had chosen to present reality in one way, but then 'transformed' that version of reality into one which differed from the original version. The original form was one in which the husband appeared as the person who was supposed to do the emptying: *Have you emptied the garbage?* In the 'transformed' version *you* had disappeared; it has been deleted by the wife, using the linguistic process of turning an active sentence into a passive one. (1993: 15–16)

This is fascinating for a number of reasons. Note the ambivalence with which Hodge and Kress characterize the reality of the situation. At the start of the extract, putting out the garbage is presented as a job that 'was to be done', but it is later described as the way the wife *first* chose to present reality; that is, it starts as some objective feature of the world, but is later treated as an understanding specific to the wife. Moreover, the objective version is ambiguous: the *was to be done* here could plausibly cover constructions of regularity (he normally does it), constructions of duty (he has agreed always to do it), and constructions of one-off intention (he said he would do it that day). This ambiguity is important, for each of these different constructions implicates a different context of accountability for the husband, and thus suggests a different sense to his retort. As we saw in Chapter 7, these sorts of constructions play an important role in script formulating activities.

Now, for Hodge and Kress the ambivalence between the objective situation and the wife's construction is not accidental. What they describe as the 'original form' of the wife's utterance (*have you emptied the garbage?*) is fitted to the actual situation: he *was* to do the job. The correlation between her thought and the reality of the situation helps justify treating this as the 'real' as opposed to the 'surface' form. The problem with this is that it turns into a moral and normative theory of language. The 'real form' is provided by an early Chomsky-style linguistic analysis which treats sentences as having base forms which are transformed in various ways. In Hodge and Kress' example, the wife's transformed utterance is obscuring this base form to head off a dispute over who should empty the garbage. Her utterance is mystifying the situation for strategic purposes.

There are three things to emphasize here. First, the 'real' situation (the husband was to get the garbage in) is invented to be just how it is. In actual research, there is not an unproblematic path to 'what the facts are' prior to their reconstruction in participants' versions. Second, this 'real' situation is central to the analysis. It is only through knowing this that Hodge and Kress are able to specify the transformation that is their central 'finding'. Third, the wife's mind is taken to contain the initial, faithful form of the utterance and then she transforms it for public consumption.

Let us continue to take this example seriously, despite its invented nature; for it is possible to give a rather different account of what is going on than is given by Hodge and Kress. In place of a linguistic analysis, consider the sequence from the sort of interactional perspective developed by conversation analysis and treat the second turn as providing an interpretation of the first.

Wife: Has the garbage been emptied?
Husband: You know bloody well I've been out all day,
               how could I have emptied the garbage can?

I suggest that the husband's response is not responding to, and thereby constituting, the wife's turn as an implicit *question* about whether he has emptied the garbage. That is, he is not orientating in his talk to what Hodge and Kress see as the sense of the utterance before transformation. But neither is he treating it as a merely *abstract* question about anyone (including him) who might have emptied the garbage (the surface form). Instead, he is responding to it, roughly, as an unreasonable complaint. This kind of analysis is focused on the specifics of what talk and texts are doing rather than on grammatical idealizations. It avoids the threefold correlation in Critical Discourse Analysis between the world, the speaker's cognitive construction of the world, and the base sentence. And it avoids the assumption that certain utterances are necessarily transformations of more fundamental pieces of language.

What this example illustrates is the way Hodge and Kress have produced a moral and normative theory; base sentences (in the Chomsky sense) are treated as more real and more honest than transformed sentences (again in the Chomsky sense) which are mystifying and strategic. The deep/surface distinction in Chomsky is translated into real/distorted, right/wrong distinctions in Hodge and Kress. Note that this is an assumption in their analysis rather than a conclusion or something demonstrated by it. It may well be that particular studies done in the Critical Discourse Analysis tradition effectively show 'transformed' sentences being used to draw attention away from particular processes, as was discussed in Chapter 7. Yet, that does not mean that the base sentences are better or more radical or more real. For example, the utterances *Has the garbage been emptied?* may be used in a range of ways in different contexts. A purely linguistic analysis treats it as obscuring the agent who should be doing the emptying, and this may certainly be something useful to consider in any analysis, yet an interactional analysis might reveal a range of other kinds of business to be going on or, indeed, other sorts of things being hidden.

Let us focus on another example and another form of transformation, in this case involving nominalization. In their analysis of newspaper coverage of labour disputes Hodge and Kress note the frequency of nominalizations (verbs that have been transformed to take the syntactic form of nouns). For example, the nominal description *picketing* may be used in place of *strikers picket factory*, which they treat as the base form. Hodge and Kress criticize nominalized descriptions because they both delete agents (the strikers) and mystify concrete 'causal process': 'an activity which was initiated and performed by the miners, in a specific place and time, now seems to have autonomous existence, and can appear as the actor in a new construction' (1993: 21).

As with the previous example, I am not suggesting that the sorts of linguistic differences between these constructions are not interesting and potentially consequential. The problems with it arise with its use of (implicit) notions of what actually happened against which to evaluate the description, and with its treatment of the base form as generally better than the transformed form. Note that the assumption that picketing was 'initiated and performed by the miners' involves judgements about precisely what is often at stake in labour disputes: who started it. Was the dispute initiated by the management through their payment of ridiculously poor wages for a difficult and dirty job? Was it initiated by the miners' leaders as part of an attempt to overthrow a right-wing government? Was it initiated by the government to generate a confrontation which would undermine the power of the union? Accounts of these kinds are commonplace in descriptions of strikes. This means that it may be highly misleading simply to equate the base form of the sentence with the real situation.

The central Critical Discourse Analysis idea that causal processes are properly represented by the base form of a sentence but mystified by the transformed form is also problematic. It is possible to argue the reverse in the case of nominalization. For example, when nominalized 'picket' ceases to be a causal process but becomes 'picketing', that is, an object in new orders of causal process: X caused 'picketing', 'picketing' caused X. However, whether this is mystifying or not depends on judgements about the world. For example, the nominal form may emphasize precisely the causal relations that are commonly emphasized in social scientific analyses of social process, where relationships between more or less abstract entities are identified that go beyond concrete events. The point is that the base form, *picket*, may hide these abstract, but nevertheless politically crucial, processes behind its empirical particulars. Such analyses are *inherently* neither radical nor reactionary. Their political consequences depend on a range of considerations.

In summary, then, I have highlighted a range of problems with Critical Discourse Analysis. It tends to make the linguistic analysis convincing by comparing the textual version with an often implicit version of what is really the case. Put another way, it departs from the principle of symmetry which has proved so important in the study of factuality. It tends to a cognitive and strategic analysis, heavily dependent on notions of what speakers intend and on the information-processing difficulties generated by some constructions. And it trades on a moral theory of language which treats certain sentence forms as more real and less mystifying than others. These features are sustained in part by a concentration on formal texts such as newspapers, where the sorts of speakers' orientations which are so important for conversation analysis are absent and it is easier to sustain claims about ideological effectiveness. Some of these issues are nicely highlighted by considering the name Critical Discourse Analysis. Criticism is treated as if it were intrinsic to the enterprise (and, implicitly, absent from other forms of discourse analysis); a less presumptuous and mechanical alternative would be to see criticism as something that might or might not be achieved in a successful analysis.

From true stories to True Stories

With the narrative logic that I have used so far in this section the obvious sequel to this overview of two flawed positions on fact criticism would be a third, perhaps more moderate position, that navigates sensibly between their extremes and corrects their faults. However, I am not going to attempt that neat resolution. Indeed, such a resolution would be hard to sustain given the broad line of argument that I have developed in the last few chapters; and there is something rather boring about advocating the moderate position. I am going to end this book with some arguments and dilemmas, hoping that these will be constructive and perhaps provocative.

To start with, take the issue of reflexivity. I postponed its discussion from the section on social science and fact construction because of its wider significance. Reflexivity concerns a set of issues that arise when considering the relationship between the content of research and the writing and actions of researchers. The most developed discussion of this issue has taken place in sociology of scientific knowledge where it was stimulated by the so-called *tu quoque* critique. *Tu quoque* can be translated as 'there's another' or 'you too'. Malcolm Ashmore's *Encyclopaedia of Reflexivity and Knowledge* defines it as the argument that 'This position (theory, argument) is incoherent (illegitimate, mistaken) because when reflexively applied to itself the result is an absurdity: self-contradiction (-refutation, -destruction, -defeat, -undermining)' (1989: 86). So the argument runs: sociologists of scientific knowledge claim to have demonstrated the socially constructed nature of scientific findings, but their conclusions must apply to their own scientific investigations also, in which case their findings too must be socially constructed, and if the finding that scientific findings are socially constructed is *itself* socially constructed it need not be taken very seriously, and thus the whole enterprise is self-defeating.

There have been various responses to the *tu quoque*. Some have involved flat disagreement. For example, Harry Collins (1981) argued that the *tu quoque* confuses constructionist *analysis* with realist *dismissal*. On this argument, demonstrating the role of constructive practices in making some scientific fact is an entirely different order of things from showing that fact is wrong. To accept the *tu quoque* is to mistake sociology of science for an enterprise attacking science, when in fact it is an enterprise that is attacking some of the simplistic stories about how science operates and about the uniqueness of scientific knowledge compared to other kinds of knowledge (cf. Collins and Pinch, 1993).

Malcolm Ashmore, Michael Mulkay and Steve Woolgar (Ashmore, 1989; Mulkay, 1985; Woolgar, 1989) also rejected the idea that sociology of scientific knowledge can be refuted by a *tu quoque* argument. In particular, they rejected the notion of logic that underpins such a refutation, and they also rejected the idea of universal standards of truth which would be troubled by a universal claim that there are no universal standards. However, in contrast to Collins, they saw the *tu quoque* argument as raising the important issue of the tension between the story of knowledge being generated by social research on science, and the timeless and universal assumptions about knowledge implied in the researcher's textual forms. Put simply, they suggested that it is hard to provide a full counter to the empiricism and objectivism of traditional accounts of science if the textual forms used in that counter are themselves constructed using empiricist and objectivist tropes.

For example, one conclusion from a range of sociology of science, and particularly from discourse analytic work in this area, is that the texts through which science is written are heavily implicated in the processes of fact construction. At this point in this book, I hope it is no longer contentious to claim that the written texts of science are not neutral, transparent descriptions of reality and scientists' actions. Rather than simply repeat the kinds of tropes that make up these texts at a higher level of social science analysis, Ashmore, Mulkay and Woolgar have tried to produce texts which use different tropes to draw attention to their own contingency and artificiality; the point was to display the operation of fact construction. Ashmore's major work in this area, for instance, includes parodies, dialogues, a lecture, an encyclopaedia, a double text, and a fake PhD viva. In each case, the textual forms themselves are a constitutive part of the argument.

This proposed dis-solution of the *tu quoque* can be seen as a broadly postmodernist move. Rather than reject representation, or realism, or empiricism or specific localized versions of these positions, the attempt is to work with them in an ironic or self-referring fashion, which highlights the tensions and fractures in referential discourses rather than trying to fix or avoid them. For example, when Malcolm Ashmore, Greg Myers and I (1995) wrote a review of the literature on discourse, rhetoric and reflexivity we used a fiction of a PhD student who had become disillusioned with her research and become interested in rhetoric and science. We produced the review as a diary of her week in the library, and in this way used a fiction to explore some of the notable absences in the standard format that social science reviews take. For instance, the reviewer was produced as a person situated in space and time, in a network of relationships; she is a person with a history and interests. It also highlighted the role of serendipity, the accomplished nature of rules of selection, and the physical space of the library. Whether it succeeded or not (whatever success would have been here) its aim was to provide a review which simultaneously commented on, and criticized, the nature of reviews. The better it worked, the better it unravelled its own basis.

Clearly, the *tu quoque* argument in (and against) sociology of scientific knowledge could be extended to the more general claims about fact construction developed in the current book. I have attempted to lay out some characteristic features of the way texts and talks are organized to present descriptions as factual. At the same time I have been concerned to show the way descriptions are produced in, and involved in, social practices. That is, I have been concerned to show how they are action-orientated. What of this text, then? What of the way *its* descriptions are worked up as factual and what of *its* action orientation? There is no time out from these practices; I do not want to claim any special exemption for the discourse in this book.

I could have reflexively explored the fact constructional practices used here in parallel to my analysis of other talk and texts, or I could have used a different textual form for the text as a whole. If this had been done well enough it would have led to a better book than this one. Wary of doing it badly, and producing a work that is even more complicated than the current one, I opted for conventional realist discourse in both review and analytic sections. My goal was in making the arguments as accessible as possible. Ideally, they will be so accessible that people will be able immediately to turn them back on this text to start to deconstruct its own tropes of fact construction. This description, too, is an account which is doing a bit of business. It makes the point while destabilizing it at the same time!

Critical and Uncritical Work on Fact Construction

I do not believe that research on fact construction is valuable solely because it can provide some sort of critical or practical intervention. As should be apparent, I think the topic is interesting for its own sake. The sophistication and elegance of the way the most mundane of accounts is put together to attend to its factual status is constantly impressive. To describe the procedures through which this is done seems to me to be an entirely satisfying, interesting and even entertaining activity. I hope some of the personal pleasure comes through in this text. Moreover, the danger of too strong an emphasis on criticism is that it can easily turn into arrogance where researchers assume that they know what is wrong in some domain, and research can become a device for passing off that assumption as research finding. None of this is to say that work on fact construction should be *un*critical, merely that its motivation can be quite appropriately an academic fascination rather than an immediate desire for change or presupposition of problem.

Nevertheless, work on fact construction does have critical potential. There are various different ways in which the notion of critique can be understood. For simplicity (rhetorical elegance?), three kinds of criticism can be distinguished: *ad hoc* practical, Critical (with a big C), and reflexive. Let me say something about each.

By *ad hoc practical* criticism I mean the sorts of practical help this set of ideas and analyses might provide for a barrister in examining a client, a viewer watching a television news programme or a wife involved in a relationship argument. Factual discourse is being built and utilized in courtrooms and classrooms, in family arguments and intimate exchanges, in political debates and scientific controversies. An explicit account of some of the procedures involved in that building, and the relations between the nature of the description and how it is used, might well assist a critical evaluation of what is going on in that setting by both participants and analysts. I would be delighted if this work made even a small contribution to people's skills at deciphering and countering factual accounts.

There are some dangers in this route to being useful, however. In the first case it might end up being patronizing. As I have emphasized, one of the features that is striking in analyses of people's everyday practices of fact construction and destruction is how subtle and skilled they are at it. Connie and Jimmy, the couple in relationship crisis who have stayed with us through the latter chapters of this book, do not come over as exceptionally articulate or intelligent on a superficial hearing. However, as we come to look more and more closely at their discussion we can see the way they draw on an intricate and embedded set of fact construction devices, and organize their versions in a way that is extremely sensitive to the various pieces of business that are being done. There is a strong sense that they do not need educating about *these* things; they may not be running their relationship very effectively, but they deserve a degree in practical constructionism. In this case, the pedagogic boot is very much on the other foot.

Another danger is that of is mis-empowering. This is the risk that tools of fact construction and destruction that might be used in a creative or critical manner can end up shoring up particular *status quos*, or being neatly slotted into the rhetorical armoury of the already powerful. An example which seems to fit this model is Max Atkinson's (1984) popular conversation analytic study of the rhetorical devices involved in successful political oratory. Atkinson introduced his book with the hope that the knowledge would provide the ordinary listeners to political speeches with the skills to be able to consider more critically what is being applauded and how that applause is being produced. Yet, a decade later, what seems to have happened is that listeners are only marginally better informed about ways of listening sceptically, but politicians have become extremely proficient in the basic rhetorical techniques. It is very rare now to hear a leading politician now failing to draw repeatedly on the devices that Atkinson identified.

The second form of criticism can be thought of as *Criticism with a big C* – as in the Critical Theory of the Frankfurt School or Critical Discourse Analysis discussed above. Here the sorts of ideas and skills in deconstructing factual accounts would be combined with theoretical and historical analysis. Norman Fairclough (1992) provides a linguistically sophisticated version of this, while John Thompson (1990) provides more sociological sophistication. Margaret Wetherell and I (1992) attempted to combine these elements in our study of New Zealand racist discourse. One of the established themes in Critical Social Science of various kinds has been the demystification of established descriptions of social arrangements, and there seems to be no reason why a systematic approach to studying fact construction should not be an aid to such demystification.

The virtue of such approaches is the power and sweep that the sociological theory provides. However, I have already noted some practical problems that can arise in my discussion of Critical Discourse Analysis. The main issue is that by its very nature such critical work is often undermining some versions of social arrangements while simultaneously presupposing others. This makes it susceptible to the kind of argument that Steve Woolgar and Dorothy Pawluch (1985) developed in their critique of a range of social constructionist research for implicit ontological gerrymandering. This critique hardly kills off such an important strand of social analysis but it does pose it searching questions. Some of these are starting to be addressed in work considering the possibility of general social Critique after the insights and doubts of constructionism and postmodernism (for a range of examples, see Nicholson and Seidman, 1995; Sampson, 1993b).

The third kind of criticism is *reflexive* criticism, which moves in a more postmodern direction. The kind of systematic and thoroughgoing reflexivity

championed by Ashmore (1989) rejects the compromises and inconsistencies that are often required in Critical work. Such work is critical in the sense
that it tends to be corrosive to all authoritative accounts, including that of the
current analyst and writer. This line of argument is not antithetical to the production of broad stories and claims, but their status *as* stories (rather than
timeless factual versions) will be sustained rather than denied. Indeed, for this
work invention can be celebrated, as The 2nd of January Group conclude in
their Postmodern Manifesto: 'The rationalists have only interpreted the
world, the point is to invent it!' (1986: 31).

The danger of this approach, emphasized by some social analysts (for
example, Parker, 1992), is that criticism may be blunted by the concern for a
fully symmetrical management of factual versions or by the turn to reflexivity. The rich and powerful will carry on exploiting the poor and powerless
while researchers, bewitched by reflexivity, explore their textual navels (cf.
Edwards et al., 1995). The reflexive worker's response to this is that one's textual navel is an excellent start point for considering the constitution and
mystification of power.

Let me end by having it both ways. So rather than proposing a choice
between these different critical courses (non-, *ad hoc*, big C and reflexive), I
would prefer to stress the value of them all, and in particular the theoretical
and analytic tensions between them. A situation where each of these positions
both complements and undermines the other is preferable to either outright
victory of one line of argument or blandly peaceful coexistence. I would like
to celebrate the tension *itself* as productive (although this pushes me along the
reflexive, postmodern course rather further than the others). I hope the dilemmas raised will as well as contributing to the vibrancy of this general field of
exploration provide a challenge to researchers in (and on, and through) fact
construction.

Appendix
Transcription Conventions

The transcription conventions used in this book are based on the system developed by Gail Jefferson (for example, Jefferson, 1985; Sacks et al., 1974). The system evolved to use symbols mainly available in a standard typewriter character set and to pick out features of talk that conversation analysts found important in interaction. Useful summaries of this system can be found in most collections of papers in conversation analysis (e.g. ten Have and Psathas, 1995). A more thoroughgoing overview and discussion of using transcript in practice is provided by Psathas and Anderson (1990).

Most of the conventions in the Jeffersonian system can be illustrated briefly using the following extract from Chapter 7:

```
1        C:   Was that the time that you left?=
2        W:   =He left the:n that was- [ nearl ]y two years ago.
3        C:                            [°Yeh°]
4        W:   He walked out then. Just (.) literally walked out.
5             (0.8)
6        C:   ↑Oka↓y. So, (0.5) for me list↓enin:g, (.) you've
7    →        got (0.5) rich an:d, (.) complicated lives,
8             I nee:d to get some his [tory to put-    ]
9        W:                          [Yyeh. mmm,=]
10            [Mmm. (.) Ye:h (.) Oh ye:h.]
11       H:   [= Yeh. (.) that's (.) exactly wha]t ih °um°
(DE-JF/C2/S1:4)
```

- Underlining (<u>walked</u> <u>out</u>) indicates words or parts of words which are stressed by the speaker.
- Colons mark the prolongation of the sound immediately before (the:n); more colons would show a longer prolongation (Ah:::).
- Arrows precede marked rises and falls in intonation (↑Oka↓y).
- The question mark in line 1 marks a questioning intonation (there is no necessary correspondence with utterances participants treat as questions).
- The full stop (for example, in line 2) marks a completing intonation (not necessarily a grammatical full stop).
- The comma in line 6 marks a continuing intonation (not necessarily a grammatical comma).
- A dash (for example, Thanks- Tha:nksgiving) marks a noticeable and abrupt termination of a word or sound.
- The brackets across lines 2 and 3, 8 and 9, 10 and 11 mark the onset and completion of overlapping talk.

- Where one turn runs into another with no interval this is marked by an equals symbol (lines 1 and 2, 9 and 11).
- Numbers in brackets (0.5) are the times of pauses in tenths of a second; where there is just a full stop in a bracket (.) this is a pause which is hearable but too short to measure.
- Talk that is quieter than the surrounding talk is enclosed by degree symbols: °Yeh°.
- Talk that is louder than the surrounding talk is capitalized (WHERE).
- Arrows in the margin (line 7) simply pick out lines of transcript for discussion in the text; they do not mark features of delivery.
- Where the transcriber is doubtful of a word or phrase it will be placed in parentheses; if no guess is plausible these parentheses are left empty.
- Clarifactory comment is placed in double parentheses: ((laughs)), ((stands up)).
- Where material from the tape has been omitted for reasons of brevity this is indicated by square brackets around three full stops [. . .].
- The code at the end of the transcript provides a range of information. For example, this extract is from a transcript produced by Derek Edwards and Jon Fong (DE-JF). The talk is from the second couple in the sample (C2) in their first session (S1) and it appears on the fourth page of the transcript.

Have, P. ten and Psathas, G. (eds) *Situated Order: Studies in the Social Organization of Talk and Embodied Activities*. Washington, DC: International Institute for Ethnomethodology and Conversation Analysis and University Press of America.

Jefferson, G. (1985) 'An exercise in the transcription and analysis of laughter', in T. van Dijk (ed.), *Handbook of Discourse Analysis*, vol. 3 (pp. 25–34). London: Academic Press.

Psathas, G. and Anderson, T. (1990) 'The "practices" of transcription in conversation analysis', *Semiotica*, 78: 75–99.

Sacks, H., Schegloff, E.A., and Jefferson, G. (1974) 'A simplest systematics for the organization of turn-taking for conversation', *Language*, 50(4): 696–735. Reprinted in J. Schenkein (ed.), *Studies in the Organization of Conversational Interaction* (pp. 7–55). New York: Academic Press.

References

Adams, P.J., Towns, A. and Gavey, N. (1995) 'Dominance and entitlement: the rhetoric men use to discuss their violence towards women', *Discourse and Society*, 6: 387–406.

Aman, K. and Knorr Cetina, K.D. (1988) 'The fixation of (visual) evidence', *Human Studies*, 11: 133–69.

Anderson, B. (1993) *Imagined Communities*. London: Verso.

Anderson, M.L. (1994) 'The many and varied social constructions of intelligence', in T.R. Sarbin and J.I. Kitsuse (eds), *Constructing the Social*. London: Sage.

Antaki, C. (1994) *Explaining and Arguing: the Social Organization of Accounts*. London and Beverly Hills, CA: Sage.

Ashmore, M. (1988) 'The life and opinions of a replication claim: reflexivity and symmetry in the sociology of scientific knowledge', in S. Woolgar (ed.), *Knowledge and Reflexivity: New Frontiers in the Sociology of Knowledge*. London: Sage.

Ashmore, M. (1989) *The Reflexive Thesis: Wrighting Sociology of Scientific Knowledge*. Chicago: University of Chicago Press.

Ashmore, M. (1993) 'The theatre of the blind: starring a Promethean prankster, a phoney phenomenon, a prism, a pocket, and a piece of Wood', *Social Studies of Science*, 23: 67–106.

Ashmore, M. (1995) 'Fraud by numbers: quantification rhetoric in the Piltdown forgery discovery', *South Atlantic Quarterly*, 94: 591–618.

Ashmore, M., Mulkay, M. and Pinch, T. (1989) *Health and Efficiency: a Sociological Study of Health Economics*. Milton Keynes: Open University Press.

Ashmore, M., Myers, G. and Potter, J. (1995) 'Discourse, rhetoric and reflexivity: seven days in the library', in S. Jasanoff, G. Markle, T. Pinch and J. Petersen (eds), *Handbook of Science, Technology and Society*. London: Sage, pp. 321–42.

Ashmore, M., Wooffitt, R. and Harding, S. (eds) (1994), 'Humans and others: the concept of "agency" and its attribution', Special issue of *American Behavioral Scientist*, 37 (6).

Atkinson, J.M. (1978) *Discovering Suicide: Studies in the Social Organization of Sudden Death*. London: Macmillan.

Atkinson, J.M. (1984) *Our Master's Voices: the Language and Body Language of Politics*. London: Methuen.

Atkinson, J.M. and Drew, P. (1979) *Order in Court: the Organization of Verbal Interaction in Judicial Settings*. London: Macmillan.

Atkinson, P. (1990) *The Ethnographic Imagination: the Textual Construction of Reality*. London: Routledge.

Atkinson, P. (1995) *Medical Talk and Medical Work*. London: Sage.

Auburn, T., Willig, C. and Drake, S. (1995) 'You punched him, didn't you': versions of violence in accusatory interviews', *Discourse and Society*, 6: 353–86.

Auerbach, E. (1957) *Mimesis*. Princeton: Princeton University Press.

Augoustinos, M. and Walker, I. (1995) *Social Cognition: an Integrated Introduction*. London: Sage.

Austin, J.L. (1961) 'A plea for excuses', in J.D. Urmson and G. Warnock (eds), *Philosophical Papers*. Oxford: Clarendon Press.

Austin, J.L. (1962) *How to Do Things with Words*. Oxford: Clarendon Press.

Baker, G.P. and Hacker, P.M.S. (1984) *Language, Sense and Nonsense*. Oxford: Blackwell.

Bakhtin, M.M. (1981) *The Dialogic Imagination: Four Essays.* Austin, TX: University of Texas Press.

Bal, M. (1985) *Narratology: Introduction to the Theory of Narrative.* Toronto: University of Toronto Press.

Bal, M. (1993) 'First person, second person, same person: narrative as epistemology', *New Literary History*, 24: 293–320.

Ball, M.A. (1991) 'Revisiting the Gulf of Tonkin crisis: an analysis of the private communication of President Johnson and his advisers', *Discourse and Society*, 2: 28–96.

Barnes, B. (1977) *Interests and the Growth of Knowledge.* London: Routledge.

Barnes, B. (1981) 'On the conventional character of knowledge and cognition', *Philosophy of the Social Sciences*, 11: 303–33.

Barnes, B. (1982) *T.S. Kuhn and Social Science.* London: Macmillan.

Barthes, R. (1972) *Mythologies.* London: Paladin.

Barthes, R. (1974) *S/Z.* London: Jonathan Cape.

Barthes, R. (1977) *Image, Music, Text.* London: Fontana.

Barthes, R. (1981) *Camera Lucida: Reflections on Photography.* New York; Hill & Wang.

Barthes, R. (1983) *The Fashion System.* London: Cape.

Bennet, W.L. and Feldman, M.S. (1981) *Reconstructing Reality in the Courtroom.* New Brunswick, NJ: Rutgers University Press.

Bennington, G. and Derrida, J. (1993) *Jacques Derrida.* Chicago: University of Chicago Press.

Berger, P.L. and Luckmann, T. (1966) *The Social Construction of Reality.* Garden City, NY: Doubleday.

Bijker, W.E. and Pinch, T. (eds) (1992) *Shaping Technology, Building Society: Studies in Sociotechnical Change.* Cambridge, MA: MIT Press.

Billig, M. (1982) *Ideology and Social Psychology.* Oxford: Basil Blackwell.

Billig, M. (1987) *Arguing and Thinking: a Rhetorical Approach to Social Psychology.* Cambridge: Cambridge University Press.

Billig, M. (1989) 'Conservatism and the rhetoric of rhetoric', *Economy and Society*, 18: 132–48.

Billig, M. (1991) *Ideologies and Beliefs.* London: Sage.

Billig, M. (1992) *Talking of the Royal Family.* London: Routledge.

Billig, M. (1995) *Banal Nationalism.* London: Sage.

Billig, M., Condor, S., Edwards, D., Gane, M., Middleton, D.J. and Radley, A.R. (1988) *Ideological Dilemmas: a Social Psychology of Everyday Thinking.* London: Sage.

Bilmes, J. (1987) 'The concept of preference in conversation analysis', *Language in Society*, 17: 161–81.

Bloor, D. (1982) 'Durkheim and Mauss revisited: classification and the sociology of knowledge', *Studies in the History and Philosophy of Science*, 13: 267–97.

Bloor, D. (1991) *Knowledge and Social Imagery*, 2nd edn, Chicago: University of Chicago Press.

Bogen, D. (1992) 'The organization of talk', *Qualitative Sociology* (special issue on ethnomethodology), 15: 273–95.

Bogen, D. and Lynch, M. (1989) 'Taking account of the hostile native: plausible deniability and the production of conventional history in the Iran-Contra hearings', *Social Problems*, 36: 197–224.

Bruner, J.S. (1990) *Acts of Meaning.* Cambridge, MA: Harvard University Press.

Bunge, M. (1992) 'A critical examination of the new sociology of science, Part 2', *Philosophy of the Social Sciences*, 22: 46–76.

Buttny, R. and Jensen, A.D. (1995) 'Telling problems in an initial family therapy session: the hierarchical organization of problem-talk', in G.H. Morris and R.J. Chenail (eds), *The Talk of the Clinic: Explorations in the Analysis of Medical and Therapeutic Discourse.* Hillsdale, NJ: Lawrence Erlbaum.

Button, G. and Sharrock, W. (1993) 'A disagreement over agreement and consensus in constructionist sociology', *Journal for the Theory of Social Behaviour*, 23: 1–25.

Callon, M. (1995) 'Four models for the dynamics of science', in S. Jasanoff, G. Markle, T. Pinch and J. Petersen (eds), *Handbook of Science, Technology and Society.* London: Sage.

Callon, M. and Law, J. (1995) 'Agency and the hybrid *collectif*', *South Atlantic Quarterly*, 94: 481–507.

Chalmers, A. (1992) *What is This Thing Called Science?: an Assessment of the Nature and Status of Science and Its Methods*, 2nd edn, Milton Keynes: Open University Press.

Chomsky, N. (1957) *Syntactic Structures*. The Hague: Mouton.

Chomsky, N. (1966) *Cartesian Linguistics: a Chapter in the History of Rationalist Thought*. New York: Harper & Row.

Cicourel, A.V. (1964) *Method and Measurement in Sociology*. New York: Free Press.

Cicourel, A.V. (1974) *Theory and Method in a Study of Argentine Fertility*. New York: Wiley.

Clayman, S.E. (1992) 'Footing in the achievement of neutrality: the case of news-interview discourse', In P. Drew and J. Heritage (eds), *Talk at Work: Interaction in Institutional Settings*. Cambridge: Cambridge University Press.

Clifford, J. and Marcus, G.E. (eds) (1986) *Writing Culture: the Poetics and Politics of Ethnography*. Berkeley, CA: University of California Press.

Coates, L., Bevelas, J.B. and Gibson, J. (1994) 'Anomalous language in sexual assault trial judgements', *Discourse and Society*, 5: 189–206.

Cockcroft, R. and Cockcroft, S.M. (1992) *Persuading People: an Introduction to Rhetoric*. London: Macmillan.

Collins, H.M. (1975) 'The seven sexes: a study in the sociology of a phenomenon, or the replication of experiments in physics', *Sociology*, 9: 205–24.

Collins, H.M (1981) 'What is TRASP? The radical programme as a methodological imperative', *Philosophy of the Social Sciences*, 11: 215–24.

Collins, H.M. (1983a) 'An empirical relativist programme in the sociology of scientific knowledge', in K.D. Knorr Cetina and M. Mulkay (eds), *Science Observed: Perspectives on the Social Study of Science*. London: Sage.

Collins, H.M. (1983b) 'The meaning of lies: accounts of action and participatory research', in G.N. Gilbert and P. Abell (eds), *Accounts and Action*. Aldershot: Gower.

Collins, H.M. (1985) *Changing Order: Replication and Induction in Scientific Practice*. London: Sage.

Collins, H.M. and Cox, G. (1976) 'Recovering relativity: did prophecy fail?' *Social Studies of Science*, 6: 423–44.

Collins, H.M. and Pinch, T. (1982) *Frames of Meaning: the Social Construction of Extraordinary Science*. London: Routledge.

Collins, H.M. and Pinch, T. (1993) *The Golem: What Everyone Should Know About Science*. Cambridge: Canto.

Cooper, D.E. (1986) *Metaphor*. Oxford: Blackwell.

Costall, A. and Still, A. (eds) (1991) *Against Cognitivism: Alternative Foundations for Cognitive Psychology*. London: Harvester Wheatsheaf.

Coulter, J. (1979). 'Beliefs and practical understanding', in G. Psathas (ed.), *Everyday Language: Studies in Ethnomethodology*. New York: Irvington.

Coulter, J. (1982) 'Remarks on the conceptualization of social structure', *Philosophy of the Social Sciences*, 12: 33–46.

Coulter, J. (1983) *Rethinking Cognitive Theory*. London: Macmillan.

Coulter, J. (1991) 'Cognition: cognition in an ethnomethodological mode', in G. Button (ed.), *Ethnomethodology and the Human Sciences*. Cambridge: Cambridge University Press.

Crittenden, R. and Potter, C. (eds) (1986) 'Confronting reality: some perspectives on documentary' *Cilect Revue: the International Journal for Film and Television Schools* (special issue), 2.

Culler, J. (1975) *Structuralist poetics*. London: Routledge & Kegan Paul.

Culler, J. (1976) *Saussure*. London: Fontana.

Culler, J. (1983) *On Deconstruction*. London: Routledge & Kegan Paul.

Dant, T. (1991) *Knowledge, Ideology and Discourse: a Sociological Perspective*. London: Routledge.

Davies, M. (1995) *Childhood Sexual Abuse and the Construction of Identity: Healing Sylvia*. London: Taylor & Francis.

Derrida, J. (1976) *Of Grammatology*. Baltimore, MD: Johns Hopkins University Press.

Derrida, J. (1977a) 'Signature event context', *Glyph*, 1: 172–97.

Derrida, J. (1977b) 'Limited Inc. abc...', *Glyph*, 2: 162–254.

Derrida, J. (1982) 'White mythology: metaphor in the text of philosophy', in J. Derrida, *Margins of Philosophy*. London: Harvester Wheatsheaf.

Dillon, G.L. (1991) *Contending Rhetorics: Writing in Academic Disciplines*. Bloomington: Indiana University Press.

Drew, P. (1978) 'Accusations: the occasioned use of members' knowledge of religious geography in describing events', *Sociology*, 12: 1–22.

Drew, P. (1984) 'Speakers' reportings in invitation sequences', in J.M. Atkinson and J.C. Heritage (eds), *Structures of Social Action: Studies in Conversation Analysis*. Cambridge: Cambridge University Press.

Drew, P. (1992) 'Contested evidence in courtroom cross-examination: the case of a trial for rape', in P. Drew and J.C. Heritage (eds), *Talk at Work: Interaction in Institutional Settings*. Cambridge: Cambridge University Press.

Drew, P. (1995) 'Conversation analysis: the sequential analysis of intersubjectivity in conversation', in J. Smith, R. Harré, L. van Langenhove and P. Stearns (eds), *Rethinking Psychology*. vol. 2: *Alternative Methodologies*. London: Sage.

Drew, P. and Heritage, J.C. (1992) 'Analyzing talk at work: an introduction', in P. Drew and J. Heritage (eds), *Talk at Work: Interaction in Institutional Settings*. Cambridge: Cambridge University Press.

Drew, P. and Holt, E. (1989) 'Complainable matters: the use of idiomatic expressions in making complaints', *Social Problems*, 35: 398–417.

Drew, P. and Holt, E. (Forthcoming) 'The role of idioms in the organization of topic in conversation', in M. Everaert et al. (eds), *Idioms*. Hillsdale, NJ: Lawrence Erlbaum.

Dreyfus, H.L. and Rabinow, P. (1982) *Michel Foucault: Beyond Structuralism and Hermeneutics*. London: Harvester Wheatsheaf.

Duhem, P. (1962) *The Aim and Structure of Physical Theory*. New York: Atheneum.

Duranti, A. (1992) 'Intentions, self, and responsibility: an essay in Samoan ethnopragmatics', in J.H. Hill and J.T. Irvine (eds) *Responsibility and Evidence in Oral Discourse*. Cambridge: Cambridge University Press.

Edley, N. (1993) 'Prince Charles – our flexible friend: accounting for variations in constructions of identity', *Text*, 13: 397–422.

Edwards, D. (1994a) 'Script formulations: a study of event descriptions in conversation', *Journal of Language and Social Psychology*, 13: 211–47.

Edwards, D. (1994b) 'Whorf's empty gasoline drum and the Pope's missing wife', *Journal of Pragmatics*, 22: 215–18.

Edwards, D. (1995) 'Two to tango: script formulations, dispositions, and rhetorical symmetry in relationship troubles talk', *Research on Language and Social Interaction*, 28: 319–50.

Edwards, D. (1996) *Discourse and Cognition*. London: Sage.

Edwards, D., Ashmore, M. and Potter, J. (1995) 'Death and furniture: the rhetoric, politics and theology of bottom line arguments against relativism', *History of the Human Sciences*, 8: 25–49.

Edwards, D. and Mercer, N.M. (1987) *Common Knowledge: the Development of Understanding in the Classroom*. London: Routledge.

Edwards, D. and Potter, J. (1992) *Discursive Psychology*. London: Sage.

Edwards, D. and Potter, J. (1993) 'Language and causation: a discursive action model of description and attribution', *Psychological Review*, 100: 23–41.

Fairclough, N. (1992) *Discourse and Social Change*. Cambridge: Polity.

Fairclough, N. (1993) 'Critical discourse analysis and the marketization of public discourse', *Discourse and Society*, 4: 133–59.

Featherstone, M. (ed.) (1992) *Cultural Theory and Cultural Change*. London: Sage.

Feyerabend, P.K. (1975) *Against Method*. London: New Left Books.

Fiske, J. and Hartley, J. (1978). *Reading Television*. London: Methuen.

Foucault, M. (1972) *The Archaeology of Knowledge*. London: Tavistock.

Fowler, R. (1977) *Linguistics and the Novel*. London: Methuen.

Fowler, R. (1991) *Language in the News: Discourse and Ideology in the Press*. London: Routledge.

Fowler, R., Hodge, B., Kress, G. and Trew, T. (eds) (1979) *Language and Control*. London: Routledge.

Fuller, S. (1995) 'On the motives for the new sociology of science', *History of the Human Sciences*, 7: 287–91.

Garfinkel, H. (1967) *Studies in Ethnomethodology*. Englewood Cliffs, NJ: Prentice-Hall.

Genette, G. (1980) *Narrative Discourse*. Ithaca, NY: Cornell University Press.

Gergen, K.J. (1994) *Realities and Relationships: Soundings in Social Construction*. Cambridge, MA: Harvard University Press.

Gilbert, G.N. and Mulkay, M. (1982) 'Warranting scientific belief', *Social Studies of Science*, 12: 383–408.

Gilbert, G.N. and Mulkay, M. (1984) *Opening Pandora's Box: a Sociological Analysis of Scientists' Discourse*. Cambridge: Cambridge University Press.

Gill, R., Potter, J. and Webb, A. (1995) 'Public policy and discourse analysis: A rhetorical approach', Mimeo.

Glasgow Media Group (1982) *Really Bad News*. London: Writers & Readers.

Goffman, E. (1979) 'Footing', *Semiotica*, 25: 1–29.

Goffman, E. (1981) *Forms of Talk*. Oxford: Basil Blackwell.

Goodwin, C. (1987) 'Forgetfulness as an interactive resource', *Social Psychology Quarterly*, 50: 115–30.

Goodwin, C. (1995) 'Seeing in depth', *Social Studies of Science*, 25: 237–74.

Grace, G.W. (1987) *The Linguistic Construction of Reality*. London: Croom Helm.

Greatbatch, D. (1986) 'Aspects of topical organization in news interviews: the use of agenda-shifting procedures by interviewees', *Media, Culture and Society*, 8: 44–56.

Gubrium, J.F. and Holstein, J.A. (1990) *What is Family?* Mountain View, CA: Mayfield.

Gusfield, J. (1989) 'Constructing the ownership of social problems: fun and profit in the welfare state', *Social Problems*, 36: 431–41.

Hacking, I. (1983) *Representing and Intervening: Introductory Topics in the Philosophy of Natural Science*. Cambridge: Cambridge University Press.

Halkowski, T. (1990) '"Role" as an interactional device', *Social Problems*, 37: 564–77.

Halkowski, T. (1992) 'Hearing talk: accomplishing answers and generating facts', *Perspectives on Social Problems*, 4: 25–45.

Hammersley, M. and Atkinson, P (1983) *Ethnography: Principles and Practice*. London: Tavistock.

Hanson, N.R. (1969) *Perception and Discovery*. San Francisco: Freeman, Cooper.

Haraway, D. (1989) *Primate Visions: Gender, Race and Nature in the World of Modern Science*. London: Routledge.

Haraway, D. (1991) 'A cyborg manifesto: science, technology and socialist feminism in the late twentieth century', in D. Haraway, *Simians, Cyborgs, and Women: the Reinvention of Nature*. London: Free Association Books.

Haraway, D. (1992) 'When Man™ is on the menu', in J. Crary, and S. Kwinter (eds), *Incorporations*. New York: Zone Books.

Harré, R. and van Langenhove, L. (1991) 'Varieties of positioning', *Journal for the Theory of Social Behaviour*, 21: 393–408.

Harris, R. (1981) *The Language Myth*. London: Duckworth.

Harvey, D. (1989) *The Condition of Postmodernity*. Oxford: Basil Blackwell.

Heritage, J.C. (1974) 'Assessing people', in N. Armistead (ed.), *Reconstructing Social Psychology*. London: Penguin.

Heritage, J.C. (1984) *Garfinkel and Ethnomethodology*. Cambridge: Polity.

Heritage, J.C. (1988) 'Explanations as accounts: a conversation analytic perspective', in C. Antaki (ed.), *Analysing Everyday Explanation: a Casebook of Methods*. London: Sage.

Heritage, J.C. (1990/91) 'Intention, meaning and strategy: observations on constraints in interaction analysis', *Research on Language and Social Interaction*, 24: 311–32.

Heritage, J.C. and Greatbatch, D.L. (1991) 'On the institutional character of institutional talk: the case of news interviews', in D. Boden and D.H. Zimmerman (eds), *Talk and Social Structure: Studies in Ethnomethodology and Conversation Analysis*. Oxford: Polity.

Heritage, J.C. and Watson, D.R. (1979) 'Formulations as conversational objects', in G. Psathas (ed.), *Everyday Language: Studies in Ethnomethodology*. New York: Irvington.

Heritage, J.C. and Watson, D.R. (1980) 'Aspects of the properties of formulations in natural conversations: some instances analyzed', *Semiotica*, 30: 245–62.

Herrick, J. (1989) 'Miracles and method', *Quarterly Journal of Speech*, 9: 321–34.

Hesse, M.B. (1974) *The Structure of Scientific Inference*. London: Macmillan.

Hesse, M.B. (1980) *Revolutions and Reconstructions in the Philosophy of Science*. London: Harvester Wheatsheaf.

Hewstone, M. (1989) *Causal Attribution: From Cognitive Processes to Collective Beliefs*. Oxford: Basil Blackwell.

Hill, J.H. and Irvine, J.T. (eds) (1992) *Responsibility and Evidence in Oral Discourse*. Cambridge: Cambridge University Press.

Hilton, D.J., Smith, R.H. and Alicke, M.D. (1988) 'Knowledge-based information acquisition: norms and the functions of consensus information', *Journal of Personality and Social Psychology*, 55: 530–40.

Hodge, R. and Kress, G. (1988) *Social Semiotics*. Cambridge: Polity.

Hodge, R. and Kress, G. (1993) *Language as Ideology*, 2nd edn. London: Routledge.

Hollway, W. (1989) *Subjectivity and Method in Psychology: Gender, Meaning and Science*. London: Sage.

Holstein, J.A. and Gubrium, J.F. (1994) 'Constructing family: descriptive practice and domestic order', in T. Sarbin and J.I. Kitsuse (eds), *Constructing the Social*. London: Sage.

Hutcheon, L. (1989) *The Politics of Postmodernism*. London: Methuen.

Jalbert, P.L. (1992) 'Charting the logical geography of the concept of "cease fire"', *Human Studies*, 15: 265–90.

Jalbert, P.L. (1995) 'Critique and analysis in media studies: media criticism and practical action', *Discourse and Society*, 6: 7–26.

Jasanoff, S., Markle, G., Pinch T. and Petersen, J. (eds) (1995) *Handbook of Science, Technology and Society*. London: Sage.

Jayyusi, L. (1984) *Categories and the Moral Order*. London: Routledge.

Jayyusi, L. (1991) 'Values and moral judgment: communicative praxis as moral order', in G. Button (ed.), *Ethnomethodology and the Human Sciences*. Cambridge: Cambridge University Press.

Jefferson, G. (1985) 'An exercise in the transcription and analysis of laughter', in T. Van Dijk (ed.), *Handbook of Discourse Analysis*, vol. 3. London: Academic Press.

Jefferson, G. (1990) 'List construction as a task and resource', in G. Psathas (ed.), *Interaction Competence*. Lanham, MD: University Press of America.

Jodelet, D. (1991) *Madness and Social Representations*. London: Harvester Wheatsheaf.

Juhila, K. (1995) 'Factual accounting in the discourse on homelessness', *Scandinavian Journal of Social Welfare*, 4: 44–54.

Kitzinger, C. (1994) 'Experiential authority and heterosexuality', in G. Griffin (ed.), *Changing Our Lives: Doing Women's Studies*. London: Pluto Press.

Knorr Cetina, K.D. (1981) *The Manufacture of Knowledge: An Essay on the Constructivist and Contextual Nature of Science*. Oxford: Pergamon.

Knorr Cetina, K.D. (1982a) 'Relativism – what now?' *Social Studies of Science*, 12: 133–6.

Knorr Cetina, K.D. (1982b) 'The constructivist programme in the sociology of science: retreats or advances', *Social Studies of Science*, 12: 320–4.

Knorr Cetina, K.D. (1995a) 'Laboratory studies: the cultural approach to the study of science', in S. Jasanoff, G. Markle, T. Pinch and J. Petersen (eds.), *Handbook of Science, Technology and Society*. London: Sage.

Knorr Cetina, K.D. (1995b) 'Liminal and referent epistemologies: the disunity of two leading sciences', In P. Galison and D. Stump (eds), *The Disunity of Science: Boundaries, Contexts and Power*. Stanford, CA: Stanford University Press.

Knorr Cetina, K.D. (1996) *Epistemic Cultures: How Scientists Make Sense*. Cambridge, MA: Harvard University Press.

Knorr Cetina, K.D. and Aman, K. (1990) 'Image dissection in natural scientific inquiry', *Science, Technology and Human Values*, 15: 259–83.

Kristeva, J. (1980) *Desire in Language: a Semiotic Approach to Literature and Art*. Oxford: Blackwell.

Krohn, X. (1992) 'Lookin' cool and talkin' tough', *Journal of Half Remembered but Plausible Research Studies*, 2: 72–82.

Kuehl, J. (1986) 'The camera never lies', *Cilcet Review: the International Journal for Film and Television Schools*, 2: 85–92.

Kuhn, T.S. (1970) *The Structure of Scientific Revolutions*, 2nd edn. Chicago: University of Chicago Press.

Kuhn, T.S. (1977) *The Essential Tension: Selected Studies in Scientific Tradition and Change*. Chicago: University of Chicago Press.

Labinger, J.A. (1995) 'Science as culture: a view from the petri dish', *Social Studies of Science*, 25: 285–306.

Lakatos, I. (1970) 'Falsification and the methodology of scientific research programmes', in I. Lakatos and A. Musgrave (eds.), *Criticism and the Growth of Knowledge*. Cambridge: Cambridge University Press.

Lakatos, I. and Musgrave, A. (eds) (1970) *Criticism and The Growth of Knowledge*. Cambridge: Cambridge University Press.

Lakoff, G. (1987) *Women, Fire and Dangerous Things: What Categories Reveal about the Mind*. Chicago: University of Chicago Press.

Lakoff, G. (1991) 'Metaphor and war: the metaphor system used to justify war in the Gulf', Paper circulated on various electronic mailing lists.

Lakoff, G. and Johnson, M. (1980) *Metaphors We Live By*. Chicago: University of Chicago Press.

Latour, B. (1987) *Science in Action*. Milton Keynes: Open University Press.

Latour, B. (1993) *We Have Never Been Modern*. Hemel Hempstead, UK: Harvester Wheatsheaf.

Latour, B. and Woolgar, S. (1986) *Laboratory Life: the Construction of Scientific Facts*. 2nd edn. Princeton, NJ: Princeton University Press.

Laudan, L. (1990) *Science and Relativism: Some Key Controversies in the Philosophy of Science*. Chicago: University of Chicago Press.

Law, J. (1994) *Organizing Modernity*. Oxford: Blackwell.

Leudar, I. and Antaki, C. (1996) 'Discourse participation, reported speech and research practices in social psychology', *Theory and Psychology* (6: 5–29).

Levinson, S.C. (1983) *Pragmatics*. Cambridge: Cambridge University Press.

Levinson, S.C. (1988) 'Putting linguistics on a proper footing: explorations in Goffman's concepts of participation', in P. Drew and A. Wootton (eds), *Erving Goffman: Studies in the Interactional Order*. Cambridge: Polity.

Lynch, M. (1985) 'Discipline and the material form of images: an analysis of scientific visibility', *Social Studies of Science*, 15: 37–66.

Lynch, M. (1988) 'The externalized retina: selection and mathematization in the visual documentation of objects in the life sciences', *Human Studies*, 11: 201–34.

Lynch, M. (1993) *Scientific Practice and Ordinary Action: Ethnomethodology and Social Studies of Science*. Cambridge: Cambridge University Press.

Lynch, M. (1994) 'Representation is overrated: some critical remarks about the use of the concept of representation in science studies', *Configurations: a Journal of Literature, Science and Technology*, 2: 137–49.

Lynch, M. and Bogen, D. (1996) *The Spectacle of History: Speech, Text, and Memory of the Iran–Contra Hearings*. Durham, NC: Duke University Press

Lynch, M. and Woolgar, S. (eds) (1990) *Representation in Scientific Practice*. Cambridge, MA: MIT Press.

Lyotard, J-F. (1984) *The Postmodern Condition: a Report on Knowledge*. Manchester: Manchester University Press.

McCabe, C. (1974) 'Realism and the cinema: notes on some Brechtian theses', *Screen*, 15: 7–27.

McCloskey, D. (1985) *The Rhetoric of Economics*. Brighton: Wheatsheaf.

McHoul, A.W. (1988) 'Language and the sociology of mind: a critical introduction to the work of Jeff Coulter', *Journal of Pragmatics*, 12: 229–86.

McKinlay, A. and Potter, J. (1987) 'Social representations: a conceptual critique', *Journal for the Theory of Social Behaviour*, 17: 471–87.

McKinlay, A., Potter, J. and Wetherell, M. (1993) 'Discourse analysis and social representations', in G. Breakwell and D. Cantor (eds) *Empirical Approaches to Social Representations*. Oxford: Oxford University Press.

Mandelbaum, J. (1987) 'Couples sharing stories', *Communication Quarterly*, 35: 144–70.

Mandelbaum, J. (1993) 'Assigning responsibility in conversational storytelling: the interactional construction of reality', *Text*, 13: 247–66.

Manzo, J.F. (1993) 'Jurors' narratives of personal experience in deliberation talk', *Text*, 13: 267–90.

Marcus, G.E. (1986) 'Contemporary problems of ethnography in the modern world system', in J. Clifford and G.E. Marcus (eds), *Writing Culture: the Poetics and Politics of Ethnography*. Berkeley: University of California Press.

Marlin, R. (1984) 'The rhetoric of action description', *Informal Logic*, 6: 26–9.

Martin, B., Richards, E. and Scott, P. (1991) 'Who's a captive? Who's a victim? Response to Collins's methods talk', *Science, Technology and Human Values*, 16: 252–5.

Martin, J.R. (1989) *Factual Writing: Exploring and Challenging Social Reality*. Oxford: Oxford University Press.

Mathews, G.H. (1965) *Hidatsa Syntax. Papers on Formal Linguistics 3*. The Hague: Mouton.

Mehan, H. (1986) 'The role of language and the language of role in institutional decision making', in S. Fisher and A.D. Todd (eds), *Discourse and Institutional Authority*. Norwood, NJ: Ablex.

Mehan, H. (1990) 'Oracular reasoning in a psychiatric exam: the resolution of conflict in language', in A.D. Grimshaw (ed.), *Conflict Talk: Sociolinguistic Investigations of Arguments in Conversations*. Cambridge: Cambridge University Press.

Merton, R.K. (1970) *Science, Technology and Society in Seventeenth-century England*. New York: Harper & Row.

Merton, R.K. (1973) *The Sociology of Science*. Chicago: University of Chicago Press.

Middleton, D. and Edwards, D. (eds) (1990) *Collective Remembering*. London: Sage.

Mills, C.W. (1940) 'Situated actions and vocabularies of motive', *American Sociological Review*, 5: 904–13.

Mitroff, I.I. (1974) *The Subjective Side of Science*. Amsterdam: Elsevier.

Moi, T. (1985) *Sexual/Textual Politics*. London: Methuen.

Molotch, H.L. and Boden, D. (1985) 'Talking social structure: discourse, domination and the Watergate hearings', *American Sociological Review*, 50: 273–88.

Moscovici, S. (1984) 'The phenomenon of social representations', in R.M. Farr and S. Moscovici (eds), *Social representations*. Cambridge: Cambridge University Press.

Mulkay, M. (1976) 'Norms and ideology in science', *Social Science Information*, 15: 637–56.

Mulkay, M. (1979) *Science and the Sociology of Knowledge*. London: Allen & Unwin.

Mulkay, M. (1980) 'Interpretation and the use of rules: the case of norms in science', in T.F. Gieryn (ed.), *Science and social structure: Festschrift for Robert Merton*. Transactions of the New York Academy of Sciences, Series III, 39, 111–25.

Mulkay, M. (1981) 'Action and belief, or scientific discourse: a possible way of ending intellectual vassalage in social studies of science', *Philosophy of the Social Sciences*, 11: 163–71.

Mulkay, M. (1985) *The Word and the World: Explorations in the Form of Sociological Analysis*. London: Allen & Unwin.

Mulkay, M. (1991) *Sociology of Science: a Sociological Pilgrimage*. Milton Keynes: Open University Press.

Mulkay, M. (1994) 'Science and family in the great embryo debate', *Sociology*, 28: 699–717.

Mulkay, M. and Gilbert, G.N. (1981) 'Putting philosophy to work: Karl Popper's influence on scientific practice', *Philosophy of the Social Sciences*, 11: 389–407.

Mulkay, M., Potter, J. and Yearley, S. (1983) 'Why an analysis of scientific discourse is needed', in K.D. Knorr Cetina and M. Mulkay (eds), *Science Observed*. London: Sage.

Myers, G. (1990) *Writing Biology: Texts in the Construction of Scientific Knowledge*. Madison: University of Wisconsin Press.

Neisser, U. (1976) *Cognition and Reality*. San Francisco: W.H. Freeman & Co.

Nichols, W. (1992) *Representing Reality*. Indiana: Indiana University Press.

Nicholson, L. and Seidman, S. (1995) *Social Postmodernism: Beyond Identity Politics*. Cambridge: Cambridge University Press.

Nofsinger, R.E. (1991) *Everyday Conversation*. London: Sage.

Norris, C. (1987) *Derrida*. London: Fontana.

Norris. C. (1988) *The Deconstructive Turn: Essays in the Rhetoric of Philosophy*. London: Open University Press.

Orcutt, J.D. and Turner, J.B. (1993) 'Shocking numbers and graphic accounts: quantified images of drug problems in the print media', *Social Problems*, 40: 190–206.

Parker, I. (1992) *Discourse Dynamics: Critical Analysis for Social and Individual Psychology*. London: Routledge.

Peräkylä, A. (1993) 'Invoking a hostile world: discussing the patient's future in AIDS counselling', *Text*, 13: 291–316.

Pickering, A. (1981) 'The role of interests in high-energy physics: the choice between charm and colour', in K.D. Knorr Cetina, R. Krohn and R.D. Whitley (eds), *The Social Process of Scientific Investigation*. Dordrecht: Reidel.

Pickering, A. (1984) *Constructing Quarks: a Sociological History of Particle Physics*. Chicago: University of Chicago Press.

Pickering, A. (1992) 'From science as knowledge to science as practice', in A. Pickering (ed.), *Science as Practice and Culture*. Chicago: University of Chicago Press.

Pinch, T. (1986) *Confronting Nature*. Dordrecht: Reidel.

Pinch, T. and Clark, C. (1986) 'The hard sell: patter-merchanting and the strategic (re)production and local management of economic reasoning in the sales routines of market pitchers', *Sociology*, 20: 169–91.

Polkinghorne, D. (1988) *Narrative Knowing and the Human Sciences*. Albany, NY: State University of New York Press.

Pollner, M. (1987) *Mundane Reason: Reality in Everyday and Sociological Discourse*. Cambridge: Cambridge University Press.

Pomerantz, A.M. (1980) 'Telling my side: "limited access" as a fishing device', *Sociological Inquiry*, 50: 186–98.

Pomerantz, A.M. (1984a) 'Agreeing and disagreeing with assessments: some features of preferred/dispreferred turn shapes', in J.M. Atkinson and J.C. Heritage (eds), *Structures of Social Action: Studies in Conversation Analysis*. Cambridge: Cambridge University Press.

Pomerantz, A.M. (1984b). 'Giving a source a basis: the practice in conversation of telling "how I know,"' *Journal of Pragmatics, 8*, 607–25.

Pomerantz, A.M. (1986) 'Extreme case formulations: a new way of legitimating claims', *Human Studies*, 9: 219–30.

Pomerantz, A.M. (1987) 'Descriptions in legal settings', in G. Button and J.R.E. Lee (eds), *Talk and Social Organization*. Clevedon: Multilingual Matters.

Pomerantz, A.M. (1988/89) 'Constructing skepticism: four devices used to engender the audience's skepticism', *Research on Language and Social Interaction*, 22: 293–314.

Pomerantz, A.M. (1990/91) 'Mental concepts in the analysis of social action', *Research on Language and Social Interaction*, 24: 299–310.

Popper, K.R. (1959) *The Logic of Scientific Discovery*. London: Hutchinson.

Popper, K.R. (1970) 'Normal and science and its dangers', in I. Lakatos and A. Musgrave (eds), *Criticism and the Growth of Knowledge*. Cambridge: Cambridge University Press.

Porter, T.M. (1992) 'Objectivity as standardization: the rhetoric of impersonality in measurement, statistics, and cost-benefit analysis', *Annals of Scholarship*, 9: 19–59.

Potter, J. (1984) Testability, flexibility: Kuhnian values in psychologists' discourse concerning theory choice', *Philosophy of the Social Sciences*, 14: 303–30.

Potter, J. (1988) 'Cutting cakes: a study of psychologists' social categorizations', *Philosophical Psychology*, 1: 17–33.

Potter, J. (1992) 'Constructing realism: seven moves (plus or minus a couple)', *Theory and Psychology*, 2: 167–73.

Potter, J. (1996a) 'Right and wrong footing', *Theory and Psychology*, 6: 31–9.

Potter, J. (1996b) 'Discourse analysis and constructionist approaches: theoretical background', in J.E. Richardson (ed) *Handbook of Qualitative Research Methods* Leicester: British Psychological Society.

Potter, J. and Edwards, D. (1990) 'Nigel Lawson's tent: discourse analysis, attribution theory and the social psychology of fact', *European Journal of Social Psychology*, 20: 24–40.

Potter, J., Edwards, D. and Wetherell, M. (1993) 'A model of discourse in action', *American Behavioral Scientist,* 36: 383–401.

Potter, J. and Halliday, Q. (1990) 'Community leaders as a device for warranting versions of crowd events', *Journal of Pragmatics*, 14: 725–41.

Potter, J. and Reicher, S. (1987) 'Discourses of community and conflict: the organization of social categories in accounts of a "riot"', *British Journal of Social Psychology*, 26: 25–40.

Potter, J., Stringer, P. and Wetherell, M. (1984) *Social Texts and Context: Literature and Social Psychology*. London: Routledge & Kegan Paul.

Potter, J. and Wetherell, M. (1987) *Discourse and Social Psychology: Beyond Attitudes and Behaviour*. London: Sage.

Potter, J. and Wetherell, M. (1988) 'Accomplishing attitudes: fact and evaluation in racist discourse', *Text*, 8: 51–68.

Potter, J., Wetherell, M. and Chitty, A. (1991) 'Quantification rhetoric – cancer on television', *Discourse and Society*, 2: 333–65.

Psathas, G. (1995) *Conversation Analysis: the Study of Talk-in-interaction*. London: Sage.

Quine, W.V.O. (1961) *From a Logical Point of View*, 2nd edn. Harvard: Harvard University Press.

Quine, W.V.O. and Ullian, J.S. (1970) *The Web of Belief*. New York: Random House.

Reicher, S. (1987) 'Crowd behaviour as collective action', in J. Turner, M. Hogg, P. Oakes, S. Reicher and M. Wetherell, *Rediscovering the Social Group*. Oxford: Blackwell.

Roeh, I. and Nir, R. (1990) 'Speech presentation in the Israel radio news: ideological constraints and rhetorical strategies', *Text*, 10: 225–44.

Roffe, M. (in preparation) 'The interactional organization of social work', PhD thesis, Loughborough University.

Roiser, M. (1983) 'The uses and abuses of polls: a social psychologist's view', *Bulletin of the British Psychological Society*, 36: 159–61.

Rorty, R. (1980) *Philosophy and the Mirror of Nature*. Princeton, NJ: Princeton University Press.

Rorty, R. (1991) *Objectivity, Relativism, and Truth: Philosophical Papers*, vol. 1. Cambridge: Cambridge University Press.

Rose, N. (1989). *Governing the Soul*. London: Routledge.

Ryle, G. (1949) *The Concept of Mind*. London: Hutchinson.

Sacks, H. (1963) 'Sociological description', *Berkeley Journal of Sociology*, 8: 1–16; reprinted in J. Coulter (ed.), *Ethnomethodological Sociology*. Aldershot: Edward Elgar, 1990.

Sacks, H. (1984) 'On doing "being ordinary"', in J.M. Atkinson and J.C. Heritage (eds) *Structures of Social Action: Studies in Conversation Analysis*. Cambridge: Cambridge University Press.

Sacks, H. (1992) *Lectures on Conversation*. vols. I and II, edited by G. Jefferson. Oxford: Basil Blackwell.

Sacks, H. and Schegloff, E.A. (1979) 'Two preferences in the organization of reference to persons in conversation and their interaction', in G. Psathas (ed.), *Everyday Language: Studies in Ethnomethodology*. New York: Irvington.

Sacks, H., Schegloff, E.A., and Jefferson, G. (1974) 'A simplest systematics for the organization of turn-taking for conversation', *Language*, 50: 696–735. Reprinted in J. Schenkein (ed.), *Studies in the Organization of Conversational Interaction*. New York: Academic Press.

Sampson, E.E. (1993a) 'Identity politics: challenges to psychology's understanding', *American Psychologist*, 48: 1219–30.

Sampson, E.E. (1993b) *Celebrating the Other: a Dialogic Account of Human Nature*. London: Harvester Wheatsheaf.

Sarbin, T.R. (1986) 'The narrative as root metaphor for psychology', in T.R. Sarbin (ed), *Narrative Psychology: the Storied Nature of Human Conduct*. New York: Praeger.

Saussure, F. de (1974) *Course in General Linguistics*. London: Fontana.

Schank, R.C., and Abelson, R. (1977) *Scripts, Plans, Goals and Understanding*. Hillsdale, NJ: Erlbaum.

Schegloff, E.A. (1972) 'Notes on a conversational practice: formulating place', in D. Sudnow (ed.), *Studies in Social Interaction*. Glencoe, IL: Free Press; reprinted in J. Coulter (ed.), *Ethnomethodological Sociology*. Aldershot: Edward Elgar, 1990.

Schegloff, E.A. (1988a) 'Presequences and indirection: applying speech act theory to ordinary conversation', *Journal of Pragmatics*, 12: 55–62.

Schegloff, E.A. (1988b) 'Description in the social sciences I: talk-in-interaction', *Papers in Pragmatics*, 2: 1–24.

Schegloff, E.A. (1991) 'Reflections on talk and social structure', in D. Boden and D.H. Zimmerman (eds.), *Talk and Social Structure*. Cambridge: Polity Press.

Schegloff, E.A. (1992a) 'Repair after next turn: the last structurally provided defence of inter-subjectivity in conversation', *American Journal of Sociology*, 97: 1295–345.

Schegloff, E.A. (1992b) 'On talk and its institutional occasions', in P. Drew and J.C. Heritage (eds), *Talk at Work: Interaction in Institutional Settings*. Cambridge: Cambridge University Press.

Schegloff, E.A. (1995) 'Discourse as an interactional achievement III: the omnirelevance of action', *Research on Language and Social Interaction*, 28: 185–211.

Schegloff, E.A. and Sacks, H. (1973) 'Opening up closings', *Semiotica*, 7: 289–327; reprinted in R. Turner (ed), *Ethnomethodology*. Harmondsworth: Penguin.

Scheppele, K.L. (1994) 'Practices of truth-finding in a court of law: the case of revised stories', in T.R. Sarbin and J.I. Kitsuse (eds) *Constructing the Social*. London: Sage.

Scott, M.B. and Lyman, S.M. (1968) 'Accounts', *American Sociological Review*, 33: 46–62.

Searle, J.R. (1969) *Speech Acts: an Essay in the Philosophy of Language*. Cambridge: Cambridge University Press.

Searle, J.R. (1975) 'The logical status of fictional discourse', *New Literary History*, 6: 319–32.

Searle, J.R. (1977) 'Reiterating the differences', *Glyph*, 1: 198–208.

Semin, G.R. and Manstead, A.S.R. (1983) *The Accountability of Conduct: a Social Psychological Analysis*. London: Academic Press.

Shapin, S. (1982) 'History of science and its sociological reconstructions', *History of Science*, 20: 157–211.

Shapin, S. and Schaffer, S. (1985) *Leviathan and the Air-pump*. Princeton, NJ: Princeton University Press.

Shapiro, M.J. (1988) *The Politics of Representation: Writing Practices in Biography, Photography, and Policy Analysis*. Wisconsin: University of Wisconsin Press.

Shapiro, M.J. (1989) 'Representing world politics: the sport/war intertext', in J. Der Derian and M.J. Shapiro (eds), *International/Intertextual Relations*. Lexington, MA: Lexington Books.

Shiffrin, D. (1987) *Discourse Markers*. Cambridge: Cambridge University Press.

Shotter, J. (1992) 'Bakhtin and Billig: Monological versus dialogical practices', *American Behavioral Scientist*, 36: 8–21.

Shuman, A. (1992) '"Get outa my face": entitlement and authoritative discourse', in J.H. Hill and J.T. Irvine (eds), *Responsibility and Evidence in Oral Discourse*. Cambridge: Cambridge University Press.

Simons, H.W. (1989) '"Going meta" in political confrontations', in B. Gronbeck (ed.), *Spheres of Argument*. Annandale, VA: SCA.

Simons, H.W. (1990) 'Introduction: the rhetoric of inquiry as an intellectual movement', in H.W. Simons (ed.), *The Rhetorical Turn: Invention and Persuasion in the Conduct of Inquiry*. Chicago: University of Chicago Press.

Smith, B.H. (1988) *Contingencies of Value: Alternative Perspectives for Critical Theory*. Cambridge, MA: Harvard University Press.

Smith, D. (1978) 'K is mentally ill: the anatomy of a factual account', *Sociology*, 12: 23–53.

Smith, D. (1983) 'No one commits suicide: textual analysis of ideological practices', *Human Studies*, 6: 309–59.

Smith, D. (1990) *Texts, Facts and Femininity: Exploring the Relations of Ruling*. London: Routledge.

Sorenson, J. (1991) 'Mass media and discourse on famine in the Horn of Africa', *Discourse and Society*, 2: 223–42.

Soyland, A.J. (1994) *Psychology as Metaphor*. London: Sage.

Squire, C. (1994) 'Safety, danger and the movies: women's and men's narratives of aggression', *Feminism and Psychology*, 4: 547–70.

Still, A. and Costall, A. (eds) (1991) *Against Cognitivism: Alternative Foundations for Cognitive Psychology*. Hemel Hempstead: Harvester Wheatsheaf.

Suchman, L. and Jordan, B. (1990) 'Interactional troubles in face-to-face survey interviews', *Journal of the American Statistical Association*, 85: 232–41.

Sudnow, D.N. (1967) *Passing On*. Englewood Cliffs, NJ: Prentice-Hall.

Tarantino, Q. (1994) *Reservoir Dogs*. London: Faber & Faber.

The 2nd of January Group (1986) *After Truth: a Post-Modern Manifesto*. London: Inventions.

Thompson, J.B. (1990) *Ideology and Modern Culture*. Cambridge: Polity.

Todorov, T. (1985) *The Conquest of America: the Question of the Other*. New York: Harper & Row.

Traweek, S. (1988) *Beamtimes and Lifetimes: the World of High Energy Physics*. Cambridge, MA: Harvard University Books.

Trew, T. (1979) 'Theory and ideology at work', in R. Fowler, B. Hodge, G. Kress and T. Trew (eds), *Language and Control*. London: Routledge.

Tuchman, G. (1978) *Making News: a Study in the Construction of Reality*. New York: Free Press.

Volosinov, V.N. (1973) *Marxism and the Philosophy of Language*. New York: Seminar.

Watson, D.R. (1978) 'Categorization, authorization and blame-negotiation in conversation', *Sociology*, 12: 105–13.

Watson, D.R. (1983) 'The presentation of victim and motive in discourse: the case of police interrogations and interviews', *Victimology*, 8: 31–52.

Watson, D.R. (1990) 'Some features of the elicitation of confessions in murder interrogations', in G. Psathas (ed.), *Interaction Competence*. Lanham, MD: University Press of America.

Watson, D.R. and Weinberg, T. (1982) 'Interviews and the interactional construction of accounts of homosexual identity', *Social Analysis*, 11: 56–78.

Weedon, C. (1987) *Feminist Practice and Poststructuralist Theory*. Oxford: Blackwell.

Wetherell, M. and Potter, J. (1989) 'Narrative characters and accounting for violence', in J. Shotter and K. Gergen (eds), *Texts of Identity*. London: Sage.

Wetherell, M. and Potter, J. (1992) *Mapping the Language of Racism: Discourse and the Legitimation of Exploitation*. London: Harvester Wheatsheaf.

Wetherell, M., Stiven, H., and Potter, J. (1987) 'Unequal egalitarianism: a preliminary study of discourses concerning gender and employment opportunities', *British Journal of Social Psychology*, 26: 59–71.

Whalen, M.R. and Zimmerman, D.H. (1990) 'Describing trouble: practical epistemology in citizen calls to the police', *Language in Society*, 19: 465–92.

White, H. (1973) *Metahistory: the Historical Imagination in Nineteenth Century Europe*. Baltimore, MD: Johns Hopkins University Press.

White, H. (1978) *Tropics of Discourse*. Baltimore, MD: Johns Hopkins University Press.

Whiteside, A. and Issacharoff, M. (eds) (1987) *On Referring in Literature*. Bloomington: Indiana University Press.

Whorf, B.L. (1956) *Language, Thought and Reality: Selected Writings of Benjamin Lee Whorf*, J.B. Carroll (ed.), Cambridge, MA: MIT Press.

Widdicombe, S. and Wooffitt, R. (1995) *The Language of Youth Subcultures: Social Identity in Action*. London: Harvester Wheatsheaf.

Wieder, D.L. (1974) 'Telling the code', in R. Turner (ed.), *Ethnomethodology*. Harmondsworth: Penguin; reprinted in J. Coulter (ed.), *Ethnomethodological Sociology*. Aldershot: Edward Elgar, 1990.

Williamson, J. (1978) *Decoding Advertisements*. London: Boyars.

Willis, P. (1977) *Learning to Labour: How Working Class Kids Get Working Class Jobs*. Farnborough: Saxon House.

Wolpert, L. (1993) *The Unnatural Nature of Science*. London: Faber and Faber.

Wood, L.A. and Rennie, H. (1994) 'Formulating rape', *Discourse and Society*, 5: 125–48.

Wood, W. and Eagly, A.H. (1981) 'Stages in the analysis of persuasive messages: the role of causal attributions and message comprehension', *Journal of Personality and Social Psychology*, 40: 246–59.

Wooffitt, R. (1991). '"I was just doing X . . . when Y": Some inferential properties of a device in accounts of paranormal experiences', *Text*, 11: 267–88.

Wooffitt, R. (1992) *Telling Tales of the Unexpected: The Organization of Factual Discourse.* London: Harvester Wheatsheaf.

Wooffitt, R. (1993) 'Analysing accounts', in N. Gilbert (ed.), *Researching Social Life*. London: Sage.

Woolgar, S. (1981) 'Interests and explanation in the social studies of science', *Social Studies of Science*, 11: 365–94.

Woolgar, S. (1983) 'Irony in the social studies of science.', in K.D. Knorr Cetina and M. Mulkay (eds.), *Science Observed: Perspectives on the Social Study of Science.* London: Sage.

Woolgar, S. (ed.) (1988a) *Knowledge and Reflexivity: New Frontiers in the Sociology of Science.* London and Beverly Hills, CA: Sage.

Woolgar, S. (1988b) *Science: the Very Idea.* Chichester: Ellis Horwood; London: Tavistock.

Woolgar, S. (1989) 'The ideology of representation and the role of the agent', in H. Lawson and L. Appignanesi (eds), *Dismantling Truth: Reality in the Post-modern World.* London: Weidenfeld & Nicolson.

Woolgar, S. and Pawluch, D. (1985) 'Ontological gerry-mandering: the anatomy of social problems explanations', *Social Problems*, 32: 214–27.

Worton, M. and Still, J. (1990) *Intertexuality: Theories and Practices.* Manchester: Manchester University Press.

Wowk, M. (1984) 'Blame allocation: sex and gender in a murder interrogation', *Women's Studies International Forum*, 7: 75–82.

Wynne, B.E. (1979) 'Physics and psychics: science, symbolic action and social control in late Victorian England', in B. Barnes and S. Shapin (eds) *Natural Order: Historical Studies of Scientific Culture*. London: Sage.

Yearley, S. (1981) 'Textual persuasion: the role of social accounting in the construction of scientific arguments', *Philosophy of the Social Sciences*, 11: 409–35.

Yearley, S. (1982) 'The relationship between epistemological and sociological cognitive interests: some ambiguities underlying the use of interest theory in the study of scientific knowledge', *Studies in the History and Philosophy of Science*, 13: 353–88.

Yearley, S. (1984) 'Proofs and reputations: Sir James Hall and the use of classification devices in scientific arguments', *Earth Sciences History*, 3: 25–43.

Yearley, S. (1985) 'Vocabularies of freedom and resentment: a Strawsonian perspective on the nature of argumentation in science and the law', *Social Studies of Science*, 15: 99–126.

Young, A. (1990) 'Appeals to valuelessness', *Textual Practice*, 4: 38–53.

Zelizer, B. (1989) '"Saying" as collective practice: quoting and differential address in the news', *Text*, 9: 369–88.

Zimmerman, D.H. and Pollner, M. (1971) 'The everyday world as a phenomenon', in J.D. Douglas (Ed.), *Understanding Everyday Life: Toward the Reconstruction of Sociological Knowledge*. Chicago: Aldine; reprinted in J. Coulter (ed.), *Ethnomethodological Sociology*. Aldershot: Edward Elgar, 1990.

Index